Something to Guard

The Stormy Life
of the National Guardian
1948-1967

Something to Guard

The Stormy Life
of the National Guardian
1948-1967

Cedric Belfrage

and

James Aronson

New York   Columbia University Press   1978

Library of Congress Cataloging in Publication Data

Belfrage, Cedric, 1904–
  Something to guard.

  Includes bibliographical references and index.
  1. National guardian. 2. Belfrage, Cedric, 1904–
3. Aronson, James. 4. Journalists—United States—
Biography. I. Aronson, James, joint author. II. Title.
PN4900.N32B44   071   78-3530
ISBN 0-231-04510-7

Columbia University Press
New York   Guildford, Surrey
Copyright © 1978 Columbia University Press
Printed in the United States of America

To the memory

of

JOHN T. McMANUS

The third man

Contents

Illustrations follow pages 84 and 244.

A Personal Note

Each of us has spent the major part of his career as a journalist. One of us now is a teacher of journalism, the other encounters a stream of young people seeking to understand the time about which we have written. Each of us has been struck by the ignorance of young Americans of their own history, as it actually happened, particularly radical history. The fault is not theirs: it is an appalling comment on how history is taught and written. This lack of knowledge, however, is more than made up for by an eagerness to know. When the key is turned in the lock of knowledge, the receptiveness of the young is gratifying and rewarding.

We wrote this book with a commitment to the theory of the continuity of history—that one learns from the past to understand the present to set guideposts for the future. We believe that the history of events in which we played an actual role can help our young friends understand and accept the link with the past—and the value of dearly held principles in the making of history.

For her editorial assistance in the preparation of this volume, our gratitude to Simone Harris.

[New York, March 1978 CEDRIC BELFRAGE and JAMES ARONSON]

Something to Guard

The Stormy Life
of the National Guardian
1948-1967

1945: A Seed Takes Root

[C.B.] It was the second "war to end war" of my life and it seemed possible, this time, that we might really bring it off and start living like civilized humans. Franklin D. Roosevelt, an intelligent President, thought so. General Dwight D. Eisenhower, our commander-in-chief, seemed to think so, judging by the directives he'd signed for us. And some of us, American–British–Canadian "press control officers" of his "Psychological Warfare Division," had the innocence to believe it too. The guarantee in the scenario was that, albeit kicking and screaming, democratic capitalism had joined with Soviet socialism to wipe from the earth the war virus in its most pestilent form—fascism.

The job we'd been doing in the wreckage of Germany, since four months before the massacre stopped ahead, was one that nobody ever did before. We were part inquisitors, part entrepreneurs but with privileges denied to a Beaverbrook or Hearst. Waving the conqueror's wand, we simply requisitioned real estate, materials, and equipment for use by the new "democratic" press we were required to create, for which we ordered German officials to meet payrolls.

Bombs and guns had brought the existing all-Nazi newspapers to a dead halt but we found their staffs going through business-as-usual motions in what remained of their plants, like so many ghosts failing to note the break of day. I recall the incredulous stares from behind desks in the *Frankfurter Anzeiger*'s "news" and "advertising" departments when, accompanied by a stentorian-voiced officer from the Bronx, I broke in upon their dream world. We told the indomitable automatons to depart in peace and they continued to sit and stare. Finally my Bronx companion broke the hush with a bellowed *"Heraus!"* They reached for their briefcases, scuttled toward hat and umbrella stands, and in sixty seconds left an empty stage set for the "democratic" press. It was a heady situation for working stiffs from Newspaper Row to find themselves in.

The inquisitorial part of our job was harder. It consisted of permanently expelling from journalism people whom we appraised as Nazi accomplices, and installing editor-publishers with "active" antifascist records and a minimum of professional competence.

Eisenhower's orders recognized that these would tend to be Social Democrats, Christian-Socialist "Centrists," or Communists of the period before those parties became quarry for the Gestapo— and that they would be hard to find. Few could have survived Hitler's twelve-year purge of left-of-center journalists, a breed once thousands strong in Germany. For my inquisitions I composed a *Fragebogen* (questionnaire) which some colleagues adopted for their own work, dubbing it the "Belfragebogen." The façade we had to pierce was that everyone who had remained in Nazi journalism could prove he loved democracy: the only "real" fascist was Hitler, who was dead.

We strove for Solomonic wisdom but couldn't read souls, only examine records and weigh testimony—and bodies, since "active" antifascists who survived had done so on garbage, in and out of jails and concentration camps; waist measures were a sound political test. It hardly occurred to us that our publishing licences were certificates of future wealth—that is, if the recipient of one could keep it in the coming "revision" of occupation policy. Some would become West German millionaires within a few years. Revisiting Germany in 1973 I found the widow of one of "my" licencees living in clover on his share of the newspaper he had co-edited. When they came into my orbit in 1945, both were skeletal bundles of nerves; he was then a Communist but had revised his politics as flesh returned to his bones.

Others whom I helped to nominate didn't keep their licences for long. There was Emil Carlebach, a young Jewish Communist survivor of Dachau and Buchenwald who, on his return from the latter, found a Belfragebogen tucked under his door by the rabbi who had told me about him. There were the Social Democratic printer Heinrich Hollands and the Christian-Socialist Wilhelm Karl Gerst, a former book and magazine publisher—both elderly men who had precariously preserved souls and bodies at the cost of frightful humiliations. And there was Dr. Theodor Heuss, a well-preserved gentleman and scholar who agreed with apparent delight to join a Social Democrat and a Communist on an editor–publisher team in Heidelberg. Heuss qualified by a whisker for a licence in 1945 but had no further use for it after he became President, in 1949, of the half of Germany "we" saved for capitalism.

By July of 1945, with Roosevelt cold in his grave, Washington's German policy was visibly changing and I became more aware of two types among my Psychological Warfare (it had by now become Information Control Division) colleagues. Those who took the war less than seriously had no problem. Our brass installed itself in the kind of castles that inspire fairy-tale illustrators, whither instantly horizontal fraeuleins flocked to share Kansas City steaks and liberated German wine with the conquerors to the strains of sweating string orchestras. To wallow in this was a path of absolutely no resistance for psychological warriors who knew nothing, and cared less, about the joint antifascist crusade.

Some of us, on the other hand, did care. We saw that the "loyal" thing now was to reinterpret the orders or just forget about them, but out in the field we stuck to them meticulously and with straight faces.

The first full-dress confrontation was in progress when Jim Aronson joined us in Frankfurt, in time for the birth of our daily *Rundschau*. Some of our brass (but with a West Point colonel and a major or two on my side) were trying to remove Carlebach and Gerst from the *Rundschau* board of licencees. The grounds were bogus enough to give us temporary victory; the real grounds, which couldn't be cited under Eisenhower's still-unrewritten orders, were plainly Carlebach's communism and the Catholic Gerst's eagerness to preside over our *Rundschau* assortment of Social Democrats and Communists. Jim, sitting in on the performance fresh off the plane from London, effortlessly smelled the direction of the wind.

To learn the ropes Jim was attached to me on visits to Heidelberg, Kassel, Stuttgart, and Bremen, where we had new papers hatching, and if the NATIONAL GUARDIAN can be said to have been conceived during those trips, the officer who cut Jim's orders must plead guilty to premature midwifery. My days in Germany were already numbered: Eisenhower would soon order me home because, as his telegram explained, I was "British" in what had become the "American zone." Actually my home and family were in New York but, having only first naturalization papers, I had been ineligible for the olive-drab and the pay that went with it, though I messed at the Lucullan American trough.

One startling thing about Jim Aronson was that he spoke fluent German—very few of our "officers" did (and no French either—we had previously "liberated" the French press), and my immediate superior, Major (later Lieutenant Colonel) Jim Chestnutt, had been carefully trained for occupation of Japan. Ten years my junior but riper in newspaper experience, Jim Aronson had been warned in advance of my existence, as I had not of his. The daily report of problems with our firstborn paper, the *Aachener Nachrichten,* had been circulated among later press-control recruits; he had asked who the hell wrote it, had learned that I did, and seemed set on seeking me out to discover what made me tick. He was the son of a Lithuanian immigrant to America, I of a London physician; he the product of Boston public schools, Harvard, the Boston *Evening Transcript,* and the New York *Herald Tribune* and *Post,* I of British "public" school, Cambridge, and the London *Express.*

1945: A SEED TAKES ROOT

Neither of us had worked on a paper's political side but we had lived through, and felt to some extent, the rehearsals of the inquisition against leftists, which began with Rep. Martin Dies's House Un-American Activities Committee (HUAC) in 1936. Having opted to live in America after first sampling it at age 21, I considered it my country as much as Jim did. Our "premature" (as it was already being called) abhorrence for fascism was as fervent as our responsiveness to Roosevelt's view of domestic witch-hunts and of the war as reflected in our orders. We both brought to Germany fears for the democratic (we hoped, one day socialist) America that we liked, and for the world to which some American plutocrats and politicians were beginning to lay imperialistic claim. Our ideas about our craft, positive and negative, were much the same. We thought there should be some pride in being a journalist but had tasted little of it. All this wouldn't necessarily have made us brothers had we not enjoyed each other's sense of humor and found that we shared an allergy—not stopping short of our left-wing acquaintances—to hypocrisy, jargon, dogmatism, and stuffed shirts. We were rather orderly people by nature, although our private lives were in temporary disorder. We were equally far from being "intellectuals" but believed we were intelligent.

Grounded by rainstorms, stalled before the ruins of bridges, groping through the bottomless mud of detours, but well stocked with *Branntwein,* Jim and I took our professional, political, and personal back-hair down and no friendship was ever more quickly cemented. To forget the cold and our sopping uniforms we sang "Peat-Bog Soldiers," "Gouttons Voir Si le Vin Est Bon," "Wir Fahren Gegen England," and "Fuck 'Em All," and harmonized ideologically with bursts of the "Internationale." I faintly recall confessing, in a dismal British mess where we were marooned near Hanover, "My dearest hope for socialism is the state withering away," and Jim replying, "You've got a long wait, brother." Less faintly, the shock—for I'd been too busy doing it to describe it—of Jim saying:

"Do you realize that what you're setting up here is journalism run by journalists?"

Yes, we were simply eliminating the potbellied millionaire who, since it was "a business like any other," reduced our craft to glorified prostitution. For the moment through which we were living, he was as dispensable in Germany as his moneybags were indispensable in America or Britain. Wasn't that almost worth losing a war for? But why should only German journalists get the chance to go straight? Why not an honest paper in America?

"People in our line have had dreams before as well as nightmares," said Jim, "and will again. In this setting the question sounds a bit less romantic. The problem will be to keep believing it's possible, and that we're not insane, when we get home."

"But suppose we did bring it off. Suppose we set up a specimen of the free press. How long would they let us stay free?"

Our licencees had accepted with joy the journalistic *Zusammenarbeit* (we translated it "togetherwork") against fascism which our directives required of them. In October, when I had left the scene, they solemnly pledged themselves to it in a conference of free German publishers—an extinct species for the past dozen years—at Marburg University. The conference resulted from weeks of work by Jim, who by then had acquired the title of press chief of the Western Military District, U.S. Zone of Occupation. Gaunt concentration camp graduates shared the podium with aristocratic types like Heuss, who had been able with small inconvenience to "sit out" the Nazi period, and with battered working-class types like Hollands, now publishing the *Aachener Nachrichten*. The banquet crowning the discussions was the first lavish meal many of them had eaten in a decade. (To avoid gluttonous ostentation in a barren land, Jim had persuaded the Oberbuergermeister to drop one of seven courses.)

The conference was remarkable for its frank criticism (not entirely excluding the "liberators") and self-criticism, friendly but candid controversy on professional and political problems, and laughter without tension. There was a unifying sense of excitement at the prospect of honest newspapers which would help to reshape the German mind and restore the country into the family of man.

Some participants wept as they spoke of their aspirations. In the foyer, a German magician employed by the American press detachment in Marburg had rigged up a symbolic Great Seal of the United States, lighted and entwined with fir branches. He had borrowed from a nearby beauty parlor a hair-drying machine which, placed upside down, stirred the Eternal Flame topping the whole.

The flame expired with removal of the hair-dryer, and the euphoria in which the publishers returned to their desks was destined to last little longer. As an integral part of the new "cold war" against the Soviet Union, socialist goats were to be separated off from capitalist sheep and quarantined—a doctrine totally at odds with, and indeed destroying, what had been agreed at Marburg. The elements who had resolved to stop socialism, and to establish an American capitalist empire by slaughtering as many people as necessary, were emerging as decisive in the "postwar" world. Reveille had been sounded for the American Century.

In the months following my discharge, Jim in Germany, and I in America, were semiparalyzed witnesses of the betrayal of fifty million human sacrifices. Jim struggled on against the wave of benevolence toward Hitler's toadies and jackals, but one by one journalists we had booted out crept back into key positions. In America the cold war clouds gathered fast, massively seeded by poison from the press. They were particularly depressing when viewed from a prone position with an inflated and excruciating testicle, diagnosed by my doctor as mumps caught on the jammed troopship. There were other developments which grated my temper: I was officially told that my right to citizenship, for which I'd taken out first papers in 1937, had lapsed. The limit for completing the process was seven years and the fact that I'd been away at a war was irrelevant. In the new political climate I dismissed as frivolous the notion of starting again. I revived some of the *Zusammenarbeit* euphoria by writing a book about the German experience,* but, while thus engaged, received my first call from

*With a Guggenheim Foundation grant, a surprising and gratifying bonanza, but no publisher could be found for *Seeds of Destruction*—and then only a fairly obscure one—until 1954.

J. Edgar Hoover's FBI. This led to two days before a grand jury trying, apparently with success, to convince them I wasn't a Russian spy. The air was thickening with such denunciations as congressional witch-hunters multiplied in set-fair weather, and President Harry S. Truman instituted an "Attorney General's list" of proscribed organizations and "Loyalty Board" inquisitions of millions directly or indirectly employed by the government. I had been one of dozens of leftists "named" by an alcoholic lady whom it was my good fortune not to know. Exposing "spies" was the game of the hour, with scores of amateur and professional players enjoying a feast of headlines.

I felt the need of a political organization but saw no place to go. In Roosevelt's party a "liberal" wing, outdoing President Truman in hostility to our late Soviet ally, was clearly in the ascendant. The tattered remnant of Eugene Debs's Socialist Party outdid both in "Iron Curtain" invective against the country that overthrew capitalism. The Communist journalist Joe North asked me to lunch to explain the upheaval in his party over "Browderism." Communist leader Earl Browder had been headily convinced, when I went overseas, that the war alliance must lead to peacetime cooperation, and members who disagreed had been expelled. When the unhappy truth dawned, colleagues on the party's National Committee, who had followed him like an echo, expelled Browder, attached his name to a new doctrinal deviation, and continued in office.

With all the respect I had for the CP as the core of the radical movement, I found this a poor way to build confidence in party leadership and party democracy. Some hundreds of thousands of Americans of my complexion, temperamentally argumentative yet accepting that socialism stems from discipline, had tried joining the party at one time or another. We had decided that "fellow traveling" (as the non-Communist, non-anti-Communist role was known to inquisitors) suited us better. I parted from Joe amicably but reinforced in that position. (We were "observed" eating spaghetti together and to this day it crops up as a sinister item in my political/police dossier.)

Only when a new Progressive Party began taking shape around Henry Wallace, who had been Roosevelt's Vice-President and Secretary of Commerce in Truman's postwar cabinet, did Jim and I feel we had a political home and a floor of sorts for our exercise in maverick journalism. Jim had returned to the *Post* in April 1946 and moved later that year to the New York *Times,* on the initiative of its assistant Sunday editor Shepard Stone who, as a major in charge of intelligence, had been among our more liberal brass in Germany. The "progressive capitalist" Wallace, too capitalist for our heartiest cheers, had been driven out into the snow as too intolerably progressive for the cold war Establishment. Could capitalist Americans live peacefully in the same world with the Soviet Union and the new Peoples' Democracies? "Incidentally" the ink was hardly dry on their pledge to do so in the United Nations Charter, but Wallace insisted that they could because they must. While they monopolized the new Bomb (successfully tested at Hiroshima), they could atomize Russia without being atomized, but since this would bring the mighty Soviet army into Western Europe, they would then have to atomize their allies. Lethal technology had passed the point where a war could be won. To this we said fervent amens while the media yelled "Communist!" and the rabble praised God and threw tomatoes.

The Free World (as America now called its crew) was to shed Mississippis and Amazons of blood in the next quarter-century before an inquisitor named Richard Nixon would, as President, bow to this simple imperative. Wallace swallowed his natural aversion to working with Communists in the Progressive Party because he saw what was implied by his stand against "this impractical, unrealistic settlement of differences between governments by the mass killing of people" (Roosevelt in 1945). Since the Soviet Union was now the "enemy," ostracism and persecution of its defenders were merely the domestic exercise of the cold war.

Wallace was a rather dour man not, as we would learn, numbering imagination among his many gifts. We ourselves were surprised by the speed with which the media entered and won the Establishment's game of identifying all Rooseveltian progressives, all peacemongers, and all socialists with communism—that is, openly or by implication, with pro-Soviet treason. Wallace was incredulous to the end that "such things can happen in America" as the concerted distortion and disruption of his campaign, with the press as vociferous cheer-leader. He hoped against hope that the scattering of Communists in his party wouldn't turn off any of the ten million Americans who, according to an early-1948 poll, intended voting for him. But in any case his platform ruled out by definition any witch-hunt within the party. Thus the Establishment, primed for sophisticated witch-hunting, had him over a barrel.

My friend Claude Williams, the Alabama preacher who had been horsewhipped and jailed for defending blacks and poor-whites, claimed that he "swam best when the water's boiling." It seemed that Jim and I did too. I had passed an exam to become a United Nations bureaucrat, but couldn't face it as long as there was a chance of launching a decent newspaper on this political geyser. Jim was now combining with his *Times* job the editorship of *Frontpage,* organ of the New York Newspaper Guild, a trade union that took longer than most to totter into the cold war camp. So I had time to begin soundings for our dream, and he had the places. Living as I did outside the city, I used the Guild office for receiving mail and the *Times* office for local phone calls.

Progressive Party officials, swarming in a shabby Park Avenue brownstone, wished us luck and returned to their Sisyphean labors. They had no plans for a party organ and anyhow we didn't favor one. A surprising number of working journalists responded with offers of free spare-time help. They saw deepening shadows over the media and over their jobs. Anti-cold war radio commentators and columnists were disappearing in a systematic purge; "liberal" papers were losing circulation catastrophically; and New York's progressive daily *PM*—an experiment in no-ads journalism financed by Marshall Field—was in rigor mortis though it hadn't dared to come out for Wallace. The Communist press's support for Wallace offered an obvious opening to the red-baiters, to create a wall between him and potential voters.

Every well-wisher for our project supplied names of Wallaceites who had money, leaving the detachment of it from them largely up to me. In 1947–48 there were quite a few such around—"Businessmen for Wallace" (the "peace candidate") whose interests the soaring war budgets couldn't serve or seemed to threaten.

Constitutionally untunable to the wavelength of the wealthy, I had never embarked on a task with so little appeal and at which I was consequently more inept. The worst of it was that, since my targeted victims wouldn't deny an interest "in principle," all were prepared to discuss the matter. As patrons of peace they applauded the principles; as businessmen they wanted to know how and when our paper would climb out of the red. Meanwhile their contributions to Wallace's campaign "stretched them to the limit," and beyond that their funds were "all tied up." I wasted countless hours weaving imaginary figures into "break-even point" presentations, but how was I, myself so unconvinced, to convince them that the paper we contemplated could ever break even in the existing climate? There were some who, inspired by Hearstian visions of themselves, seemed really to believe it could—if they ran it. In a mansion breathing his genius for golden gimmickry, a perfume magnate said: "What we must put out is a progressive *Daily News*" (referring to the most fraudulently populist of American tabloids). A man clipping coupons in Rockefeller Center promised $7,500 for a paper we would run, if six others would put up the same. At session after session in his office we always got stuck at five—as, perhaps he may have shrewdly calculated. Eccentric "mass market planning consultants" offered brilliantly unfinanceable advice, but no checks.

Any smart operator in an air-conditioned glass eyrie could see that Jim and I had no head for business, and our lack of someone who did was the flaw detected by all. Jobless leftists who heard of our insanity, and began to straggle in wanting to join us, itched for typewriters and flinched at the thought of juggling bank overdrafts and fending off creditors. But Mel Bernstein, the cartoonist we had collected from *PM* as art editor, had a friend named Peter Hodgson. A chronically unemployed but politically semirespectable business type, Hodgson would take it on because he believed Wallace had a chance for the Presidency. When our project was still but a gleam in our own eyes, he already showed his pale political colors and Jim and I doubted if the marriage would be consummated. His nose for business proved better, at any rate, than his electoral prognosis. Some time later, when our ship was afloat without him, he was seen cruising down Fifth Avenue in a Rolls-Royce. It seemed that on a visit to a chemist friend he had played with some waste product lying around the lab, rolled it into a ball, and found that it bounced and had other curious properties. He packaged and marketed it as "Silly Putty" and became another emblem of the American Dream.

"The only way to get something done," I droned bromidically to Jim, "is to do it." By early summer of 1948 we had abandoned the mirage of six-figure capitalization and accepted the fact that our politics fixed us in poverty row. With all work except printing donated, we would rely on one or more sample issues to bring enough subscriptions for continuation. We outlined a paper simple in appearance and style, aimed at the broadest possible progressive audience, avoiding sensationalism, condescension, political cliches, and tendentious use of words, reviving the traditional but moribund humor of the American left, and above all insisting on brevity. We would encourage reader opinions, editorialize mainly by quoting authorities on issues, and be sparing with polemics but target it exclusively at the enemy, Free World reaction. Concentrating on news that was elsewhere distorted or suppressed, and interpreting it by the way it was handled, we would cover socialist countries' actions and policies as adequately as their defensive censorship systems would permit. With the Progressive Party we decided against commitment to socialism, for we hoped to win a public beyond the "converted," "starting where they are" and leading them by subversively rational steps to where we were.

Every anti-Establishment journal, fundless in a world fueled by advertising, has the problem of making potential readers aware that it exists. If for us there was a solution to this, it lay in the cadres of the Progressive Party—the "Jimmie Higginses" of the left who traditionally rang doorbells for something they believed in. Scattered as the tribe was through countless cities, towns, and villages, we could reach them with our samples, at home or at Progressive Party meetings, to the extent that printing and mailing costs could be raised.

As for American intellectuals, we expected little from them and got less. Ten years earlier they had overwhelmingly defied the inquisitors in defending Spain against fascism. In 1948 they were resisting the tiderace of unreason less than businesmen or union leaders or farmers, less than German intellectuals in 1933. Lillian Hellman gathered a prosperous few of the remnant at her home to hear our plans. If they had been bankers, they couldn't have challenged us with tougher break-even-point questions nor ticked off with gloomier meticulousness the past failures of left journals. The documentation of this fruitless rendezvous is a letter from Jim to Lillian, mentioning inter alia that "the security risks that the people in your livingroom worried about" weren't the only ones: "a lot of us—while we may not have much money—are making considerable sacrifices with regard to our livelihood."

Jim added that "in perhaps the most critical period of America's history there isn't one strong voice raised to fight for decency in the whole field of journalism." He slightly exaggerated. In York, Pa. (pop. 59,000) a stubborn Pennsylvania Dutchman fought on for it in his *Gazette and Daily*. Josiah Gitt was among the few Americans of some stature who stood up with Wallace in defiance of red-baiting. In each geographical and occupational area there was one or a handful of these—ranging politically from loyal Rooseveltian to socialist—though all wouldn't stay the course. They included the New Deal governors of Puerto Rico and Minnesota, Rexford G. Tugwell and Elmer Benson; United Electrical Workers President Albert J. Fitzgerald; Williams College Professor of Government Frederick L. Schuman; Iowa Farmers Union President Fred W. Stover; New York Congressman Vito Marcantonio; Paul Robeson, W. E. B. DuBois, and the well-known Yugoslav-American writer, Louis Adamic.

Suddenly that summer Jess Gitt spoke sweet music from York. He would come in as publisher of a weekly *National Gazette* and underwrite a 70,000-copy preview issue. In addition to separate sales, the paper would be a weekend supplement to the *Gazette and Daily*. Nine of us now began a series of solemn huddles, with minutes ending "The Meeting Rose at 8:30," at the home of Jack Turner, a businessman addicted to our form of lunacy. Hodgson, Bernstein, Jim, and I had signed a document as "directors," with Gitt as chairman, of "National Gazette, Inc." O. John Rogge, a former U.S. assistant attorney general backing Wallace, housed us in his law office on Lower Broadway to prepare "preview" copy and send it down to York. Later someone lent us a summer-vacated apartment on upper Madison Avenue. There I bent to what would be my chief task for the next years: making little ones out of big ones for breadth of range in narrow space and for ease of reading by busy people. Deluged with articles from heretical journalists we had solicited around the country and the world, we saw that curing some of them of longwindedness and jargon would be a long haul, and prepared for the cross every editor must bear—the fury of those left out.

In late July Jim and I were in Gitt's printery giving birth to an amorphous but, we thought, bright infant. Gitt, like a model publisher, offered no editorial interference. Our *Gazette*'s sixteen tabloid pages, with cartoons and drawings two or three to a page by fifteen artists listed on the masthead, contained some sixty text items. Most were bylined, a few attributed, the rest round-ups by unpaid but hopeful "office staff" (at that time Elmer Bendiner, Robert E. Light, Helen Scott, and Leon Summit). Health, sports, housing, taxes and prices, religion, veterans, labor, movies, radio, books, and the press were covered in addition to national and international politics and the domestic witch-hunt. Adamic described the interracial euphoria of the Progressive Party convention just held in Philadelphia; Wallace's speech was summarized (the only full-page item). Bernard Shaw, in an interview with a purged radio commentator, called Wallace "the only American figure today who knows what it's all about." (Shaw described Stalin and Einstein as the world's only living great men apart from himself.)

From North Dakota Don C. Matchan told how the business community had bounced him as editor of the Valley City *Times Record* for his coldness to the cold war, and from Harviell, Mo., Owen Whitfield looked at the Presidential elections through his fellow black sharecroppers' eyes. Fragments of "testimony" before Truman's "loyalty boards" vied for comic honors with James Dugan's satire, "How to Build a Dewey" (Thomas E., the Republican mechanical man and favored candidate for the Presidency). The bombastic but perilous futility of the then-raging "Battle of Berlin" was examined by Fred Schuman, British MP Konni Zilliacus, and Max Werner. (The Labor Party was about to oust Zilliacus for overfriendliness with Communists; Werner, whose *PM* column had proved him America's shrewdest military analyst, fell into our lap by default of the wishful thinking press, which couldn't stomach his accuracy about socialist military power.) Anna Louise Strong, buttressed by our correspondent Peter Townsend in Nanking, wrote that "all the billions of aid cannot save" Washington's Chinese footman, Chiang Kai-shek, and Eleanor Wheeler reported from Prague on pro- and anti-American views of Czechoslovaks commemorating Huss. Rogge documented the unconstitutionality of the Smith Act under which U.S. Communists were about to be tried and jailed. Our Washington man, John B. Stone, quoted prophetically from the co-author of the Mundt-Nixon bill (later McCarran Act): "The heart of the red conspiracy," Rep. Richard M. Nixon warned, wasn't the "known Communists" indicted under the Smith Act, but "secret operators." We didn't miss the point that this meant every opponent of the cold war, every potential reader of our paper . . . it meant us.

One afternoon that fall Jim and I stood on a downtown sidewalk debating what to do next. The $10,000-odd response to our offer of five 13-week subs for a $5 bill (or a year for $4) promised to get us off the ground soon; and Vic Levitt, a friendly printer of trade union journals, had given us office space on upper floors of his Murray Street plant near City Hall. But as we approached the building Helen Scott ran out with our correspondence files stuffed under both arms.

"The list, the list!" she panted. "Hodgson and Bernstein have barricaded themselves in the office with it and say they won't let you in!"

"The list" was the only solid capital we had, the subscriber names and addresses. This was the outcome of our crescendoing argument with Hodgson, who still dreamed of a more imposing financial setup than our bootstrap approach if we would only tone down our radicalism. Jim and I were even more insistent that the radicalism was not only what brought the subs, but the sole reason for the paper. We believed that weakening before the anti-Wallace barrage had decisively contributed to the death of *PM*.

Rather than try to enter by force majeure, we decided to take next morning's milk train to York—as we suspected Hodgson and Bernstein would also do. Our fate lay in Gitt's hands. Either our New York "partners" didn't think fast enough or overslept; anyway we had a clear field. When Hodgson and Bernstein finally huffed into Gitt's office around noon, his face told them they had lost. Gitt, frank as always, had confessed to us that our paper's complexion was a bit too red for him; he didn't object to it, but had political headaches enough with the *Gazette and Daily* and wanted out. He outvoted Hodgson and Bernstein as to who should get "the list," and we left with his blessing.

A double victim of the cold war in journalism was John T. Mc-Manus, film critic of the defunct *PM,* ex-president of the New York Newspaper Guild. A majority of Guild members, tenderized by the red scare, had voted him out early in 1948. At the same time the new Guild officials urged Jim to remain as editor of *Frontpage;* he had agreed and then, with what he called "incredible cheek," they put it out that he—by more than implication on instructions from Moscow—refused to quit. Jack went to Washington as administrative assistant to Representative Leo Isacson, one of the House's only two Wallaceites (the other was Vito Marcantonio) and remained in touch with Jim. There was a project for a "new *PM*" called New York *Star;* both Jim and Jack were offered jobs on it but neither was enthusiastic.

Turning up at our office after the attempted Hodgson putsch, Jack proved to be the one and only journalist willing to take on business management. At least he had the experience of running a trade union, and he was strong on the quality needed for shaking money off trees—gall. He also had a breezy journalistic flair which his "Reports to Readers"—mainly cajolings for cash—would show off at its best. His approach to major money-raising was that affluent persons who claimed to share our beliefs should be persuaded or bludgeoned, if necessary, into seeing a great truth: that while he who didn't work shouldn't eat, he who didn't eat couldn't work. The son of a Tammany politician, he was an eminently Irish-American phenomenon, pink-faced, white-haired, laughter-loving, easily flappable in many situations but never in a crisis. As I came to know him, he was twice as mulish as myself and his obstinacy perforce mellowed mine. For example, while he never joined the CP, his respect for it—even when he conceded its frequent wrong-headedness—made him its most consistent defender in our Anglo-Jewish-Irish trinity.

With frequent, heated, but eventually resolved arguments about policy, the trinity would remain solid until a heart attack felled Jack in November 1962. The only coincidence in our backgrounds was that we had all been film and theater critics. The unifying elements were political conviction, mutual trust, and inquisitorial harassment.

It was a good omen that we agreed so easily on what to call the paper. From the entourage came every conceivable proposal suggesting a bugle call to man the barricades. The fact that we'd already established a name which we couldn't use, but which we could adapt, was decisive among arguments for something quieter and less exotic. Of all possible words beginning with G, "Guardian" appealed to us as a tribute to one of the best pioneer left journals by our standards, the *American Guardian,* which Oscar Ameringer used to publish in Oklahoma City. The name had some appropriateness for a paper that—as we said in a recollective first-anniversary editorial—"thought it had something to guard. If anyone wanted to know what that was, we referred them to Tom Paine, Tom Jefferson, Abe Lincoln, and Franklin D. Roosevelt. We had to guard the decent popular tradition of America."

We were right in thinking that if people liked the package, they would quickly accept any reasonable label under which it came. But one quaint result of our choice was a sub or two from people who had to be told we weren't the organ of the National Guard.

Postscript [**J. A.**] In July 1948 I wrote to Jack McManus in Washington. As a charter staff member of *PM* his job on the *Star* was guaranteed, but I had a hunch he had no Star in his eyes. I said that if he still hadn't unraveled the question of his future, he might "be interested in a permanent tie-up with us."

Our cordial but not close relationship had begun in the early Newspaper Guild years when Jack was reviewing films for *Time* and I was doing time on the New York *Post*. When he became president of the Guild I was editor of its journal *Frontpage* on leave from the New York *Times*. He had been elected president as a compromise "neutralist" candidate in a stalemate between the Guild's left and right wings. It soon became apparent that there was nothing neutral about Jack when it came down to defending the rights of working staffs against publishers, and that was enough for the right wing to begin lumping him with the "reds." This kind of mindless characterization was the surest way to move Jack's stubborn mind to find out what the "reds" were all about.

A few weeks after my letter, when we were recovering from the ordeal of York, Jack appeared unannounced at our office on Murray Street. A green leprechaun hat was perched on his close-cropped, prematurely white hair. He put the hat on an old-fashioned standing rack, mentioned that he'd just read the *Star* editorial throwing support to Truman for the Presidency, and said: "What's cookin'?" We told him, and his hat stayed on the rack. Next day he wrote the *Star* not to expect him.

Yes, the arguments ran very hot indeed as the three of us thrashed things out. And it was just the kind of open, undevious working-out of ideas and problems that created the respect we had for one another—a rare relationship in the savagely competitive atmosphere (as we had all known it) of a newspaper office.

Jack had an unshakable faith in the GUARDIAN. From the day he walked in that August to the day he died, he never stopped thinking, doing, talking, writing, and dreaming for the paper; and he was a man who dreamed in Technicolor, as he said. I could always sense the imminence of a McManus fantasy which might have had a horizontal origin in bed around 4 A.M. Jack would loom in the office doorway, fasten you with that leprechaun look, and say: "Are you sitting down, Hugo? I have had a vision." There followed the outline of an outlandish scheme for circulation-building, promotion, or fund-raising, which you knew couldn't work—except that Jack's enthusiasm, chutzpa, and intelligence usually made it work.

He saw the GUARDIAN as both a news medium and a service medium. Well, we all did, but for him the most impressive intellectual achievement was valueless unless it was applied to practical situations. Leo Huberman, the late and much-lamented co-editor of *Monthly Review,* once called Jack "the intellectual as hero." He was committed. He cherished the GUARDIAN staff and was respectful of their work, yet he felt that no story was so indispensable that it couldn't be trimmed by a few inches to make room for news of an urgent picket line in Washington or San Francisco. And if such an item was left out, mighty was his wrath.

In staff discussions he played devil's advocate to the very edge of an explosion. Then, at the strategic moment, he would say: "I think your position is very sound." Once in the midst of an argument he said to me: "You know, Jim, your name should be O'Ronson—you've got such an Irish temper." "You know, Jack," I responded, "your name should be McManischewitz—you argue like an oriental Jew." That broke up the argument.

Politics was a way of life for Jack. Rarely was there a man who so genuinely enjoyed the bustle and maneuvering of politics, or who tried more earnestly to turn it into an honorable profession. He knew more about the science of government than most persons in office. In the Korean War hysteria of 1950 he ran as American Labor Party candidate for governor of New York, on the ticket with W. E. B. DuBois for Senator and Vito Marcantonio for an eighth term as congressman. After a spirited campaign paid for in the people's pennies, he described himself as "the best-licked governor New York State ever had." There was more to the remark than Jack's typical humor. The office was one that he deserved and would have honored. Had he lived to be elected to it in a time of sanity, he would have helped mightily to dispel the stench that envelops the word "politics."

Jack applied his political theories to the paper itself, and helped to shape it into a never-yielding advocate of unity for independent political action by the American left. He had all the patience in the world for argument and debate; he had no tolerance for divisiveness, truculence, or intellectual snobbery.

He was an avid student of world politics too. He knew much about the Bolshevik revolution, understood very early the significance of the Chinese revolution ("Maps," he would shout, "let's have maps of China!"), and was captivated by the Fidelista movement in Cuba in the 1950s. His favorite political philosopher, Finley Peter Dunne's Mr. Dooley (circa 1898), didn't fail him for comment on Washington's exertions to avoid losing Cuba to the Cubans:

> "Well, sir," said Mr. Dooley, "dam thim Cubians. If I was Gin'ral Shafter, I'd say to Gin'ral Garshy, I'd say, 'I want you;' and I'd have thim all down at the station and dacently booked be the desk sergeant befure the fall iv night. The impydince of thim!"
>
> "What have they been doin'?" Mr. Hennessy asked.
>
> "Failin' to undershtand our civilization," said Mr. Dooley.

Jack understood our civilization very well indeed: the kind of understanding that was needed then, and is needed now, by anyone seeking to change it.

There were three originators of NATIONAL GUARDIAN; there should have been three authors of this book. Jack McManus was the third man in the standard definition: "A player first in the line of defense."

1945: A SEED TAKES ROOT

2

Our Lady of the Lake

[**J.A.**] Jess Gitt was magnificent. He agreed to be responsible for any outstanding debts of National Gazette Inc., and to circularize all preview subscribers at his expense announcing our continuation of the project as NATIONAL GUARDIAN. Subscription money would go to the GUARDIAN unless the sender wanted it back. I don't recall any who did.

Changing the name of our offspring before it actually walked was not agreeable, but we had much to be grateful for. The preview issue had demonstrated the ability of our editorial, circulation, and office crew to produce a paper. We had a yardstick by which to judge ourselves and to plan for the future.

Through August and September, with the after-hours help of our working wives or husbands and other volunteers who showed prodigious stamina, we sent out bales of letters seeking editorial and financial help. Other progressive publications were falling by the wayside: *Scope, Salute, '48.* All were of the magazine type, trying to compete with million-dollar publications in expensive outward show while camouflaging their "progressive" ideas in various ways. We were interested rather in providing news and information that people could get their teeth into without having to bite through layers of masking tape. "The press could disseminate goodwill," Henry Wallace was saying. "It could be objective—it could work toward world understanding. But the press has abdicated this supremely important function. It's an old, old story." We were trying to write a new story.

After York, people were subscribing at a rate of two hundred a day. Comments accompanying the $1 introductory subs were enthusiastic and sometimes startling: "A breath of fresh air at last". . . . . "The most exciting political event since they killed Mussolini." Businessmen whom we asked to advise us on circulation-building, promotion, and fund-raising methods kept warning us that anything less than a $300,000 "nut" represented a "shoe-string operation." As one of these put it, "people I ask for money gripe that newspaper people aren't business people." What else is new? Jack said. It was suggested that we put out more trial issues instead of starting in regular business in October. Vic Levitt, manager of Trade Union Service, wanted to print and house us and radiated enthusiasm. "No project can be less risky," he told the businessmen with a straight face, and we felt like hugging him. A great pre-election rally was planned for the Progressive Party in Yankee Stadium and we printed 60,000 flyers. Wallace was reported favorably disposed to the idea of assuming the publisher role after the election on November 1.

The trouble with the businessmen was that they knew too much about the kind of business ours would never be. Despairing of agreement on a practical plan for pre-publication financing, we got ourselves incorporated as Weekly Guardian Associates Inc. (lawyers' advice: we could go bankrupt and stay out of jail), counted the money from the preview issue, banged on doors for a few thousand more, and set the target date of October 18 for the first issue.

We determined on an inexpensive, five-column, tabloid format, combining a review of the week's news in departmentalized fashion (WORLD, NATION, BETTER LIVING, OTHER PEOPLE'S LIVES, etc.) with articles and cartoons providing background, interpretation, satire, criticism, and humor. The news-review material was to be set in distinctive, larger-type, two-column measure in running continuity from page to page, distinct from the rest of the paper. The purpose of this technique, aside from its attractiveness to the reader, was to present the news in organized fashion along with appropriate sidelights, rather than in the jumbled, catch-as-catch-can manner of most newspapers then and still today. Reproduction of cartoons from the foreign press, especially those showing America as others saw us, was to be a regular feature—plus original line drawings by American artists. Robert Joyce, who had been with *PM,* joined us as art editor and created our symbol, the Guardian Angel, who assumed various irreverent guises (including Stalin, may the holy fathers forgive us) to illustrate news stories and fund appeals.

Jack, Cedric, and I gave ourselves the titles of General Manager, Editor, and Executive Editor, although our functions overlapped and we would all do some writing. Jack would be responsible for business and public relations and coordination between business and editorial sides; Cedric for passing on all copy, with the right of final decision in the event of disagreement; I for layout and production and for seeing that editorial conference decisions were carried out. At the weekly conferences the whole editorial staff would plan the next issue and criticize the last; both staff members and editors would offer ideas and assignments would be made. Particularly when basic policy was at issue, discussion was open to all hands. This innovative procedure would continue until I left the paper in 1967. It was participatory democracy years before the term was "invented" in the 1960s by the "New Left"; but of course, then as now and for evermore, no newspaper can make its deadlines without someone having the last word.

A month before we began regular publication, *Time* magazine gave us a send-off in its Press section with a story headed: "Pink Shoestring." It quoted Jack: "We're starting out very modestly on the shortest possible shoestring," and noted suspiciously that the "leftish ex-President of the New York local of the American Newspaper Guild" was "mum on who supplied the shoestring." The masthead "had a heavy list to port." Among the contributors, "sportswriter John Lardner and his screenwriter brother Ring Jr.

(one of Hollywood's 'unfriendly ten')," and Anna Louise Strong, "untiring apologist for Russia." General conclusion: "It looked as if the GUARDIAN's complexion would be something between pink and rosy red." A smart-ass scalpel treatment demonstrating *Time*'s permanent list to starboard. We expected worse to come in the press about us—and got it on every occasion when we were mentioned at all, which was not often in our first years.

Volume 1 Number 1, dated October 18, 1948, came off the press on schedule. In the bound volume of early issues it looks remarkably fresh today, except for the page edges turning golden brown like good ale. On page 1 was a cartoon of Winston Churchill, holding aloft the symbol of the atom bomb, with a caption quoting Labor MP Emanuel Shinwell: "Of course Mr. Churchill is a great war leader. That's why he wants another war." The drawing was by Antonio Frasconi, today one of America's leading artists, then struggling in the world of commercial art. To avert danger to the income by which he supported his serious work he used his Bolivian mother's name, Carbona. Henry Wallace, in an article titled "The Egg and Us," described his egg-pelting ordeal during a Southern speaking tour when he refused to address segregated audiences. He wrote: "The deceptions which other men may seek to practice upon us are powerless unless we also deceive ourselves into silence. And self-deception in this atomic age leads not to the comfort of illusion, but to annihilation."

Featured with Wallace was "A Credo for the Living," by Norman Mailer, whose first novel, *The Naked and the Dead,* had just won critical praise. Mailer then saw—but would soon lose— "hope in the fact that there is a political party, the Progressive Party, to poll the protests against the campaign to make America fascist." Anna Louise Strong, an innocent then en route to a nightmare in Moscow (see chapter 5), wrote movingly of a visit to Lidice, the Czechoslovakian village which the Nazi occupiers wiped out in World War II. And on page 2, over the signatures of Cedric, Jack, and myself, a statement headed: "This is NATIONAL GUARDIAN." It said:

We present our publication humbly, in the conviction that the times call for a voice in our nation which without fear or reservation will bespeak the cause of peace, freedom and abundance. We ask the indulgence and support of all who share that conviction.

NATIONAL GUARDIAN will have no editorial page. But it will certainly have an editorial point of view. This editorial point of view will be a continuation and development of the progressive tradition set in our time by Franklin D. Roosevelt, and overwhelmingly supported by the American people in the last four elections.

We believe, with FDR, in expanding freedoms and living standards for all peoples as the essential foundation of a world securely at peace.

We believe, with FDR, that peace can be secured only by seeking areas of agreement among nations, rather than seeking areas of disagreement.

Since FDR's death we have seen a succession of manufactured crises and negations of people's rights and freedoms. These convince us that his political successors and his Republican opposition—now joined in bipartisan policies which are not in dispute in the 1948 elections—intend neither to seek agreement in world affairs, nor to establish freedom for any peoples except on terms dictated by American big business.

With FDR, we believe that: "The liberty of a democracy is not safe if the people tolerate the growth of private power to a point where it becomes stronger than their democratic state. That, in essence, is fascism."

We believe that the world's greatest productive machine has been created in America by the people of America, out of their own resources; that monopoly's increasing grip on that machine threatens the security of the farmer, small businessman and wage-earner alike; and all these must combine to carry forward the greatest American political tradition—the battle against concentration of private power.

We believe that our country's resources should be used to create an abundant life for the people who developed them, with freedom and opportunity for all. We believe that the interests of property should never and nowhere be respected above the interests of people.

These objectives and concepts are not espoused by any segment of the American press, most certainly not by a national newsweekly.

The Wallace-for-President movement this year, with its rallies, radio addresses and literature, has managed to keep the Roosevelt program before the people despite this national press blackout. However, such cannot be the case once the campaign is over. Therefore, the need for continuing, progressive publication devoted to these ideals becomes one of the most pressing needs of our future.

NATIONAL GUARDIAN begins its existence as the campaign comes to a close. It is the purpose of NATIONAL GUARDIAN's editors to further these ideals by giving the inheritors of Franklin Roosevelt's America an uninterrupted flow of facts to fight with in the continuing battle for a better world.

Our second issue published a hopeful secret poll of New York State showing vast indecision among voters who would choose among President Truman, Governor Dewey, and Wallace. The third issue, bridging the election, looked ahead to "the next four years" and promised that whatever happened the GUARDIAN "will be in the ring, doing what it can to see that the people aren't fooled all the time." We predicted that progressives "are going to be tested by fire. Every conceivable and inconceivable means will be used to make them run for cover—to say with Cain, 'Am I my brother's keeper?' " The statement continued:

The German people, submitted to exactly the same propaganda barrage about "Communism" that we are getting now, answered that question with Cain's bloody negative. It is the sourest joke in history that, having indicted the Germans as a nation for their cowardice which led to such frightful years, and having beaten them in a war, we are only three years later telling them in effect that they were right all the time. But they were not right. And since we know the results of such cowardice—and they did not—our sin is far greater and possibly fatal if we make the wrong answer.

"We" did make the wrong choice—to a large extent because Truman, in the last weeks of the campaign, fooled millions of Americans into believing that he bore the Roosevelt mantle. Soft-pedaling the cold war and its grim domestic implications, he appeared to take over most of the Progressive Party platform. The odds-on favorite Dewey was beaten; the Wallace vote was just over a million, half of that in New York State.

Newspapers with approximately 79 percent of the total daily circulation backed Dewey, 10 percent Truman, 10 percent no choice, and one-tenth of 1 percent Wallace. The pollsters, way off the mark, were haunted by a photograph of a grinning Truman holding up the first edition of the Chicago *Tribune* with the banner headline: DEWEY ELECTED. James Reston accurately set forth the lesson in the New York *Times:* "The great intangible of this election was the political influence of the Roosevelt era on the thinking of the nation . . . and we didn't give enough weight to it. Consequently, we were wrong, not only on the election but, what's worse, on the whole political direction of our time." Having stated this truth, Reston, along with his fellow pundits, continued marching in the wrong direction.

How dangerous that direction was, became rapidly clear. Domestically, for the first time in history, one American official had been elevated by the media to godhood beyond criticism—the fanatical political policeman J. Edgar Hoover. In November Cedric wrote about Operation X, the beginning of America's cloak-and-dagger campaign to destroy socialism in eastern Europe. Early in December, Jack told how the CIO labor leadership in convention had "ordered its 6,000,000 members into the cold war camp by unqualified endorsement of the Marshall Plan and the Truman Doctrine"—twin pillars of the antisocialist crusade. Two weeks later I was on page 1 with an article about "The Great Pumpkin Spy Melodrama," the "discovery" by Richard Nixon of documents on Whittaker Chambers' farm in Maryland which would prove to be Nixon's ticket to the White House. Accompanying the piece was a cartoon by Fred Wright—a "Congressman Snoop" with a copy of *Time* in his coat pocket, standing before a pumpkin-headed psychiatrist, faithful pumpkin-head dog lying beside the desk, pumpkin-head Dr. Freud looking down from the wall, Snoop saying: "Everywhere I go I see pumpkins, Doc." The humor was blacker than we knew.

A test of principle for us at the GUARDIAN came in mid-January 1949 when twelve leaders of the Communist Party U.S.A. went on trial under the Smith Act for "conspiring to advocate" overthrow of the government. We had had no discussions, formal or informal, with the Communist leadership about our plans for NATIONAL

GUARDIAN. We assumed that some organizers of the Progressive Party and many of its activists were Communists. We did not inquire, we did not care. But it was also apparent that some in the Communist leadership looked at our venture with a wary eye. They did not know us except by what we said, and our independent way of saying certain things was not pleasing to them. Stalin had already read the riot act to Marshal Tito of Yugoslavia, as we had not (see chapter 5). We might also, if we succeeded in attracting a mass readership, become a threat to the circulation of the CP's *Worker*. When the CP came under fire, however, none of this was in our minds; we had our eye on something larger, something that could extinguish not only the CP but all dissenting opinion in the United States. Thus, on January 24, we departed for the first time from our no-editorials intention with "An Editorial: Who's On Trial?"

We pointed out that the twelve were "openly doing business" as CP leaders and that "what they are charged with doing—having certain ideas and spreading them—has been done in full view of the nation." We knew of "no statements by them that the government should be overthrown by force" but recalled: "A century ago, a Republican said in a famous speech that it was the people's right to overthrow the government." We referred of course to Lincoln's first inaugural address. We didn't believe the Republican Party should be put on trial because of Lincoln's words, and the same applied to the CP, even if it had "conspired to advocate" as charged. But "the idea that the tiny U.S. Communist Party could succeed in such a coup, even if they desired it, is absurd on its face."

Any honest reading of history [we continued], compels the recognition that on the major issues of the past 20 years the Communist Party has been right more often than it has been wrong. . . . The Communists were taking active steps to expose and destroy fascism—and to avoid World War II—long before most of their critics came out of their coma. They were found leading the heroic resistance to fascism in every country occupied by Hitler and the Japanese. They speak up for the poor and those least able to defend themselves against flagrant denials of democracy in America. In China today, the Communists are, with complete justification and utmost competence, doing what Lincoln said a democratic people can do when a government no longer satisfies them.

If their doctrine is as false as President Truman says it is, it is remarkable, to say the least, how often it has led them into morally commendable positions and actions.

As for the twelve Communists now making front page news all over America, it is not they who are on trial. If they are convicted, almost all Americans will feel it where it hurts. Read the history of other countries where the Communist Party has been outlawed. In every case this has been the curtain-raiser to attacks on the people's living standards, on their unions and their civil rights, including those of the very people who joined the hue and cry against the first victims.

Ideas cannot be killed by putting the people who hold them behind bars. They have never been and never will be. It is the common sense of America that is on trial in New York's Federal Court.

That set the policy for our relations with the CP. We sought to maintain it—certainly in print—from that point on, despite serious differences with the CP leadership, particularly on an effective political-action strategy for the American left, Communist and non-Communist. After the conviction, futile appeals and imprisonment of the Smith Act victims, we raised thousands of dollars through our pages to ease the plight of their families. I doubt whether the majority of CP leaders ever understood how vital it was for them to have the support of a non-Communist radical publication like ours, but if they did not, the rank and file of the CP did.

Our coverage of the trial provided an understanding of the basic issues for our 25,000 paid subscribers (our circulation by February 1949) and for newspapers abroad which increasingly reprinted the interpretive GUARDIAN articles. But despite the rapid circulation rise we were finding it ever more difficult to meet operating costs. Staff salaries were low—no one got more than $75 a week, some weeks nobody got anything—and babies insisted on being born and getting fed. Vic Levitt ran a union shop and had to pay his printers. He was suffering too: since the CIO had joined the cold war, unions were pulling their papers out of his shop (oddly, the publication in Italian of the Catholic archdiocese of Brooklyn remained). The Progressive Party national office, regrouping after the election, seemed to be the logical "court of appeal" for our means of survival, and there we went. If the PP was going to stay in business, surely it would acknowledge the necessity of helping to maintain a national weekly espousing its cause.

The reception was cool. It was a bad time for money-raising for any progressive cause, we were told, and even if it weren't the PP had a deficit to pay off and state offices to support; the GUARDIAN not being a PP project, PP resources could not be called upon to keep it from going under; although Wallace and the former Businessmen for Wallace had agreed to sponsor a function to obtain loans for the GUARDIAN, the leadership would oppose this as not in the PP's direct interests; we should not, in effect, "poach on PP preserves," no matter how great the demand of PP membership for a reliable publication. The leadership was unwilling to consider the danger of our hanging separately if we didn't hang together. The framers of this "go look for funds elsewhere or drop dead" policy were, we knew, in or close to the CP.

Jack was livid; his feelings boiled over in a memo he wrote after the meeting: "I think I need not stress the utter cynicism of this outlook, which in my opinion has characterized the top-level operations of the PP from the very start. Terms such as 'selfish' and 'short-sighted' and 'dog in the manger' do not begin to describe this attitude. It means obviously that we must build the GUARDIAN without the help of the PP, since its paid administrative level will scuttle any attempt we make to have Wallace or any authoritative leader extend us any help in obtaining financing. In proceeding on our own, however, we must in my opinion curb any impulse to drag this stupid situation out in the open in any way that might disaffect the PP membership or further any splits now existing among its leadership. We shall simply have to go out and convince enough money people that the creation of a progressive press is of topmost importance to the PP, despite the refusal of the PP leadership to render more than lip service to this conviction."

A generally charitable man, Jack had uncharitable reactions to two participants at the meeting. One was a hard-boiled fund-raiser who lamented to us about the falling price of men's shirts, since "this means a recession for some of our money people." Jack's comment: "This despite our stated objective of lower prices. Wow!" The other was an extremely rich woman who had admonished us to "stop milking the same cow." Jack's comment: "I propose we start by a private collection to send Mrs. —— her $500 back and wish her well on her trip to Deauville." (I had a similar reaction to this woman when, on a pre-publication money hunt at her East Side town house, she shoved a box of candies across the livingroom rug toward Cedric with her foot. He graciously declined to select one.)

As the February winds howled through the canyons of lower Broadway, the mood in the GUARDIAN office was bleak. There just wasn't any money to be had anywhere and we were mentally writing the obit of our fledgling weekly. We owed $15,000 in printing bills—a paltry sum to those familiar with publishing ventures, but life-and-death to a small firm like Vic's. Circulation was steadily rising and we had taken over the 8,000 readers of the expiring progressive *Illinois Standard*. The *Star* was folding in New York and we hoped to pick up readership there. But nothing could be done without cash to pay the printer and promote the paper. We decided on one last urgent appeal to our readers.

We threw out an already prepared page one for the issue of February 7 and substituted a message, in large type, taking up the entire page: A CALL TO ACTION NOW! THE PROGRESSIVE PRESS IS IN PERIL. We laid out the situation in cold blood and concluded:

"Suspension of NATIONAL GUARDIAN would not only leave the Wallace–Progressive movement without a single sympathetic national publication. It would force upon the American people a choice between the alternatives of only the Communist Party press on the left and the commercial press—overwhelmingly hostile to liberal American tradition—on the right. The editors and staff of NATIONAL GUARDIAN do not propose to let this happen without a fight and without inviting our readers to join that fight. Therefore, we place our situation squarely up to you."

And then, to us nonbelievers, it happened: The Miracle of Our Lady of the Lake. On February 10 this telegram arrived at the GUARDIAN:

> YOUR NATIONAL GUARDIAN OF FEBRUARY SEVEN IS COM-
> PELLING. WOULD YOU SEND ME TELEGRAPH COLLECT SOME IN-
> FORMATION I GREATLY WANT. I AM GREATLY MOVED BY ITS
> OUTLOOK AND I WOULD LIKE TO KNOW THAT THE CONTENTS
> CONTAINED IN THAT STATEMENT WILL BE SAFEGUARDED UNTIL I
> MAY HAVE A CHANCE TO FIND OUT WHETHER I MAY BE OF SOME
> HELP TO THAT END. KINDLY WIRE ME COLLECT ALL THAT YOU
> THINK BEARS ON MY QUESTION. ALSO PLEASE SEND ME A DOZEN
> COPIES OF THAT ISSUE. YOURS SINCERELY.
>
> ANITA BLAINE, 101 EAST ERIE ST., CHICAGO, ILL.

The message was given to Jack first. His boiling point had not elevated appreciably since the session with the Progressive Party leaders, and all hands were walking around him gingerly. He came into our office and handed the telegram to Cedric, who read it and handed it to me. We looked at Jack. "This isn't some kind of a gag, is it?" he said. "I'm not in the mood for pranks." So wary were we that we checked the authenticity of the message with Western Union.

Anita Blaine was no less than the daughter of Cyrus McCormick of the great reaper fortune. She had become the belle of Chicago's Gold Coast society when she married Emmons Blaine, son of the "plumed knight" James G. Blaine, who was defeated for the Presidency by Grover Cleveland in 1884. Emmons Blaine, a lawyer, died in 1892, leaving his young widow with a son, Emmons Jr., who was to die in 1918. With the death of her husband a change came over Ms. Blaine. She gave up the glittering life and took charge of her great holdings at her own office on Michigan Avenue—a most unusual step for a society woman in those days. Daily, in widow's black, she rode in a carriage to her office.

She became interested in American schools and got herself

elected to the Chicago Board of Education. There she took on the politicians, creating a storm at a meeting of the National Education Association when she chided teachers for their "bread-and-butter" attitude and urged them on to higher principles of instruction than "the mad rush for money." She rushed several millions of her own money to support her principles by founding the Chicago Institute, which later became the famed Francis Parker School, espousing the progressive educational ideas of the principal of Cook County Normal School for whom it was named.

When "Aunt Anita," as she was known to her friends, made up her mind, one of them said, "money means nothing." Among recipients of her generosity were the League of Nations, the School of Education of the University of Chicago, the families of miners killed in accidents, and the poor children of the area fringing her lakefront mansion. The mansion, looking like a museum and normally with the hush of one, was the scene of Sunday afternoon parties, always run on "democratic principles," for these children.

A deeply religious woman, Ms. Blaine applied her beliefs by helping a wide range of institutions from settlement houses to the Foundation for World Government. "The human race," she said, "the whole world, is in perhaps the worst situation in its history. The need is terrific. We in the United States are in the middle of the whole crisis. We must do something for the human family." When China was struggling against Japanese occupation, she walked into the Drake Hotel in Chicago, handed Mme. Chiang Kai-shek a check for $100,000, and said: "You are to use this in any way you see fit." She instituted the eight-hour day for her household staff, to the discomfiture of her "class" friends.

Her dress remained turn-of-the-century, with odd little hats fastened with a hat-pin. She advised against women's hats weighing more than four ounces. "A larger hat causes mental strain," she said, "and women certainly need all their mental equipment to get by in the world." Eccentric she was, in a spectacularly sane fashion. In 1936 she spent thousands of dollars for full-page ads to help FDR's reelection campaign, and although she was against war to the point of pacifism, she insisted in 1941 that Congress must declare war against Nazi Germany. It was this concern with the encroachment of fascism and America's predatory foreign policy after World War II that attracted her to Henry Wallace. She said of him: "In the deep and vast problems that face us today, he is an honest and enlightened guide—conservative and not radical."

These facets of Anita Blaine were little known to us that day in February 1949 as we read and reread her telegram in something of a daze. But we recovered quickly and sent her a wire, including a statement of the GUARDIAN's founding principles, a description of ourselves and the staff, and a report on the first results of our February 7 appeal: "There is evidence of tremendous determination among our readers not to let us down . . . We have at least a few weeks of reprieve. Will you permit one or all three of us to come to Chicago to discuss this situation in full detail?"

Next day came this message:

I thank you heartily for your reply to my telegram in which all questions were understood. . . . I have been suffering with Henry Wallace and his helpers over the possibility of the avenues of light going out. That evening the whole picture afflicted me newly and I reached out for existing or future help. The next day you came running. Now, in outline, the possibility of sharing and sending real light is at stake. I have been in consultation with Henry Wallace concerning his next plans and thoughts. I am wondering whether this emergency can be serviceable to us all—perhaps in addition to the talks you suggest—two talks, one for a few to look over the field of the best possibilities, another to acquaint a wider group to look further into that. It might be wonderful and extend farther than we think.

I am, faithfully yours,
Anita Blaine.

The following Sunday afternoon we flew to Chicago, taking along Vic Levitt who, after all, had the biggest lien on us; in addition, he was one of the few businessmen who had faith in us. We were met at the airport by a liveried chauffeur with limousine for a drive to the Park-Sheraton, where a suite had been reserved. On the drive in from the airport, Vic, a New Yorker to his marrow, observed: "Chicago is like Queens, except that you never get to

OUR LADY OF THE LAKE

Manhattan." The limousine, we were told, would pick us up the next morning for a meeting with Ms. Blaine at 101 East Erie. The elevator at the hotel sped us up to the penthouse Bamboo Suite, an elegantly exotic arrangement complete with beaded curtains—a perfect setting for a seduction, but our intentions were honorable. In the livingroom were flowers and baskets of fruit and a bottle of Old Fitzgerald, a bourbon of graceful age which was to become for us later a ceremonial libation to our Lady of the Lake.

Cruising on Monday morning down a stately street that led to the lake, we disembarked outside the huge, gloomy mansion for our rendezvous. Anita Blaine came down a curved stairway to greet us in the foyer. She was then 82, dressed in a long simple black dress with white lace collar, her white hair caught in a bun. She wore metal-rimmed glasses. In her hand she carried a gold clock with large hoop. She extended her hand to each of us and said, with tears in her eyes: "You don't know how happy you have made me by coming." I had never met anyone remotely like her: noble and, at the same time, most touching.

Then the butler went twice to the door to admit two handsome and courtly gentlemen. Their aroma was that of men given to handling large sums of money with discreet but firm resolution. They were Ms. Blaine's attorneys, Richard Bentley and William Warfield III, of Tenney, Sherman, Bentley, and Guthrie, a prestigious La Salle Street firm. Their suave masks could not quite conceal an episcopal suspicion about our odd quartet of supplicants at the shrine.

We took our places in the living room and Ms. Blaine asked us to lay out our situation. Jack made an admirable presentation, punctuated by polite questions from Messrs. Bentley and Warfield and encouraging interpolations by Vic. Cedric and I were a modulated Greek chorus. There followed a luncheon of filet mignon, served on little tables at our places, which moved Vic later in the downstairs washroom to confide to me: "I'll tell you how they got that piece of beef. They took a cow, scooped out the choicest six-inch hunk, and threw the rest of the animal away." I had no reason to doubt his version.

Ms. Blaine's questions, and the respectful attitude of her attorneys, established two facts: while she must have been inundated with requests for assistance, she was not an "easy mark"; while her attorneys almost surely disapproved the political complexion of some of the petitioners, they had learned to accede to their eccentric client.

What we asked was the advancement to us of $3,000 a week for a six-month period, actually the cost of putting out the paper—payroll, printing, mailing, and promotion—each week. Income derived from circulation and other sources would be placed in a separate fund for use only when necessary. The plan would provide us with both security for the ongoing operation and a nest-egg for an emergency. Ms. Blaine agreed with an enthusiasm and speed which left us dizzier than her first telegram. We had never before been in such a cordial situation with a prospective angel. The remainder of the discussion was taken up with reminiscences and talk about newspapers, particularly the Chicago press. With seemingly innocent guile our hostess dissected "Cousin Bertie"—Colonel Robert R. McCormick, publisher of the Chicago *Tribune*—whose person and policies she could not abide. Even as a child, she said, Cousin Bertie was a most unpleasant companion, and all the little McCormicks avoided playing with him on the rooftop playground of the mansion.

We returned to New York by overnight train in a manner befitting newspaper publishers who had just settled their affairs for a half-year ahead, and ordered Old Fitzgerald in the dining car. Next morning Ms. Blaine called and asked Jack for a letter giving the essence of our agreement. "You are manager of the paper completely," she said. "I don't want to infringe. I simply accept the whole thing laid before me. If you accept my word over the telephone, we are now in this together. We are partners because you have accepted my word and I accept yours." She said the money would be a gift, and we were relieved. We could envisage a situation in which a loan might be called in because of unforeseen circumstances, and we would be, as we used to say on the sandlot ballfield, out in left field without a glove. Jack complied with a businesslike letter, then added:

OUR LADY OF THE LAKE

The foregoing is the formal part of this letter; the rest is partner to partner. You have no idea of the tremendous, buoyant lift your interest and generosity have given the people of NATIONAL GUARDIAN. Now we know we can settle down to our tasks with no fear of the future. Our trying months have not been in vain. We have our GUARDIAN; we have a grand new ally in the fight for a truthful, peace-loving press and a better life for people everywhere. . . . This, to us, means the fulfillment of a dream—a dream of opportunity, as journalists, honestly to serve the people through the medium of a truly free and responsible press. We are deeply gratified at the confidence you place in us; we shall do all in our power to justify that confidence.

Ms. Blaine called almost daily, with great excitement, for the next several days, often opening the conversation with expressions such as, "The world is wide, and it's all ours. I just wanted you to know." On February 27, delivered by hand, was an envelope addressed to the three of us, enclosing a check for $78,000 and this note: "Dear Guardian: I am sending my gift to reach you by the date we made together. May it be enabled to fulfill all our wishes for it. Ever yours."

Jack had a dream of one million readers at 50¢ a year—a genuine "penny press"—and he saw the new money as a way to realize the dream. Being of a more cautious nature, I was skeptical; I wanted to hoard our new-found security against the risk of natural and unnatural disaster which the political climate seemed to portend. Perhaps more than anyone on the paper, since I was the one who saw it through to the presses each week, I was impressed by the enormous effort of putting out a 12-page tabloid with inadequate staff and increasing costs. Would it not be wiser to invest in quality staff and promotion, and ease our way slowly into the future? What would happen if one day Our Lady vanished with the miracle into the Lake?

But Jack's imagination was infectious. We reduced the sub price of the paper from $4 a year to $2, with a special introductory sub of 40 weeks for $1. The rate of subscription more than doubled; one reader sent in $64 with 64 names. We added to the staff editorially as well as promotionally. The paper's editorial quality improved and we basked in the glow of comment that we had moved from being a "good" paper to an "indispensable" one. Unfortunately the promotional and business additions did not match the editorial improvements. Fast-talking mass-market "experts"—the kind who inspire awe exclusively in left circles ("he would be a $50,000-a-year man with any corporation if he were willing to sell his soul")—found their way on to the staff. Chronically at liberty and immediately available at the sniff of the green, they dazzled with their "analyses" and "potentials." We worked such long hours and ended each week in such a state of exhaustion, that we were oversusceptible to dazzlement and welcomed a respite from our role as inexpert entrepreneurs. Jack walked about humming, "If I had a million . . .", but by May the circulation was only 50,000—an impressive increase since the dank February days, but a long way from home. And the money was running out. The mass-marketing schemes and both proper and improper demands by the staff (see chapter 3) had made large dents in the reserves.

So back we went to Ms. Blaine with a new proposal: $5,000 a week beginning in June to take us into the winter of 1950—a total of $150,000. Ms. Blaine agreed, and a new gift check arrived on June 7. While Cedric and I concentrated more on the editorial side, Jack devoted himself increasingly to circulation-building and securing the paper's future—and began to nurture a new dream. Late in June he asked me if I had Dickens' *American Notes* at home. I brought in a copy and knew that sooner or later it would turn up in the paper. The following week Jack's "Report to Readers" came to my desk. He had been browsing through Dickens on a recent day off, he wrote, and had come upon this description of the American press of the 1840s:

> Good strong stuff dealing in round abuse and blackguard names, pulling off the roofs of private houses, pimping and pandering for all degrees of vicious taste, gorging with coined lies the most voracious maw; setting on, with yell and whistle, and clapping of foul hands, the vilest vermin and the worst birds of prey.

Jack made a quick survey of the press a century later and found remarkably little change. What was the answer? "A profit-free press, without the requirement of subservience to the demands of the business interests which subsidize our present press. There is no decent reason for the press to be a profit-making institution, nor the radio. Both are grants by the people. Both should exist solely for the interests of the people. This is the age of foundations. We see foundations for cancer research, for curbing heat, disease, for peace—for all manner of things in which our economic and political system has ignored the people's needs. Now let us have a foundation for a free and responsible press; free of advertiser or business domination; free of concern over its own economic security; free of any restriction save only that of operating in the people's interest. And let all profit be turned back to the foundation for further extension of a truly free and responsible press in America instead of a subsidized chain of house organs for greedy enterprise.''

In our eyes it was an eminently sensible proposal. Only two years before, a commission headed by Chancellor Robert M. Hutchins of the University of Chicago had published the results of a three-year study of the press—financed largely by Henry Luce of Time, Inc., who surely didn't know what was coming—in a volume titled *A Free and Responsible Press*. The report by this prestigious commission, made up entirely of non-newpaper people, criticized American newspapers so devastatingly that the press rose up in arms. Col. McCormick financed a book to discredit the report, in a campaign whose echoes still reverberated in June 1949. What Jack was proposing, in effect, was that the recommendations of the commission to make the press responsible be implemented. But in view of the press's obvious unwillingness to police itself, an alternative in the form of a nonprofit foundation could be an answer.

Since all roads seemed to lead to Chicago, Curtis MacDougall, a professor of journalism at Northwestern University, was approached to draw up a prospectus on the needs for a foundation. And since Ms. Blaine had shown her continuing interest in the press, by refinancing our operation and giving a much larger sum to Ted O. Thackrey to publish the New York *Compass* (about to be born), the road ultimately led back again to 101 East Erie. With Ms. Blaine's blessing two conferences were held in July to discuss the foundation plan, and out of these came a decision for a larger conference to be held early in September with Ms. Blaine.

Basically, the idea was to improve the means of information reaching the American people with these main proposals: 1) subsidize liberal daily newspapers, magazines, radio programs and stations (the effectiveness of television was not yet appreciated), and other communication media—an opposition press which would not depend on big business for its existence; 2) support a continuing study of the extent to which American journalism lived up to or fell short of its responsibility; 3) institute public education about the reading and evaluation of newspapers; 4) encourage the training of principled men and women for active participation in dissenting journalism. Among participants in the wider conference would be, in addition to Ms. Blaine, the GUARDIAN editors, the management of the *Compass*, Professor MacDougall, Roger Lee of the Harvard Corporation, Dr. Linus Pauling, Henry Wallace, and C. B. ("Beanie") Baldwin, secretary of the Progressive Party.

Various obstacles prevented the meeting from taking place on schedule, but there was a new spurt of activity in the early fall and a document for a certificate of incorporation for the "Anita Blaine Fund" was worked out. A meeting scheduled for late November again had to be postponed. That was a relief for me because a new baby was scheduled (and arrived) at our house on November 22. She was named Anita, and Ms. Blaine sent a potted plant to mark the occasion. Finally, December 17 was set for a full-dress conference.

Early in December we wrote to Ms. Blaine for a separate sit-down with her to discuss the GUARDIAN's own situation. The refinancing money was dwindling, along with the dream of a million subscribers, as the domestic counterpart of the cold war machine spread its climate of fear. On December 9 Ms. Blaine fell ill and the foundation meeting was put off again. A week later she wired the intended participants that the meeting would have to go over to the first of the year: "I have had some sort of breakdown for which I ask forgiveness. The one thing I would hope for most

40

definitely would be that no real interruption takes place in the line of thought which we have held and in the purposes which have been ours since the beginning." She felt that Jack fell naturally into place as leader of the venture. We sent her flowers and she wired: "Your violets speak to me of a lovely day."

But the violets wilted as Ms. Blaine underwent surgery on December 20. After the operation she telegraphed: "WILL CALL YOU ON RETURN HOME." The call never came. In response to an urgent letter from us, attorney Warfield wrote that no business matters were being placed before Ms. Blaine and it was therefore impossible to bring the GUARDIAN's problems to her attention. A gracious but noncommittal response came also from Nancy Blaine, Ms. Blaine's niece and closest surviving relative, who went daily to visit her in the hospital. On February 13, 1950, attorney Bentley sent us an ominous-sounding letter noting the payment of $150,000 to us the previous June, and requesting "detailed information not otherwise available to me at this time as to the basis on which the payment was made."

We supplied the information and asked for a meeting with Nancy Blaine and Bentley, which was granted. Jack as our emissary set forth the GUARDIAN's situation and needs. It was not till May that we received a reply from Bentley. On the eve of her operation, he wrote, Ms. Blaine had told him there were "puzzling questions in her mind with regard to various organizations, and I am quite sure from the context of her remarks that this referred to the GUARDIAN, even though it was not discussed." Bentley did not reveal the inspiration for his clairvoyance, and the letter puzzled us, but our own oracles indicated that Ms. Blaine's advisers and possible heirs would not be sympathetic to a continuing arrangement with us. The yellowing files reveal no further communication from Ms. Blaine.

Three years of silence from Chicago set in, broken only by a letter in January 1953 from a Chicago firm of accountants: it noted an "indebtedness" on our part to Ms. Blaine for "loans" of $228,000, a sum which in that Year of McCarthy seemed as elusive to us as Jack's million readers. We wrote that the money was a gift, and enclosed copies of the "letters of gift." A similar letter from the same accountants came in January 1954.

Ms. Blaine died in May 1954. That November William S. Warfield III called us when he was in New York on other business and asked about the money. Same reply. A year later Bentley wrote to us: "As I am sure you realize, it is the duty of the Executors to collect all claims due to the estate or to satisfy the Probate Court as to why they are not collected in whole or in part. In the case of a claim where the debtor takes the position that no payment is due, it is usually necessary to resort to the courts to determine the matter. I understand that there has been considerable stringency in the financial situation of NATIONAL GUARDIAN. If this would have a bearing on the collectibility of the claim (assuming we could convince a court it is due), it would be useful both to you and to us if we were furnished with definite information as to its relevance."

Bentley seemed to have lost neither his discretion nor his courtliness in the years since our first meeting in February 1949, but we detected also a certain compassion. He seemed to be saying: Just write us a letter saying you can't pay. We did, of course, insisting however that we owed nothing because Ms. Blaine had clearly specified the money as a gift. On January 19, 1956, Bentley wrote: "On the basis of the information now on hand, we will regard the claim of the Blaine estate as uncollectible, and we have no present intention of pressing it."

Ms. Blaine left an estate of $41,364,236.05. The GUARDIAN didn't get even the nickel.

Postscript [**C.B.**] Chicago . . . Two Colonels: I never met "Cousin Bertie" McCormick, the Chicago *Tribune* publisher whom Anita Blaine found as personally nasty as his newspaper (impossible, I thought); yet he lingered on for me as a more real character than Ms. Blaine. Right after the Soviets "got the Bomb" in 1949 he pioneered the "atomic defense" hoax-hysteria by fortifying the *Tribune* building with a warning system, "command post and nerve center," stockpiles of aspirin, and arrangements for barricades of newsprint rolls to avert radiation of the staff. Every

American schoolteacher thereafter had to drill children in ducking under desks, a backyard-shelter business boomed, and anyone failing to scuttle for shelter at the sound of a siren was arrested. The sirens continued for years as a feature of American life, each shriek a salute to Cousin Bertie, whereas Ms. Blaine vanished so suddenly back into the Lake that she came to seem like something I dreamed. Even my New York jail home in 1955 had a shelter but was a surprising island of sanity: when the siren blew, nobody moved. "If one of them things falls," a screw confided, "you're dead anyway."

But there was another colonel associated with Chicago, and for a long time with Ms. Blaine, who was as different from McCormick as she was. God knows why Chicago should have produced around the turn of the century a strain of wealthy Americans who saw—and acted—beyond their investment portfolios, but one of them was Colonel Raymond Robins. Like Ms. Blaine and the other do-gooders, as orthodox millionaires dubbed them, Robins was a religious person who took his Bible seriously. Little versed in Marxism, he believed that godless rebels and revolutionaries also contributed to God's work. By the time I met Robins (I wanted to write his biography), he was a cripple living on a Florida estate and an ardent GUARDIAN booster with what remained, after all his benevolences, of the fortune he dug up in the Klondike gold rush. The historians' neglect of Robins, an American original if ever there was one, is shameful. The post-Klondike highlights of his life, which began as a barefoot farm boy, were two trips to Russia, Bible in hand, with missions to Lenin and Stalin. Officially as a Red Cross emissary, unofficially to make contact with the Bolsheviks, he was a witness of the revolution in Petrograd in 1917.

In many conversations he tried to convince Lenin that he was a Christian without knowing it. This particular task was hopeless, but he reported back in Washington that the revolution, led by a man Robins bracketed with Jesus and Jefferson as a giant of history, was worthy of America's support. The normal public vilification by a congressional committee followed. In 1933, when Roosevelt contemplated diplomatic relations with the Soviet Union, he sent Robins back there for an up-to-date survey. This time it was recognition of the USSR that followed. Robins told Stalin prophetically: "The situation forces us above all to follow our own interests . . . we are interested in development of U.S. exports. The only big market with great possibilities and not really utilized is the Russian market." Stalin thought this sound but, like Lenin, declined the honorary Christianity that Robins would have conferred on him.

The "Blaine papers" preserved by Jim restore our Lady of the Lake to nebulous reality for me: her irrepressible aversion to Bertie, for whose journalistic crimes she felt she must atone; her "reaching out for help" to "share and send real light" with her fortune; her enchanting telegrams with their 10-to-1 ratio between superfluous and necessary words. The thought that her first telegram was a practical joke came naturally to us paupers, but only someone who never had to give money a thought—except for how to give it away responsibly—could have sent it and its successors.

"Deeply religious" really describes her, in the only good sense of that tortured phrase. She probably assumed that we three were all atheists but, since we were "Christians without knowing it," there was no need to ask. In this way she was like my mother, a country parson's daughter with fewer farthings than Ms. Blaine had thousands of dollars, who was stricken when I stopped worshiping her God but grew in conviction that whatever I did, even if it landed me in jail, must be "for the best." I recall Ms. Blaine's description of how her attention was drawn to the GUARDIAN's plight. Our crisis issue lay on the floor at the foot of that manorial staircase; as she came down, her feet were "guided to it" and she picked it up. She was a subscriber but papers tended to get lost in that immense pad and this, miraculously, was the issue to which she was "guided." Such things came out of her simply and straight. I detected no guile in her mind, nor gush in her eyes when they filled with tears.

Jim and I couldn't argue against Jack's noble thought of directing the Blaine bonanza, not merely into the GUARDIAN, but into a national press reformation. My Scots forebears and Jim's Jewish ones shuddered in their graves, but that was the sort of partner we had. The way we went through our money was very Irish. The consolation is that it didn't have time to corrupt us much and, forced back into the bleakest self-reliance, the GUARDIAN made it anyway.

We had to raise funds the hard way, a job calling for endless resourcefulness and patience and determination. But thanks to such heroines as Theodora Peck and Vita Barsky (to name the chief ones through the years), the impossible was achieved.

*   *   *

Did we overstress the "FDR" motif in our first issue statement? For all the details about his Presidency that we know now and didn't know then, I don't think we did. Even looking at him in relation to White House tenants of the next three decades, I would submit that his eminence isn't wholly due to the flatness of the surrounding country.

Report from the Interior

[**J.A.**] The golden wand from Chicago, and the illusion of affluence it created in us, vanished just when the supreme offensive
against all cold war opponents began. When I think back on it, almost invariably in my mind I join Pete Seeger singing "Wasn't
that a time to try the soul of man?" One had to sing to keep up
one's spirits—and sang with all the gusto appropriate to the fact
that both songs and singers were marked as subversive. That particular song in 1955 would qualify as an "exhibit" in the record of
Pete's appearance before HUAC, which led to a one-year jail sentence (later thrown out) for the GUARDIAN's favorite entertainer.

Haunting the nation's capital was the specter of the Soviet
Bomb, first announced at the end of 1949. The corollary of course
was: Who gave *Them* the Bomb? With their peasant mentality the
Russians could not possibly have discovered the formula for nuclear fission without assistance from spies in the United States.
The Communist Party leaders were doomed to prison, Alger Hiss
was convicted of perjury after a second trial, his denouncer, Whittaker Chambers, was nominated for sainthood by the liberal intellectual establishment, and Richard Nixon was on his way to the
Senate. John Foster Dulles, Republican lawyer for international
and especially German corporations, was named foreign policy ad-

viser to President Truman to compound the mendacity of Secretary of State Dean Acheson and emphasize the bipartisan solidarity of cold war policy. On the hustings for the 1950 mid-term elections, Democrats vied with Republicans to present before a bewildered electorate a record of unimpeachable anticommunism.

In the "popular" press—Hearst and Scripps-Howard—the theme was: Kill a Commie for Christ (i.e., capitalism); in the "respectable" press—the New York *Times* and Washington *Post,* for example—the crusade against the international communist conspiracy assumed a cathedral quality: editorials were solemn masses evoking the satanic essence of socialism, with a celestial choir celebrating American virtue and godliness. And as the giant organ thundered the overture, Senator Joe McCarthy of Wisconsin stood before the Republican women of Wheeling, W. Va. (an audience whose hats I am sure violated Ms. Blaine's four-ounce limit), flourishing some folded sheets of paper and saying: "I hold in my hand a list of names that were made known to the Secretary of State as being members of the Communist Party and who nevertheless are still working and shaping policy in the State Department." It was the night of February 9, 1950. In the beginning, there was darkness. . . .

At the GUARDIAN we were compiling other lists—names of angels with chubby fingers to plug the dike of financial disaster. But let me go back a bit to present the situation in its fullest flavor.

In the fall of 1949 our staff expressed a wish to join the New York Guild. Appreciating their almost uncomplaining acceptance of the early bumps, and strong advocates of organization in the newspaper field (after all, Jack and I had both been Newspaper Guild functionaries), we encouraged the staff's move and they all joined. In addition to the obvious protections of unionism, the staff felt that the infusion of a group of militant radicals might stiffen the increasingly flaccid spine of the Guild's leaders in face of the cold war onslaught against labor's rank and file.

Thus, in November 1949, a contract was signed with the Newspaper Guild with provisions similar to those prevailing at the New York *Daily Compass* (the successor to *PM* and the *Star*), which had been founded by Ted O. Thackrey, former editor of the New York *Post*. Thackrey had been divorced from both his paper and his wife (*Post* publisher Dorothy Schiff) after their falling-out over the 1948 Presidential elections. Thackrey had been for Wallace, Ms. Schiff for Truman. Financing for the *Compass* had come from Ms. Blaine in a very generous amount. Salaries did not approximate those on the *Times,* but were quite respectable and, in the commercial departments, almost equal. The contract provided for a five-day, 35-hour week, generous holidays, four weeks' severance for every year employed, four weeks' vacation after three years' employment, six weeks' sick leave at full pay and six weeks' at half pay, and six months' maternity leave with six weeks' pay.

There was an innovation also which struck some traditionalists as a bit much for an enterprise as shaky as ours: paternity leave. "In the event a birth occurs in the family," the contract read, "the father shall be given a week off with pay for the purpose of taking care of the household." Since working wives of staff members were making the utmost contribution so that their husbands could stick with the GUARDIAN, this bit of premature women's liberation philosophy was implemented without severe dislocation to work or male ego.

The contract, however, was short-lived as far as wages were concerned. Money ran out at the beginning of 1950 and almost immediately it became a question of continuing on a drastically reduced level or shutting down. Since no one wanted the latter, we established a joint staff-management committee to seek ways to preserve a maximum of jobs and maintain union shop conditions within the limits of our ability. The staff agreed to a setup in which all basic pay would be $40 a week, plus $10 per dependent; management was subject to the same conditions. Thus there were times when a subscription clerk took home more than the editor.

With staff consent, in February we laid out the situation to Thomas J. Murphy, Guild executive secretary, with whom both Jack and I had worked. He understood he wasn't dealing with the *World-Telegram,* he said, and anything that could be worked out with logic would be agreeable. He would send an organizer down to talk it over. The organizer arrived next day and accepted the staff–management arrangement, plus a plan to defer wages (the difference between what the employee got and what the contract said he should get) until the joint committee felt conditions had changed sufficiently for the balance to be paid. The staff representatives would have a voice in deciding on all actions necessary for the life of the paper. The Guild was formally notified of the arrangement.

Three months later the Guild's secretary-treasurer M. Michael Potoker (he subsequently was appointed to a municipal judgeship) informed us that the Guild refused to recognize any agreement modifying the original contract. The cold war obviously had taken over. An exchange of correspondence followed, but the Guild was adamant. It preferred charges against its GUARDIAN members (without consulting the members in advance) and gave staff and management 48 hours to comply under threat to "take the necessary steps to obtain enforcement of the contract."

A bargaining stalemate at the Hearst and Scripps-Howard papers preoccupied Potoker and the Guild for several weeks, but they found interim ammunition in the monthly newsletter of the Bartenders Union of New York (Local 15, AFL) which tried to slip us a mickey. Under a headline, COMMIES' "MILITANCY" EXPOSED AS PHONY, the June 1950 issue of the newsletter reported: "Employees of the NATIONAL GUARDIAN . . . agreed several weeks ago to 'lend' approximately 50 percent of their pay to their employers. It's the old 'kickback' story. . . . Part of the situation that points up the phony militancy of the Reds is the fact that John T. McManus, general manager of the NATIONAL GUARDIAN, was president of the Newspaper Guild of New York three years ago, before the membership cleaned the Commy-following officials out of the Guild. When he was a Guild official McManus was a red-hot militant. If a kickback had occurred when he was in the saddle, he would have screamed to high heaven. But this is different."

The difference became apparent in September when the Guild

officialdom, relieved of its bouts with Hearst and Scripps-Howard, instituted a "trial committee" to hear charges against the staff involving contract violations. The staff denounced the move as politically inspired because they had often taken issue with Guild policies, and because the policies of the GUARDIAN were at variance with the politics of the CIO leadership (the CIO had not yet merged with the AFL). The Guild leaders would not budge: they were out for the kill. The staff perceived this without difficulty and resigned en masse from the Guild to save the paper from certain death. Our staff–management committee continued in operation and all provisions of the contract remained in effect, except wages. Paternity leave was preserved.

Early in 1950 we shifted gears back from Blaine to Bootstrap—Operation Bootstrap, to be precise, and it described itself perfectly. For three months we became a 16-page biweekly, then for several months an 8-page weekly. Our readers responded, but the Progressive Party leadership remained impermeable. The one political figure who understood the importance of the GUARDIAN to the movement was Congressman Vito Marcantonio. As head of New York State's American Labor Party, he sought to help us enroll its 160,000 members as subscribers in a plan which would also raise funds for the ALP. In a circular letter he wrote: "The GUARDIAN is a must in the hands of an ALP voter every issue."

The campaign was not successful because things were hotting up too fast. The Supreme Court refused to hear an appeal by the Hollywood Ten; Louis Budenz, former editor of the *Daily Worker,* surfaced as a prime McCarthy stool pigeon; Harry Bridges of the West Coast Longshoremen—most defiant of labor leaders, whom the government was set on deporting—was sentenced to five years in prison (the court later threw the case out); John Foster Dulles and his Homburg hat were scurrying from London to Berlin to Tokyo to Seoul to contain the Red Tide, and the media were whipping the jingo spirit to a frenzy. In the struggle for the hearts and minds of America, our David-like GUARDIAN was confronted with a super-Goliath.

The staff felt the pinch badly. SOS messages came with increasing frequency to the "disbursing council" of the staff–management committee empowered to make special outlays for the ultra-needy. One memo said: "Mortgage due (with interest yet) on the 18th. Will you okay $71.60 to keep the foxes away from the porch?" Another: "The FHA loan on my furnace is due. $100 would tide me over." All requests were granted. Vic Levitt resumed his pleas for back printing bills. One came on May Day: "This is a helluva day to wash out a progressive paper. We will do no further production work unless you can positively assure that the old bill will not increase. . . . I guess you know how I feel. Don't get sore."

Under Operation Bootstrap we sought to organize our readers in 1,000 communities for single or group pledges of sustaining units of $100. And despite our financial adversity, we had the healthiest spread of circulation of any radical paper since *Appeal to Reason*.* So it was to the *Appeal* that we turned for inspiration in a "Last Ditch Appeal to Reason" in the issue of January 23, 1950, one year after the page-one SOS that had attracted Ms. Blaine. We reviewed our first year, set forth the current situation as we saw it in the world, the nation, and on Murray Street, and talked about the job ahead. Readers sent in precious dollars out of relief checks and old age pensions. Within weeks we had raised $30,000; the spread is indicated by the fact that the average contribution was $3.

It was clear that the Progressive Party leadership would continue to look the other way. We did not even get press invitations for our reporters to major PP rallies and dinners. The hierarchy, without our knowledge, was dickering behind the scenes to obtain financing for the *Compass*. Our circulation was three-quarters outside of New York State and we did not regard either the *Compass* or any other new publication as competition. Quite the contrary, in

---

* In the halcyon days before the Russian Revolution transformed American socialists into "Soviet agents," *Appeal to Reason,* of which Socialist presidential candidate Eugene Debs was a contributing editor, achieved circulations ranging from several hundred thousands to a million a week.

our desire to build the movement, we said the more the merrier. And, ironically, we had been instrumental in deciding whether or not the *Compass* would actually come to life.

One day Ms. Blaine had phoned Jack to tell him about a peremptory call from a PP wheel giving her four days to make up her mind about supporting a new New York progressive paper. The message apparently was that her failure to support it would kill the project. She knew neither the name of the paper nor anything about the man she was to call back. She was offended by the deadline approach and was not inclined to help. Jack told her that deadlines have a way of "popping up" and she might reproach herself later if she let that stand in the way of supporting such a worthy project. He suggested she send one of her lawyers to talk with Thackrey the next day and, at her request, Jack alerted Thackrey to the visit. Ms. Blaine then financed the *Compass*.

Our fraternal attitude toward publications on the left was not often reciprocated. Our fellow travelers on the press run to brotherhood preferred the more traditional competitive methods and attitudes of capitalism. They may not have tried actively to cut our throat, but generally there was a leg out for us to trip over.

In that "Last Ditch Appeal" issue I wrote in the Report to Readers:

I can remember mornings in the 12 years I worked for the commercial press, how I hated the idea of going into the city room. I can remember how my stomach tied in knots when I saw how a story or a headline I wrote was twisted after it left my hands—to supply the slant I refused to give. I can remember the bull sessions we used to have after an edition when we'd dream about breaking out and doing something we believed in (but where was there for a newspaperman to go?). I can remember decent, even brilliant, newspapermen drinking themselves into a sodden mess out of sheer frustration. . . . There's none of that in the GUARD-IAN.

Not that we were any exception to the rule that newspaper people drink, but we had no sodden messes for the simple reason that we were not frustrated and we were much too busy with work we believed in. Well, who were "we"?

We came together, for the most part, by magnetic impulse, not knowing each other but wanting the same thing, and for the most part we stayed. From the beginning, or from shortly after the beginning, "we" were:

- Elmer Bendiner—from *Esquire* magazine and *Flying Age,* the *Newark Ledger, Brooklyn Eagle* and Paramount Pictures. In manner and sometimes in personal style a journalist who might have been at home in Victorian Fleet Street. He wrote fast, scratched his editing in almost illegible hand; the copy, when deciphered, proved to be graceful and often delightful prose. He was well liked on the staff and became naturally a leader. A frequent and rigid political antagonist in the early days, he mellowed with time and events.
- Robert E. Light—young and fresh out of the World War II infantry, frail of health (he was to die early), willing and inventive, quick to anger and as quick to fun. From a brief background with jazz and TV magazines, he joined us as a commercial-editorial jack-of-all-trades, settled down as a senior staff writer and, with guidance which he accepted gracefully, became an able and versatile journalist.
- Lawrence Emery—seasoned in the radical movement and press, a veteran of four prison years (for organizing lettuce pickers in California's Imperial Valley), withdrawn, sometimes bitter, but straight as a die. A man of unyielding habits: two boiled three-minute eggs each morning; a pint of blended whisky (oddly named Press Club) during a day, without perceptible influence on his meticulously clean and workmanlike copy.
- Tabitha Petran—from Radcliffe, *Time, PM,* the New York *Post* and *New Republic.* An indefatigable researcher and picker of brains, with problems of applying her own obvious intelligence to the mass of acquired material. She regarded editors as enemies but learned to live with them. She was a solitary person, but her view was as global as her relationship with colleagues was restricted.
- George Evans—from the Navy Department and the Veterans

Administration. Thin, intense, and serious, mainstay of the circulation and business department, quiet in his observations (almost always shrewd and valid), the kind of stalwart without whom the ship could easily founder.

● Robert Joyce—*PM* alumnus. A man of many talents—artist, photographer, philosopher—who never quite settled for concentration on any of them. Became our art director at the start, designed the logo, created the Guardian Angel, which delighted us and the readers more than it delighted him.

● Ione Kramer—daughter of Wisconsin farmers, devoted, didactic, hard-working. She would marry and go to Peking with a Chinese engineering student and resume her journalism career in China.

● Kumar Goshal—Bengali-born, actor, lecturer par excellence, author of books on colonial India and Asia. He could talk out a foreign policy article with a radiance that dimmed when the words went from voice to paper. But he took editing well.

● Marcelle Hitschmann—our UN correspondent, at first under the pseudonym Ali Hassan to protect her precarious permit in the United States. A diminutive, exotically dressed woman of Italian-Egyptian birth, who had married a Czechoslovak. Fiery in temperament, informed, courageous, with short shrift for journalistic boors, diplomatic bores, and sectarian leftists.

● Stanley Karnow—brought to us by Norman Mailer in 1948 as a fledgling seeking a start in journalism. Got it as a GUARDIAN correspondent in France and Spain, immediately showed professional quality but moved into big-time media in 1950.

● Jean Norrington—young widowed mother who joined us as librarian in the first year. Combined the Trade Union Service morgue with our own and doggedly and skillfully selected and catalogued the record of two tumultuous decades without which this book could not have been written.

● David Reif—veteran of the wars of the left, oldest person on the staff, an "anything for the cause" man who must have been the prototype for "Jimmie Higgins." Entirely without malice, loyal to the core, suffering all the world's sorrows in his own soul.

● Lillian Ryckoff—a wise and tested woman (physically as a polio victim from childhood; intellectually from her wide reading and experience), who presided over the Buying Service and advertising departments with exemplary patience.

The attraction of the GUARDIAN to young journalists—and the kind of journalist who was attracted—may be seen in the story of Egon Pohoryles, who joined us in 1949. Born in Cologne the son of a caviar merchant, he was 11 when the family fled from German antisemitism in 1936 through Czechoslovakia, Austria, and France to England, then to Cuba (where visas were for sale) and finally to New York. Firsthand encounters with the Nazis gave him an early political education and, at 13, he ran away from St. Paul's School in London to join the defense of Spain against Franco's fascists. He was caught and returned home.

He volunteered for service in the U.S. Army soon after arrival but was too young—and an "enemy" alien to boot. He was drafted at 18, imbued with "an overwhelming desire to fight fascism." When he expressed this desire in applying for Officer Candidate School, the examining officers "looked at me as though I were a dangerous maniac." Refused permission to join the infantry, and kept in strictly noncombatant activities, he was finally assigned to guarding German POWs "by carefully hiding the fact that I spoke German." His education was advanced by listening to U.S. personnel and German prisoners discussing the number of Jews they would kill after they returned home. These Army experiences turned him into "as militant an anti-militarist as anything could."

On his discharge, Egon resumed his studies at New York University and became involved in the battle to reinstate Dr. Lyman Bradley, one of the university's most popular teachers, who had been fired for opposing the developing cold war. (It was through Bradley that I met Egon.) The losing battle for Bradley made Egon aware of "the menace of thought control sweeping NYU" and of the "atmosphere of fear and suspicion which pervades it, duplicated to a greater or lesser extent at every other school, and beyond the schools in every phrase of activity." In his job application he wrote: "All this you know and have, since the founding of the GUARDIAN, fought against. My reasons for wanting to join the GUARDIAN can be summarized quite simply by saying that I want to join your fight."

This was the quality of the early staff, and virtually all were to stay at least until 1960, when the pressures of growing families particularly forced some to seek greater incomes elsewhere. Not one of the originals left because of political disagreement, but there were differences and arguments aplenty in the weekly editorial discussions about the contents of the paper, quality of articles, and problems of circulation and promotion. Periodically we held all-day meetings on weekends when we could discuss things fully away from office pressures: how to reach trade unions that were resisting cold war takeover, the black communities, peace groups, civil liberties organizations? Should we offer the paper for public ownership with a board of advisers? Should we publish a New York edition (we did for a brief period)? How could we get better Washington coverage? meaningful cultural coverage? improved science news in an increasingly technological age? The goal, we felt, was broadening our approach without watering down our political point of view—that the main source of tension in the world was Washington. While tensions were originating elsewhere, including the Soviet Union—and we could not blink them—our main job as an American publication was to inform and enlighten Americans about the centers of power in our own country where we lived, worked, and voted: the only country whose decision-making processes we could possibly influence.

We were building a first-rate team of foreign correspondents, mainly women as it turned out, some Americans in exile, and Europeans and Asians who had lived and worked in the United States (as correspondents for papers abroad or with the UN Secretariat) and were familiar with American journalism and reading habits. Most had full-time jobs but wrote for us because they believed in what we were doing. Among them were two German-born women who had come to the United States as refugees from Hitler, become U.S. citizens, worked for the United Nations, then left the United States in political disagreement with American policy and domination of the UN. Anne Bauer settled in Paris and became our correspondent there after Karnow; Ursula Wassermann, author of *I Was an American*, became a roving correspondent, reporting for some years from Israel where her critical (but sympathetic) articles got her into trouble, and from eastern Europe, before settling in Switzerland.

The problem of national and regional correspondence was harder. Except in the planning stages and the first months of the paper, working journalists in the United States shrank from associating themselves with a radical publication and, as the repression became more severe, their reluctance increased. But our search for competent correspondents yielded several who shared our point of view and reported for us on local events of national interest and on left activities in their areas. This enabled the GUARDIAN to serve as an information lifeline for the radical movement, many of whose members believed they were about to go underground against the new imperial power in civilian guise in Washington. In effect we became a clearing house and forum for the American left and for non-leftists with open minds: they had to read our paper to know who was doing what and why, and what was being done to them for doing it.

Among other precedents we established was payment, however modest, for all articles by non-staff members. This tradition maintained through the nineteen years of our association with the paper was based on a born-of-experience distaste for exploiting radical journalists, especially those without other means of income—a custom which regrettably persists to this day. Recipients of these small checks often returned them, in shocked gratitude, to the general fund or used the money to subscribe for others.

Growing external tensions were inevitably reflected internally. Frayed nerves caused short tempers and arguments flared. Whenever cracks appeared in our managing triumvirate, we resorted to written memos until the cement of calm could be applied in person. It was a rare occasion when managerial decisions were not unanimous. We understood the urgency of compromise under battle conditions.

A segment of the staff proposed a change in our structure from corporation to cooperative, and lengthy discussions ensued, one lasting from 7 p.m. to 8 a.m. the following day. Our triumviral view was that there could hardly exist a more de facto cooperative than the GUARDIAN, with management taking all the bumps with the staff and more, and with full staff participation in decision-making. The vigor with which the proposal was pressed led us to suspect a hidden factor: that the CP leadership had encouraged their members on our staff to gain a dominant voice in GUARDIAN councils. We knew that a debate was being mounted within the CP about political action policy. A growing number of influential Communists were arguing against independent radical politics as futile in an entrenched two-party system. We did not hold with that view. Our triumvirate successfully shelved the cooperative proposal, which under the circumstances seemed ominous, but it was a long time before full harmony was restored.

I recall an emotional outburst by one lingering mass-market expert, whose zeal for GUARDIAN-building had declined in proportion to our exchequer. How, he asked, could he continue to work for a corporate enterprise and look his trusting five-year-old son in the eye? Our expert rescued the child from worse than death by departing the premises shortly thereafter, but not until we had determined he was using GUARDIAN phone, postage, and supplies to plan a newsletter of his own. We learned also that he had written to Jess Gitt in York (whose goodwill was still a valuable asset to us) that the GUARDIAN was being poorly run, that our policy was too "left-sectarian," and that perhaps Gitt might like to support his projected newsletter. There were fortunately few such incidents during our early years.

We reasserted our independent political action view vigorously in the aftermath of the 1950 elections, in which Progressive candidates running for congressional and local offices fared wretchedly:

You can't throw an empty pop bottle away today without hitting someone with a set of lessons to be drawn: The progressive movement of this country is never going to get to first base unless it can get its program before the people. And the truth is that the progressive leadership

REPORT FROM THE INTERIOR

throughout the nation has failed thus far to take the first, simple step in that direction. That simple step is the building of a publication which will be the voice of the whole movement. . . . We of the GUARDIAN propose our paper for the job. We set up the paper for that purpose in 1948, staffed it with straight-as-a-string progressive craftsmen and women, opened its columns from the very first issue to the leaders and spokesmen of the progressive movement, to the program of the Progressive Party and all its branches.

No other people's political movement that we know of has survived on the crumbs of publicity it could garner from the commercial press. Today more than ever no campaign for peace, freedom, and abundance can hope to win attention if it is geared publicity-wise to the obtaining of a paragraph on page 29 of the New York *Times* . . . Time spent deploring the fake of our "free" press is time wasted.

We urged our readers to go into their organizations and raise the question of a progressive press; if they were brushed aside, to raise it again, and again. But in the course of the next two years, looking toward the presidential elections of 1952, there would be fewer and fewer forums in which to raise it.

The severest blow of the 1950 elections was the defeat, after twelve years in Congress, of Vito Marcantonio. A coalition of Democrats, Republicans, and Liberals, a district reorganization to reduce the Hispanic and black population, plus a vicious press campaign, did the job. The ammunition was supplied by an unprecedented consolidation of money power of the kind usually employed in presidential elections. The Establishment recognized Marc as an effective and unyielding enemy. It was he who had said at the time of the Smith Act arrests: "The defense of the Communists is the first line of defense of civil liberties in America." And it was he who, four months before the election, stood alone in the well of the House of Representatives to denounce U.S. intervention in Korea. Now that last voice was stilled in the Congress. The irony of the election was that James G. Donovan, the victor, campaigned on only one issue: that Marc "followed the Communist Party line," at a time when Marc was having serious disagreements with the CP.

These disagreements (to project this theme to its end) would lead to his resignation as chairman of the ALP in 1953. The root cause was the CP's promulgation of the "mainstream" policy after the minuscule vote for the Progressive Party's Vincent Hallinan–Charlotta Bass presidential ticket in 1952. Since the bulk of American workers were in the Democratic Party (the CP reasoned), all progressives should go where the workers were and seek to move the Democratic Party to the left. Behind perfunctory campaigns for Communist candidates the CP generally supported Democratic candidates, particularly in national elections, thus further muddling efforts to build a viable political alternative.

NATIONAL GUARDIAN held with Marc and insisted on sustaining the effort to build an independent political movement. It fought against dismantling the ALP in New York (again opposing CP policy) and consistently declined to support a Democratic candidate for President. In fact, the last candidate for governor of New York on the ALP ticket in 1954 (he had run in 1950 also and gathered 208,000 votes) was our own Jack McManus.

The CP leadership had urged Jack to run. I was opposed to it because Cedric at that point of pressure was battling deportation, and I worried about neglect of the paper's managerial problems if Jack were drawn into a campaign. Further, I did not trust the CP's importuning in light of their rejection of independent political action. Jack, however, was spoiling for one last fight to maintain the ALP as a ballot party (50,000 votes were required), and I yielded. The CP, behind the scenes, encouraged support of the millionaire Democrat Averell Harriman, thus shifting away from the ALP its necessary margin of votes to stay on the ballot. Jack's vote was a few thousand short of 50,000. That episode led to a confrontation between a CP delegation and Jack (I was a witness)—a magnificent display of Irish wrath in which Jack denounced the CP for their duplicity/stupidity and then, typically for him, rejected a break in relations. Rather, we would continue our efforts toward independent political action and challenge the CP to prove us wrong.

Our twin convictions on the electoral question held firm. First, the two major parties offered no alternative. Second, a constant campaign of information and education—despite poor showings at the polls—was essential to awaken in the electorate a sense that, in a system offering only recurrent cycles of war prosperity and peacetime recession, something was grievously wrong.

By the same token we insisted that we had no enemies on the left, however great the disagreement on certain tactics or policy. We felt that the history of the American left had been marked by divisive polemics which had rendered it almost useless as a political force through the most critical periods. We considered the CP as part of the left. They were not our enemy, and we knew who was.

Postscript [**C.B.**] The Blaine largesse landed us firmly in a "management–staff" relationship, sparring with people we wanted to deal with as colleagues about who should get what slice of pie from a week's togetherwork. On that level it was a relief when the pie took wing and disappeared. Having been a mere dues-payer in the National Union of Journalists in Britain, I wore the "management" hat awkwardly and was grateful for the executive trade-union experience of Jack and Jim. They were able to bargain patiently and effectively on demands which astonished us all (including some of the staff, as they privately confessed) but which left me gasping for air. Jim is still able to record with un-raised blood pressure the "paternity leave" demand, a benefit then unheard-of in the most lucrative newspaper's union contract. As a symbol of an attitude, it poised me between laughter and tears. Were we, or weren't we, socialist stargazers in a capitalist world?

Of course part of the explanation was the romantic view of trade unions which the whole left traditionally shared. If it was proper—as it was, although almost ruinous to us—to publish in a union shop with handsomely paid printers, it seemed to follow that a rebel paper's editorial staff should enjoy the benefits for which "commercial" journalists—including management's Jack and Jim in their pre-GUARDIAN phase—had fought. But the eventual stance of the Newspaper Guild showed how far on the wrong side trade unions were becoming politically. The interest that "organized" (more and more for, not against, capitalism) labor had in our troubles was to make our survival impossible.

Fortunately the people dominating our staff committee came to recognize this, but we seemed to see another set of motivations behind their maintenance of the pressure for a "cooperative." The Communist Party was very uneasy about a paper which insisted on friendliness to it and to the Soviet Union, but over which it had no control—a new phenomenon in American journalism and an impossibility from the inquisitor's eye-view. What was worse for Communist policy makers, the GUARDIAN *was* controlled by people uncomfortably familiar with party methods in such situations. The Communists wouldn't want to kill us if they could help it, rather they wanted to push us into the background or take us over; although just what purpose another party-line organ could serve, only they knew.

In any case I decided on a confrontation with V. J. Jerome, the party's "cultural commissar," as the best contribution I could make. I had had a nonparty relationship with him over his proposal that I write a biography of his former (deceased) wife, Rose Pastor Stokes, a still-unsung heroine of America's progressive movement. We had talked this over at various times after I studied the mass of her letters and other documents which he gave me, but I had finally had to plead the priority of other work.

V. J. was an outwardly mild man with a unique blend of the poetic with party-line austerity. I had little doubt that, if there was any scheme to take over the GUARDIAN through a staff "cell," he would know all about it. He professed to know nothing and agreed effusively with my contention that a GUARDIAN controlled by us was more advantageous to the Communists than one controlled by them: a friend was someone who supported you reserving the right to differ, I said, and where else in journalism could they find one?

Among other disruptive internal phenomena I mentioned an office rumor that had drifted my way—circulated, as I believed, by the same staff members who led the "cooperative" performance—that I was a secretly continuing British spy and that the

GUARDIAN was an arcane plot of British Intelligence. He threw up his hands in incredulity and I left him with a plea, in effect, to call off his shock-troops. He protested to the last that he had none: a disturbance in our nest was the very last thing the CP would want.

It seemed to me that tension with the staff relaxed markedly from that day on. This could very well have been my imagination, but at least the gossip that the GUARDIAN was a boring-from-within tactic by Her Majesty's Secret Service was heard no more around the shop.

The Extended
GUARDIAN Family

[**C.B.**] When Jim, Jack, and I were hauled into the inquisitorial labyrinth in the GUARDIAN's fifth to seventh years, we responded with incantations of the Fifth Amendment to the U.S. Constitution. Our readers well understood our reasons for this performance and might have disapproved any other. Yet how easily it could be interpreted as at worst conspiratorial, at best ignoble, by those who did not, or pretended not to, know the nature of the labyrinth! The trap was artfully baited. If we represented high journalistic principles, why didn't we take the opportunity to proclaim them before America?

The short answer is that we could only do so at the peril of jail for "contempt" or "perjury," and that, in our case, would mean the paper's death. But even so we would only have been feeding our own egos, for there was no opportunity to proclaim anything beyond the inquisitorial chamber's walls. The only forum we had was the GUARDIAN. The media were themselves in the witch-hunting vanguard. They even rejected paid advertising for radical causes and, until the signal came from above to turn and rend Joe

McCarthy, almost all ate from his hand. They could be trusted to distort anything we said that they didn't suppress.

Under the inquisitors' ground rules, the "witness" answering any one question in an "area" must answer all others. Thus to identify ourselves as publishers of the paper was to open the trap-door for questions about anyone or anything connected with it, so we didn't admit even that "on the grounds [no other was acceptable] that it might tend to incriminate us." We shared the shame of this with America.

And there was plenty to ask about the GUARDIAN family, for it embraced the last activists in a period when the movement was thrown mainly on the defensive.

Of course we knew by then only too well that the browbeatings for names were largely a formality: almost everyone in our extended family must have already been honored with a police dossier. Subscribers? The Post Office supplied Hoover with the list, and most of the more articulate and active ones signed their names on our Mailbag page. Writers? A handful used pseudonyms with dubious effectiveness. Sub boosters, consultants, large or small financial angels? If any were still unknown, only shoddy work by the hawkshaws who tapped our phone and inspected our mail could be responsible. As producers of an openly prepared and circulated newspaper we were by definition in a goldfish bowl, and the remotest member of the extended family was perforce there with us. Even an interview granted to the GUARDIAN, or a speech published with permission—even an outside mention of the paper without anathematizing it—was a dossier-worthy action conferring family membership of a sort.* Consider the fact that one of the "charges" later brought against myself was "authoring a novel praised by the *Daily Worker.*" Hoover's men combed through everything that might help build up a conspiratorial network.

No, the inquisition's game in cases like ours was not the extrac-

---

* Many "top people" abroad granted interviews, hardly any in the United States. Honorable mention to Arthur Garfield Hays of the American Civil Liberties Union, the only "respectable" lawyer willing to answer in 1949 a questionnaire on the constitutionality of the Smith Act. We published speeches by (among others) Isaac Deutscher, Albert Einstein, Eugene Genovese, Fanny Lou Hamer,

tion of names as such, but the public self-defilement of the victim in giving them. And we weren't going to play. What was hard for us Fifth Amendment invokers to take was the self-styled liberals' abandonment of us to whatever fate our stubbornness might bring. And this although the threat of concentration camp and torture chamber was never available to American inquisitors, as it was to Germans before them and South Americans, Greeks, Iranians, and Koreans after them. With only unemployment, deportation, and jail to fear, at least before the Rosenberg case, America's liberals fell silent when they didn't actively cooperate: self-defilement by default.

So much the greater our pride in our extended family, cheerfully taking the consequences of cooperating in whatever way they could. Our refusal to talk about them reflected that pride, and our own standard of what defiles a man, rather than any illusions that we could conceal them.

While jail hung its shadow over them all, for some it became a reality, and they wrote from behind the bars or wrote or spoke for us upon reemerging. First of these political prisoners of our period was author-publisher Carl Marzani, a most effective GUARDIAN fund-raiser. The last was Willard Uphaus, locked up for a year for withholding the guest list at his World Fellowship Center. Others were Alvah Bessie, Lester Cole, Ring Lardner Jr., and Dalton Trumbo of the Hollywood Ten; Spanish International Brigade veteran Steve Nelson, novelist Howard Fast, who later repudiated his radical connections (but not under inquisition); Louisville's Carl Braden (twice jailed) and his wife Anne; George Crockett, Vincent Hallinan, and other lawyers jailed for defending radicals; and labor leaders Harry Bridges (whose fight against deportation was a GUARDIAN campaign) and Clifford Jencks of the New Mexico miners, a devoted sub booster with his wife Virginia.* The World

Tom Hayden, William M. Kunstler, Owen Lattimore, Staughton Lynd, Arthur Miller, Carl Oglesby, H. H. Wilson.

*The strike committee led by Jencks circularized the miners (mainly Chicanos) with *Guardian* samples: "This national paper that tells the story of OUR strike is a paper for ALL the people, and stands for peace and progress for all of us regardless of nationality or race or politics. See if you can't afford $1 so you can read FACTS about REAL PEOPLE, news you can't find in the 'Funny Paper,' the daily press. Viva la Unión! Vivian los Huelguistas!"

War II resistance hero and editor Manolis Glezos wrote from a death cell in Greece. William Pomeroy became a GUARDIAN correspondent after our campaign against his death sentence for aiding Huk guerrillas in the Philippines.*

W. E. B. DuBois, Corliss Lamont, Harvey O'Connor, William Patterson, John W. Powell, Pete Seeger, and Paul Sweezy were tried or "cited" for trial by inquisitors, but fought successfully to stay in circulation. Lamont, humanist philosopher and tireless defier of inquisitors, was a contributor and our most consistent financial angel over the years. Economist Sweezy wrote for the GUARDIAN before founding *Monthly Review* with Leo Huberman, who spoke at our functions. Author O'Connor, active challenger of the inquisition, boosted GUARDIAN funds and subs with his wife, Jessie Lloyd. Seeger, blacklisted pied piper at subversive songfests, was a major fund-raising magnet for us.†

Among legal consultants and contributors, defending the GUARDIAN and causes it espoused, were Gloria Agrin, Nat Dambroff, and Blanch Freedman, who gallantly attempted the impossible in my deportation proceedings; Leonard Boudin, William Patterson, Royal W. France, the Rev. A. A. Heist (Los Angeles chairman of the Citizens Committee to Preserve American Freedoms), and Abner Green of the American Committee for Protection of Foreign Born. All of these stood in the front lines under inquisitorial fire, where they were in the company of such American members of the family as:

Louis Adamic, Yugoslav-American writer (a suicide, 1951, after being "named" as a "red spy")
C. B. Baldwin, secretary of the Progressive Party
Elmer A. Benson, witch-hunted ex-governor of Minnesota
Emanuel Bloch, whose ouster was sought by the Bar Associa-

* For details about some of the people above and below, see later in the text. Apologies to those omitted for reasons of space from this far from comprehensive list.

† Other performers at *Guardian* affairs were Martin Balsam, Irwin Corey, Sarah Cunningham, Barbara Dane, Howard da Silva, Jay Gorney, Al Hammer, E. Y. Harburg, Irma Jurist, Judith Malina, John Randolph, Earl Robinson, Martha Schlamme, and Ellie Stone.

tion of the City of New York for defense of the Rosenbergs

Richard O. Boyer, Communist writer purged from the *New Yorker*

Angus Cameron, purged publisher, founder of Liberty Book Club

Rhoda de Silva, pro-Rosenberg American journalist, kidnapped by U.S. agents from her Ceylon home

Rev. Clarence Duffy, blacklisted Catholic priest

Barrows Dunham, philosopher purged from Temple University

Clifford and Virginia Durr, distinguished New Dealers under inquisition for Southern civil rights activities

Rev. Stephen Fritchman, pastor of witch-hunted GUARDIAN-reader-infested Los Angeles church

Hugh Hardyman, farmer-educator, leader of illicit China tour by Americans

Albert E. Kahn, author of exposé of U.S. inquisitors and fascists

Mary Jane and Philip Keeney, UN functionary and professor, both witch-hunted out of jobs

Florence Luscomb, women's liberation veteran, defier of Massachusetts witch-hunts

Vito Marcantonio, congressional holdout for peace and the Constitution

F. O. Matthiessen, Harvard's "greatest rediscoverer of our literary past" (New York *Times*), suicide, 1950, under FBI hounding

Rev. William Howard Melish, Episcopalian ousted from his Brooklyn parish

Karen Morley, blacklisted film actress

Philip Morrison, inquisited Nobel laureate

Linus Pauling, inquisited Nobel laureate and peacemonger

Victor Perlo, Marxist economist, veteran of subversive lists

Anton Refregier, painter whose murals aroused art purgers' fury

Rose Russell, leader of witch-hunted New York Teachers Union

Agnes Smedley, denounced as "spy" by General MacArthur

Anna Louise Strong, a "spy" in reverse

Lionel Stander, blacklisted film actor

Fred W. Stover, leader of witch-hunted Iowa Farmers Union

Dirk W. Struik, Marxist mathematician suspended by M.I.T.

Rev. Claude Williams, de-frocked Presbyterian minister.

Any cooperator with us took at least an economic risk, but a few had or found ways to cooperate and survive without direct inquisitorial confrontation. The survival was generally tenuous for such writers as Fritz Silber, David Wesley, Jennings Perry, Arthur Hurwich, John Lardner, Sidney Margolius, Truman Nelson, Heinz Pol, Frank Scully, John B. Stone, J. Alvarez del Vayo, William Worthy, and Richard Yaffe. I. F. Stone was the only cooperating journalist who (with his *Weekly*) made an economic success of confronting the inquisitors.* Writing for us about religion made Guy Emery Shipler, editor of the progressive *Churchman,* and Union Theological Seminary's Harry F. Ward—the inquisitors' chief devils in that field—little more vulnerable than they already were. The same went for the maverick U.S. Brigadier General Hugh B. Hester, for Mary van Kleeck of the Russell Sage Foundation, and for artists like William Gropper and Robert Gwathmey. Olin Downes, the New York *Times*'s dean of music critics, wrote for us and kept his job; likewise Frederick L. Schuman, Williams College professor of political science. Israel Epstein, one of our writers on China, went to live there before the axe could fall; another, Ilona Ralf Sues, moved to Poland. Before his *New Masses*–GUARDIAN dossier could explode in his face, James Dugan, last of America's great radical satirists, took a dive into Europe, where he wrote successful sea and undersea books. Only Stanley Karnow, foreign correspondent and Far Eastern specialist,

---

*Objecting to some of our politics, Stone didn't contribute but advertised his *Weekly* with us and defended our right to be wrong both in the *Weekly* and at a Belfrage "Fight-Back" rally.

made it from the GUARDIAN to the journalistic big time. Norman Mailer, whose wife Beatrice raised initial funds and subs for us, wrote once and disappeared from our horizon.*

The worst that America could do to our extended family abroad—correspondents, Mailbaggers, interviewees, sub and fund boosters—was to declare them inadmissible, a chastisement which they survived. In Britain these included J. D. Bernal ("the wisest man in the world," according to Julian Huxley), Bertrand Russell, J. B. S. Haldane, Sean O'Casey, Dean of Canterbury Hewlett Johnson, London County Council member Peggy Middleton, Queens Counsel D. N. Pritt, Gordon Schaffer (Lenin prize for peacemongering journalism), Ella Winter (self-exiled American), and Konni Zilliacus, MP. In the Americas, novelist (later ambassador) Carlos Fuentes, Clive Smith (British veteran of International Brigade in Spain), Guyana Prime Minister Cheddi Jagan, muralists Diego Rivera and David A. Siqueiros, and poet Pablo Neruda. In Europe, Emil Carlebach and John Peet (Germany), Ralph Parker (Moscow), Professor Margaret Schlauch (American in Warsaw), Eleanor and George Wheeler (Americans in Prague). In the Far East, Peter Townsend (British) and Wilfred Burchett (Australian). In South Africa, Hilda Bernstein—under a pseudonym until her escape from house arrest to London.

At GUARDIAN annual dinners, 1949–1967, our honor guests included:

John Abt, defense attorney in witch-hunt trials
Harry Bridges
David Dellinger, pacifist and Chicago Seven defendant

---

*Calling himself "an ignorant Marxist . . . to the left of the PP and right of the CP," Mailer saw both light and shade in the USSR and ridiculed the "Soviet war threat." He saw the United States as "a moral wilderness, torn between a Christian ethic now enfeebled, a capitalist ethic, and a new sexual ethic whose essence is sadistic"; a land of "staggering frustrations and animosities" where, however, two facts encouraged hope—"that there is resistance . . . to fascism and war" and that U.S. "economic rulers have their problems too. They have satisfied temporarily the spiritual frustration of American life by feeding Americans upon anti-Russian hysteria, but hatred . . . is only a temporary food." As the inquisition reached its zenith, the sadistic essence of the new sexual ethic came to preoccupy him.

THE EXTENDED GUARDIAN FAMILY

J. Alvarez del Vayo, former foreign minister of Republican
   Spain
James Forman, executive director of SNCC
Ruth Gage-Colby, Women's International League for Peace and
   Freedom board member
Maxwell Geismar, author and critic
Eugene Genovese, professor of history and author
Fanny Lou Hamer, Mississippi Freedom Democratic Party
Tom Hayden, founder of Students for a Democratic Society
John O. Killens, novelist
William Kunstler, civil liberties attorney
Mark Lane, attorney, pioneer investigator of John Kennedy as-
   sassination
Staughton Lynd, author, activist against Indochinese wars
Edita Morris, novelist
Robert Moses, SNCC leader
Truman Nelson, author
Carl Oglesby, president of Students for a Democratic Society
Dr. Samuel Rosen, ear surgeon, and wife Helen, scientist
Margaret Russell, founder of Women Strike for Peace
Miriam Schneir, co-author, *Invitation to an Inquest* (Rosenberg
   case)
Rev. Michael Scott, director of Africa Bureau, London
I. B. Tabata, a founder of African People's Democratic Union
Sir Robert Watson-Watt, developer of radar
Dr. William Appleman Williams, historian.

Vincent Noga, Scappoose, Oregon . . . Louise Harding
Horr, Brisbane, California . . . A. Garcia Diaz, New York City
. . . George F. Curry, Martins Ferry, Ohio . . . Al Amery, East
Pepperell, Massachusetts . . . "A Dirt Farmer," Gretna, Virginia
. . . Clara M. Vincent, Chattanooga, Tennessee . . . Irma C.
Otto, Center Sandwich, New Hampshire . . . Rev. M. E. Dorr,
Dayton, Iowa . . . Dr. Ralph R. Sackley, Chicago . . . Dorothy
Butler Howells, New York City . . . John J. O'Neil, Bay City,
Michigan . . . Theodore S. Behre, New Orleans . . . Mrs. Har-

vey Sydow, Lyons, Nebraska . . . Ernest Seeman, Erwin, Tennessee. . . .

Those names and hundreds more wove themselves for us into a Whitmanesque poem and, perhaps dangerously for our political equilibrium, stimulated romantic feelings about America. ("They *are* America," we told ourselves.) Most of the people we never met, most of the places we could only imagine, but as "regulars" of The Mailbag they were the editorialists and commentators of NATIONAL GUARDIAN.

We pruned to the bone and used our smallest type, and it was curious how Mailbaggers in the remotest places got the point fastest—that we were inundated with mail—and wrote the best letters in fewest words, leaving maximum space for others. For as Jim wrote in a Report to Readers, The Mailbag was "the link between embattled progressives surrounded in many communities by a hostile sea of misunderstanding and ignorance," a weekly reminder that "their kind exists in the thousands all over the country." A "lifeline of decency," Jim called it, "the proof that when all the muck of a sick culture is cleaned away, cooperation and brotherhood remain the core of human nature." In other words, despite its corruptions America retained a certain purity which it was (and is) fashionable to mock as innocence.

The breadth of unselfish concern, the common sense and wit and indomitability with which it was expressed, recalled the Committees of Correspondence before the Revolution: Americans defying tyranny as publicly as circumstances allowed, with the difference that now the rebels who wouldn't be silenced were all nobodies.

As the inquisition intensified, "Name Withheld" letters (sometimes also "Place Withheld") began to be scattered through the vast majority of signed ones. The writers of these identified themselves to us and we respected their reasons for anonymity. A Clevelander began it in November 1948 with this apology for not signing her well-chosen words about demagoguery: "Sorry, but I haven't the confidence in the liberalness of the present Administration that many people have, and I want to continue eating for a while longer to see how you fare in this world. The Lord bless you and keep you." In the Korean War letters from anonymous beleaguered draftees appeared with "Camp ——" and "Somewhere in Korea" datelines.

But everyone took a chance merely in writing to us, for there were legions of men "going round taking names" and the mails weren't immune to J. Edgar Hoover's attentions. (The first intimation that the FBI was demanding our sub lists from post offices came in August 1949: a California postal worker wrote that he had resigned rather than surrender it—and been told he must go to Washington to "clear himself of disloyalty.") Over every head hung a Damoclean sword with many edges: political police intimidation, public contumely, broken family, dishonorable discharge, unemployment, blacklist, jail, deportation if not native born. For this there was recurring evidence although Mailbaggers seldom wrote about their personal problems.

A Marine lieutenant wrote from Quantico, Va., signing his name; not long afterward we were reporting his ordeal before a military inquisition. In our third month "Mrs. (name withheld)" wrote from Minnesota that her GUARDIAN had been arriving in her RFD box "neatly torn in two in the middle, and then not at all. Please mail my paper in my son's name to his college, he'll bring it home to me." The same Mailbag page carried our first obituary of a subscriber: schoolteacher Minnie Gutride of Staten Island who, depressed after a day before the academic inquisition, put her head in her gas oven.

In August 1949 we got our first letter from a political deportee, an American union leader banished to Budapest. (He reported that newsstands there sold our paper "for the same price as six cigarets or two ozs. of candy.") In 1950 County Circuit Court Judge Norval K. Harris informed us from Sullivan, Ind.: "I am defending myself against criminal charges here but pledge $10 a month to your fund." (The crime, of which he would be convicted: "Contempt" for not naming his associates in a National Non-Partisan Committee to Defend the Rights of Communist Leaders.) From Bayard, N.M., Virginia Jencks, wife of union leader Clinton Jencks, who was to get a five-year term for his politics, wrote:

"The courage, the care, the effort that go into publication of your paper inspire the rest of us. As long as I can take it weekly from my mailbox I feel there is hope. But the time for mere words is long past. I am a young mother of two children. My husband volunteered in the war against fascism, and was willing even to die in such a cause. I ask other young women who face the destruction of those they love to act with me. No matter how great the odds may seem, ask yourselves, What are the alternatives? There are none. Peace is the only answer to hope for the future. I want my children to live; I want life for your children too. Organize in whatever way you can in your own communities to speak for peace. War is not inevitable. It is not necessary. War is criminal. Do we not have the right to act in our own self-interest?''

In a gesture that warmed our hearts, since he had broken the connection with us, Jess Gitt dealt roundly with red-baiting abuse in our first weekly issue. A Philadelphian ''liberal small business man'' detected ''the 100 percent Communist line'' in our Preview issue because it contained ''nothing favorable about our government.'' Gitt replied: ''To me Americanism means the right to have opinions whether or not they are the opinions of those in power. . . . I am opposed to President Truman because I think he is leading us down the road to war; opposed to a number of other U.S. policies for the same reason. If that makes me a Communist or is 100 percent Communist line it is news to me. In my opinion that is the American line—the line that all who appreciate what was done for us by our forefathers will follow. . . . May I say that I don't think you could possibly be a liberal or you would not have written as you did.''

William Tucker Dean Jr. of New York then notified us that ''until you criticize the Soviet Union . . . I do not want to receive your paper, even gratis.'' A Detroit lady wrote: ''I am returning your vile publications—they are a disgrace to our nation.'' And Dr. H. S. Grubschmidt (Internal Medicine) from St. Helena, Calif.: ''If I am not dropped from your subscription lists effective immediately I shall most certainly take this matter up with both my lawyer and postal authorities.'' *New Republic* publisher Daniel Mebane, voicing admiration for the Hiroshima A-bomb, wanted instant "removal from your subscription rolls" because we publicized the Stockholm Peace Appeal—a subversive document which tens of millions in scores of countries signed. Evidently some Guardian Angels were filling out our "5 trial subs for $5" coupon with more enthusiasm than discrimination.

This was run-of-the-mill stuff for the period, emanating as we assumed from people who saw sinister motives in others because they were unsure of their own. Average readers had no trouble understanding what we were doing and why. Publishing such letters was apt to pay off in the form of two or three or more new subs for the one lost, sent in by avenging replenishing angels. Perhaps it was because of this (as shown in succeeding Mailbags) that the abusive correspondence dried up.

Always, too, there were readers to help out when a would-be subscriber abroad wrote that his government didn't allow sending dollars (or when a domestic one wrote, "I like the paper but haven't a dollar"). They would subscribe for him and get a kick out of extending our Committee of Correspondence into infidel lands. In short order we had reader-Mailbaggers in Britain (most frequent correspondent: Lieutenant Commander Edgar P. Young, RN retd.), France, West and East Germany, India, Canada, Mexico, Peru, Poland, Israel, Australia, South Africa, and Monte Carlo—often thanks to some Angel in Chickasha, Pahokee, or Tonasket. The only circumstance preventing this first-aid was imprisonment of the would-be reader. When Dr. Edward Barsky, an American surgeon who had saved the lives of countless antifascist fighters in Spain, was serving time for his politics, the warden of his jail requested that we "cancel the subscription and make a refund to the person who subscribed for him, as it cannot be delivered to the prisoner." A Puerto Rican reader who subscribed for Deusdedit Marrero, a political prisoner there, sent on to us a letter from an Independence Party leader: "Where the hell do you think you're living—in a free country? Marrero won't be allowed to receive it. Even Christmas cards to Nationalist prisoners were rejected by the authorities because they had the Puerto Rican flag."

Labor officials had no inhibitions about writing to us as long as their unions stood against the storm. Collegiate correspondents, in the prevailing climate of political lassitude, were rare; but one wired from the University of California at Richmond, "CAMPUS BAN ON GUARDIAN RESULTED IN GREAT INTEREST. SEND FIFTY COPIES AIRMAIL SPECIAL," and 45 Chinese students wrote from Cambridge, Mass., blasting Chiang Kai-shek. A bank president in Parkston, S.D., wished "more power to you boys who are laboring under such terrible difficulties to bring us the truth." If he wasn't kidding, he failed to spread his zeal to others of the tribe. Clergymen wrote from small towns—in our first year two from Iowa and one each from Missouri, Saskatchewan, Massachusetts (a retired missionary), and New York State (a rabbi)—and many Mailbaggers salted their letters with Bible or other religious references. In one early issue a New York Catholic quoted the Pope against Cardinal Spellman's strikebreaking, a Mailbagger in Tuckahoe, N.Y., "prayed with all my heart for God's blessings on Wallace," and another in Evanston, Ill., confessed: "My religion is the Fatherhood of God and Brotherhood of Man, sure to qualify me as a 'Communist' for HUAC. I'm scared so send $1."

Others wrote in defense of Mormonism or invoked upon us "the blessings of Allah." An Oakland, Calif., Christian Scientist claimed hers as "the most progressive religious sect," citing Mary Baker Eddy to show that "apathy is not incurable." The GUARDIAN's positive attitude toward religious people involved in social action owed much to the influence of Claude Williams, our Alabama preacher friend who saw no conflict between religion and Marxism. And although most Mailbaggers were probably atheists, none questioned our position, unique in contemporary left journalism. Nor did anyone object to a very constructive letter from John J. O'Neil of Bay City, Mich., raising the question of Marxism itself being a religion. Far from being a mere economic tract, O'Neil wrote, "*Das Kapital* fairly burns with the biblical cry for social justice and dire forebodings for those who 'grind the faces of the poor.' " The only Mailbagger we actually knew to be a Communist was William Patterson of the Civil Rights Congress, who always encouraged us. Presumably some others were, but

THE EXTENDED GUARDIAN FAMILY

Marx and Marxism were as rarely mentioned in The Mailbag as in the body of the paper. We made our position on Marxism sufficiently obvious (we liked it) but our wavelength was America.

Religion was in fact one of the areas in which we were constantly bombarded for "more news." Other "More, pleases" were humor (but some wanted less), poetry, movies, television, "an article on roaches," and "a Henry Wallace column." S. L. Reese of Crawfordsville, Ore., advised us "not to cripple yourselves, as some fine publications as good as yours have done, by loading them down with rubbish." A Bronx reader admired some of our headlines but urged us to "blaze it across the top of the page. Use blue or red ink. You can't fight the poison of a Hearst or Roy Howard with modesty. You've got the stuff for a great newspaper, so dish it out." To all these we had to reply that the paper was already bursting at the seams. The solution? "More readers equals more pages equals no more missed boats."

Readers were ever alert (excessively in the case of Owen Whitfield—see chapter 7) for phrasing that smacked of racism. And although we observed the linguistic "proprieties" of the time we gave occasional offense. A Ms. Robinson of Fallon, Nev., liked the paper but asked: "Is it so necessary to print the exact swear word, as in reporting on the CIO convention: 'Curran rose to answer. He said he wanted Bridges "to keep his g– d— nose out of our union." ' Personally I'm no prude."

Subjects covered in the paper which aroused most Mailbag controversy were the Anna Louise Strong "case" (criticizing and defending her with equal vigor), the Soviet geneticist Lysenko (finding us too uncritical), Henry Wallace's defection in the Korean War (overwhelmingly anti-Wallace), independent political action, and the evergreen question of whether or not the United States was headed for fascism. Recurring general themes included "the woman question" and dietetics. Over the years the small but vociferous fragment of left-oriented diet buffs never failed to alert fellow-readers to the poisons that a heedless government compelled them to ingest in water, sprayed fruits and vegetables, etc. The most gallant defender of women from our first issues was

Dorothy Butler Howells. She wrote six-page longhand letters in green ink, containing some highly extractable nuggets but mainly concerned with the vindication of Casanova as a great liberator of her sex.

As a "male admirer of all that women have fought for and won," K. M. Price of Providence, R.I., wondered why "after chaining themselves to fences and throwing themselves under horses' hoofs to get these rights, the women haven't done more with them now they've got them. If the male politicians are all set on an atomic World War III, why don't the women stand up and tell us they won't go along? What's the use of fighting for something and then falling over dead?"

Dorothy Goodman put Price in his place from Chicago: "Every liberal meeting I've attended in four years has had an overwhelming majority of women present. Most were organized by women. At one, on the subject of the United Nations, women outnumbered men four to one and the issue became how to get the men interested. Men's political freedom dates back thousands of years. Besides educating themselves politically, women have had to educate their men in the rudiments of manhood and this may have slowed them down in the 30 years since they got the vote."

Postscript [**J.A.**] To paraphrase a famous classified ad slogan ("I got my job through the New York *Times*"), I rediscovered my country through the NATIONAL GUARDIAN. I believe I read just about every letter-to-the-editor that came into the shop for nineteen years and, with Cedric and Jack, replied to thousands of them. I also made about a half dozen cross-country speaking tours for the paper during which I met hundreds of Mailbaggers and innumerable other readers too self-conscious to write.

I went from fund-raising affairs in well-appointed livingrooms of doctors and lawyers in Westchester County to a spartan meeting room in Minneapolis where the temperature outside was 29° below zero and GUARDIAN readers drove 75 miles through the cold night for a report from New York. From there to a chicken-farm community in Petaluma, Calif., and an elderly audience most of whom must have had a youthful hand in the aborted 1905 revolution in

Russia; at long tables covered with white oilcloth we ate (chicken) and talked. Then up the coast to Santa Barbara, Fresno, Portland, and Seattle; across to Denver, Chicago, Detroit, Buffalo, Philadelphia—and home, physically exhausted but spiritually renewed.

After each trip I reported to the staff with missionary zeal which must have been suspect to them: why didn't all the enthusiasm cause circulation to rise to Jack's vaunted million readers? The answer came from one of our most valued Mailbaggers in 1958, a farmer named Hobart McKean of Circle, Mont. He wrote in response to an annual letter we sent broadside to the readership— a kind of Report to Stockholders on the year past, suggesting as gracefully as we could that, frankly, sir, or madame, as the case might be, we still needed money. In this particular letter we volunteered that if the times got to be a bit less pressureful, we might put out a more "affable" paper. McKean wrote:

"Congratulations on your nine years of uninterrupted service. The business of a crusading journal is not to attain success as measured by circulation figures, and its freedom from financial difficulties. Under our present social system, such success is synonymous with failure. I would like to be wrong in my apprehension that your desire to become a more affable paper means a failure to fulfill the need which the GUARDIAN has fulfilled so significantly in the last decade.

"I would be the last to deny that times change, but not all change is necessarily to the good of humanity, nor does it ensure service to mankind to attempt to conform with modern ideas and practices, just to achieve more readership and financial gain. I am only a farmer, caught in the cost–price squeeze too, and whatever I can contribute to educational purposes must go to the most needy. The GUARDIAN's future affability may well obviate the necessity to further sacrifice on my part."

Needless to say, the times did not take a turn auspicious to affability and, even if they had, we most likely would have spurned the opportunity in the face of Hobart McKean's chastening letter. Nor was the necessity of his sacrifice obviated; he remained a loyal friend.

I could add endlessly to Cedric's list of postmarks: Elkview,

W. Va., Wetumpka, Ala., Pueblo, Colo., Tochigi-Ken, Japan, and lots more. We had to assure New Yorkers we were not making a special selection for publication to maintain geographical distribution—like an Ivy League college admissions office. There was no discrimination against the East Coast Radlib Establishment, as America's most loathsome Vice-President would characterize it years later. Readers in the hinterlands simply insisted on being heard—and what stories they had to tell.

Take Elizabeth Burrow, for example. She was the editor of the twice-a-week *Spectator* in Ozark, Ark., and was suffering from an incurable cancer. While she was in the hospital for an operation in the fall of 1958, there was some unpleasantness in Ozark over the integration of two black girls in a public school. She recovered sufficiently to resume her page 1 column (The Last Straw) with a piece headed: "A Malignancy Worse Than My Cancer."

"Aren't you big, brave people," she wrote. "Where is your intelligence? Of course the two little colored girls will make it all right. But the worry is over *our* conscience. Will we white people make it all right? Here's a malignancy worse than my cancer, and I wouldn't swap with you."

We reprinted Elizabeth Burrow's piece, and I wrote wanting to know more about her. It was the beginning of a warm friendship, although we never met. She told us we were putting out a fine paper and that some of her most encouraging letters had come from GUARDIAN readers. She wrote:

"I hope you realize that Faubus [Governor Orval Faubus who had barred the door personally to black children in the confrontation at Little Rock in 1957] and his following are a small part of Arkansas. My great-great-grandfather was a member of this state's first legislature . . . I am descended of slave-holders on both sides of my family, and I like to think that the position I hold is pretty typical. I have a debt that cannot be paid to the Negroes who stayed with my mother's family after the Civil War. Except for them she would have died and I would never have been born."

We blessed the day Elizabeth Burrow was born, and we mourned when the correspondence ended: her own untraceable malignancy prevailed where the induced cancer of race hatred could not.

Walt Whitman, yes, and Eugene Debs too. In May 1963 a letter arrived from Tonasket, Wash., in the bold firm hand of J. P. Douglass:

"In 1897 I carried a copy of the old *Appeal to Reason* from the Yakima Valley, Wash., on a bicycle trip of 3,000 miles to southern central Minnesota (Fairmont). Took subs all the way. Afterward took subs for the *American Guardian*. For some years have taken NATIONAL GUARDIAN. Am a 'tired radical' (be 91 in July). Cut me off your list. I knew the whole score 70 years ago. What we need is Hoover, Hell, and Hard Times. Enclose a small check to make sure I'm quitting in good form. Have spent much time and money trying to educate the American fools. You might as well talk to the family cow or the family car or truck."

J. P. Douglass had earned his rest. But there were feisty folk, some of them not much junior to Douglass, who wouldn't give up. One such, in Coeur d'Alene, Idaho, was Thomas B. Wood, representative from Kootenai County to the House of Representatives of the state of Idaho. He commented on the 1950 national elections:

" 'The mountain labored and brought forth a mouse (rat).' The above quotation can very aptly be ascribed to the results. Prostituted editors, radio commentators and others looking for a reason for the swing toward the ultra-reactionary Republican Party give us all kinds of reasons, all of them wrong. . . . Thank God there are a few voices that refuse to be hushed, a few publications that are not for sale, a few patriots who place a higher value on truth, honor, decency, and justice than on the lust for gold and the specious but false plaudits of their parasitic master. NATIONAL GUARDIAN is in that company. Keep up your good work."

Grand phrases? Perhaps. But we remembered that Tom Paine had preferred to call it common sense. It was that common sense that kept us going for the long haul. As I said, we were rediscovering America.

Some Small Communities with NATIONAL GUARDIAN Readers/Mailbaggers, 1948–1955

	Under 1,000 pop.	1,000–5,000 pop.	5,000–10,000 pop.	10,000–20,000 pop.
Ala.	Helena			
Ariz.	Elgin			
Ark.	Imboden	Eureka Springs Mountain Home		
Calif.	Montgomery Creek	Brisbane St. Helena Cypress		
Colo.	Victor Cedaredge	Fruita		
Del.		Stanton Arden		
Fla.	Captiva	Pahokee Zephyrhills	Titusville Kissimee	
Idaho		Orofino St. Maries		Coeur d'Alene Nampa
Ill.		Lemont Byron Greenup		Ottawa
Ind.	Greens Fork	Sullivan		Crawfordsville Wabash Jeffersonville
Iowa	Dayton	West Liberty Osage Montezuma Hampton Shell Rock	Centerville	
Kans.	Spring Hill West Mineral			
Ky.			Hazard	
La.	Dodson Newllano	Leesville		
Maine		Yarmouth		Biddeford
Mass.		Abington Cohasset Pepperell		
Mich.	Alger Alto Honor	Algonac		
Minn.	Gully Willernie	Blooming Prairie Frazee Warroad	Eveleth	

	Under 1,000 pop.	1,000– 5,000 pop.	5,000– 10,000 pop.	10,000– 20,000 pop.
Miss.				Pascagoula
Mo.	Mountain View			Moberly
Mont.	Noxon West Glacier	Scobey		
Neb.	Lyons	Oshkosh		
Nev.	Jarbidge Overton	Fallon		
N.H.	Center Sandwich			
N.J.		Kenvil		Moorestown
N.M.		Bayard		
N.Y.	Rensselaerville			
N.C.		Spruce Pine		
N.D.	Lignite			
Ohio	Danville	Leetonia	Worthington	Berea Fostoria Martins Ferry
Okla.	Ketchum	Weatherford		Chickasha
Oreg.	Scappoose Rogue River Crawfordsville			
Pa.	Port Matilda	Trucksville Library	Media	
R.I.			Westerly	
S.D.	Baltic Hosmer	Parkston		
Tenn.		Erwin Loudon Tracy City		
Tex.	Port Aransas	Farmersville Midlothian		
Utah	Aurora Moroni	Parowan Tooele		
Va.	Gretna			
Vt.	East Burke			
Wash.	Tonasket	Chelan Mercer Island		
W. Va.		Follansbee		
Wisc.	Argonne	Cumberland	Portage	

Note: Postmarks not in gazetteer: Janesboro, Ark.   Page, Ill.
Blue Jay, Calif.   Macomb, Mo.
Spivak, Colo.   Grand Forks, Neb.
Old Matchlock, Conn.   Ransomville, N.C.

High Winds from the East

[C.B.] Like most ideas whose time has come, our exercise in external fellow traveling and internal togetherwork required several kinds of bravado. In loftier moments we might compare ourselves with Columbus splashing into the unknown. Often we felt more like the Jumblies of the children's poem who went to sea in a sieve.

We had launched our craft into a gathering storm without illusions about the reef to starboard—the fact that subscribing to the GUARDIAN wasn't a mere clip of a coupon but a possible invitation to the police. In addition to that fact of life and the financial rocks never far ahead, there was an ugly shoal to port, the contentiousness among left sects. With an optimism that political Cassandras called starry-eyed, we had hoped to avoid getting into battles with any of them—but especially the Communist Party, still dominant on the left—by stressing common perils and goals. Instead, two new extensions of the shoal reared up when we had hardly set the sails.

The birth of People's Democracies in Europe and Asia after World War II had ended the isolation of socialism within Soviet borders. The idea that countries building socialism could fight among themselves never occurred to Marx or Lenin, but by 1948 it

July 1945—the signing of a contract for the first licensed newspaper, the Frankfurter *Rundschau*, in the American zone. Dedicated to preventing former Nazis from regaining control of the German press and again spreading fascist ideology, the paper was behind the idea of the founding of the NATIONAL GUARDIAN in the United States. Wilhelm Gerst, chairman of the editorial board, signs while Lieutenant Colonel James G. Chesnutt, Cedric Belfrage, and Major Oscar D. Cully (seated) look on.

The GUARDIAN's Executive Editor James Aronson (seated) and John T. McManus, General Manager. cr. Robert Joyce

NATIONAL
GUARDIAN
the progressive newsweekly

Vol. I, No. 1   NEW YORK, N. Y., OCT. 18, 1948   10 Ce

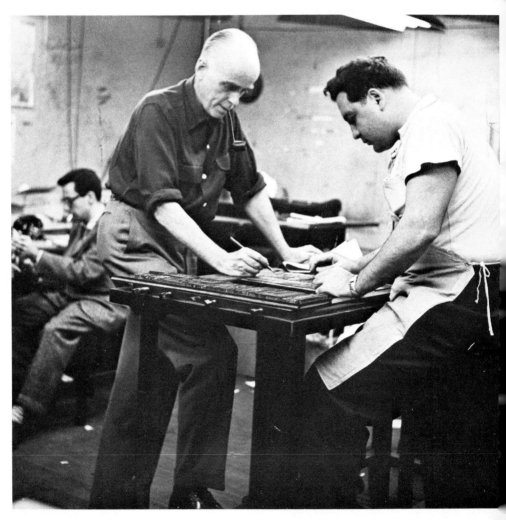

GUARDIAN Editor Cedric Belfrage in the composing room.

onson, Belfrage, and McManus talk with
ogressive Party presidential candidate Vin-
nt Hallinan in 1952.

The GUARDIAN always backed Congressman
Vito Marcantonio of Manhattan's East
Harlem area.

Aronson and Belfrage in the GUARDIAN office.

A thoughtful McManus queries a reporter.

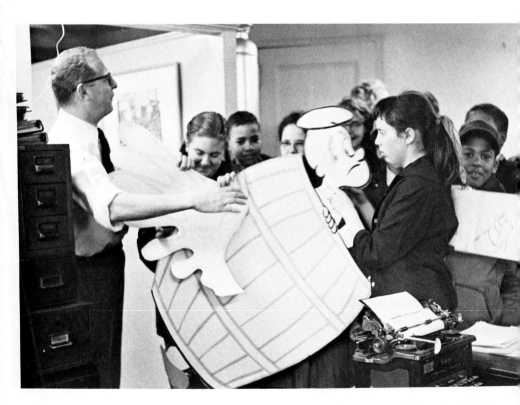

Aronson introduces visiting school children to the GUARDIAN angel. cr. Robert Joyce.

W. E. B. Du Bois.

Belfrage with Choon Cha and Chungsoon Kwak. The "disappearance" of this couple remains a mystery still to be solved.

NATIONAL
GUARDIAN
the progressive newsweekly

McManus and Dr. Du Bois.
cr. William Price

Dr. Du Bois and Belfrage.

NATIONAL GUARDIAN

the progressive newsweekly

Vol. I, No. 1   NEW YORK, N. Y., OCT. 18, 1948   10 Cents

"Of course Mr. Churchill
is a great war leader.
That's why
he wants
another war."

—Emanuel Shinwell,
Labor M.P.
October 11, 1948

[See WORLD
ROUNDUP
—Page 3]

Henry Wallace

'THE EGG AND US' Page 6

Written Exclusively
National Guardian

Norman Mailer

'A CREDO FOR THE LIVING' Page 7

By the Author of
'The Naked and the Dead'

Anna Louise Strong Visits A Lidice Reborn...Page 3

**Harry, Harry, quite contrary, how does your garden grow?
Distorted facts, Atlantic Pacts, make crosses row on row.**

Early on, the paper fought against racial injustice, the decay of the cities—and war.

Drawing by Fred Wright

**"Jones, you've been changing that tool 20 minutes ... Grogan, that's
your second trip to the men's room ... Berger, who gave you
permission to leave your machine?"**

was happening and socialists everywhere had to learn to live with it. Yugoslavia was the only European country that, rather than being liberated from fascist occupiers and from capitalism by Soviet troops, had liberated itself under the popular leader Tito. And it was the Yugoslavs whom Moscow now began accusing of treason to socialism, citing a decade of perfidies by Tito. Yugoslavia in turn accused Moscow of trying to run the People's Democracies like an old-fashioned empire. Outside the storm center, this brought "Titoist!" said or written with a snarl, to join "Trotskyite!" and "Stalinist!" in the arsenal of left-wing curses.

Konni Zilliacus, the left-wing Labor MP who wrote for us from London, had become Tito's friend during war service as a British liaison officer in Yugoslavia. In the mild early stage of the Moscow–Belgrade brawl he did an admiring GUARDIAN profile of Tito as "Yugoslavia's George Washington." We ignored the brawl for several subsequent months until the rising shrillness on both sides showed how serious it was, and then we tried to report both with due calm. Readers seemed grateful that we mounted neither wave, but the shoal and the rocks were ominously linked: a wealthy angel whom we could ill spare heaved anchor and departed because we wouldn't side with Moscow.

Events nearer home were, in any case, far more demanding upon our space. The procession of American political prisoners to jail had begun. Congress was preparing to cap the disgrace of the Smith Act with the Mundt-Nixon-McCarran monstrosity, providing for concentration camps and perpetual imprisonment of leftists failing to register as agents of a foreign power. Under the umbrella of the Taft-Hartley Act, which compelled union officials to swear they weren't Communists, stoolpigeons and finks and goons—often with the blessing of labor's leaders—systematically defused the labor movement and handed it on a leash to the Establishment. Spectral pumpkins hurtled across front pages as Nixon earned his witch-hunting diploma by digging microfilms from that humble vegetable on Whittaker Chambers' farm in Maryland. This strange fruit was supposed to show that Chambers, who claimed to have been a Moscow agent, had once got material for his masters from

Alger Hiss, a former State Department official. The melodrama that finally put Hiss behind bars for "perjury" was too outrageous to conceal the gamesmanship from anyone looking for it. Along with Hiss, Roosevelt (whom he had accompanied to Yalta in 1945) was convicted of "treason" for the postwar coexistence arrangements with Stalin.

And in New York the first Communists were being tried, under the Smith Act, for "conspiring to advocate overthrow of the government by force and violence." While our small voice strove to revive America's common sense, the giant media cooperated to the hilt of dishonesty with the clowns and elephants of this grim propaganda circus. At the same time they were accustoming Americans to the idea that their government, with immaculate conscience and regardless of cost, could indulge anywhere in any violence and crime it fancied. It was building the most grandiose clandestine machine in history to perpetuate capitalism all over the world by massacre, assassination, threat, fraud, and corruption. And the good folk of America moved to the beat of the media drum from astonishment to approval to apathy.

The next hurricane blew us almost out of the water. Moscow arrested and deported Anna Louise Strong as an American spy. This Seattle clergyman's daughter had gone to the USSR for the Quakers during the postrevolutionary famine and epidemics, and remained to become its stoutest interpreter–defender in the English language. Her *I Change Worlds* and other books, in which she also introduced Mao Tse-tung and his rebel army, were primers in every library for open-minded Americans. In her 62d year she had called at our office to get acquainted, and returned to Moscow as our correspondent. Traveling through "the American zone" (West Europe) in the fall of 1948 she had found varying degrees of hysteria about "the coming war with Russia." But "as soon as one passes the 'iron curtain,' " she reported accurately that November, "the war talk dies."

For a quarter of a century she had been a star by-line in the radical press and anathema to Establishment media; now the roles were reversed. On a February night in 1949 a mob of photographers and red-menace specialists gathered at New York airport to greet her as another disillusioned radical. Hearst had sent a man to fly in with her from Gander, remind her of "the very fine job you did for us as a Moscow correspondent" in 1921–22, and offer a blank check to Tell All. No one else awaited the plane except myself, our businessman friend Jack Turner, who brought me in his car, and a phalanx of cops. Anna Louise's old CP friends either believed the unbelievable or submitted uneasily to discipline. Articles she was contributing to the *Daily Worker* had stopped in mid-series. Party researchers were scanning her associations and writings through the years for "evidence" of Moscow's delusions. Surprisingly, though, no one coined the term "Strongite" as a new malediction.

From our two or three meetings the previous fall I knew her as a formidable, dedicated woman who commanded everyone to drop what he was doing and concentrate on what Anna Louise was doing. But I was amazed by her performance when the journalistic wolf pack engulfed her at the airport. With quivering voice after her life's greatest trauma and three bedless nights, she scorned her tormentors for trying to "use me to inflame international friction. News today is like an atom bomb. It can explode and destroy worlds." Of the Soviet political police she said: "Official stupidity isn't a monopoly of any country." (I wondered if in the circumstances I could have thought of anything so devastatingly sensible.) And of the Soviet Union in the GUARDIAN (March 1949): "It's not a model that I should like America to copy, but I still think it carries the great hope of mankind . . . as a mother carries a child toward birth."

Although there was no visible discord then between Moscow and Peking, her dogged insistence on going to China when it was "inconvenient" had apparently helped to madden the Soviets; but her correspondence with Trotsky in the early 1920s, which police found in her flat, must have been a potent assist. She had admired Trotsky then, but by 1949 every Soviet cop knew him as Satan. Whether the Soviets really believed the charge for which they would apologize six years later, we never knew. We did know that paranoias on both sides of the "curtain" were growing by leaps and bounds, fattening on each other.

Only among fellow-travelers of the GUARDIAN school could Anna Louise hope to heal her wounds, and this she gradually achieved in the bosom of Stephen H. Fritchman's church in Los Angeles, a Unitarian congregation of free-wheeling heretics. The Communists refrained from attacking us in print because we didn't cross swords with them. Our approach—to state our own position positively and cut the polemics—was still new and strange to them. Their private war against us, however, was waged vigorously.

The going was rough with the political group that we had resolved to defend as a matter of principle, but we were surer than ever of the principle: keeping our eye on the real enemy. From the opening in February of the 1949 lynching season in Georgia, mob violence against blacks and their consistent defenders—the left—filled more and more of our columns. It climaxed that summer in a murderous attack, with racist tribal yells and state-trooper assistance, on people attending a Paul Robeson concert near Peekskill, N.Y. The law looked the other way and many concluded that fascism adapted for "democracy" from the Hitler model was next on America's agenda. The government seemed to have symbolically endorsed it in acquitting Ilse Koch, the "bitch of Buchenwald," and opening America's door to Nazis while shutting it to anti-Nazis. At best, the government-media use of the Hiss and Smith Act trials to fan "spy" hysteria confirmed the all-out war against the left, regardless of sect.

"The work, my friends, is peace. More than an end to this war—an end to the beginning of all wars; yes, an end forever to this impractical, unrealistic settlement of differences between governments by the mass killing of people."

Franklin Roosevelt's words had become treasonable four years after he spoke them, as America forged the first unholy alliance against its former ally. Zilliacus wrote in the GUARDIAN: "NATO throws overboard the UN Charter and reverts to balance-of-power and arms race. It is clearly untrue that everything has been tried to come to terms with the Soviet Union. The U.S. is an eager convert to the errors and abominations of Europe's power politics, which I spent many years of my life fighting as a League of Nations official, and which the American people had so heartily denounced throughout most of their history.''

Yet out of what seemed like another world Roosevelt's voice echoed in more hearts than we knew. Under a tornado of "atom spy" scarce-headlines some 550 American intellectuals and professionals sponsored an across-the-curtain peace conference in New York, organized by the National Council of the Arts, Sciences, and Professions (ASP). It set off a chain of conferences in Prague, Paris, Havana, and Mexico through the spring and summer of 1949. Americans could still get passports to attend them, but only "hard core" peacemongers dared to go.

As if only Communists were concerned about the dumping of the UN Charter, the media denounced these gatherings as transparent Moscow plots. You had to read the GUARDIAN to know what actually happened. We mobilized our whole staff to cover the conference panels at the Waldorf-Astoria hotel: science, education, fine arts, religion, mass media, writing and publishing, public health, sociology and economics. All in all, the discussions were on a high, serious, and positive level.

As Thomas Mann, in the last stage of disenchantment with the land that sheltered him from Hitler, remarked that spring: "The word peace might get you on the Attorney General's blacklist provided you're not yet on it." The ASP, whose organizing geniuses Hannah Dorner and Joe Joseph staged the conference, was already on it and marked for death. But the sponsors and participants were naive enough to think that, if a "Western" war with the Soviet Union was to be prevented, they must talk it over with "Western" and above all with Soviet fellow intellectuals. Only the subversive ASP offered them the chance.

Surprisingly few were intimidated in advance, but the Establishment saw to it that all except the "hardest core" would be when they went home. By way of cannily underlining the "Communist plot" thesis—not that much canniness was needed to hold the media's devotion—the State Department denied visas to "Western" delegates (France, Britain, Italy) while admitting all the "iron curtain" ones, headed by Soviet composer Shostakovich. Reformed Marxists, veteran russophobes since before the antifascist war alliance, were brought into service inside the hotel: Professor Sidney Hook (favorite hatchet critic of the New York *Times Book Review*) in an "Intellectual Freedom" counterblast bureau, Dwight Macdonald to lead the bedeviling of the Russians. Stalin's cruelly enforced intellectual conformity, about which the bedevilers were better informed than most of the audience, afforded cynical grounds for their heckling. While participants of differing views inside the hall projected proposals to relieve East-West tensions, organized anticommunist groups paraded outside screaming for Red blood. And that was what got into the papers. Most of the sponsors and participants of the Waldorf conference were in *Who's Who* but not in the thick of cold war politics. For the first time they saw the blueprint with which we were already familiar. They were being put on notice that to consort with Communists was to be one, and that a Communist was a traitor. They were being shown the implications of persisting, and few would venture forth again for many years.

With the bewildered Russians' departure, the lights almost dimmed out in America's groves of culture. ASP went into its death-throes and Hannah Dorner, like Thomas Mann, retreated to Europe—to mobilize blacklisted Hollywood talent for an enormously successful TV film series about Robin Hood.

The GUARDIAN pushed ahead, striving to maintain some equilibrium in a rush of noble or sordid and perplexing events. Within two fall weeks of 1949 it was our joyful duty to herald the triumph of the Chinese revolution, and our painful one to report the "treason" trial in Hungary. Eight top Communists there confessed abjectly to improbable crimes, and were sentenced to death, after the style set in Moscow in the late 30s. It was the first of a similar series of trials in the People's Democracies, paralleling the series

HIGH WINDS FROM THE EAST

of Smith Act trials in which America merely sentenced its political heretics (sometimes along with their defense attorneys) to prison.

Automatically defended by every Communist, these trials in eastern Europe were the severest test of nonaligned socialists throughout the world. To appraise them, no newspaper had any yardstick but the victims' open-court confessions and its own wishful thinking about socialist justice. Soviet CP Secretary Nikita Khrushchev would admit in 1956 that they were a *grand guignol* devised by Stalin—the confessions extracted by torture—to purge colleagues whom he suspected of less than doglike loyalty to himself.* Western "Kremlinologists" expressed this view at the time, but their long record of lying about the Soviet Union suggested that whatever they said, the opposite was probably true. If we believed that such grisly frame-ups were against socialism's very nature, we could only report them, for lack of hard information, with our bewilderment as well as bias showing, and hope for the best.

A dismaying aspect of the Hungarian trial was the introduction of Noel Field as an agent of imperialism in socialist pastures. Since the summer of 1949 an attractive, sympathetic woman, Dr. Elsie Field, had been visiting our office and filling us with embarrassed frustration. Her brother Noel was an American in Warsaw whom, on Zilliacus's recommendation, I had asked in 1948 to report for us. In August of that year he had accepted enthusiastically, saying that he wanted to make a study of all the People's Democracies and expected to travel around that area. In October, without having written a line for us, he had begged off on a strange plea of ill-health and incompetence.

His sister, aware of our proposal to him, was desperately seeking light on Noel's disappearance in May 1949 on a flight from Warsaw to Prague. The two letters—all we had, for we had never met him—offered no clue. All they indicated was a man ap-

---

* Years later the British establishment journalist Stewart Steven offered strong circumstantial evidence of how the CIA fed Stalin's suspicions through double agents and black propaganda. Sensationalist as it is, Steven's book *Operation Splinter Factor* (New York: Lippincott, 1974), is the first gleam of light on this vital aspect of the frame-up trials but has been almost entirely ignored.

parently as devoted to the good cause as Zilliacus said he was. No one knew then that he had been in a Hungarian jail ever since, under third degree for a confession to crown Stalin's melodrama. His adopted daughter had disappeared in Germany and his wife Herta and brother Hermann, going in search of him, likewise vanished—into the same jail as we would learn. The little we knew about his background was that during World War II he had "worked with refugees" for the Unitarian Service Committee in Switzerland. Having had a similar function for the British in New York, I understood this to mean that he recruited people for parachuting into German-occupied countries of which they were citizens. And—in view of the American propaganda that he was a "Communist" and a friend of Hiss—that his recruiting standards must have been similar to mine: left convictions were the best guarantee of reliability and courage against the fascist enemy.

In the Prague "treason" trial ending the series in 1952, a more familiar name turned up as an "imperialist-Titoist-Zionist" plotter against socialism: Konni Zilliacus himself. Only after many years could we fit together the pieces of this nightmare, or rather see how Stalin's henchmen fitted them together. With regard to Field, men now highly placed in the People's Democracies had been among his wartime recruits and, disastrously for him, the chief with whom he coordinated this part of his work had been Allen Dulles, then groundlessly supposed to be working for the antifascist alliance and now (in 1949) head of the CIA. As for Zilliacus, he had done wartime service for British Intelligence as liaison with Tito, now chief villain in the melodrama. Thus the "contacts" for the "plot" were complete.

Had the prosecutors known that Zilliacus recommended Field as our correspondent, we realized, the GUARDIAN could have been lumped with all the others into the plot. (Zilliacus had a high regard for Field since their days as fellow League of Nations officials in Geneva.) Yet from our longer acquaintance I was even more sure of Zilliacus' socialist honesty than of Anna Louise's. If either was an imperialist agent, I was ready to become a navel-contemplating hermit.

After the Hungarian trial (when Zilliacus was merely identified by the Communist establishment as a "Titoist," not yet as a plotter), Elsie Field's tear-streaked face already became for me a symbol of some furtive horror which everyone was distorting for shameless propaganda. I slept badly and, by way of composing myself, started a "personal and confidential" correspondence with Zilliacus in London. The Labor Party had expelled him for being overly friendly with Communists who, of course, had ostracized him as a "Titoist." By 1950 his GUARDIAN by-line read "ex-MP" as Vito Marcantonio's read "ex-Congressman." Nevertheless he remained Britain's most active and optimistic socialist as well as its loneliest. At the end of a letter late in 1950 describing three vacation weeks with Tito, he wrote:

"I saw I. F. Stone in Belgrade. He is bringing his wife and children over to England and hoping to settle here permanently. He says he can't stand America any longer—it's impossible to be a journalist and to keep sane and honest, so he's becoming a political refugee."*

Zilliacus gallantly and logically argued for calling the shots on Soviet misdeeds as the best defense of socialism. I congratulated him on his fair assessment of the Stalin–Tito dispute and sought to justify our own position. Convinced as I was then that the Anna Louise charges and at least some of those against Tito were false, I still clung to the hope, when Zilliacus emerged as a "plotter," that this was a mistake in an otherwise fair prosecution. But we could no longer delude ourselves that socialism and frame-ups were a contradiction in terms.

The essence of our position was that "the great hope of mankind" was still in the womb of the Soviets who, only producing their first bomb at the end of 1949, were critically vulnerable to America's atomic arsenal. As long as this was so, how could we

---

*Stone nevertheless managed to remain sane, honest, and in America although the papers he wrote for kept dropping dead under him. He had made his name as a columnist on *PM* (1940–48) and the New York *Star* (1948–49) and had gone to Europe on a roving assignment for *PM*'s second successor, the New York *Compass*. After the *Compass* expired in 1952 he launched his successful *Weekly*.

even appear to join the hue-and-cry led by the West's vilest people and most shameless liars? In any case, whatever was wrong in the socialist world, we knew no way in which it could be put right by foreigners: for if on the record they were enemies of the Soviet Union, Moscow could turn an attack by them into a justification; and if on the record they had been friends, they promptly became enemies in Soviet eyes. The tremendous East-West tension left no room in between.

"The ultimate good of world socialism and the particular conditions in which we find ourselves" must be our test, I wrote to Zilliacus. "We feel compelled to suppress a moral conviction because we think we'd do more harm to what we most deeply believe in by expressing it. I would be sorry if at least somebody of your stature hadn't taken your position, but by taking it we would separate ourselves from the movement in this country, poor and weak as it may be. I suppose it's thoroughly jesuitical, but it's the best we can do in a period of many confusions, in a world already littered with broken hearts. I hope we can keep in touch. Your honesty and forthrightness remain a great tonic to us."

Czechoslovakia's "treason" trial of top leaders, in the winter of 1952, stressed the "Zionist" role in the "plot." Since eleven of the fourteen victims were Jewish, propagandists in America went to town with charges of "socialist antisemitism" (as usual, without a hint of the racism in their own country). A man we had met in New York and liked, Foreign Minister Vladimir Clementis, was now among the defendants in court. The trial was on the eve of America's execution of the Rosenbergs (as we thought—there was a further stay) who, even at the cost of orphaning their children, wouldn't save themselves by false confession. Unable to conceive how Clementis could be induced to confess falsely—and not even save himself—we reported the trial with our socialist bias painfully showing. This time we had our own correspondents on the spot, Eleanor and George Wheeler, and they were as innocent as we. Their last dispatches before the trial had described the calm pleasures of family life in Prague and a polka and square dance peace march in which they joined. On the trial, they stressed the Czech government's denial of antisemitism (backed by Prague's chief rabbi, Gustav Sichl) and the contented "comments in Prague": "Although the defendants were in key positions they were not able to stop the country's advance . . . [and] although they managed to get into top jobs, they were caught." We left it to our roving correspondent Ursula Wassermann, in Tel Aviv, to throw doubt on the trial's genuineness. (She proved equally insightful just before the Hungarian events of 1956.)

In Prague jails the victims were summoned in the night, from icy cells where they were forbidden to lie down or even lean against the wall, to be confronted with Zilliacus' picture. To deny knowing him was, if anything, more fatal than to admit it. This, and much more, Zilliacus would hear years later from the lips of victims who survived; and so would I. At the time Zilliacus could only torment himself with guesses. But he needed no convincing that at its worst the GUARDIAN never approached the daily jesuitry of the *Times* of London or of New York, and he continued as a correspondent and brother who never let us down. Although no exaggerator of his own importance, he had the pleasure in 1956 of reporting the Soviets' public apology to him and his welcome—a somewhat ghoulish one—back to Prague.

Stalin certainly strewed no roses on the hard bed we had chosen. In the fall of 1949 Professor Frederick L. Schuman reviewed for us Isaac Deutscher's *Stalin,* a biography of "the 'man of steel' who is Pontifex Maximus of communism and the anti-communist's Devil Incarnate," and we settled for the Deutscher view. "No 20th century potèntate," Schuman wrote, "has evoked more love and hatred nor has any other, through purely political leadership, affected more profoundly—for evil and for good—the destinies of more human beings. Deutscher, an ex-Communist who doesn't earn his living by confessing his past sins nor soothe his soul by spitting venom at the erstwhile object of his adoration, sets himself the task of understanding Stalin, not praising or denouncing him." As Schuman quoted Deutscher's final evaluation:

"Hitler was the leader of a sterile counter-revolution, while Stalin has been both the leader and exploiter of a tragic, self-contradictory but creative revolution. . . . The better part of his work is as certain to outlast Stalin himself as the better part of Cromwell and Napoleon have outlasted them.''

The Chinese victory was the noblest event we reported through the years. Washington and the media bewailed America's "loss" of China, feverishly hunted scapegoats, and found them in State Department officials and advisers who had simply told the truth in their reports. Our correspondent Peter Townsend had described from China the disciplined onrush of Mao's troops as city after city was liberated. When they reached Canton, Agnes Smedley traced for us the Chinese people's century-long struggle to repossess their land from warlords, crooks, Western bloodsuckers, and Japanese assassins. They had triumphed and set a star in the sky for other oppressed peoples, Agnes wrote, because they could learn from history and the oppressors couldn't. The GUARDIAN began frequently quoting Mao on plans for the People's Republic, while the media transferred the title "China" to the island of Taiwan whither Chiang Kai-shek had fled. In effect, America declared the world's largest nation nonexistent now that it was socialist.

Agnes was a lionhearted woman, reared in the grimness of Colorado mining camps, whose perception of the brutality of imperialism had landed her early in a New York jail. She had been more than a press correspondent in China, trudging over thousands of miles in a Red Army medical corps uniform, and cooperating perilously against China's Japanese invaders while Washington supplied materiel for their atrocities. I had met her in Los Angeles when she came home in 1941, low in health, with no gainful outlet for her work, but retaining a great sense of fun which would burst through her intensity of conviction. There we organized together a mass meeting for her friend the bishop of Hong Kong, who followed on her heels, to expose Japanese imperialism (they called it "co-prosperity") on the Asian mainland. I lost sight of her during the war but when we started the GUARDIAN she was in New York, living miserably (which we could do little about) but struggling to complete her biography of Chu Teh, Mao's comrade in arms.

To top the contempt with which her country treated her, insofar as it knew the name of one of its finest women, General Douglas MacArthur, Washington's proconsul in Tokyo, denounced her as a "Soviet spy" who was "still at large." The American occupiers were by then fraternally cooperating with the Japanese (as with the German) political police, seasoned experts in the pursuit, torture, and elimination of antifascists, from whose files this information presumably came. Agnes publicly promised a libel suit against MacArthur for this "despicable lie" if he would "waive his immunity," which of course he wouldn't. She was too sick and depressed to write much for us and the dream of returning to China kept her alive, but she was in the same boat with many others: America would neither let her earn a living nor leave. When intercessions through Congressmen finally won her a passport, she got as far as a British hospital. She died there after an operation in May 1950, and ended her journey in the revolutionary heroes' cemetery in Peking. She had written us from the hospital: "Reading of American fascism day by day, I don't care much if I go to join the spirits of my ancestors." America's inquisitors pursued her beyond the grave. It was suggested in the Congress that the Russians had "liquidated" her because she "knew too much."

The British Marxist journal *Labour Monthly* had published in March a prophetic article by Agnes—her last—which we reprinted. Through Chinese, Hong Kong, and left Japanese sources available in London she had got wind of "a dreadful war plot being hatched in the Far East" by Chiang in Taiwan, MacArthur in Japan, and Japanese militarists whom MacArthur was rehabilitating. An imminent new turn in antisocialist "brinkmanship" was suggested by the feverish comings and goings of these people and of America's pharisaical Secretary of State John Foster Dulles, by the U.S. fleet concentration in China's coastal waters, and by the stepped-up bombings of Shanghai, Foochow, and other Chinese cities. It was reasonable to suppose that Asian nabobs frustrated by Mao's victory were goading American hawks to invade China and get their war with the Soviets through the back door.

Agnes noted that Vietnam, where Washington was spending billions to help the French destroy Ho Chi Minh's republic, also figured in the "plot." We had followed Vietnam developments in the GUARDIAN since 1948, but with America's "roll-back" policy making the whole Soviet periphery highly explosive, Korea had almost escaped our attention.

Postscript [**J.A.**] NATIONAL GUARDIAN, we warned in an editorial on March 28, 1949, "its readers and the whole progressive movement in America may shortly find themselves in the eye of an ideological hurricane occasioned by the writings and lectures of author-reporter Anna Louise Strong, following her recent experiences in the Soviet Union." Anna Louise was indeed besieged with offers to write, for fancy remuneration, what the offerers expected to be a blast against the USSR. That, however, was not what she had in mind, so she rejected all proposals except one, by the New York *Herald Tribune* syndicate—on the conditions that the articles would not be tampered with and would be introduced by a noninflammatory descriptive paragraph. She specifically rejected a characterization of the USSR as a "police state."

The $5,000 payment for the series was consigned to the office of John Rogge, acting as Anna Louise's attorney, for disbursement to causes selected by her. Her first contribution was a $1,000 check to the Communist Party to help the Smith Act defendants. With the contribution went a message from Anna Louise: "To the American Communists who are getting as raw a deal from American justice as I got from the USSR, from a fellow victim of the cold war." Instead of sending the message separately, Rogge's office inscribed it on the back of the check, thus forcing the endorser (the CP) in effect to subscribe to the statement. The CP sent the check back.

A second $1,000 check went to the Civil Rights Congress for the defense of the Trenton Six (see chapter 7). It was returned, resubmitted, and finally accepted by William L. Patterson, CRC director. Obviously this was less thorny than the gift to the CP, and common sense prevailed at the CRC. Patterson told us that the news of the offer brought more calls on the Trenton case than any other event—and from newspapers which had previously ignored the case.

The *Herald Tribune* went back on its word. It published the first article with an introduction headed "The Police State," describing the series as "the most damning documentation which has become available in this country." Actually the articles were, in the circumstances, a remarkably dispassionate description of a country busy with postwar reconstruction and worried by the cold war; they attributed Anna Louise's troubles to her persistent demands on an already harassed press department. But the articles themselves evaporated in clouds of emotion that had gathered over the affair, and the hurricane broke in our Mailbag page and throughout the progressive movement. One of the directors controlling the fate of Trade Union Service, the GUARDIAN's printer and landlord, threatened to have us thrown out. He said he had evidence from the Soviet Union, buttressing the charge against Anna Louise. We offered to publish it but, since there was no such evidence, nothing was forthcoming. Counterbalancing this threat was the support of another director, Corliss Lamont. The day after our editorial defense of Anna Louise's right to report and be published, he came by our office and said: "Good for you!"

But it was a bad time for Anna Louise. Once it was clear that she was not about to launch a new career as a professional anti-Sovieteer, the offers to write and lecture stopped coming. In March 1950 she received a bid to speak at her alma mater, Oberlin, an academically elite school almost entirely divorced at the time from the real world. More than 1,000 persons came out to hear her talk on world revolution. Her reception was enthusiastic, the student leader of Young Progressives of America wrote to us in a letter describing the event.

Troubled by Anna Louise's isolation and the obvious (to us) injustice of her treatment at the hands of old friends, we made copies of the letter and sent it to persons prominent in the movement. A covering letter from Cedric urged them to reconsider their stand at a time "when the need for active cooperation from all who can help the progressive cause is so great." Among the recipients was Joseph Starobin, then the *Worker*'s foreign editor, whose reply arrived three weeks later.

"Dear Belfrage," he wrote, "I found the letter from Oberlin indicative of problems which Miss Strong is creating; my own impression is that she does less than that in other places. On the substance of the matter: I don't share your opinion that the treatment of [Ms. Strong] constitutes a major bone of contention in the Left. In my own mind, the question is closed, and I cannot agree that any considerable body of opinion is really exercised over her present or future activities. I don't think the broadening of the progressive movement requires any different treatment of Miss Strong than the one which logically follows upon her expulsion from the Soviet Union. That's my view."

In the margin of the original letter in my file, Jack had written in his firm hand: "Tecumseh has spoken. Ugh!" Starobin's closed-mind view prevailed for years thereafter, solidly in the CP and quite widely in the movement in general.

The effect on Anna Louise was devastating, as her letters to us showed. In private, she grappled with herself to find a valid reason for her expulsion, but she could not come up with one. She herself did not believe that her pestering of the press department for clearance to China was a sufficient reason, but it was the best she could do. "For my own soul's sake," she wrote, "and for the sake of the USSR's reputation, I had to find some reason to justify them. It has done me harm."

She moved from the Connecticut home of her old friend, Dr. Emily Pierson, who had nursed her back to health, to California—from Palo Alto to Los Angeles to San Francisco, always hoping that things would change and she would be able to resume a useful career. For long periods she could not write: "I could use a bushel of words trying to explain why, but none of them would really explain. . . . Partly it is that the deep personality split that took place on my expulsion from Moscow, in which most of me was killed and a small piece was trying to start over, never got resolved. I never got accepted by 95 percent of my friends who then threw me out. And this has gradually had certain psychological results which I seem powerless to prevent."

She wrote many times in the early 1950s to Soviet authorities asking for a review, but never got an answer. She cabled Georgi

Malenkov, who succeeded to the leadership of the Soviet Union after Stalin's death—no answer. "Perhaps," she wrote to us, "if you were to ask some time of the Soviet ambassador, whether anything can be done, perhaps you might get an answer, but only perhaps. . . . I don't think the Russians give a damn." Then, in a frightening evocation of the psychological pressures on the Communists who were tried in Budapest and Prague, she wrote: "I am beginning to share [the Russians'] opinion of myself . . . that, deep down, there must have been some basic flaw in me because I just can't seem to care for anything any more."

These letters touched us deeply. Not only because of the injustice involved, and the seeming deterioration of a valuable human being, but because, to prevent the new holocaust we saw developing, every sane voice was needed—and here was a most brilliant one being silenced.

We persisted quietly in our effort to persuade the Soviets to acknowledge a grievous error. Soviet correspondents to whom we spoke listened sympathetically but said they could do nothing. Diplomatic representatives from eastern Europe seemed embarrassed by the subject—except one.

Josef Winiewicz, Polish ambassador to the United States, had been a journalist before becoming a diplomat. A charming man of unusual intelligence, he spoke excellent English and traveled frequently in the United States to lecture—and to listen. In the early 1950s, at a lecture in Los Angeles, a white-haired woman rose from the audience to ask a question. He recognized her as Anna Louise, addressed her by name, and went out of his way to pay tribute to her. It was an act of humanity and courage. It registered with the audience. When Winiewicz told me this story, Cedric and I decided that he might be the catalyst, and I invited him to dinner with Cedric at my home. It was on the eve of his return to Warsaw for reassignment.

Winiewicz came to my house from the New York airport, where he had joined the diplomatic corps gathered to honor the remains of Andrei Vishinsky. The Soviet delegate to the United Nations had died two days before, and his body was being sent back to

Moscow. Vishinsky, ironically, had been the USSR's chief legal officer at the time of Anna Louise's arrest. We told Winiewicz of our concern and said that if there was no break soon we would feel duty bound to present the entire case in our pages, as we had done with the Rosenberg case. Anna Louise was an American who had earned the trust of socialists, and it was right for us to protest against injustice to her anywhere or by anyone. Winiewicz asked us to forbear for a while longer: he would almost surely be going to Moscow soon, and he would take up the case with appropriate officials. This was in the spring of 1955.

In July, I received a call from a friend at the Associated Press. "Thought you'd like to know the Russians have cleared Anna Louise Strong," he said. I asked him to read me the story, then hung up and called Anna Louise in Los Angeles. "I know," she said jubilantly, "I just got a call from the Hearst paper here."

That fall Winiewicz came to the United Nations for the General Assembly session and we met at a friend's home. Sure enough, he had been the catalyst. He had brought the matter up with a Moscow official who said: "Anna Louise Strong? That case was closed long ago; everyone knows it was a mistake." Why didn't you say so publicly? Winiewicz had practically screamed. That seemed a novel idea to the Russians, but they finally got the point.

I met Konni Zilliacus in 1958 in London, where I had gone for my first reunion with Cedric since his exile in 1955. Zilliacus took us to tea on the House of Commons terrace. His Labor colleague Sydney Silverman also was there, a diminutive man looking for all the world as though he had remained too long undusted in an attic. Zilliacus: buck teeth and constant smile, one of the most cheerful men I ever met. Finnish father, American mother and stepfather, California-born wife, a Yale man. I asked if he would one day accept the invitation of a Harvard man to come and speak in the United States. Sure, he said, he had no prejudices. Gales of laughter.

I did send an invitation, in September 1961, for Zilliacus and his wife to be honored guests (he would speak) at the GUARDIAN's annual dinner in New York November 10. We wanted to salute him for a lifetime of effort toward sanity in the world through negotiation and discussion. He was traveling in Europe at the time, and among the people he was seeing was Prime Minister Khrushchev. He had learned of the Soviet decision to resume nuclear testing (a jolting decision of which the GUARDIAN editorially disapproved) the night before it was made known to the world. We published an exclusive account of his interview with Mr. K.

On September 25 Zilliacus cabled his acceptance. We wrote to several men he wanted to see: Senators Hubert Humphrey of Minnesota, Joseph Clark of Pennsylvania, Under-Secretary of State Chester Bowles, Professor James Macgregor Burns of Williams, Adlai Stevenson, and Cyrus Eaton. Two weeks later he applied at the U.S. Consulate in London for a visa covering the period November 8 to December 15—for the dinner, lectures, radio and TV appearances, and dates with these men. "I believe it important," he wrote to the consul, "for British MPs to keep in touch with American opinions and policies; doubly important for those of us who specialize in international affairs, and trebly important for those who, like myself, are on the left wing of the Labor Party and more or less opposed to official Anglo-American policies." That was Zilliacus—straight out.

Later he wrote to Stevenson: "As I told the consul, I have always been in the Labor Party except in 1949 when they threw me out or suspended me. They threw me out for sticking to my election pledge, as I saw it. At the same time I was bawled out in Moscow and the whole Cominform press and radio, and was later pilloried at the Slansky trial in Czechoslovakia as the agent-in-chief of the Anglo-American intelligence services. . . . At present I am having a spot of bother with my noble leaders because they did not like the terms of a letter retorting to their strictures in an article on the Labor Party I had written in the *World Marxist Review.*"

We proceeded with the dinner plans and arranged for lectures in several cities. Days went by, and no visa. Consul in London was "sympathetic" and sent several cables to Washington (he said).

Still no visa. We asked for intervention by Humphrey and Clark; Professor Burns was particularly helpful. On November 6, in exasperation, I wired Secretary of State Dean Rusk spelling out the urgency of the situation. Two days later came this reply:

YOUR TELEGRAM NOVEMBER SIX K. ZILLIACUS. APPLICATION RECEIVING URGENT CONSIDERATION. HOWEVER IMPOSSIBLE TO COMPLETE PRIOR TO NOVEMBER 10. (signed) ROBERT F. HALE, DIRECTOR, VISA OFFICE.

The telegram meant only one thing: the State Department was deliberately delaying Zilliacus' trip so he would miss the dinner. And since there was no guarantee he would get the visa in any case, the lecture dates had to be canceled. This was President Kennedy's New Frontier a year after his election, six months after the Bay of Pigs, and in the midst of preparations for sending American "advisers" to Vietnam. The press had no interest in the Zilliacus story but gave full coverage to a 3,000-mile flight by C. D. Jackson, publisher of *Life* magazine, to apologize to the leader of the Christian Anti-Communist Crusade for a *Life* story suggesting that said leader was more interested in the Crusade's financial side than in doing battle with the Red Menace. At the GUARDIAN dinner I read a message from Zilliacus. Here are excerpts:

I had hoped to be with you tonight to look at the New Frontier. But I couldn't get past the Statue of Liberty. The State Department knows all about me. All they had to do was to make up their minds whether they wanted to let me in or not. Instead, they kept me and those who invited me on tenterhooks for over a month. As I cannot believe that even the State Department can be so monumentally inefficient as that, the only possible conclusion is that this was a hypocritical way of turning me down again. [He had been rejected in 1949 after an invitation to join Henry Wallace on a speaking tour]. All this of course is going to reinforce my feeling, already widespread and strong in Britain, that the New Frontier is remarkably like the Old, and that Joe McCarthy is not dead, or if he is, his ghost is commuting between the State Department and the Justice Department.

I send my admiration and affection to you all, comrades-in-arms in the great fight for sanity and survival. I am heartbroken that I cannot be with you this time. Maybe you will invite me for next year. If so, I will apply for a visa right now and maybe we'll wear 'em down. Or maybe by that time that candy-manufacturing S.O.B. who finances the John Birch Society and the Pentagon and Dr. Teller will be running the country, and defending freedom so hard that you'll all be in prison, or we'll all be dead.

A year later John F. Kennedy was still running the country but we all came close to being damn near dead. The GUARDIAN's 1962 dinner took place just days after the Missile Crisis in Cuba, with its threat of nuclear war between the United States and the Soviet Union.

6

The First Asian Crusade

[C.B.] Before Agnes Smedley's remains reached Peking, America launched its "United Nations police action against aggression" in Korea. The victors of World War II, having put an end to Japan's brutal colonization of Korea, had split the country in two. The northern half, bordering both China and the Soviet Union, proceeded to build socialism under Kim Il Sung, who had been the guerrilla leader against the Japanese. In the south the class who had co-prospered with Japan, enthusiasts for capitalism under any flag, welcomed the massive occupation force and the President—Syngman Rhee, a long-time U.S. resident—sent in by Washington.

As later in Vietnam, dividing the country with an IOU for reunification had its advantages: concrete efforts by Koreans to eliminate the "frontier" between them and their sisters, cousins, and aunts could be presented as "aggression" by their half against the other half. There had in fact been constant sniping across this "frontier" from both sides, but by 1950 Washington, in the event of a showdown, had nothing to worry about propagandistically. Although few Americans even knew where Korea was, the five-year media buildup of Stalin's "aggressiveness" and the subservience of his "bloc" would place beyond a doubt guilt upon the North.

The other side of the story—indeed, all the developments in North Korea since 1945—no more existed for the media than did People's China. Anna Louise Strong and other Americans who had been in North Korea, and correspondents in Japan and China, filled our readers in. Among the oddities reported by Anna Louise was that at the time of her visit, 1947, the Northern government's top officials after Kim Il Sung "were two Protestant preachers, products of American mission schools." The facts showed with what good reason North Korea suspected the dovelike motions of an overwhelmingly U.S.-controlled United Nations, which wouldn't even accept it as a member. Yet in the face of Rhee's terror against genuine peacemongers including diplomats, the North had tirelessly sought unification talks with the South.

Incomplete as the available background information was, it more than sufficed to convince us which side we were on. The "UN police action against aggression" was a monumental hoax. The reality was that the turn from cold war to hot, moving from threat to massacre for the imposition of capitalism, had arrived.

The isolation to which this conviction condemned the GUARD-IAN (apart from the Communists' automatic partisanship) was greater than we expected. In the past, distinguished citizens had faced the consequences of opposing America's clearly imperialistic wars and the barren bloodbath of World War I. Now mature liberals separated themselves even further from realities than the uninformed youth who would be shipped to kill and die in Korea. Our readers were the core of an opposition so small as to be barely heard. Many of them felt on their own hides the wrath of their media-drugged communities. Merely to read the other side in the GUARDIAN was to ensure a threatening visit from the FBI. In the war's first weeks (July 1950) circulators of the GUARDIAN were arrested on Long Island, N.Y., to face trial with a possible two-year jail sentence.

In the Congress, Marcantonio spoke up. "My words," he said in a deadly silence, "do not adequately describe the consequences of this disastrous course." He was the prophet totally without honor among his peers. He described the South Korean government as a police state imposed by force of arms but, whatever it was, "you cannot split into two countries a people united culturally and racially over centuries." As for China, the fiasco of Chiang Kai-shek had shown that "no amount of billions will defeat the desire of 400,000,000 Chinese to establish their own form of government." Most ominous of all for Americans, "the power to make and declare war has today been usurped by the President from the representatives of the people. . . . This declaration by President Truman is an acceptance of the inevitability of war. I stand here and challenge that doctrine."

He spoke alone, the media dismissed him with a passing expectoration, and a Democrat–Republican gangup defeated him for reelection before the year was out. In his last speech, against the McCarran Internal Security Act, he told the House: "The governing factor in the ruling circles of America is fear—fear that has impelled men and women to beat their breasts and declaim against communism, to make sure that no one will have the slightest suspicion that they may be called communists."

"My country, right or wrong" (or "my mother, drunk or sober," as G. K. Chesterton paraphrased it) was the prevailing spirit, heated by the lists of "traitors in high places" which Senator Joe McCarthy waved before America's bloodshot eyes. We salted our coverage with Mark Twain on wartime witch-hunting and his "I was from Connecticut" reflections on loyalty, Bernard Shaw on resistance to the herd instinct, and other recent but forgotten nuggets of sanity. Jack McManus came up with a magnificent passage by Finley Peter Dunne's Mr. Dooley on "Westhren Civilization's Xmas Cillybration in Peking."

Chesterton's disease spread to Henry Wallace and, although the only foreign troops in Korea were American, even I. F. Stone, who later wrote the definitive work on the hoax,* lumped the blame on Moscow. But the majority of the Progressive Party's na-

*The Hidden History of the Korean War (New York: Monthly Review Press, 1952).

tional committee went our way and, using six-point type, we crammed their statement and Wallace's into the paper with our own terse manifesto in between. We recalled that we'd always been "an independent publication based in the American progressive movement, striving to reflect the views of its rank and file. We feel we can correctly appraise these views because of constant contact with active progressives in thousands of communities."

Losing Wallace, the only ex-Vice-President ever to lead a left coalition, was politically sad and economically near-disastrous for us but no great surprise. The "police action" once accepted, Wallace's subsequent behavior was par for the course. He would soon be bewailing his entrapment by Communists from the outset, but too late to restore himself with the Establishment. Even inquisitors yawned. Rogge, the lawyer who first gave us a roof and had been a busy peacemonger, also clutched the flag and jumped off our non-bandwagon with both feet. Soon he would be establishing clubby relations with the FBI as lawyer for the Rosenberg trial informers and as government witness against DuBois. A frequent contributor, we had thought of Rogge more as "family"; his last GUARDIAN piece but one (in November 1949) had been on "How to Build Anti-Fascist Unity," and we never had a clue as to what changed him and when.

On the positive side, we kept documenting the advantages for Americans of living and trading peacefully with socialist peoples instead of escalating the billions to kill them. The unprecedented (but clearly fatal in the long run) national prosperity promoted by the war economy made this doctrine hard to sell, and anyway the billions had soared into a stratosphere far beyond the plain citizen's comprehension. Trying to make the statistics intelligible the little Marine Cooks and Stewards Union, about to disappear under an inquisitorial avalanche, reckoned that at the average current wage a worker would have had to start on the job 300,000 years before Christ to earn just one billion. From respectable circles came one echo of our position in the form of a "piercing shriek" (New York *Times*) by Senator Paul Douglas of Illinois. A liberal cold warrior, he seemed fleetingly to get the point when his colleagues proposed adding another $5 billion to a war budget that had already risen by $55 billion in thirteen years. But he was soon back on the reservation, pushing for concentration camps as a cure resort for America's heretics.

When Hitler attacked the Soviet Union in June 1941, and American experts agreed he would take Moscow by Christmas, Max Werner had written: "The Red Army cannot be beaten." The secret of his record of correct military analysis was his grasp of the vital political element, which made him embarrassing to the media and restricted his wisdom to the GUARDIAN. On Korea his immediate response was that, no matter how much blood was shed, the crusade was militarily hopeless. The U.S. fighting services' traditional qualms about involvements in Asia had never been more justified, he wrote. The counter-arguments that won the day had a fatal flaw—blindness to the "military renaissance" in Asia, "the idea of the mass army, the army of the people." Max was right again. The primitively armed "Mongol horde" so scorned by MacArthur failed to collapse under the supermen's hail of bombs and napalm. Instead, swelled by determined Chinese who stormed into the fray when MacArthur approached their border, despite repeated warnings from Peking, they swept the crusaders back in a near-rout. America's European allies were so appalled at MacArthur's effort to turn the Korean War into an inevitably disastrous world war, that Truman had to remove him from the command.

Three years later the war petered out just where it began. The promise to "go to Korea" and bring peace swept Eisenhower into the Presidency in the 1952 elections. Over 54,000 young Americans came home in coffins. Beneath the ground of North Korea lay 3 million roasted and shattered corpses. Above it, hardly a tree remained standing. And North Korea, not to mention China, had its feet far more firmly on the socialist road than ever. But long before the Korean truce was signed America was already stirring the fire in Vietnam, where the French, scenting the collapse of

THE FIRST ASIAN CRUSADE

their effort to suppress socialism, were angling for a peace settlement with Ho Chi Minh.

Max Werner died in the Korean War's eighth month, insisting to the end on the impotence of super-technology against armies of the people. He was irreplaceable in America. Our left took literally the song "Ain't Gonna Study War No More" when it most needed studying, and the GUARDIAN settled for borrowing "Colonel X's" analyses from the Paris *Tribune des Nations*.

As the war with its horrors and hypocrisies progressed, the media reached their all-time low. The obscure radicals Ethel and Julius Rosenberg were sentenced to death in 1951 for "giving the atomic secret to Moscow" and "causing the Communist aggression in Korea." The extravagances of McCarthy and of Hoover's paid stool pigeons removed the last restraints from inquisitors, who wrecked countless lives and drove some victims to suicide. Intellectuals vied in sanctimonious jingoism with union leaders while the few who remained defiant were hounded and blacklisted. In the first wartime elections in 1950 DuBois and McManus sought to bring sanity to a broader public by running for senator and governor in New York on the American Labor Party ticket. They were swamped along with Marc, and DuBois was brought to trial for advocating peace. The media reported none of these things with a vestige of honesty. Meanwhile the last of the old-style radical muckraking sheets, George Seldes' *In Fact,* expired from collapsing circulation. America's most obscene press baron, William Randolph Hearst, followed *In Fact* to the tomb and we commented:

Why tell the truth when there is more money in lies? As the *Wall Street Journal* put it in 1925, 'a newspaper is a private enterprise owing nothing whatever to the public which grants it no franchise' . . . Today Hearst's standards are the standards not only of the American press, but of "America." The final Hearstian triumph came last week when the U.S. rejected the UN treaty on freedom of information because "Asian and Near Eastern governments" insist on the right to suppress material inflaming sentiment for war or racial and religious hatred.

Looking as newspapermen still proud of our craft at the picture to which Hearst has so generously contributed, we can only say: Thank God for the "Asian and Near Eastern governments." . . . Our newspaper is NOT a private enterprise. It owes EVERYTHING to the public, which alone grants it a franchise.

During the long "truce talks" with bomb and napalm accompaniment, when the white Titan strove for a formula to conceal his frustration by "gooks," government and media laid down a barrage of fakery about American POWs in North Korea. All the names, with photos of the POWs in the camps where they were held, were appearing in the *China Monthly Review,* published in Shanghai by the American John W. Powell Jr. who had grown up there. Also messages from POWs to their families, and wives' and mothers' letters found on American dead. Powell was sending advance proofs of his lists to the American media, but they found them un-newsworthy even as "enemy propaganda" and continued, with appropriate editorial umbrage, to feature Washington's concoctions about atrocities committed on "our boys" and about thousands "missing in action." We were happy to take advantage of this exclusive-by-default on the names, photos, and messages, although sometimes, when poverty reduced us to eight pages, they crowded out of the paper almost all else except "war and peace," the inquisition, and our battle for the Rosenbergs' lives. Publication of the POW material brought hundreds of grateful letters from "disappeared" GIs' families. It also brought proposals that we accompany our Jewish traitor friends the Rosenbergs to the deathhouse and, finally, the compliment of attacks by the Hearst and Scripps-Howard press. The latter called for FBI action against our "dirty work" in publishing the names. After some months Washington, forced to act by the bitter fury of the GIs' families, confirmed the correctness of our lists.

Late in 1952 some New Zealand delegates to a peace conference in Peking obtained there, and sent to us, a firsthand "Western" account of North Korean POW camps. The source was Wilfred Burchett, an Australian who had covered World War II in Asia, and the People's Democracies after that war, for the London *Times* and *Express* and the *Christian Science Monitor.* Among other feats

THE FIRST ASIAN CRUSADE

putting him in the top rank of reporters, he had scooped the world with an eye-witness story from atomized Hiroshima. Like many journalists he was a socialist; like few, he had quit the bourgeois press in disgust for its mutilation of his copy. To cover the Korean War he had joined the French Communist daily *Ce Soir,* which landed him on the Northern side and enabled him to tour the POW camps and meet the inmates.

Considering the conditions under which the camps were maintained—for the bombing of what remained of North Korea never stopped—Burchett had reason to be impressed. While the Koreans' diet consisted of millet, convoys with other food for the Americans came down from China under "continuous U.S. strafing." The POW's had considerable freedom for recreation and outings, which some of them abused. "Self-criticism"—"brainwashing" in the U.S. media—was imposed for misbehavior, and for "bad crimes" (robberies or attempted rape) they were locked up alone for a week and deprived of tobacco and sugar rations. Burchett talked to "hundreds" of POW's and "heard of none being shot or having disappeared, nor any rumors of such." He did report a prevalent "fear of going home . . . linked with a fear and distrust of each other. None feels secure from denunciation by some one reporting him as friendly to the Chinese."

Logically enough, only a handful of Americans would opt to stay in China (their only alternative) after the truce, but the treatment of returnees "reported friendly to the Chinese" would show that the fears weren't groundless. Washington, meanwhile, wove a massive propaganda campaign from the "refusal to go home"— for fear and hatred of socialism—of North Korean and Chinese POWs. When prisoners were exchanged in 1953, hundreds of men captured by the "UN" forces failed to turn up. They had died under the hands of Rhee's torturers, or in wholesale massacres, which were the techniques for eliciting "refusals to go home"in the South Korean–American camp on Koje Island. Surviving Koje inmates gave Burchett enough documentation of this for a book.*

* And Alan Winnington of the London *Worker,* the only other "Western" correspondent on the Northern side.

We summarized it with the same sort of editorial note on Burchett that accompanied his American POW story: in view of his relations with *Ce Soir* and the North Koreans, "the hysterical [and] those whose propaganda collapses if the description is true . . . may discount his report in advance."

Burchett's reporting of the "truce negotiations" at Panmunjom near the North–South "frontier" made him an ever pricklier journalistic celebrity whom we took into our family with pride. The American military negotiators were so clearly stalling that they gave flimflam briefings to correspondents on their own side, compelling them to get from Burchett each evening his version of what had gone on. The media, with warnings about the implications of his apostasy, began using and naming him as a source. His stuff always turned out to be true.

Under J. Edgar Hoover's baton a monstrous regiment of Macs— Senate inquisitor Pat McCarran, Attorney General J. Howard McGrath, and Senator Joe McCarthy—provided domestic orchestration for MacArthur's crusade against red Asians. McCarthy having emerged to media super-stardom four months before the war, returned to grimy obscurity a few months after the truce when he began finding traitors in the U.S. Army high command. The war hysteria and the inquisitor who (because historians attached his name to the era) won most enduring fame fed sumptuously on each other.

McCarthy's "reds in the State Department" weren't even in the State Department, which had been meticulously "loyalty-testing" every charlady, clerk, and ambassador for years. The GUARDIAN headed McCarthy's charges, LUNATICS AT LARGE; EVERYBODY AND HIS SISTER IS A RED. Jennings Perry in his column called them "purely silly, a disgrace to the people of Wisconsin who are mainly decent at heart"; and the story of the arrest of the Good Soldier Schweik as Top Russian Espionage Agent, which we borrowed from Karel Hasek's classic, made our point better than any editorial. We listed McCarthy's fascistoid big-business backers and signs and portents that, in the general lunatic context, his "dangerously sinister side" shouldn't be overlooked. The only an-

THE FIRST ASIAN CRUSADE

swer to him was plain common sense but, still incredulous that the public could be panicked into taking him seriously, we reckoned without the media. Beginning with the Hearst and Scripps-Howard chains, McCarthy soon parlayed his nonsense on to the "responsible" press's front pages and (with mildest reservations) into its view-with-alarm editorials. That is, it was the people he named, not McCarthy, whom they viewed with alarm.

For some eighteen months we left McCarthy Circus reporting up to the media, which headlined it almost every day. We felt that further comment on our part was secondary if not superfluous. Our readers seemed to agree: there was one complaint from Portland, Oreg., that he was "tearing the Catholic Church apart," but he rarely made it into the Mailbag. The other Macs needed coverage more urgently, especially the Nevada senator who claimed credit for the McCarran (1950) and McCarran-Walter (1952) acts. (The first authorized "emergency" concentration camps for "communists" and ordered "registration," and diclosure of all members' names, by organizations which a Subversive Activities Control Board might identify as part of a "world-wide conspiracy." The second provided for deportation of "subversive aliens" outside the jurisdiction of courts of law.) In 1952 Sen. Pat McCarran began inquisiting and purging Americans on the United Nations staff. Abe Feller, the UN official assigned to cooperate with him, committed suicide.

McCarthy returned to our pages when he campaigned for Eisenhower and Nixon in that year's presidential elections. The Republican victory turned him from a maverick inquisitor into a committee chairman, with Democratic colleagues giving his committee a "liberal" complexion. This we could hardly ignore since we were ourselves among its early customers.

By way of footnote on McCarthy's lunatic context, we started in mid-1952 a "How Crazy Can You Get?" feature for which readers were invited to send candidates. The prize for the week's craziest item clipped from the press was a year's free subscription. Nothing McCarthy ever said himself was crazy enough to win; he was outdone by the media. The only time Joe made it was when the United Press reported in November 1953 that he had "received the 'Bill of Rights' medal from the Wall Street Post of the American Legion."*

The press could, however, also "go too far" as McCarthy did, though it was difficult. We assumed that an October 1951 issue of *Collier's* helped to kill what had been America's second largest mass weekly. With a GI on the cover standing guard outside a UN-flagged "Moscow Occupation Headquarters," *Collier's* outlined "The War We Do Not Want"—to take place in 1952—as seen by *Times* military analyst Hanson W. Baldwin, *Christian Science Monitor* editor Erwin D. Canham, Robert E. Sherwood, J. B. Priestley, Walter Winchell, and other authorities. Max Werner had made it abundantly clear to GUARDIAN readers that, irrespective of "our" wants, "we" had no more chance of raising "our" flag over Moscow than Hitler.

These are a few of the lowlights we reported during the Korean carnage years—the first three years of a decade of "happy days

---

*For the GUARDIAN's lighter side we tried to work up a politically flavored competition feature in the style of London's *New Statesman*, but "How Crazy" was the only such feature that caught on. We tested the water with this competition sample in November 1949, shortly after the Free World signed the NATO pact:

WHO SAID THAT?

1) "The conclusion of today's agreement is an epochal event. It is a turning point in the struggle of all nations which love order and civilization against the powers of destruction. . . . This agreement is a guarantee of peace for all the world."
2) "The Pact has no hidden aims. It is directed against no one. It is an instrument placed in the hands of peace and civilization."
3) "This Pact is a powerful defense arrangement. It is not directed against anyone."
4) "The shadow of our planes will darken the sky."
5) "The shadow of our air power can be cast over any part of the world."
6) "We must never forget that the regents of present-day Russia are common, bloodstained criminals; that here is the scum of humanity which . . . has exercised the most frightful regime of tyranny of all time."

The answers were: 1) Nazi Foreign Minister Ribbentrop after signing Anti-Comintern Pact, Nov. 1936; 2) Mussolini's Foreign Minister Ciano, same period; 3) British Foreign Minister Bevin, 1949, referring to NATO; 4) Mussolini after signing Anti-Comintern Pact; 5) US Air Force chief, March 1, 1949, referring to arrival in UK of his A-bomb squadron; 6) Adolph Hitler, *Mein Kampf*.

THE FIRST ASIAN CRUSADE

filled with innocence and the promise of even better days to come": *

- War hysteria fanned by compulsory "atomic defense drills," forcing schoolchildren to huddle under desks. A Seattle school superintendent: "We are making every effort not to disturb the children emotionally, especially the little tots." Some children taken by court order from politically heterodox parents. *Catholic Worker* editor Dorothy Day arrested for leading modest sit-downs against "drills."
- Inquisitors begin years-long harassment of Linus Pauling, Nobel Prize scientist and "Rooseveltian Democrat" peace-monger, as a ringleader of California teachers resisting "Loyalty Oath." Small student protest at San Francisco State, but teachers standing on constitutional rights fired nationwide.
- American Friends Service Committee (Quakers) under Clarence Pickett sets forth peace alternatives in pamphlets and in a "Time for Greatness" film which, "exposed" as "red" by "responsible" media, dies unscreened. The Quakers' unheard argument: "The Asian revolution would be going on today even if Communism and the Soviet Union didn't exist."
- Rev. Claude Williams of Alabama, named as arch-witch in church inquisition, recklessly "registers" with President Truman as "agent of a foreign power, the Way of Righteousness." (Unfrocked, 1954.) Rev. Clarence Duffy of New York, publicly opposing war in defiance of his superior Cardinal Spellman, mauled in the street by loyal Catholics.
- Eugene Moy, editor of the New York-based *China Daily News,* only Chinese-language newspaper in U.S. opposing Chiang and the war, tried (jailed, 1955) for helping Chinese-Americans send money to relatives at home—"an international racket involving murder and torture." The overt act: publishing an ad in his paper for a mainland bank with branch in Hong Kong.
- Foreign-born radicals, especially union militants and foreign-

* Description of the 1950s in the introduction to a television series, 1974.

language newspaper editors, picked up all over U.S. for deportation.

• To jail for their politics: Hollywood Ten (screen writers and directors); 11 leaders of committee for Spanish Republican refugees; Civil Rights Congress chairman George Marshall; American-Soviet Friendship Council leader Rev. Richard Morford. For refusing to name contributors to CRC bail fund—Dashiell Hammett, novelist; DuBois associate Alphaeus Hunton; radical millionaire Frederick Vanderbilt Field. Steve Nelson, International Brigade leader against fascism in Spain, sentenced to total of 25 years.

• Lawyers jailed for "contempt" in defending radical clients: all five in first Smith Act trial, Progressive Party presidential candidate (1952) Vincent Hallinan. Others disbarred from their profession, making lawyers almost unobtainable in political cases.

• Hallinan's client, radical Australian-born longshoremen's leader Harry Bridges, jailed and bailed out 1950. Government's effort to denationalize and deport him (finally aborting due to undependability of paid informers) goes into 18th year, 1952.

Elmer Bendiner of the GUARDIAN, who made a Latin American tour for us and described President Arbenz's ill-fated "New Deal" in Guatemala, was briefly a guest in an Argentine jail in 1951. William Pomeroy, an American friend of staff member Lawrence Emery, and his wife Celia got life terms (commutation from death sentences) in the Phillippines for helping the Huk guerrillas. We campaigned with eventual success to free them, and Pomeroy became a GUARDIAN correspondent from London and Moscow.

Campaigns on all these fronts needed money. While the GUARDIAN hovered on the edge of bankruptcy, we thought that as the largest-circulation radical paper we couldn't discriminate between our own campaigns and those of outside radical groups. Thus, during those happy, innocence-filled days with the never-failing promise of worse to come, we took fund-appeal advertising from a number of organizations as well as making their needs and addresses known editorially. Almost every issue contained some new coupon to clip and attach to a check or greenback. These included the Rosenberg defense committee, formed in 1951 and promptly denounced by (among others) Jewish bourgeois groups and the American Civil Liberties Union; the DuBois defense in the same year; the Bayard, N.M., "Chicano" miners' strike (basis of the film *Salt of the Earth*), which went into its thirteenth month in December 1951; the American Committee for Protection of Foreign Born, the only group fighting political deportations, to which we gave most of an issue in 1952; the Harry Bridges defense—and I. F. Stone's *Weekly,* which advertised for subscribers in December 1952, just before its birth.

The CP was thrown almost entirely on the defensive by endless arrests and trials of its own leaders, for which all the funds and legal talent it could muster were not enough. After we invited help for the families of Communists in jail, they saw that they needed us as much as we needed them. They advertised for contributions to the Smith Act defense fund, with emphasis on their national committeewoman Elizabeth Gurley Flynn. We greatly admired Flynn's record in trade union battles through the decades, and expressed it editorially.

Meanwhile, on a generally rising and rarely falling note of urgency, we bombarded readers with pleas to save the GUARDIAN itself from the graveyard. The readers took the barrage without flinching and it was from the meagerest savings that the decisive response came.

Postscript [**J.A.**] Korea, our "other war" in Asia, was a turning point for the GUARDIAN in the arena of world politics, matching in importance, if not in immediate drama, our involvement in the Rosenberg case. But there was personal drama too, in the fate of two Koreans we came to know and love—Choon Cha and Chungsoon Kwak.

Choon Cha was born in Seoul and studied music at Korea's leading school for women. Chungsoon, born in Pyongyang, was a child-prodigy violinist who became concert master of the Seoul

Central Symphony orchestra while still in high school; he graduated from Chosun Christian College in 1934. Both were featured soloists whose recordings sold widely in Korea. Having studied and absorbed their native culture, it was natural for both to be patriots who took part in strikes and demonstrations against the ruthless Japanese rule of Korea.

Choon Cha came to the University of Michigan in 1938 on a scholarship and received a degree in 1941; the next year in Ann Arbor she married Chungsoon, who had come to the United States to further his studies and had graduated in 1940 from the Chicago Conservatory of Music. In Chicago, and later in New York, they were leaders of the Korean student movement opposed to Syngman Rhee (then also in the United States). Chungsoon was also chairman of the board of trustees of the Korean church in New York where Choon Cha was choirmaster.

When the United States went to war with Japan, the government sought their services: the Korean emigrants in the United States had a vital stake in a war which could free their country from the Japanese. Chungsoon became chief of the Korean censorship office of the U.S. Armed Forces Information and Education Division, with Choon Cha as his assistant. They won an "excellent" rating for their work directing the editing and publication of all Korean-language material used by the armed forces. After the war they served with the Voice of America, then under the State Department.

In June 1949, a year before the outbreak of war in Korea, Chungsoon was abruptly fired (Choon Cha immediately resigned). No reason was given, but it was obvious: Washington had set up Syngman Rhee as President of the southern half of Korea; the Kwaks had openly opposed Rhee and the partition of Korea, and had refused to register as "South Korean" nationals. They had become an embarrassment to Washington.

What followed was far more sinister than the loss of two jobs. The Kwaks had come to the United States on student visas, which were transferred, at government request, to visitors' visas. In 1948, under the law, they applied for permanent residence when

THE FIRST ASIAN CRUSADE

the last of their visitors' visa extensions (previously granted in routine fashion) was due to expire. An answer came in September 1949: the Immigration Service converted their application into deportation proceedings on the ground that they had "overstayed their visitors' permit." As Chungsoon put it: "We were blamed— a most curious form of logic—for not having something which it is only in the government's power to grant, and on which the government had not acted."

Deportation to South Korea meant delivery to Rhee's butcher shop in Seoul. The Kwaks appealed and asked for permission to leave for a country of their own choosing. This was denied. In April 1951 they were arrested at their home in New York and held on Ellis Island for two weeks. They were released on bail, took menial jobs to maintain themselves and to support their fight against deportation aided by attorney Ira Gollobin and the Committee for Protection of Foreign Born. They had to report to Ellis Island every two weeks.

In October 1951 they requested a stay of deportation proceedings under a provision of the Internal Security Act precluding deportation if physical persecution would result. The matter dragged on. At a hearing several months later they produced documentary proof of their opposition to Rhee, cited the violence and death suffered even by mild opponents of Rhee in South Korea, and said:

"We are citizens of the People's Democratic Republic of Korea [North Korea]. . . . We believe and we did say and write publicly that Syngman Rhee and his cohorts are the enemies of the Korean people . . . [that they] were collecting dollars by putting Korean flesh and blood on the auction block . . . As the enemies of the Korean people [they] are our enemies. They know it as well as we do."

Attorney General Herbert Brownell knew it too. In March 1954, after further legal sparring, he ordered the Kwaks to surrender at Ellis Island for deportation to Seoul on April 7. Their attorneys went into court to reverse the order but the government decided to wait for an opinion in a similar case to establish a precedent. The case was decided against the government but Brownell refused to move in the Kwak case. Meanwhile David Hyun, a brilliant young Korean architect living in Los Angeles, won his fight to go to a country of his own choice. It was obvious the government had it in for the Kwaks—they knew too much about U.S. involvement in Korea.

Cedric and I met Chungsoon a scant two weeks before the April 1954 deportation date, when he came to the GUARDIAN office to talk about his case. He spoke quietly, almost apologizing for regarding his personal affairs as important. We listened, and decided—as we had so often before—that it was "our" case and we must do something about it. In the issue of March 27, 1954, Cedric wrote the first story on the case to be printed in a newspaper of general circulation, accompanied by a request for reader intervention with Brownell—and for the inevitable funds.

A few days later we met Choon Cha. She had just come from a showing of the film *Salt of the Earth*. The story of that brave little band of Mexican-American mine workers in New Mexico had so moved her that it was hard to bring her out of her mood and get her to talk about herself. A tall, graceful woman, she proved to be quick to laughter and fun; her personal modesty could not hide a wide-ranging familiarity with politics and cultural matters. I wondered, as I observed them a few days from scheduled doom, how it was possible for them to behave so normally. How would I react under similar circumstances?

The first story sparked a Kwak defense committee and a national campaign of considerable proportion. We persisted with the case until the day in January 1956 when the government yielded under the pressure and allowed them to leave for Czechoslovakia, which had granted them visas. Ironically, Cedric, who had written that first story, had been forced to leave the United States five months earlier.

During the campaign my wife, Grambs, and I had become fast friends with Chungsoon and Choon Cha. With Grambs (who had been born and raised in China) they shared a love of things oriental. Choon Cha was a magnificent cook and her Korean table was superb. They had no children but lavished their affection on a neurotic cocker spaniel, who always retired under the table at dinner. As an amateur mimic I would entertain the Kwaks (an appreciative audience) with imitations while the dog (most unappreciative) would howl his protest. That always sent the Kwaks into gales of laughter. I introduce the cocker here because of subsequent events.

We held a celebration/farewell meeting (at which DuBois spoke) for the Kwaks only days before their departure. I told the audience of friends and supporters of my mixed feelings about the evening: "On the one hand I have been involved, ever since that day in March 1954 when they came into the GUARDIAN office with their story, in trying to help get them back to their homeland in Korea.* On the other hand, their leaving fills me with a sense of sadness at losing the friendship of two of the most wonderful human beings I have ever come to know. But once having known Choon Cha and Chungsoon, one never loses them—or their friendship."

We had arranged before the Kwaks left for them to send us articles from Pyongyang. They in turn asked us to send them the GUARDIAN through Israel Epstein, our correspondent in Peking, since there was no direct mail to North Korea; they expected to see Epstein on their way to Pyongyang.

The Kwaks flew to Prague early in February, spent two weeks there, then went to Moscow from which they wrote to Cedric in London on February 20: "We have very little regret to leave the United States. However, we could not help feeling sorrow to leave so many good friends behind. No more the brutal hands of the U.S. government choking our necks. In the U.S. we were told so often of 'free world.' Now we really taste the air of free world . . . We want you to know that you and all our friends have been the source of our strength. Without your love and encouragement we could not have withstood the ordeal. Now, for the first time in many a long year, do we feel peace within ourselves. Perhaps before too long you may be able to visit Korea."

* Since Czechoslovakia recognized North Korea and there were flights between Prague and Pyongyang, the Kwaks could reach North Korea without trouble.

On February 26 they wrote to my wife and myself from Moscow. They spoke warmly of the help given them by our correspondents in Prague, George and Eleanor Wheeler. In Moscow, where they were rounding out a ten-day stay, they had been under the care of the North Korean embassy, which had looked after all their needs. They had seen the Bolshoi theater and gone to many concerts and operas ("Who would think that in a place where so-called Western culture is so far, far off there could be such beautiful Verdi, such graceful Mozart?").

Their original plan had been to fly from Prague to Pyongyang via Peking, but the United States had launched propaganda and spy balloons ("You may not have any idea about the size and weight of these balloons") over Eastern Europe which, the Czechs charged, had caused plane crashes; so the Kwaks were advised to proceed by train to Valdivostok. They left their beloved cocker spaniel with the Wheelers, planning to send for her when they reached Pyongyang. Their letter to me said:

"We are leaving for Pyongyang this evening. We shall be [there] in two weeks. You will be hearing about us through the Wheelers, I am sure. . . . And we want you to know this also. Nearly $1,500 left over from the money we had [collected for their fight against deportation] we intend to spend for reconstruction or some sort of aid in Korea. So please tell our friends. We miss you very much and talk about you very often. We regret that we shall not be passing through Peking, because we know Eppie would have messages for us. But we are sure we can make contact with Eppie easily. Keep well, friends. Let's hope we can see each other before too long, and we will work very, very hard for the date. Our respect and greetings to the staff of the GUARDIAN. And our love to you both."

That was the last word that any of us ever got from Choon Cha and Chungsoon.

For some months we were not overly concerned. It would take them some time to become adjusted and communications, even via Peking, would be difficult. But when the silence persisted we began to worry. We queried the Wheelers and Epstein. They had heard nothing. The Wheelers were concerned because they still had the dog.

In 1957 Cedric went to China to report for the GUARDIAN. He learned that the Kwaks had never contacted anyone there and their GUARDIANS were piling up at Epstein's. At the North Korean embassy in Peking Cedric expressed a desire to visit the Kwaks and to see Korea "through their eyes." He left for a "field tour" of China and, on his return, went to see the same Korean embassy official. Nothing had been heard about the Kwaks, the official said, but Cedric was welcome to visit Korea and the embassy would make the necessary arrangements with Pyongyang. Cedric emphasized his wish to see the Kwaks and said that, in the absence of news of them before his departure, he would pursue his inquiries in Pyongyang. A few days later the embassy informed him that it could get no word from Pyongyang about the Kwaks and that, this being the case, perhaps it would be better not to make the trip. Under the circumstances, Cedric wrote me later from London, he felt it was wisest not to go. He must have thought about the Field family, swallowed up one by one as they went in search of the missing Noel.

By this time we could not doubt that something had gone terribly wrong. The feeling was shared by George Wheeler, who wrote from Prague in January 1958: "I hate to think of the possibility of good people 'sitting' as the result of circumstances when they sacrificed so much to be honest progressives." He suggested a formal letter of inquiry, detailing the situation, which he would present to the Koreans in Prague. I complied. It was two years since we had heard from the Kwaks.

In March Cedric wrote to a member of the central committee of the Korean Journalists Union with a full background report, asking their help in tracing our two friends. There was no reply. That July I went to London for my first reunion with Cedric since his deportation in August 1955. While I was there a letter arrived from Stockholm from Ralph Parker, who frequently wrote for the GUARDIAN from Moscow. Parker reported a conversation about the Kwaks he had in Stockholm with the head of the Korean Peace Committee (who also was president of the Korean Writers Committee) at a meeting of the World Peace Council. He wrote:

"I have good news for you. . . . He replied without the slightest hesitation, 'They are working in the Conservatory at Pyongyang and are in good health.' . . . He said he was glad if his information helped remove any misunderstanding. He could not have been pleasanter and I felt quite confident he was being frank. I don't see why people should not write to the Kwaks at that address."

We wrote to the conservatory; no reply. In the fall of 1959 Cedric went to Tashkent, via Berlin and Moscow, to cover an Afro–Asian Writers Conference. In Berlin he broached the matter to a group of Korean journalists. One of them immediately said he knew the Kwaks well, was working with them, and they were doing fine. He assured Cedric that he would get them to write to us as soon as he got home. Cedric's comment in a letter to me: "It sounded completely on the level, yet if we do hear from the Kwaks it will be the biggest surprise of a lifetime."

In Moscow Cedric went over the whole matter with Wilfred Burchett, who by then was our accredited Soviet correspondent, and together they put the case to a Korean journalist friend of Burchett. The Korean embassy was unavailable for a visit because of a holiday, but Cedric wrote a formal letter to Premier Kim Il Sung, enclosing a note to Kim from Monica Felton, a British leader of the left-oriented Women's International Democratic Federation and a friend of Kim, asking for his personal intervention. Persistent as ever, Cedric wrote me from Tashkent:

"I got my interpreter to have a word about the Kwaks with the chief of the Korean delegation. He was very abrupt when the subject was mentioned and indicated he was fed up with being questioned about the Kwaks. It turned out that he was the same man with whom Parker had spoken in Stockholm. I then discussed the matter with some of the top Soviet writers present, and Boris Polevoi especially. . . . Polevoi pointed out that this of course was an internal Korean matter in which the Russians could hardly intrude themselves. He also said that if such a thing had happened four or more years ago [it was after the 20th Congress of the Soviet CP and the ensuing thaw] there might be serious cause for concern, but he didn't think we should be too greatly worried in the present period. At the same time he would not dispute that something has clearly gone wrong and evidently the Kwaks have been under some sort of suspicion.''

Three more months went by without a word. Burchett said his Korean friend, "looking embarrassed" every time he saw him, promised to inquire at the embassy and phone him, but no call came. Entirely frustrated, we decided that we would prepare a factual report on the case, have it set in type, and send proofs to the Korean authorities, informing them that we would publish the article unless we had some legitimate news from them about the Kwaks.

Even as we made our decision, Burchett wrote from Moscow on April 2, 1959: "Tonight I had a phone call from the Korean colleague whom Cedric and I had visited together. He said he had received word from the Kwaks that everything is 'just fine.' He is working at the Publishing House for Foreign Languages. She is teaching at the Conservatory of Music. Just recently they moved into a new flat and they are both very happy. I hasten to inform you of this because of the article you are preparing."

We were encouraged to a degree but noted that while earlier reports placed both Kwaks at the Conservatory, this latest report put Chungsoon at the Publishing House. Oddly, the same mail brought a letter from George Wheeler in Prague reporting on a two-hour meeting at the Korean embassy:

"One man told us that [the Kwaks] were 'all right and teaching.' Then he added: 'Like any Korean citizens, they could write to you if they want.' I told him frankly no American would believe that—and that I did not. I said that they *had* written from Moscow and promised to write again as soon as they had an address. I had every reason to think that they would have written us and their many other friends if they could."

All the messages were essentially the same as the one Parker had received, but they did not make much sense: if the Kwaks were free to circulate and write, why had they not written? Surely reports from people who knew American tastes would be worth infinitely more to the Koreans than official magazines with language incomprehensible to Western readers and studded with solemn photos of Kim Il Sung? And our personal friendship with the Kwaks was as strong as our trust in them. But, as Wheeler wrote of his encounter at the embassy: "It was like talking to a stone wall."

And stone wall it was from that point on. Nothing except a direct communication from the Kwaks themselves—with reasonable evidence that it was freely written—would convince us that they were not under some kind of duress, or worse. Yet there was no way through the wall. It was hard for us to believe that out of a whole population pulling together with such courage and spirit to rebuild their war-devastated country, these two Koreans should be singled out for a fate we did not want to imagine.

And yet we had precedents: Anna Louise Strong in Moscow, the absurd accusations against Zilliacus, the nightmare of Noel Field and his family and, above all, the ghastly fate of the innocent men tried and executed at the Budapest, Sofia, and Prague trials. True, it was another time—Stalin was dead, and the victims were being "rehabilitated" in the capitals of Eastern Europe. But . . .

Could the Kwaks possibly have been American agents whose secret role was discovered? All we can say is that everything in our long and close relationship puts that completely beyond our belief. It is perhaps more conceivable that, because they were dedicated socialists and knew too much, through their work with the U.S. government, about American involvement in Korea, they were unknowing pawns like Noel Field in a web woven by Western intelligence. In that case they would indeed be better dead than red—for Washington's purposes. In a tinderbox situation like Korea, it would not be impossible to plant the seeds of suspicion in a North Korean government alert to any snapping twig in the forest.

But we did not know. We had no proof that the Kwaks were in

prison or dead. We had no proof that they were free and thriving. It was this indecision that motivated our hesitancy to publish the story. In a media world salivating for such material, we weighed the harm we might do in the absence of any facts.

As a new decade arrived, and with it the black liberation movement at home and the gathering clouds in Indochina, our attention was drawn away from the past and the fate of individuals to focus on the second round of Washington's genocidal campaign in Asia. Yet I have never been easy in my mind about not publishing the story.

Over my desk in my workshop at home is a silver-point drawing by Grambs of Choon Cha Kwak. It was unfinished when the Kwaks left the United States, and Grambs planned to send it to them when we had an address. When I look at that strong, pensive, lovely face, I recall my words at their farewell: "Having once known Choon Cha and Chungsoon, one never loses them."

I still hope I was right, that the portrait will one day reach its destination. But I suppose it is by now not a hope, but a dream.

W. E. B. DuBois and
the Color Line

[C.B.] A street in Trenton, N.J., late summer of 1948. A leaflet lies in the gutter and the woman's aching feet come to rest as she picks it up. "Civil Rights Congress," it says, with an address.

The name sounds hopeful enough to quicken her pace; she is not quite frantic, still capable of hoping. She finds the rumpled office in Manhattan and is courteously received by its director, William Patterson. Clad in the best that the Lord vouchsafes to a garment worker, she doesn't feel uneasy in the presence of this business-suited lawyer, who is a bit blacker than herself.

"My young brother, Collis English," she says wearily. "They're going to kill him and five other of our boys. There was a white man murdered, the law came with guns and took them away and beat them to confess, and they're waiting to be executed. They don't know any more about it than I do."

Bessie Mitchell had spent the summer vainly scouring New Jersey and New York for someone to defend the six. Although they had repudiated the "confessions" at the trial, and tried to describe how they were obtained, their state-provided defense had been a parody; and how could she raise the fee for a lawyer who would

130

take the case seriously? Black ministers in Trenton would do nothing. The National Association for Advancement of Colored People said, "Sorry, we don't handle murder cases." She had phoned all the newspapers without result.

In the GUARDIAN's first month William A. Reuben, who would become our special investigative reporter, got the story from Patterson and brought it to us. It was a Northern parallel of Alabama's "Scottsboro Boys" case in the 1930s: nine sentenced to death for "rape," all eventually spared thanks to a campaign by the left. We gave it the gun and, together with Patterson, got John Rogge as lawyer in an appeal action and Paul Robeson for a mass protest meeting in Trenton.

Patterson was a Communist, his organization under attack as a "Communist front." He warned Bessie Mitchell of the mark of Cain on himself and all of us radicals, which would rub off on anyone we defended. Nothing could have seemed less relevant to her, an innocent untouched by the political witch-hunt.

"I didn't have much schooling," she told Reuben. "But you don't have to be educated to tell when something smells bad." Her education came fast and made a different woman of her. To her amazement, protests began pouring in from all over America and from countries she never heard of. Reuben had pieced together how the charges were fabricated—from interviews with the condemned men's families and alibi witnesses, with lawyers and jurors and prison officials. Our readers had opened a letter barrage in all directions, newspapers abroad had picked up the story, and thus the GUARDIAN had provided the Civil Rights Congress with the publicity that was vital but elsewhere unobtainable.

In the eighty years since they were slaves, black Americans had been held down by racist theories and practices including the lynch rope, generally administered when some white female cried "Rape!" This phase of "the Negro problem" was petering out when the GUARDIAN was born. The last phase before the explosion of the 1960s (which wouldn't end it) was in full flower: the law taking over from the mob.

The propaganda inseparable from World War II, a war against

brazen racists, had pulled "the Negro problem" well out from under the rug. Millions of white citizens who never gave it a thought had become uneasily aware that the problem was theirs, and that their ancestors had made certain Constitutional commitments. But as soon as the war was won, blacks who fought for their rights, and whites who supported them, faced an ingenious new obstacle on top of the traditional one, the media curtain. The media had always needed formidable prodding to take notice of a legal lynching. Now hardly a day passed when J. Edgar Hoover and his disciples didn't imply that black militancy or white association with blacks was prime evidence of treason against the Free World. The media gratefully accepted this patriotic justification for looking the other way.

Thus our charges of frame-up in Trenton didn't rate a line of type in the American newspapers to which we sent galley proofs or marked copies. After three months the New York *Times* buried in the jungle of its first edition (and yanked in the second) a paragraph about the impending human sacrifice. The *Times* had sent a star reporter to Trenton, we learned. He had determined that the six were guilty and "the Communists are using the case for agitation." The conscience of America's greatest newspaper could rest easily.

Yet the world was paying attention. Three radio commentators were moved to mention the appeal proceedings (one, CBS's Don Hollenbeck, even gave credit to the GUARDIAN), and a new trial was ordered in June 1949. The *Times* then published some details with warnings (in which the American Civil Liberties Union joined) about the "Communist-led" defense campaign. Two trials and two years later, the murder conspiracy by the six was declared imaginary by a jury. The "conspirators" had been in jail for three years and four months. The *Times* still pointed to the defense as an example of Communist efforts to "exacerbate race relations."

Even then lynch law didn't give up: there had been no conspiracy, but two of the victims had to remain behind bars for participating in it. Collis English's failing health didn't permit him to serve much of his life term, and his sister only got him back to bury him. All of the six belonged to America's predominantly black army of near-illiterates, but English and Ralph Cooper were the most militant. We had little doubt that this, as manifested in Bessie Mitchell's fight-back associations, was the real crime for which they had to continue paying. In the common Southern phrase about blacks, they were "uppity."

That they would all have been dead if Ms. Mitchell hadn't picked up a Communist "front" organization's leaflet, no one could honestly doubt. Some day, perhaps, a historian will give Communists their due credit for defending black fellow-citizens, not always wisely but with great courage. Where they went overboard in their zeal, it was on an issue that was more vital for American society, and more neglected by it, than any other.

The CP had worked out a plan, based on Stalin's "national question" theories, for a nation within a nation—"Self-Determination of the Black Belt," comprising parts of several Southern states. It was a novel and challenging idea which would be more broadly advanced in the 1960s and into the 1970s, but which we thought impractical both from black and white standpoints. At the same time we needed no convincing that America's most oppressed people took special precedence in the movement. Since the Communists understood and upheld this more than anyone, we went out of our way to avoid offending their super-sensitivity on the subject.

In those days, for example, almost any use of the word "black" could aggravate them. The only respectful term was "Negro," and this was offensive if (as in Southern and some Northern journals) the "N" wasn't capitalized. Communists frowned on any collective term except "the Negro people." Inattention to these and kindred details could provoke fiercer charges of "white chauvinism" than improper social behavior.

We started in 1948 a "Cotton Patch Charlie" column dealing humorously, but I thought devastatingly, with life as seen from the South, where most blacks then lived. It ranged from Uncle Toms, jimcrow buses, and "doodlum book" plantations (paying in company-store scrip, piling up sharecroppers' debts) to stool pigeons, warmongers, and pompous politicians in the North. Even iron curtains:

> Every day someone escape from some iron curtain and our Brass Hats jes gathers them in their arms, flies em all over our country in them delux airplanes to tell about the hunger and slavery they jes escaped from. If these Guys from behind these Curtains think theyve lef behind all slave-drivers, liars, hunger, ignorance, sickness and death, jes let them settle among us poor whites and blacks as one of us, behind that long curtain that stretches plum across the U.S. called the Mason Dixon line.

Yes, the column called them "blacks" and mostly took the form of conversations while "chawin, spitin, and pickin" in the boss-man's fields. "Cotton Patch Charlie" wrote as he did (we corrected some of his spelling) because he was one of them, a black southeast Missouri sharecropper with 13 children named Owen H. Whitfield. He was also one of the bravest and wittiest Sunday preachers in the South, and an ingenious organizer with a *guerrillero*'s instinct for matching black brains against white power. He had once planned and led a "strike" which put share-croppers, America's forgotten men and women, on national front pages. By simply camping along the highway to parade their misery where "the laws" dared not attack them, they—that is, nearly all the demonstrators except the ringleader—had obtained decent housing from the federal government.

But inside and outside our office Whit's column built up a head of steam about the slur on the Negro people's dignity. There were whispers that I, the only one who knew Whit personally, was a white chauvinist. We compromised with the title "The Cotton Patch," then "Owen Whitfield Says" with vernacular totally bowdlerized; then we dropped the column. I put up a struggle for it but, on balance, don't regret my surrender. There were already enough bones of contention, and bigger ones, at our weekly staff meetings. Whit took it philosophically "for the cause" and continued collecting GUARDIAN subs in the sharecropper zones. He reported from Tennessee:

> My expenses to date [a few dollars] is far more than I intended due to the terror existing in Memphis. Couldn't get free lodging as I used to get.

Everything is more or less going underground. I was talking to the Rev. A. B. Kyle, Progressive Party candidate for Congress, and two white girls were in another room of his office folding papers. Police swooped down on the place, drove the girls out, put them in a car and carried them someplace, dumped them out and dared them to be found on Beal St. again. I ran into a closet and they missed me. Dr. Kyle was molested. This gives you some idea how it is. Hope I can cut expenses from here on.

Later Ernest Seeman of Erwin, Tenn., one of our most sagacious Mailbaggers, did a piece for us on election day in the Tennessee backwoods. The dialect was twice as thick as Whit's and no one objected. Seeman and the people he described were white.

We had guidance on the "problem" from men who knew different aspects of it rather well. One of them, Claude Williams of Fungo Hollow, Ala., was white with a bit of Cherokee: a sharecropper's son, self-cured of ancestral racism, a preacher of brotherhood who was beaten and jailed for practising it as a union organizer. When in 1949 the House Un-American Activities Committee denounced his antiracist People's Institute of Applied Religion as "one of the most vicious Communist organizations ever set up," Jack McManus insisted on excerpting my Williams biography to run as a serial.* Claude's later adventures in the religion of brotherhood, regularly followed in the GUARDIAN, included "de-frocking" by a Presbyterian Church court. (He commented on that occasion: "If they hadn't fired me, I'd have fired them.")

There were black leaders in our orbit who kept their and our feet on the ground. A GUARDIAN explosion in August 1952 by Eslanda Goode, Paul Robeson's anthropologist wife, offered a refreshing pause in the white chauvinism furor which continued distorting the "problem's" realities. She was "fed up," she wrote, not only with white chauvinism but with "endless discussion of it." She had been fighting that poison all her life but didn't "plan to spend 24 hours a day getting mad." She told of a serious middle-aged woman with a long militant history who, exasperated by the chat-

---

*A Faith to Free the People (New York: Dryden Press, 1944), published originally as Let My People Go (London: Gollancz Left Book Club, 1939), and in 1941 (New York: Modern Age), as South of God.

ter of two young women behind her at a meeting, told them to "shut up." From that point on the evening's business was forgotten in favor of declamations against white chauvinism which ended with the older woman being thrown out. She was white and the two chatterboxes were black. With commendable restraint Ms. Robeson commented: "Now I submit this was carrying things too far." The black women had undoubtedly "taken a lot of the poison" and were right "to be on the alert for more of the same, but I do not think this was more of the same." On their part "the white woman and all white people have got to bear the burden of the long history of humiliating, insulting, arrogant, offensive, and murderous behavior toward the Negro people. But I do not think this was more of the same."

Paul Robeson, the son of a man born into slavery, grown world-famous in concert and theater, had been influenced for the rest of his life by the experience of "walking this earth in complete human dignity" on socialist soil. His participation in European peace congresses in the late 1940s gave him undisputed precedence on the official U.S. list of black traitors. The media virtually ignored these congresses but picked out one remark in Paul's speech in Paris, that Negroes had every reason not to fight for U.S. imperialism, for distorting headlines and foaming editorials. By 1949 he was probably the most widely known and loved American outside America, especially in socialist and colonial countries, where his recordings sold by the millions and were constantly played on radio programs. "Behind the curtain" he was greeted by ecstatic multitudes as the symbol of "the other America"; an ironical best-seller in that area was the patriotic chorale written for him by Earl Robinson, *Ballad for Americans*. In his own land the only hall or theater that would book him was Washington's inquisitorial bear garden, and his passport to accept engagements abroad was canceled in 1949. He gave an open-air concert near Peekskill, N.Y., in that year and dozens of the attending men, women and children left the field for hospitals, after an attack by mobs screaming, "Commies, nigger-lovers, kikes!"

This nightmarish scene was followed by riots in Chicago, where the mobs likewise coupled blacks with Jews because some of the latter defended the former. Our Chicago correspondent, Rod Holmgren, reported the remark of a cop who stood by watching the onslaught: "One batch [of victims] were properly beaten because they were Communists." Asked how he identified them as such, the cop said: "Because they were Jews."

Yet before and after Peekskill no GUARDIAN contributor wrote on a more upbeat note than Robeson. He believed, when Communists and many other progressives no longer could, that fascism wouldn't come to America. He projected "What it *will* be like when Negroes have freedom in their own land." With this theme in 1952 he began publishing the monthly tabloid *Freedom*, edited by Louis Burnham, who later joined the GUARDIAN. From the outset we had devoted most of an issue each February to Negro History Week—an occasion hitherto (and for years afterward) celebrated almost exclusively by Communists, since for most of the "white" press Negroes had no history. We borrowed most of the 1952 material from *Freedom*—articles by W. E. B. DuBois, Burnham, and other black writers—and threw in a *Freedom* sub coupon. Robeson made a coast-to-coast tour for his paper that summer, singing in churches or wherever he wasn't deemed to pollute the air. He couldn't cross into Canada but sang from one side of the border in Washington State to 40,000 Canadians on the other.

William Edward Burghardt DuBois began writing for us on Africa in 1948, introduced our first Negro History Week section and, in our first financial crisis, joined white social worker Mary van Kleeck as GUARDIAN "fund administrator." A world traveler for more than half a century, he commuted from one peace congress to another—New York, Paris, Moscow, Prague—until the State Department bolted the door on all peacemongers. He and his colleagues in a Peace Information Center, Elizabeth Moos and Abbott Simon, were indicted as "agents of a foreign power" while DuBois was running for the U.S. Senate from New York on the American Labor Party ticket. His Negro History Week contribution just before the trial in 1951, at which Marcantonio defended him without fee, was an evocation of John Brown. The evidence that the Center was a Moscow plot came from O. John Rogge in whose home it had been launched. Since the Justice Department could find no one to confirm this, and Rogge happened to be an "agent of a foreign power" himself (attorney for the Yugoslav government), an embarrassed judge threw the case out.* DuBois continued holding forth in the GUARDIAN on such themes as "The Right to Think," "The U.S. Needs No More Cowards," "A Nation Going Mad" and the overriding need, despite the setback to the Progressives, of independent political action. He recognized that without access to the media only a superhuman door-to-door effort could put it over. But he saw "no other hope for America." In all, he wrote 130 articles for the GUARDIAN in fifteen years. Almost no one else would publish him.

Of all our family DuBois was the one we most cherished. He was more than a dignifier of his own black people and of America. Slavery had just been abolished when he was born and he had seen every cruel phase of "the Negro problem" since; but his had been the prophetic voice crying ever since 1900: "The problem of the twentieth century is the problem of the color-line," not just to America but to the world. He had given steadfast leadership, through trial and recognition of error, in all of the country's decisive battles for the family of man to which he truly belonged. This he could do because luck offered him in the 1880s a good education by white standards, and he had not only the will and intelligence to profit by it but the modesty to perceive the responsibility it laid on him.

When he supported Henry Wallace in 1948 he, who more than anyone had built the NAACP, was fired by that organization in its pursuit of a respectable way to fight for blacks. Then he courted red-baiting, and got it in full measure, by joining Paul Robeson in a Council on African Affairs. Finally, as a globe-trotting and then

* See chapter, "Oh! John Rogge" in DuBois's In Battle for Peace (New York: Masses and Mainstream, 1952), for his genially contemptuous account of Rogge's role.

shackled apostle of peace, he became the exclusive property of us political heretics by courtesy of the inquisition.

We loved him as a sage who didn't know how to be stuffy, as an irreconcilable who enjoyed each moment of life and work, but with an affection always tinged with awe. I never heard anyone— not even Shirley Graham, the writer who married him on the eve of his trial and efficiently superintended him to the end—call him by his first name. A few of us went as far as "W. E. B.", but he was generally addressed and referred to as "Dr. DuBois."

Universities, occasionally with polite excuses, ignored him. A few white intellectuals promised to write about him when he faced imprisonment, but more pressing duties always intervened. A few black journals paid him the respect of declining to red-bait him, others joined in the game. He and Shirley journeyed twice across America to raise the $35,000 cost of his defense. He was too familiar with the black class structure to be more than gently discomfited by well-to-do Negroes' coldness; the response came mostly in pennies from poor blacks and whites alike. He had no book publisher but the Communists, no journalistic outlet—not even for a letter-to-the-editor—except the GUARDIAN, and consequently no money. Dangerously stretching our budget, we paid him up to $25 for his articles, later raising it to $50 for longer ones.

All heretical groups vied for him as a speaker at meetings— always for nothing, for they were penniless and fighting for survival and their leaders on or near the brink of jail. Accepting as many invitations as he was physically able, he never turned down the GUARDIAN. He was the "keynoter" at our fund-raising affairs and often the chairman. In that capacity he earned our gratitude, and that of all conscientious objectors to long harangues, by the dictatorship he exercised over the speakers. No matter if they were in mid-sentence when they exhausted their time, he rose to his feet with an expression and posture that none could challenge. He himself read from a text meticulously tailored to the time-limit, yet held the audience better than any who spoke extemporaneously. On each occasion he said just what needed saying, without equivocation and with extraordinary and rousing eloquence. The timbre of his public-address voice was as thrilling in its way as that of Robeson's singing voice. He wrote and spoke like an Old Testament prophet. That he only got as far as handcuffs and the prisoner's dock, never into jail, was a source of his constant and urbane surprise.

But he was no Methuselah, and died in Africa in 1963 at ninety-five, too soon to see himself "rehabilitated" in his own country. The intellectual and black establishments, which reduced him to a phantom in his last two decades, were soon reprinting his every word, including his GUARDIAN pieces and the entire collection of *The Crisis,* the NAACP journal he edited and built. Everyone lauded him to the skies, and there was no one whom we would more devoutly have wished to be Up There listening.

Late arrivals at the shrine missed what made us so treasure his companionship and comradeship; his humor, olympian and earthy, sharp with no trace of vulgarity or unkindness. He was a model of graceful aging; there can't be anyone who ever spent a tedious moment in his company. He listened to everything of interest that others had to say, and could show himself to be more youthful in heart than the young. Silence was for him preferable to the risk of monopolizing a conversation, although the hush was instantaneous when he spoke. When he laughed, it was with the whole of his compact body and sometimes to the point of tears. He took himself, others and his monstrous government as seriously as he and they deserved, and no more.

With respect bordering on the religious, and with no hint of the events that made him a living phantom and his widow an exile, the *New Yorker* reported the fashionable reception in 1973 at New York's Plaza Hotel where the University of Massachusetts at Amherst paid her $150,000 for his papers. Such are the advantages of being dead. But surely some fragment of him must have floated above the Plaza that day, with tears that were almost but not quite all tears of laughter.

From year to year DuBois watched through the GUARDIAN and the Communist press the procession of legal lynchings and savagings of people who tried to stop it. The "cases" were uniformly outrageous in that especially bizarre way reserved for blacks, but rarely enough so to make a media "story." North Carolina sentenced the Daniels brothers, aged 16 and 17, casually picked up in the vicinity, for a murder which they could no more possibly have committed than the Trenton youths. In Georgia Rosa Ingram, a widowed sharecropper, violently attacked by a white neighbor, was defended by her three school-age sons and the neighbor died from a blow on the head; she and the two older sons, aged 16 and 13, were jailed for life, leaving nine other children parentless. In the same state a Ku Klux Klan group killed the husband of Amy Mallard, a schoolteacher, in her presence; at his funeral, she was arrested and charged with the murder. Later she identified one of the group and he was acquitted with flying colors after a parade of witnesses testified, "Amy is bad." She was unafraid to tell us about it on the phone. "If it takes my life," she said, "I want the world to know" what it was like to be black in America. The frame-ups pursued each other beyond our power to cover more than samples.

Georgia was the scene in 1949 of one of the last old-fashioned lynchings, but the law made its contribution everywhere. A police terror in the black section of Brooklyn culminated with cops killing two blacks on the streets. Nothing happened to the cops. Meanwhile a Martinsville, Va., white woman complained of being raped by "thirteen or fourteen" blacks, and seven youths, whom she couldn't identify, were rounded up to sign prepared "confessions" and receive death sentences. The second Trenton Six trial was beginning when Patterson and some friends, including the GUARDIAN's Rod Holmgren, went to Virginia to try to stop the executions. They came home in bandages for their pains.

A few weeks later we were happy to announce that Illinois had freed, with a gift of $10, a black who had spent twenty-six years in jail for an imaginary rape. But then a correspondent in Groveland, Fla., reported a vast "rape" manhunt that was going on there. A woman had conveniently said she was raped, but the quarry were in fact $3-a-day logging-camp workers who had asked for more money. One was shot dead and three were beaten to "confess" and held for trial. A Florida NAACP man, Harry Moore, tried to do something about it. An "unknown hand's" bomb blew up his home with himself and his wife in it, killing both.

The GUARDIAN made as much noise about these "cases" as space would permit. Trenton was our only success, but among the others our campaign for Willie McGee of Mississippi got the broadest response. All that it achieved—perhaps all that could have been hoped when official America was so thirsty for black and "communist" blood—was the delay of McGee's execution for five years while the case moved to the Supreme Court. Lawyers who intervened in Mississippi for the delays, and reporters accompanying them, were savagely beaten and threatened with lynching.

His crime was "rape"—in consenting to sleep with a white woman. There were "save McGee" picket lines in New York, protest processions in London. In Paris, "French" African leaders addressed a huge mass meeting, and when McGee was electrocuted the Assembly of the French Union stood for a minute in silence. Eminent Free World citizens who had flooded U.S. embassies with petitions got the official answer: "McGee's trial was in the best American tradition." As other such immolations claimed our attention, we wound up the McGee story with his farewell note to his wife, Rosemary, whom he left with four children:

"Tell the people the real reason they going to take my life is to keep the Negro down. They can't do this if you and the children keep on fighting."

In the summer of 1952 Louisiana executed Ocie Jugger and Paul Washington, a returned participant in the Korean crusade, on "rape" confessions repudiated in court. The state provided the usual farcical defense. We noted that these were the thirty-third and thirty-fourth young black lives similarly liquidated by Louisiana since 1907—the third and fourth in 1952. In Florida Walter Lee Irvin awaited the same fate on the same charge. For the few Americans who heard of it, the process was losing its horror through familiarity. The protest came more and more from abroad. In an article recalling the broadly based, persistent campaigns to save Mooney and Billings, Sacco and Vanzetti, the Scottsboro Boys and others, Lawrence Emery asked in the GUARDIAN: What has happened to America's conscience? The question was rhetorical for most of our readers. America's conscience was drowning in fear—fear of the consequences of "subversive associations."

William L. Patterson of the Civil Rights Congress had laid before the United Nations a charge, richly documented from his own experience, of "genocide" against the U.S. government. Shortly after doing so he was brought to trial for the second time, for "contempt" in refusing to name his associates. By then the inquisitorial harassments which led to such indictments had become routine for him. On the last occasion one congressional inquisitor, Republican Henderson Lovelace Lanham, had rushed at him with clenched fist crying, "You black son of a bitch!" Semantic perspective (see comments above on use of the word "black") is required to appreciate Lanham's fine choice of words to insult Patterson twice in one phrase. On the other hand the state—or rather a few percent of its white citizens—that sent Lanham to Congress made it more of a compliment. He came from Georgia.

In preparing such trials the government, confident that it was a pushover to convict a black Communist, was getting careless. Some judges had retained through all the hysteria some old-fashioned views about court procedure, and so it was with the "case" against Patterson. Marcantonio, as his attorney, exposed the holes in it às expertly as he had done in the "case" against DuBois. Unable to doubt that the government would try again, Patterson returned to his subversive task in his rumpled office.

At this stage, a decade before the Black Power movement erupted, few questioned that joint interracial struggle was the answer, but frustratingly little was achieved in that direction. We thrashed around a lot to explain why, despite DuBois and Robeson and our emphasis on the purgatories of black Americans, our readership remained overwhelmingly white. It wasn't very consoling to reason that literate blacks with a spare dollar were mainly middle-class or trying to be, and that for all of them a subscription to the GUARDIAN was more dangerous than for whites. Perhaps we gave too much thought to our responsibilities, and too little to our limitations, as a white paper "trying to help." Perhaps we intertwined too closely the problem of posture toward blacks with that of posture toward the CP. But we saw no other course and the final "perhaps" is that there was no solution.

Jack, Jim, and I wrote each other memos for after-hours rumination, trying to fix our ideas on this and on our "political line" in general. One memo I wrote after a trip south has survived and suggests my particular state of mind. I think it was in the year of Peekskill and that I had gone, primarily, to see Colonel Robins in Florida (see chapter 2) about writing his biography. I reported talks with blacks and whites leading to gloomy conclusions about the movement in the South:

The CP after many years appears to have far less than 100 members in Georgia and Alabama. The Progressive Party is to all intents and purposes dead in both states, the Georgia chairman having taken off to engage in red-baiting. Don West, the Georgia poet, says this chairman was a decent but politically innocent professor, maddened by the fact that his whole committee seemed to be orthodox CP-ers who would make no compromise with his less mature yet useful and sincere viewpoint.

The fault of progressives has been over-anxiety to show the "mature" people that We are "correct." But the mature lot aren't important, they are converted already. The problem remains of reaching the people in such numbers that the Left can become a power.

And in the South at least, the black who would be the object of any American fascist genocide was the key, my memo said: "We ought to give continual guidance as to the lesson to be learned from [Hitler's] Germany. Left sectarianism has been tried and failed, and is unnecessary and improper for *progressives*. The main issue here today, as in Germany in 1932, is the possibility of complete fascism which involves *all* progressives. . . . That is the issue to unite on, no matter how much we may differ on the Soviet Union, etc. Claude Williams quotes this from the Bible: "I have many things to say unto you but ye cannot hear them now." The CP position demanding complete equality and elimination of all segregation is "correct." But Southern whites (there are millions of good ones and I've talked to many) aren't ready for complete desegregation, and Negroes are frightened off by this demand. They say: "We want equal citizenship, equal pay, equal schools"; if they get those things they know the end of racial segregation will follow.

Before it's too late we have to find ways and means to "stop the drift" of good Americans into the progressive movement and out of it again. This continuing drift means not only losing allies but making enemies.

Such were the confusions, with a chink of light here and there, of a white mind in those gray days.

Postscript [**J.A.**] Whenever I called DuBois about writing an article for us and suggested an outline, he would answer like this: "Yes, I will do it. How many words do you want, and when?" He never went beyond the limit and never missed a deadline. Accompanying the completed articles would be a note on a half-sheet of paper: "Here is the article you requested; use it or edit it as you will. If not, consign it to the wastebasket." No basket was ever graced by a DuBois manuscript, but I could not help comparing his attitude with that of indisputably lesser figures demanding to see any changes in their masterpieces before publication. We had wastebaskets brimful of theirs.

Cedric cannot recall anyone calling DuBois by his first name; I can recall very few whom DuBois called by *their* first names. Shirley, of course, was one, Paul (Robeson) another, and Cedric himself was a third. That was a mark of affection and respect. I myself was enormously pleased to reach the middle echelon when DuBois dropped the "Mr." in his letters to me and I became simply "Dear Aronson."

For all his reserve about his own emotions, I sensed in his last years in the United States a smoldering anger at the power establishment for its determination to bury him alive. It was expressed clearly in his acceptance of President Nkrumah's offer to come to Ghana to live and direct the compilation of a massive encyclopedia of Africa. Just before leaving for Ghana he took another step—publicly joining the Communist Party U.S.A. We knew he had differences with the CP, yet, as with us, these differences were secondary to the common struggle against the main enemy. This latter act was at once an expression of his contempt for American imperialism and his solidarity with its victims.

One of my most memorable evenings in DuBois' presence was at the Schomburg Collection in the 135th Street Library, just off Lenox Avenue in Harlem, on a May night in 1957. The Schomburg is a special kind of collection devoted to black life and history; it grew out of the treasures of Arthur A. Schomburg and was presented to the New York Public Library in 1926.

To get there you go through streets of tenements that fill you with anger and break your heart. Stenciled in white paint on walls next to the entrances of many buildings is the legend: "This building condemned. Habitation is unlawful." The signs are put up by the City of New York—and the buildings are full of people who have no other place to live that they can afford. Across from the tenements are wastelands of rubble.

Lenox Avenue is alive with people, lights, taxis, and noise; you cross it and climb a few steps to the modest reading room of the Schomburg Collection. It is a most unusual night: the customary library hush has been replaced by an excited hubbub, the tables have been removed, and the room is filled to standing with expectant people. It is the occasion of the unveiling of a DuBois bronze bust executed by the sculptor William Zorach.

The chairs are occupied by people whose faces you know in an instant—a well-known novelist, a great historian, a world-renowned basso—and by people whose faces you never saw before but are glad to see—a straight-backed grandmother and her teen-age granddaughter, an African student, a little boy sandwiched between his mother and his aunt reading a book tucked under his coat on his lap.

An independent Hollywood producer filming a life of DuBois (whatever happened to it?) has set up hot lights to record the event in color. Van Wyck Brooks with ruddy face, intelligent eyes, and white walrus mustache, the literary conscience of America, tells of

W. E. B. DUBOIS AND THE COLOR LINE

DuBois, the Harvard undergraduate, going with his philosophy professor William James to the Perkins Institute for the Blind in Boston to meet a 12-year-old girl named Helen Keller. Brooks, a neighbor of Ms. Keller, says that when he told her he was going to speak at the unveiling, she recalled the meeting in Boston and told him she felt even then that she was in the presence of a great human being.

DuBois was the first to see, Brooks tells the audience, "that the darker peoples of the world would overthrow the world unless they got their share of democracy." E. Franklin Frazier, the distinguished sociologist, asks for a return to real scholarship in America. Zorach tells how he accomplished his work, and the bust is accepted by the Collection's gracious curator, Jean Blackwell. The drape is drawn, revealing the bust, and there is long fervent applause. An artist in the audience watches Zorach's face and reports: "He nodded, pleased, as though to say, 'It is a good thing I have done.' " Messages are read—from Mordecai Johnson, president of Howard University, and from Nkrumah, who speaks of his love for DuBois and his "lovely consort," Shirley Graham.

Finally DuBois speaks. In the many times I have seen him, he has never seemed so visibly touched. He says (and I believe it) that he was at a loss about what to say this night, and he decided to talk about books and libraries. He tells how he started his own library at 10 in the town of his childhood, Great Barrington, Massachusetts; how he felt the day the first public library opened there ("I may not have been first in line, but I surely was among the first"); how he bought Macaulay's five-volume *History of England,* paying 25 cents a week until it was his ("It is still in my library"). DuBois' words are a song of love to books and learning, and the joy of using knowledge to help others learn.

After the ceremony people move about greeting one another, basking in the glow of a great scholar. It is as though each person there hoped secretly that a touch of the greatness had rubbed off on him or her, to be nurtured for a lifetime.

Six years later, on a sun-baked field in Washington, D.C., I stood in silence with a quarter of a million of my fellow-

Americans, black and white, as Roy Wilkins of the NAACP announced the receipt of a cable reporting DuBois's death in Ghana. It was August 28, 1963, the day of the great March on Washington for Jobs and Freedom, the day Martin Luther King Jr. made his celebrated "I have a dream" speech.

"It's like Moses," an old black woman said, weeping. "The Lord had written that he should not enter the promised land." I was there as a reporter, an observer supposedly without emotion, but I wept with her.

It was appropriate, as a bitter comment on the America of his birth, that DuBois should have died in Africa whose children's children he had inspired to freedom. That as a prophet without honor in his own country he should have been given a state funeral in the capital of Ghana, and buried outside Government House, where Nkrumah had welcomed him in 1961 as the father of pan-African independence.

In a GUARDIAN article in February 1958 marking his 90th birthday, DuBois wrote: "I do not apologize for living long. High on the ramparts of this blistering hell of life, I sit and see the Truth. I look it full in the face, and I will not lie about it, neither to myself nor to the world . . . Socialism progresses and will progress. All we can do is to silence and jail its promoters. I believe in socialism. I seek a world where the ideals of communism will triumph— to each according to his need, from each according to his ability. For this I will work as long as I live. And I still live."

In the planning stages of the GUARDIAN we had sought out no one for the staff; it came together through the magnetism of the idea of the paper. Those who came at first were white. This paleness worried staff and management both; I was particularly concerned, as a veteran of the battle for greater black representation on the editorial staffs of newspapers where I had worked, but I found the idea of token representation distasteful (there had been "one of them" on the New York *Post* when I was there, and one on the New York *Times,* which employed a few hundred black maintenance workers). Actually one black journalist would have represented 20 percent of the GUARDIAN editorial staff.

Jean Norrington was a constant as librarian and there were black employes in other departments of the paper. Black contributors were frequent from the start. But when the GUARDIAN was well launched, we consciously sought out black journalists as full-time staff members. Three outstanding ones were Eugene Gordon, Louis E. Burnham, and Joanne Grant.

Gordon represented the past. He was a veteran of the Boston *Post,* a longtime Communist who had been with the *Daily Worker,* an angry man, not easy to friendship, and resistant to change. His experience came out of the time of Scottsboro and the life of a black Communist in the 1930s and 40s.

Grant represented the future. She was young, a product of a white community and white newspapers in upstate New York, and so fair that her "blackness" was difficult to discern. She brought to the paper a fresh understanding of the ferment among the youth, black and white; and if her blackness was not apparent, it was deeply felt—she went through her own enlightening baptism of fire in a Southern voyage of discovery as a GUARDIAN reporter in the spring of 1960, a few weeks after she joined the paper. It was the first of many trips into troubled areas, North and South, which she undertook with such enterprise and involvement that at times she was a "case" as well as a reporter for us.

Burnham represented the bridge between past and future, and his contribution in this respect was great. As Claude Williams said of him after his premature death in 1960 at age 44: "The place had found its man, and the man had found his place."

Fresh out of City College of New York, Lou Burnham became Southern organizer of the American Student Union in 1936, then from 1941–48 was a leader of the Southern Negro Youth Conference. He became the Progressive Party's Southern organizer in 1948 and remained in this job until 1951, when he was named editor of *Freedom,* the monthly paper published by Paul Robeson. *Freedom* died in 1957 and Lou joined our staff the next year.

That is the bare bones of his formal career. Within its outlines was a man touched with grace, easy to be with and reassuring. In his writings, lectures, and conversation, he never dissembled. His seriousness, manifest in his painstakingly careful speech, was leavened by high humor. The love that people bore him was demonstrated in his hosts of friends—from the teenagers on his Brooklyn block, through the bearded youngsters who came to him for counsel, to the patrician figure of DuBois, his mentor and his colleague.

Burnham's life and work were a bridge between the races which withstood misunderstanding and ignorance. There was anger in his being and plenty of sorrow, but little hate. It pained him to hear blacks pit all whites as their enemy. And even when a white would say to him that this was understandable, he would reply: "Perhaps, but it cannot be." He had enough patience and trust to take white friends into his confidence—and thereby open to them a new insight into race relations. Therein lay his greatest achievement.

In the GUARDIAN's Negro History Week issue in February 1960, Lou wrote his last testament without knowing it. It was prophetically addressed, in the ninety-seventh year of the Emancipation Proclamation, to "white and black America." Much of what the black fights for, he said, "is not to gain new ground but to restore positions once dearly won and foully taken away." And those who "stand to suffer by the Negro's gain, though powerful, are but a numerically minuscule part of the whole American nation." He concluded:

"But what of the white worker at the lathe and on the farm, the teacher, the doctor, the housewife, the cook in the restaurant, the seaman, the miner in the pit—the vast majority of Americans? What have they to lose from the Negro's forward march? Their prejudices? Yes. But oh, how much to gain; nothing less than a new nation to gain."

That spirit infused Lou's reports from the South, from Little Rock, Chicago, Detroit, and Harlem—and above all, the thoughtful interpretive articles when he returned from those trips.

On the night of Lincoln's birthday in 1960 Lou stood at the lectern of a small meeting in New York marking Negro History Week. His subject was "Emerging Africa and the Negro People's Fight for Freedom." His resonant bass voice sounded fatigued, his words were slow. He said: "I know you get tired of the continuing struggle sometimes. We all do—and then there are reversals in situations—but we must not despair, we must not rest too long. Tomorrow's new world beckons. Tomorrow belongs to us."

A few moments later his voice faltered and stopped. He sat down to rest. An hour later he was dead—of a heart seizure—in the emergency room of the Polyclinic Hospital. I was called to identify his body, and I still recall my resentment of the unshaven, sloppy doctor as we stood in the squalid room with Lou's body. He wasn't responsible, but everything seemed to pile into that room that night—all the meanness and injustice of a valuable life snuffed out too early.

At a memorial meeting for Lou that April, DuBois said: "I knew Louis Burnham for about twenty-five years. There are many matters of which I might speak concerning him; of the work he did; of the work he was doing at the time of his death; and of what he might yet have done had he lived. Above all, none can forget his honesty and utter sacrifice. I speak, however, only of one matter which seems to me of the greatest moment. What I want to say has to do with the saving of lives like that of Louis Burnham; the stopping of the vast and reckless waste which goes on each year in this country and others, and deprives the world of irreplaceable help for the tasks which we have to do."

DuBois's words were both a reproach and a warning to the radical movement. They charged a responsibility to the individual, to his friends, and to a delinquent state, but mainly DuBois was saying: We are few enough; let us look after one another and not stand by as the lifeblood of our comrades drains out.

In Lou Burnham's case it was particularly appropriate: a stern finger pointing to the unnecessary loss of a man needed for one of the most urgent tasks of the day—making white America understand its stake in black freedom.

Lightning Before Thunder

[**C.B.**] Publications like ours began in the 60s to call themselves "underground," borrowing a term from countries that don't permit printed resistance to the government. Due to strategic cold war imperatives, the Free World has embraced countries where the term is completely valid, but in America it has more validity than appears on the surface to citizens who never had to cope with the economics of periodical publication.

American "underground" publications are in fact neither under nor over, but occupy a twilight zone of economic prostration. The main basis of their claim to subterranean distinction is that outfits devoted to the profit system will, most logically, not advertise in papers that oppose it. And since the public has become accustomed to paying less for a paper than it costs to produce, with advertising revenue supplying the difference and the profit, this removes the element that makes publishing without perishing possible. New York's *PM* was the first and last attempt to balance a newspaper's budget by gearing its sale price to its production cost. Its millionaire backer, Marshall Field, learned dearly the lesson that this doesn't work against the competition of papers maintained by advertising.

But America has freedom of the press, and it would be unthinkable to deny any newspaper publisher access to the mails with a reduced second-class mailing privilege. The duty accompanying this privilege is to publish once a year a notarized paid-circulation statement, which may not be fudged with free samples and copies that bounce back from distributors. That moment of truth can be uncomfortable for a journal that must do a lot of whistling to keep up its readers' courage.

Having entered the field with few illusions, we were pleased by the GUARDIAN's notarized score of 35,336 at the end of our first year and 75,595 at the end of our second. For reasons we knew well, these figures didn't represent our full readership by a long way. We reckoned that for every copy sold we had about three more readers, consisting of people who dared not receive the GUARDIAN directly: the least vulnerable in a circle of subversive friends would subscribe and pass it around. The Mailbag left no doubt that our paper pleased the public at whom we aimed it. But without money to advertise it, we depended on the ability of one subscriber to recruit others under steady bombardment from the enemy. Thus more than anything the figures measured the intensity of the political inquisition. Approaching its zenith in our third year, the inquisition made that 75,000-odd a figure we could never top.

When *In Fact* expired in October 1950, the GUARDIAN became America's largest-circulation left paper, but we said goodbye sadly to George Seldes's weekly "antidote to poison in the press." It had long and effectively raked the muck of capitalism which escaped the attention of the advertisement-bloated media. Naturally, *In Fact* had been a target of Representative Martin Dies and his pioneer inquisitors before World War II. The comparatively open climate of the New Deal had nevertheless enabled Seldes—with his four leaflet-size pages and minimal overhead—to achieve economic viability, reaching a six-figure circulation. Seldes gruffly charged apathy as the cause of *In Fact*'s steady decline since the war. Our own far from apathetic family encouraged hope that he was mistaken, and some angels were prepared to buy for GUARDIAN sub solicitation the country's biggest list of radical readers.

We had built our circulation on a "Have You Got 4 Friends?" coupon with space for four prospects' names, but most readers were nearing the bottom of the barrel with friends who, financially and inquisitorially, could afford to subscribe.

Seldes was in too morbid a mood even to negotiate for the *In Fact* list, which might conceivably have abated the crises flaring on to page 1 of the GUARDIAN. There they were adorned by a Fred Wright cartoon that became our crisis trademark: a worker standing nude before the boss and saying, "Frankly, sir, I need more money." No device existed to avert the periodic ultimatums by Vic Levitt, who had to pay his printers the union scale regardless of what we got or didn't get. He would stalk down into our office with scarlet face and, I am sure, breaking heart to shout: "A grand [or two, three, four] by morning or the press don't roll!"

For Jim and me this meant leaving desks to visit our few and already exasperated angels, in the hope of squeezing something out of them that Jack couldn't. I attribute most of the appeasement of the Levitt volcano, however, to the fact that he shared Jack's passion for chess. Jack developed a genius for luring him with apparent casualness to the board when he was about to erupt. Returning empty-handed from our missions, Jim and I might find Vic too absorbed in a game to ask how we made out. Jack would signal with a glance that we were probably on dry land again for another week. Beneath the inevitable flare-ups between him and Vic, they loved each other tenderly.

Jack's was the kind of ingenuity that flowered when the mortician stood at the door, as he almost always did. Had this stalwart partner of ours been disposed in that direction, he would have made an excellent planner of bank robberies. Entirely unversed in financial wizardry, Jim and I would sometimes despair of a solution to an immediate problem; Jack, equally unversed, would say: "Never fear. There's always a way."

For example, a thundercloud that loomed over us quarterly was payment to the government of the "employer's" (that was us) Social Security withholdings on payroll. This ran into thousands of dollars, which had already been handed over to Vic for printing arrears. On the last possible day Jack would mail a check for the amount due to a New York address long since abandoned by Internal Revenue. He nicely calculated at about two weeks the wanderings of this check through the postal system before it arrived back marked "Addressee Unknown." Then, the money to cover it having somehow been accumulated, a new check was mailed along with the returned envelope as manifest of the goodwill of Weekly Guardian Associates Inc. (our corporate name). A gimmick further extending the "grace" period was mailing the check at a remote Long Island post office, known only to Jack, from which no letter reached its destination in less than a week. The bank privileged to handle our preposterous account belonged to a fairly friendly trade union, but Jack's pacification of it was another aspect of his genius.

All our sources of revenue were by definition "political," with all that this implied. When we began taking ads early in 1950, the problem was not to solicit the announcements of subversive meetings and publications (they came easily enough because we were almost the only "bulletin board") but to collect the bills from organizations as bankrupt as ourselves. As radical America became more and more an undefined ghetto, our advertising columns were modestly swollen by inmates who depended on taking in each other's washing. GUARDIAN readers, assuming that an advertiser must be a fellow subversive, went out of their way to patronize him although the insurance, appliance, bottle, or record they wanted could be bought around the corner. Some advertisers were recognizable as teachers, journalists, etc., who had been hounded from their professions and were running laundromats or auto-repair or house-moving services to pay the rent. Thus GUARDIAN advertising yielded unique results and the bills, small as they were, were mostly paid.

It was typical of Jack that, just when he was running for governor of New York in 1950, he came up with a GUARDIAN Buying Service scheme to produce extra headaches for him. The idea was that if we offered bargains, we too could cash in on the loyalty of subversive consumers. We started with "beautifully figured and woven linens imported from Russia, Czechoslovakia, Belgium, and Ireland.'' Russia's and Czechoslovakia's roles in this were clear enough since the Establishment declined to trade with them, but how Belgium and Ireland got into the act I never knew. By spring of 1952 we were peddling coffee tables, Guatemalan skirts, "Kantwet" baby beds, belts, and razor blades. Part of the office became a packing and wrapping stockroom requiring more hired help and producing small returns for much labor.

The GUARDIAN back file shows no circulation statement in October 1951, when McCarthy was in full rampage. Jim thinks we just forgot to publish it, and the hounds may have been snoozing in the autumnal sun. Jack reported to readers that the paper now covered "4,000 American communities," and fired a "salute of 50,000 guns to those who have made our third bouncing birthday possible. . . . Never in U.S. history has it been more 'impossible' to keep the voice of truth ringing out. The terrific economic pressure of, for, and by the corrupt press against the progressive press has been many times intensified. To this pressure has been added the flouting of our Constitution by the highest organs of government to slander publicly, to hound and fling into jail—and now [with the Rosenberg case] even to sentence to death—Americans who 'cry peace when there is no peace.' '' The conclusion of this address to our troops was that, having fought so hard for the Trenton Six, they should fight twice as hard for the Rosenbergs.

I am amazed as I look through the file—and probably was at the time—by Jack's cheery vision the following May of "A MILLION READERS IN 1952!—Not a dream, a political imperative." Elections were imminent, and the massive sub-drive mailing we then put out was based on a rainbow of faith in the Progressive Party. With a presidential candidate (San Francisco attorney Vincent Hallinan) nominated while in jail, and a black woman (Los Angeles publisher Charlotta Bass) for Vice-President, it seemed possible that the party could win enough votes to acquire heft as a balance of power. For months "Jimmie Higginses" had been collecting signatures day and night to put the party on state ballots, with impressive results: in Massachusetts they had got over 80,000, far more than were necessary. And this with little help from Communists, who were offering their own candidates—mostly in or en route to prison—and platform.

We published an eight-page pictorial supplement on the Progressive convention in Chicago. The best Americans—white, black, brown, and assorted, unscared by political and personal harassments—jammed the hall in a scene which we all allowed to raise our hopes. Four years after its founding convention, with its original leader lost, the party could still create a living replica of democracy as children read about it. In fact, while the delegates came from most parts of every state, the people they represented were a bold and informed drop in an ocean of fear and ignorance and still dwindling. No doubt a substantial quota of FBI agents joined in the Chicago euphoria.

Jim went on from the convention to a Midwest fund-raising tour while Tabitha Petran and I did the same up and down the West Coast. It was one of the very few times I left the shop from which I would eventually be hauled under escort. The meetings were always enthusiastic and overflowing but, having run out of friends cajolable for subs and donations, our farflung family could only dig deeper into their own pockets. In October we had an "URGENT—GUARDIAN NEEDS QUICK $10,000" crisis in issues dotted with fund exhortations for a spectrum of causes: to stave off a proposed frame-up of Earl Browder, to get a foreign-born trade unionist off Ellis Island, to keep the CP's Elizabeth Flynn out of jail, to save longshoremen's leader Harry Bridges from deportation and the Rosenbergs from death.

Under the circumstances our notarized circulation of 47,374 seemed remarkably healthy—still more so the decline of only 2,000 in 1953. But in November 1952 we were SOS-ing all hands to deliver us from a "threat of being shut down ever since Labor Day" which, out of respect for the election drive, we had hesitated to mention before.

The electoral disaster left no doubt that the Progressive Party as we had known it was breathing its last, yet we welcomed the article on "The Job Ahead" by its executive secretary, our friend

Beanie Baldwin. We took a dim view of the new CP line of "working within the Democratic Party where the people are." The people weren't visible in either of the Establishment parties and we thought that the Republocrat whale would digest Jonah if it didn't promptly regurgitate him. We saw no alternative to battening down in our trench until conditions would be more propitious for a third party—clearly a long wait.

Jack's high-spirited report to readers at the turn of 1952–53 showed that the family was in the trench with us and could still find some ammunition. He cited Wilkins Micawber's account of his finances in *David Copperfield* as a reasonable reflection of our plight and philosophy: "Annual income twenty pounds, annual expenditure nineteen nineteen six, result happiness. Annual income twenty pounds, annual expenditure twenty pounds ought and six, result misery." Our income and outgo were both a bit higher and the gap between them greater on the misery side. "But our state of mind isn't one of misery but of satisfaction, because for our $160,000 we've been able to print and circulate some 3,250,000 copies of the GUARDIAN."

The Establishment cared too much about its Free Press image to gun down in public a stray tomcat like the GUARDIAN, but was expert in devious skinning methods visible only to the cat. On the one hand, the media: their public contribution was simple to ignore us, with a disdain that stood firm against almost all of our taunts, challenges, and provocations. Their backstage role was to make certain that the GUARDIAN wouldn't appear on 99 percent of the newsstands, lest passing innocents might be tempted by awareness of our existence. Newsdealers who would have handled the GUARDIAN were told that if they preferred to sell our paper rather than the ones that provided their daily bread—the *Times, Time* or whatever—well, it was a free country.

The government brought Internal Revenue into the performance with constant inspections and queryings of our accounts, while post offices succumbed to FBI importunings for our subscriber lists. We then began to get cancellations of a kind that no respectable journal receives, often without explanation but conveying the sensation that they were splashed with tears. Dollars for our survival fund accompanied the cancellations or were delivered by hand. Knowing that their phones and mail were liable to be tapped and opened, these dropouts left us to draw the obvious conclusions or let us know the circumstances indirectly: they had been visited by the FBI with warnings of the consequences of receiving "this paid Moscow propaganda." It was futile for them to point out our many differences with the CP: could there be surer proof that we were the "secret operators" identified by Nixon as "the heart of the conspiracy"? The decisive point made by these apparitions at subscribers' doors—instantly recognizable by their square suits and haberdashery and the fact that they came in nunlike pairs— was: "What would your employer say if he knew?" The question was rhetorical: the government was offering a last, sporting chance to continue drawing a paycheck.

We too, of course, assumed that our phones were tapped, and this was confirmed by a friendly Bell Telephone employee. He called to suggest, with evident concern, that some staff members were being less than discreet in their conversations. With the beginning of the Korean War harassment of GUARDIAN workers, extending out to their families and friends, reached crude proportions. FBI agents accosted them on the street as well as visiting their homes, and the police were openly hostile when our reporters were out on a job. The office received a rising tide of "hate" mail, and of provocative and improbable phone calls seeking information which could only be useful to the government. At the homes of our people, building superintendents and janitors reported curious inquiries. Staff members with listed phones were badgered by calls at regular intervals all through the night. When the receiver was lifted there was dead silence at the other end—not even obscene heavy breathing. Apparently right-wing organizations recruited the services of night workers to spread this silent terror. Again a cooperative telephone worker came to the rescue with advice about dimming the ring. We met silence with silence. When we took up the Rosenberg case (see below) the harassment increased. Metal scraps and tools were thrown into the presses of the printing plant, forcing a careful inspection before any press run.

We were in a sense a guerrilla force living among the general population, with a daytime (and often nighttime) encampment at the GUARDIAN office. The main difference with standard guerrilla operations was that everyone knew where we were, and we had no intention of disappearing. At the same time we knew that our smallness made us no more than a potential threat to be watched, not worth the sacrifice of the Free Press image.

Meanwhile, already in 1949, the uncomfortable feeling that I might be a liability to the GUARDIAN had begun to haunt me. That was the year, six months after our debut, when prospective jurors at the New York Smith Act trial were challenged with the question: "Are you or have you ever been employed by or associated with or have you contributed to the NATIONAL GUARDIAN?" "Are you or have you ever been?" was the prescribed inquisitorial formula for unmasking radicals as Communists, so this meant that—as far as the government was concerned, if not the media—we had arrived. But later the same month Rep. George A. Dondero of Michigan, maintaining a decorous silence about the GUARDIAN, filled seven *Congressional Record* pages with a blast at myself (at Jim only by inference). It was becoming clear that when the storm struck the GUARDIAN, it would do so at our weakest point and that, as an "alien," I was it. Nor was I any ordinary alien from an inquisitor's-eye view, for Washington had me registered, with fingerprints, as one trained by a foreign government (Britain during the war) in undercover techniques.

Dondero's theme, in cooperation with the penitent ex-Marxist Dwight Macdonald, was my work in Germany in 1945. Who knows what inspired Macdonald's choice of me as that particular month's sample of Muscovite perfidy; but to make his invariable point, his journal *Politics* had featured my punctilious obedience of my commander-in-chief, General Eisenhower. We had heard of Macdonald but not of the author of the article, one Peter Blake. To Macdonald's documentation of the plot to kremlinize Germany,

LIGHTNING BEFORE THUNDER

Dondero added his own findings on "the record of Cedric Bel-frage."

Macdonald (whose emergence twenty years later as a spokes-man of the Vietnam peace movement has baffled me) should have been embarrassed to find himself in red-baiting partnership with Dondero—an inquisitor of such singular ineptitude that an attack on the GUARDIAN by him might have doubled our circulation. Dondero's bid for fame by exposing some of America's best artists as "red termites in the art world" was the super-flop of the Mc-Carthy era. Certainly our efforts in Germany were a handle for getting at us through the back door, but he had no idea how to grasp it as McCarthy did later. The conclusive proof of treason was, of course, our nomination of the Communist Emil Carlebach for a newspaper license in Frankfurt.

A word here about Emil. He had been a leader of the Buchen-wald underground which, with exemplary heroism and in-telligence, had liberated the camp from Hitler's sadists before the U.S. Army turned up there. Later, in Frankfurt, some anti-Com-munist survivors of Buchenwald had charged him with partisan cruelty to them in organizing the camp resistance, but the great majority of his available fellow victims credited him with saving thousands, of all political persuasions, from death. The camp regi-men was so frightful that no one who hadn't experienced it could decently judge the conduct of people who had; but the Information Control Division brass had listened to the testimony pro and con, and on the weight of evidence had had to "clear" Emil. His real offense being his politics and readiness to work with anyone against fascism, a presentable excuse under our directives for can-celing his licence was hard to come by. In fact none was ever found, but by 1947 it didn't matter. U.S. Military Governor Gen-eral Lucius D. Clay, the liberator of "bitch of Buchenwald" Ilse Koch,* finally fired Emil for "unsuitable political views and traits of character," and there was no one of importance around to ob-ject.

In rehashing all the Buchenwald "charges" against Emil, Mac-

* Clay's compassion for Frau Koch so embarrassed the Germans that they put her back in jail for a while.

donald–Dondero ignored both his "clearance" by Information Control's commanding general and the fact that he had been our German correspondent since the GUARDIAN's first issue. He was indeed a much valued one, with journalistic talent which he was incapable of using for professional "success." He devoted it above all to fulfilling the Buchenwald survivors' vow to their tens of thousands of massacred comrades, that the lessons of Nazism should not be forgotten.

Dondero's "record of Cedric Belfrage" competed in lameness with Clay's grounds for firing Emil. The congressman from Detroit accused me of signing a cable to President Roosevelt against the blockade of republican Spain in 1938, speaking at a Young Progressives of America affair, being the author of a novel "recommended by the *Daily Worker*," and, a year before Pearl Harbor, joining a Long Beach, Calif., picket line against America's largesse of scrap-iron to the Japanese, who turned it into weapons to kill Americans. The GUARDIAN placed these charges before the bar of the public opinion it could command (no other journal did, not even Macdonald's) with two stipulations: that I wasn't in the Long Beach picket line but would have been had I known about it, and that we would wrap the matter up the following week by publishing "the record of George Dondero"—a most dismal one not otherwise rating a precious GUARDIAN inch.

Such scuttlebutt was normally purveyed to congressmen by J. Edgar Hoover, and this bore his unmistakable trademark. I concluded that Hoover was beginning to make up for his failure to discover, up to the year 1943, that the Belfrage neck was one he should have been breathing down. In that year, as British Intelligence liaison with the FBI, I had had the unusual experience of inspecting his miles of filing cabinets by invitation of one of his agents, on a visit to his headquarters in Washington. Naturally I took the opportunity to check my own dossier. I couldn't expect it to be very impressive (otherwise I wouldn't have been there) but was surprised by its meager contents. A fraction of a millimeter thick, it showed a deplorable standard of political-police work in prewar Los Angeles, where I had been most active in antifascist organizations. This was encouraging, but one could hardly rely on its continuance in the future.

After Dondero's ineffectual noises the Immigration and Naturalization Service, the division of the Department of Justice now increasingly devoted to moving bodies out of rather than into America, informed me that it would investigate my "associations and background" and, with a candor I still thought remarkable, my "writings." If any such "investigation" followed, I knew nothing of it. I only knew that, while preservation of the Free Press image ruled out my present activities—full time on the GUARDIAN—as ammunition against me, my "contacts" in the daily round could provide handy leads into the past.

For example, my appearance at the gate of Danbury penitentiary in 1951, to greet my emerging friend, Lester Cole, could have led Hoover's sleuths back to Los Angeles for a less perfunctory "probe" of the company I kept there. Lester, a screenwriter, was one of the Hollywood Ten who had been scare-headlined as the epitome of political villainy in the movie colony, and had earned jail terms early in the "Are You or Have You Ever Been?" game. The inquisition was now the feeding trough for a stable of Hollywood stool pigeons who had "named" hundreds of people as Communists, but not me. I was proud of the fact that none of these informers was ever a friend, but I recalled some of them, and a jog to their memories could bring out that I consorted not only with the Ten but with every Los Angeles subversive worth knowing. Other crimes of mine in those years would no doubt be bared, such as my Hollywood Anti-Nazi League activity, my co-editorship of the left-literary journal *The Clipper;* my collaboration with Theodore Dreiser on a book opposing U.S. aid to Chamberlain's Britain, and—who knew?—my chairmanship of a diary co-op which brought milk to the consumer as it came from the cow. All this, on top of the spaghetti with Joe North and the grand jury probe of the "Russian spy" charges in 1947, could provide an inquisitorial embarrassment of riches.

When I last saw my dossier in 1973—but only across the desk of a Mr. Karp, the U.S. consular official in Mexico who had to "question" subversive visa applicants—I estimated its thickness at three inches, and most of it seemed to be typed single-space on thin paper. Its Pandora's box of half-truths, buffooneries, and inventions produced a deep melancholy even in Mr. Karp. But it was a tribute to the compound interest with which a dossier expands once the political police get into stride: one "reliable source" leads to another and only a revolution can stop the process. Yet events in 1953 showed that the inflation in my case didn't really begin until the middle of that year. Not that the government hadn't already decided to send me back where I came from, but that Hoover found he was taking too much for granted. He thought it could be done simply by announcing that I "was or had been" a Communist, a fact, for him, too obvious to need confirmation. To his legitimate indignation—for the media had endowed him with infallibility in these matters— a judge would ask him to prove it.

Lacking access to the FBI morgue since my "liaison" days, I have only been able to speculate on what specifically sparked the drive to deport me. The evidence is circumstantial but strong that it was the GUARDIAN's defense of Ethel and Julius Rosenberg and Morton Sobell, beginning in 1951. By 1952 this was stirring manifest wrath in Establishment circles. It emerged in the form of violent calumnies, very rarely mentioning the GUARDIAN, against the defense committee which our campaign brought into being, and which the FBI penetrated with little delay. (One penetrator ended by "confessing" and sought to drown his remorse in gin.) Some of the calumnies were disseminated by respectable champions of civil liberties. The defense was accused of everything from cynical exploitation of the Rosenbergs' Jewish origin to deliberately sabotaging the case to provide the American CP with martyrs. But whatever motives were attributed, anyone defending Ethel and Julius and Morton was automatically a Moscow agent or tool.

The facts were somewhat different. When the Rosenbergs were sentenced to death as "atom spies"—"causing the Korean war," the judge put it—the curtain of fear was so dense over America that not one voice was raised. The media having effectively hidden the outrageousness of the trial, not even radicals had grounds for questioning the verdict. The CP, to which Ethel and Julius and Morton were routinely alleged to belong, seemed too preoccupied and threatened by its own leaders' trials to come to the defense of these obscure people. The Rosenbergs' lawyer, Emanuel Bloch, came to us as the very last hope when they had been awaiting death for three months, and when our debts augured the same sentence for the GUARDIAN from week to week.

Our reactions to a first study of the trial were shame for our inattention when it was in progress a few hundred yards from our office (our report of it had, however, stressed the Rosenbergs' insistence that they were innocent scapegoats), and unanimous desire to put up a fight as long as we could stand up. This might well prove the torpedo to sink our ship since, if the Rosenbergs were innocent as Bloch was convinced and we suspected, we would be exposing no less than calculated murder by the U.S. government. If that was indeed what we confronted, the motive wouldn't be difficult to fathom: to silence once and for all, through two typical rank-and-filers of the movement, the opposition to the government's imperialist war policy. Yet at that stage even Bloch couldn't face the possibility of such ugliness by the inheritors of the Declaration of Independence. For him the trial was an outrage but still not a premeditated one.

Moreover there was no clue as to how our extended family would respond. While the media published loyal citizens' felicitations to the government on its alertness for spies, our Mailbaggers continued sounding off on other matters until a voice broke the silence from Martin's Ferry, Ohio, in July 1951. The Russians having been our allies at the time, under what clause of the Constitution, wondered George F. Curry, could Americans be electrocuted for allegedly giving them information? Other readers echoed the cry of horror against the sentence, one of them noting that "even Dorothy Thompson" (a "liberal" syndicated columnist) had called it "unbelievable."

That was all until the GUARDIAN's dissections of the trial, beginning in August, opened the floodgates. We soon saw that our decision to seek out the truth and proclaim it had been as inevitable as fate. What were newspapers for? And if not we, who?

The trial had done what the government intended it to do, with the cooperation of the ever-reliable media. Nowhere had the travesty of justice been so much as hinted at in print, any more than the Nazi press hinted at the horrors of Buchenwald and, now as then, ordinary citizens knew by sniffing the air that it was unwise to inquire. As for still-unreconstructed progressives, they were already living with the knowledge that their politics could land them in jail. Now they were put on notice that it could land them in the electric chair. For some this was all they could take and the movement never heard of them again. Others had been waiting with understandable caution for someone to give a lead. Thus we found that our campaign, far from scaring off most of the GUARDIAN family, put new heart into it.

Protest committees sprang up on every side and, amid almost nonstop ultimatums by Vic over the printing arrears, the postman brought more money than we'd ever seen—almost all in small amounts and earmarked for the Rosenberg defense fund, which was where it went. Through our contacts the uproar spread from country to country, becoming far louder abroad than the residue of unscared Americans could make it at home. It was too big for any left group to stay out, and the world Communist movement took it up and gave it a formidable impulse. Wherever they went U.S. diplomats were needled and taunted on behalf of Ethel, Julius, and the two little boys whom it was proposed to orphan. The Establishment's response, that the trial was the quintessence of justice and the protest a red plot to defame America, failed to convince even the Pope. He added his voice to the outcry of celebrities and nobodies demanding, from dozens of lands, at least clemency for the young parents.

Or did he? The New York *Times* reported one day that he did, and next day that he didn't.

Postscript [**J.A.**] Two meetings come to mind. Both involved Jews as victims; both evoked the smell of burning flesh. One was in Bad

Homburg, Germany, in July 1945; the other in the basement Co-Op Cafeteria on Murray Street, New York, in July 1951.

The central office of Information Control Command, Supreme Headquarters Allied Expeditionary Force, U.S. Army,* was in the Schoolhouse on the grounds of the Kaiser Wilhelm Bad, a stately watering place gone slightly to seed in Bad Homburg near Frankfurt-am-Main. The Schoolhouse was surrounded by some thirty villas reserved for the American conquerors and a swimming pool, all of this in turn circled by idiotic barbed wire.

Once German ladies and gentlemen suffering mainly from self-abused stomachs came to drink the curing waters and take the sulphur baths. Now the American cultural commissars, guiding post-Hitler Germany to democracy in the areas of press, radio, film, theater, music, publishing, and vaudeville, walked the gravel paths to their own watering places in the compound, where brandy sold for 10¢ a glass, and to offices in the Schoolhouse, where papers bearing General Eisenhower's signature were shuffled endlessly. Here in temporary uniform were some of the celebrated names of Madison Avenue and Hollywood Boulevard—for example, Colonel William S. Paley of CBS with silver-top walking stick, and Colonel Billy Wilder of Hollywood, looking in pink officer's uniform exactly like a film director. Presiding over this army of play-soldiers, secretaries, clerks, technicians, and GIs waiting impatiently for their orders to ship for home, was Brigadier General Robert A. McClure, chief of Information Control Division.

Into this enclave I was dumped in mid-July 1945 after a flight from London. The atmosphere was stifling, the activity sluggish, the talk predominantly about the day's quotation for a carton of American cigarettes on the black market. In the press section, however, there was a certain stir of excitement about the August 1 target date for birth of the *Frankfurter Rundschau,* the first newspaper to be published by German licensees in the U.S. Zone of Occupation. This was Cedric's baby, and he and his crew had

---

* Later incarnation of SHAEF Psychological Warfare Division (see chapter 1).

labored long and hard to bring together a compatible and untainted board of Germans to direct the paper. Among them was Emil Carlebach (Dachau Class of '38, Buchenwald '45), one of two board members describing themselves as Communists when that party had still to be reconstituted.

I had read Cedric's Aachen Diary describing the genesis of the first postwar German paper before the four powers demarcated their Zones, and had been briefed on the search for clean Germans in Heidelberg, Stuttgart, and elsewhere. Everything seemed in order for Frankfurt. Then, twenty-four hours before the presses were to roll, there was disorder. The case against Emil Carlebach had been reopened. His political enemies seemed determined to get him thrown out of the *Rundschau* operation on the ground of "collaboration" with the Buchenwald camp commanders. The other side of the story was that he had been an outstanding leader of the resistance which, of course, depended for its success on the arts of cunning. A full-dress meeting of the ICD high command was ordered on July 31 to hear the charges.

The meeting lasted all day. The evidence was reviewed, the reports of ICD intelligence presented, as well as the findings of an impressive investigation by ICD's Frankfurt detachment. The high command retired to consider its verdict. It came late that afternoon: Carlebach was cleared, the *Rundschau* could go to press. It was a strange and exhilarating spectacle: a West Point general and his deputy, who had been a Republican lieutenant-governor of New Jersey, voting to approve the appointment of a concentration camp Communist to management of the first free newspaper in the U.S. Zone of post-Hitler Germany.

I did not meet Emil till mid-August when I went to inspect the *Rundschau* on assignment from headquarters. It was becoming an effective newspaper, trying to balance its coverage of U.S.-Soviet relations (growing steadily worse) while insisting on a cleanup (much to the annoyance of the vulnerable mayor, and of American Military Government officers who were shacking up with the English-speaking daughters of SS men and Wehrmacht generals) of Nazis still floating freely around Frankfurt. I liked Emil from the start, and was amazed at the sanity and humor of this man who had spent eleven years in concentration camps. The signs of those unspeakable years were the incredible leanness of his body for one so full of energy, the deep set of his dark eyes, and a shoulder twitch. I visited him as often as work would permit, and we became friends.

One day in September 1945 we were sitting in his drafty office in the *Rundschau* building on Schillerstrasse when Cedric came in to say goodbye: he was going "home" to America. (I would see him later for a final farewell at the Frankfurt ICD detachment.) I watched as the two men shook hands and Emil accompanied Cedric to the door. He turned back to me, moved but not wanting to show it; he had had much training in that department. He looked at me and said: "Das ist ein Mensch." It took a man to know another one.

About the first of July 1951 I received a phone call from an old friend who was on the staff of the New York *Mirror* (circulation 1 million). The *Mirror,* a now defunct Hearstling, was then the home base for Walter Winchell, whose column alternated between calls for the blood of the Rosenbergs and the body of Belfrage. (It is an interesting commentary that the "reddest" units of the Newspaper Guild in those days were in the Hearst chain.) Could we have lunch? my friend asked; there was someone he wanted me to meet. We set a date.

The someone turned out to be Manny Bloch. We sat for two hours in the Co-Op cafeteria across the street from the GUARDIAN, as Bloch poured out the story of the Rosenberg ordeal and his own Ancient Mariner's odyssey seeking help to keep Ethel and Julius alive. There were few lawyers to whom he could turn for guidance; scientists who could testify with authority about the delicate atomic evidence fled at his approach; the media had shut their doors and their conscience. I listened in almost complete silence, asking only a question here and there.

Finally my friend spoke. You have worked for three newspapers in this town, he said, and know many more newspaper people because of your work in the Newspaper Guild. How can we break through with this story? Can't we approach people on the papers and try to get them to do something? Not a chance, I said. Those with the guts to speak up would become suspect to their editors. And even if an editor would listen and present the matter higher up, he would be given a sermon on the Gospel according to St. J. Edgar. It looks as if this has been a political case from the start, I said, and if so that's how it will end. I asked for a few days to think it over. As I saw it, unless an independent and unencumbered newspaper like the GUARDIAN would take up the case, Ethel and Julius would go to their deaths—and their co-defendant Morton to jail for thirty years—without a murmur of protest.

I sat for a time at the table after my companions left, but actually Manny remained to haunt me—his urgent speech, heavy head thrust forward to emphasize his agony, intense eyes under thick brows fixed on my face. The way he took the case to his own heart was startlingly un-lawyerlike. I was sorely troubled.

I crossed the street to the GUARDIAN and sat down at my desk without greeting Cedric, who sat across from me. It was not my custom. He peered up, pipe in mouth, from an editing job and said: "You were a long time. You all right?"

"Is Jack in?" I said. "I've got a story to tell you both." The three of us met in a cubbyhole room we used for private conferences above our very public newsroom. This time I talked nonstop and they listened to what Manny had told me. When I finished, Cedric said: "When do we start, and how?" Jack nodded. There was complete agreement, even though in each mind there must have been some foreboding of the consequences.

Then next day we called in Bill Reuben, who had first come to us with the Trenton Six story and had doggedly tracked the facts down to victory. We told him to get the Rosenberg trial record (890 pages) and study it; talk to everyone involved in the case who would talk; sit down with Manny Bloch and his associate Gloria Agrin; visit the Rosenberg, Greenglass, and Sobell families for background and possible clues; check out the witnesses whose testimony seemed contradictory—and be ready to turn in the first article in a month.

On August 8 we prepared our readers with a story about Michael (8) and Robby (4) Rosenberg, who had just been allowed an hour with their parents in Sing Sing deathhouse. On August 15 this headline ran across page 1:

THE ROSENBERG CONVICTION
Is This the Dreyfus Case of Cold War America?*

The following week Reuben's by-line appeared over the first of seven consecutive articles. Long before the last one went down to the composing room, the storm broke.

---

* Some aspects of the Rosenberg case almost paralleled the concocted case against Dreyfus. For example, a note filched by French counterespionage from German espionage referring to "D———," an agent of the latter, could be used to make the cap fit Captain Dreyfus of the French General Staff, who was the ideal scapegoat for reactionaries of the day. In the Rosenberg trial Elizabeth Bentley and Harry Gold, two self-declared spies, testified respectively to phone calls from a "Julius" and to an "atomic secret" rendezvous where the password was, "I come from Julius." At neither trial was any weight given to the well-known fact that espionage apparati endow their important agents with pseudonyms: Bentley and Gold themselves made much of this in other testimony, but it was accepted without juridical or public qualms that on these key occasions the "master spy" used his own name. The absurdity was compounded by the introduction, as proof of the Gold assignation for the spy "coup of the century," of hotel registration forms with the name "Harry Gold." These were forged but, of course, had Gold been represented as registering under another name as he would clearly have done, they would have been valueless.

The French reactionary establishment brazenly defended the forgers of the concoctions against Dreyfus, and hounded and jailed his defenders, even after the forgers were exposed and began committing suicide; but at least the scapegoat's neck was saved so that he lived to be rehabilitated. Six decades later the land of "liberty under law" killed the scapegoats and promoted the forgers.

1953: The Year All Hell Broke Loose

[J.A.] It was our custom, amid the encircling gloom of the times, to present the brightest possible face to readers in each year's first issue. Happy New Year, we would bravely wish them on a front page framed by a cavorting Guardian Angel, our nude and impudent mascot. But when 1953 rolled in we had neither heart nor stomach for levity.

The issue dated January 1 carried a banner line across page 1: THERE IS ONLY ONE WEEK TO SAVE THE ROSENBERGS FROM DEATH! Ethel and Julius had been scheduled to die during the week of January 12. Under the headline was a lovely photograph of Michael and Robby Rosenberg, and under that a silhouette of the electric chair at Sing Sing.

In the lead story, the atomic scientist Harold C. Urey confirmed to the GUARDIAN that he had written to the trial judge, Irving R. Kaufman, urging judicial clemency, and also to the New York *Times,* making public his doubts about the case. "I am just not happy about the evidence in general," he said. Urey's indirect connection with the case was indeed one of its most extraordinary aspects. He was one of several top atomic physicists whom the government had announced it would call as witnesses, presumably to verify the scientific "evidence," but never called. The device had effectively kept defense attorney Emanuel Bloch, who knew nothing about physics, from trying to dispute that "evidence," which was about as scientific as a Tinkertoy.

In view of Kaufman's summing-up statement that the Rosenbergs "caused the Korean war" (at Moscow's behest, naturally), there was irony in another story on the same page 1. America had awakened on Christmas Day to learn from the *Times*'s James Reston that Stalin, in response to Reston's questions, had expressed willingness to "cooperate in any diplomatic approach to end" that war. Stalin also rejected the notion that war between the United States and the Soviet Union was inevitable.

"Stalin's offer stirs new hope in the world," we headlined this story, but the *Times* itself had already begun the campaign to dash that hope. From Washington its bureau chief, Arthur Krock, wrote testily that no one in government or on Eisenhower's team (he was within three weeks of inauguration as President) had any knowledge that Reston was putting questions to Stalin. The *Times* complained that "the Kremlin's 'peace offensive' presented difficult problems for the West." In the *Times,* Soviet peace gestures were always confined within quotation marks.

Not least of the problems was how "the West" could electrocute Ethel and Julius at a time when their "sponsor" was offering to sit down and talk the whole thing over. The *Times*'s quotation marks, however, could not conceal the disenchantment of the nation with the Korean War. What then was to be done? Increase the tension, of course. And in this effort the media again rallied to the spirit of "the West."

Not a single wire service except the British Reuters (which carried a reduced version) reported Dr. Urey's actions. From Europe, where the clamor for clemency was growing daily, *Le Monde* asked: "Can it be that there is a conspiracy of silence?" A 24-hour clemency vigil began in Washington. Einstein associated himself with Urey's plea, and 1,500 clergymen signed a clemency petition to President Truman. The GUARDIAN devoted pages to these developments, but the "conspiracy of silence" did not yield. Give-'em-Hell Harry checked out of the White House, leaving the fateful Rosenberg decision to Dwight Eisenhower.

Pressure mounted on Ethel and Julius to "confess." William L. White, a board member of the American Civil Liberties Union, proposed in the *Times* that "in atonement [the Rosenbergs] make what the FBI would recognize as a full and complete confession"—barring that, "let them die." Judge Kaufman, after granting a month's stay of execution for new legal pleas, reset the date for the week of March 9. Dispelling the self-inflicted confusion in the media over whether the Pope had or had not intervened, *Osservatore Romano,* the Vatican's official newspaper, said that Pius XII had indeed spoken out for clemency. The U.S. Court of Appeals extended the stay of execution till March 30 to allow Bloch to appeal to the Supreme Court, which had twice rejected reviews. As one of his first presidential acts, Ike set up a putting green on the White House lawn.

Leonard Lyons in his syndicated column, and Walter Winchell on radio, reported that Julius and Ethel had rejected the services of Sing Sing's Jewish chaplain. At Sing Sing, the rabbi nailed the lie, but by then it was no longer news. New York *Post* columnist Max Lerner, looking for scare items about the "Jewish angle" in the case, went to the Flatbush section of Brooklyn to report on a clemency meeting. Looking around the room, he saw "vultures and victims," the former "the half-pint commissars, exploiting the emotions of unsuspecting Jews," the latter, the rest of the audience, "huddled together in their anxiety." A "little orthodox rabbi . . . the prize catch of the cynical men who ran the meeting" was the main speaker. "Why did he let himself be used by them?" Lerner asked. The rabbi was available, but Lerner never put the question to him. It served better as a prize piece of rhetoric by a cynical columnist for an unsuspecting readership.

Lyons moved again to the front with a charge that the deeply moving Death House letters between Ethel and Julius had been ghost-written. In fact the GUARDIAN, which had published many of the letters, had taken them either from the originals supplied by

Bloch or from photostats of their handwriting. Julius wrote to Ethel: "I am amazed at the fabulous newspaper campaign organized against us. . . . It is indeed a tragedy how the press can mold public opinion by printing . . . blatant falsehoods. The pressure campaign is in high gear and many weak people will be scared off. . . . There is a new whipping boy in our land." It sickened the Rosenbergs as much as it pleasured the Establishment to know that the whip frequently was in willing Jewish hands. But for Jews who scorned the whip there was another treatment: Sydney Silverman, the British MP, offered to speak at a clemency dinner in New York but was refused a visa to come.

Overall, the role of the media could only be described as murderous. For the Scripps–Howard syndicate, Robert C. Ruark wrote that he had no way of knowing whether "they'll pull the switch" on the Rosenbergs, but "I certainly hope so." To the Hearst press the death sentence was "the scalpel" to remove "the Red cancer in the American body politic." Headlines, news stories, columns, and editorials fostered the belief that the charge against the Rosenbergs was treason (it was "conspiracy to commit espionage," and no concrete piece of evidence had been presented to support it). As for the "responsible" media, the New York *Herald Tribune* ignored the Rosenberg committee's press releases along with every other paper in the city, and refused to see a committee delegation. The *Times* and its radio station, WQXR, rejected all advertising on the case. Whenever there seemed to be a faint chance of clemency or judicial review, the media let loose a new burst of fury.

Then, in our issue on April 13, two years almost to the day after the convictions, the GUARDIAN carried a new banner line on page 1: SENSATIONAL NEW DISCLOSURE IN ROSENBERG CASE. We called it sensational because it was. Our reporter Leon Summit, after months of digging, had located the missing console table, a piece of evidence which the government never produced at the trial but employed with devastating effect to get the convictions. The government had charged that the table was a gift to the Rosenbergs "from the Russians" for their services, and that it was "hollowed out" to conceal an apparatus for microfilming secrets for Soviet agents. This description had come from David and Ruth Green-glass, Ethel's brother and sister-in-law, whose testimony had been the key to conviction. Julius had testified that he bought the table for about $21 at Macy's in late 1944 or early 1945.

An examination of the table showed it to be an ordinary inexpensive piece of furniture with no hollows. Macy's purchase records for those years had been destroyed, but an affidavit from a Macy representative, subpoenaed by the defense, confirmed that the table had been sold at the store in 1944 for $19.97. The price appeared in chalk marks on the bottom of the table, along with other special store markings. The affidavit supported Julius's testimony to the hilt. The table had been kept, along with some other nondescript furniture from the vacated Rosenberg apartment, in the basement of the home of Julius' sister. It was so shabby that none of the family had even thought to connect it with the expensive piece described by the prosecution. Finally it was used to furnish a sparse apartment set up for Julius' mother and the Rosenberg children. There our reporter discovered it.

We felt a great excitement over the discovery and hoped (against hope) that it might reopen the case, on the basis of new evidence, even as the appeal for a new trial was being taken to the Supreme Court. The conspiracy of silence in the media remained unbroken: only the GUARDIAN published the news of the table's discovery. The Supreme Court recessed late in April without a decision. The Pope made a third appeal, reproduced on page 1 of *Osservatore Romano*. The media blacked it out.

There was a response to the new evidence—not unexpected, but not precisely what we had wished for. At the end of April an advance man for Representative Harold H. Velde, chairman of the House Committee on Un-American Activities (HUAC), showed up at our office with a pink slip—a subpoena for Cedric to appear before the committee in New York in the first week of May. Velde, on the floor of the House a year earlier, had called the GUARDIAN "a propaganda arm of the Soviet Union" exerting "a sinister effect on Americanism." He had called then for an investigation, but nothing happened. Now the auspices were favorable.

It was a glorious time for the forces of darkness in America, that brilliant spring of 1953. Senator Joe McCarthy was at the peak of his power. The government was quietly encouraging his exposures of reds under every bed to cover the failure of the "United Nations police action" in Korea. Richard Nixon was in the Vice-President's chair, a niblick shot away from the White House. Attorney General Brownell was busy with new repressive legislation and roundups of aliens who insisted that the Constitution protected them too. Roy Cohn and David Schine, McCarthy's chief assistants, had just returned from a "fact-finding" tour of Europe in search of American subversives abroad. Their trip had taken them to Bonn, Berlin, Frankfurt, Munich, Vienna, Rome, Paris, and London. Secretary of State John Foster Dulles had asked all diplomats to cooperate with them. Among their activities reported by a dazed European press was a pantless chase around a hotel lobby in Frankfurt during which they batted each other over the head with rolled-up newspapers. Their Rhineland journey, as Cedric and I were soon to discover, would lead to a Walpurgisnacht for us. But at the moment we were observing the strange performance of another journalist in Washington.

The New York *Post* had annoyed McCarthy by publishing in 1951 a seventeen-part series titled "Smear Inc.—A One-Man Job." Joe had contented himself at the time with an "exposé" of the Young Communist League membership of the *Post*'s editor, James Wechsler. But that was hardly a sensation. Wechsler had for fifteen years been making a ritual performance of his break with the Communists in 1937, and by 1953 had certified anti-Communist credentials. But Joe had his own way of doing things. So late in April 1953 Wechsler was summoned before the McCarthy committee, ostensibly because his books were on the shelves of U.S. Information Agency libraries abroad.

Wechsler arrived with reams of clippings and documents testifying to his Americanism, among them a testimonial from Representative Richard Nixon for a Wechsler editorial on the Hiss case. He had, Wechsler proudly told Joe, given perhaps the first editorial support in the nation's press to Whittaker Chambers' charges against Hiss. Also presented were denunciations of Wechsler in the *Daily Worker* (in his inimitable fashion Joe asked Wechsler whether he had had a hand in causing them to be written). After hours of this desultory exchange, Wechsler asked that the transcript of the hearing be made available for submission to the American Society of Newspaper Editors to determine whether there had been a violation of freedom of the press. That could be arranged, Joe said, but there was a piece of unfinished business: he had asked Wechsler to submit a list of persons he knew to be Communists during his YCL days, and Wechsler had not yet complied. The *Post*'s editor pondered the matter over a weekend, then delivered to McCarthy a list of fifty-nine names. "Joe McCarthy wanted silence, not submission," Wechsler said, "and I was determined not to walk into his trap."

While we were disgusted but not surprised by Wechsler's failure to keep his own trap shut, the GUARDIAN nevertheless appraised the Wechsler summons and hearing as what they were—an attempt to silence all press critics of King Joe. The HUAC summons to Cedric and the McCarthy foray against the *Post* were strands in the same rope.

The general press did not see it that way. The *Times* rallied to Wechsler's defense and ignored a statement we issued about Cedric's subpoena—as did the *Post*. On May 4 a thousand people turned out for a Belfrage Fight-Back rally. Speakers included Marcantonio, Dorothy Day of the *Catholic Worker,* Rose Russell of the Teachers Union, and Angus Cameron, recently purged chief editor of the publishing firm Little Brown. (Angus still wanted to publish subversive authors and was doing so from poverty row.) There was not a word in the press about the meeting.

On May 6 Cedric appeared before HUAC in the Federal Courthouse on Foley Square, where the Rosenbergs had been tried, convicted, and sentenced. Cedric asked that the klieg lights be turned off. Velde said he would so order if Cedric promised to answer all the questions. That depends on the questions, said Cedric. The lights went off but the questions went unanswered. Cedric said he preferred to stand on his First Amendment rights but was forced to invoke the Fifth—"the shield of innocence . . . it is this innocence that I seek to protect. . . . I have no confidence in this committee and I believe, on its past record, that whatever answers I would give would be used to crucify me and other innocent persons.'' With the GUARDIAN's lawyer Nat Dambroff at his elbow, he proceeded to admit gingerly that he existed; the scores of unanswered accusations in the form of questions included his authorship, in 1940, of an article about nudist camps entitled ''Nude Without Being Rude.'' ''For the first time,'' he said afterwards, ''I realized how much we owe to the authors of the Fifth Amendment, and what the 'witches' at the Salem trials felt like without it. If they denied copulating with Satan they were hanged because they couldn't prove the denial, and if they admitted it without naming fellow copulators they were hanged anyway. But now you can't be pressed to death beneath heavy stones for refusing to answer.''

There was considerable oratory from the committee side of the table about this alien enjoying the golden corn of American democracy while continuing to subvert unsuspecting natives. When Velde left the hearing room, Representative Kearney of New York (who long since passed into well-deserved oblivion) took over. He said to Cedric: ''I'm going to contact immigration authorities and find out why you are still in this country. I think you're the type to be deported immediately.'' The handwriting was on the wall.

And the hand was the hand of Joe McCarthy. One week after the Un-American performance Cedric and I were both served with summonses by a U.S. marshall, commanding us to a session before the McCarthy committee in Washington. The summonses came at deadline time on a Tuesday, and a decision was made to hold up the issue two days to include a report of our appearance.

We spent the four-hour train ride to Washington arguing with Dambroff—a genial but watchful man who was also a personal friend—for the right to invoke the First Amendment rather than the Fifth, and make it a free press battle. He listened with a sphinxlike expression but, as the train approached Union Station, said:

''OK, you heroes, you take the First and go to jail for contempt of Congress, as the Hollywood Ten did. Then who's going to put the paper out?''

The point was as unpalatable as, in the temper of the times, it was persuasive. People much better than ourselves had gone to prison for a principle, and would again. What worried us was the incredible expense of battling our way through unfriendly courts and the probability that the GUARDIAN could not survive such a war of attrition. But the decision involved more than that: faith had to be kept with the thousands of people who depended on the paper as a lifeline to the beleaguered groups of dissenters everywhere in the country. It was all they had. Would a noble stand for the First Amendment (with the certainty that anything noble about it would go unreported) profit the struggle for honest news and opinion if the GUARDIAN died? That was what we had to decide. We chose silence. Jack, who joined us in Washington to observe and report, concurred.

The actual title of McCarthy's committee was "Permanent Subcommittee on Investigations of the Senate Committee on Government Operations," and since Joe was shrewdly aware that even in 1953 it was unwise to engage the First Amendment head-on, the subject of the inquiry was "United States Information Centers" in Germany. That was where we came in, with a shove from Cohn and Schine. Once the questions were put about our activities in postwar occupied Germany, it was clear that Joe's slapstick assistants (the London *Financial Post* called them "scummy snoopers . . . distempered jackals") had met with former Nazi publishers whom we had proscribed but who, thanks to the flourishing cold war, were now back in the saddle. When you get back home, these publishers almost surely had said, you might check out two chaps named Belfrage and Aronson. So we were checked out and McCarthy struck red gold: two subversive army officers who, after laboring to create a "red press" in Germany, had returned to establish one at home—a paper now leading the fight for the Rosenbergs, at whose trial Cohn had been an assistant prosecutor. The circle had come full.

We encountered Joe McCarthy first in "executive session," and sure enough Cohn, as counsel to the chairman, was at the master's elbow. Also present were Joe's Democratic colleagues, Senator Stuart Symington of Missouri, then a perfervid cold warrior, and

Senator Henry (Scoop) Jackson. I was first. I answered routine questions about my work in Germany and about my past newspaper employment, then stopped dead at all inquiries about the GUARDIAN and my political beliefs and associations. If I had responded to a single question in an "area"—for example, conceding even that I was the GUARDIAN's executive editor—I would have been forced, under threat of a contempt citation, to answer *all* questions in that "area." The next questions would have been: Who are the other staff members? Are they Communists? Who contributes financially to the paper? Will you produce your subscription files? Such questions were in clear violation of the First Amendment, and to answer them would be a violation of faith with staff and readers. We had an obligation to keep the trust of privacy, and the only way we could maintain that trust and our right to continue working was by invoking the silence of the Fifth Amendment. Our work and our beliefs were none of the committee's damn business.

Outside the glare of publicity, Joe was all grace and charm. He apologized to me for the lack of a private room where I might consult counsel, and generously offered me the opportunity to meet privately with the FBI, in a session in which I could bare my soul for Hooverian absolution. I could think about that overnight. Symington confined himself to asking how I rated myself on the Americanism scale, but Scoop bore in. He pressed me about my answers to a War Department questionnaire eight years earlier as to whether I belonged to any organization that advocated violent overthrow of the government, etc. I had given negative answers, and I trust it will not diminish my standing in the community if I note here that I was cleared by both the FBI and Army Security. Jackson seemed determined to nail me as a liar, but in the midst of the foray Joe intruded: "I think the statute of limitations has run out on this fellow." This unexpected assist puzzled me until I realized that Joe simply didn't want Scoop stealing his headlines.

Cedric's private session was more abrupt. After the usual preliminary skirmishing, during which Joe established that Cedric had been careless enough to get born in London of British parents, he said he would demand the presence at next day's public hearings of a representative of the Immigration and Naturalization Service to explain why Cedric was still in the United States. That was the chief topic of discussion with counsel in our hotel room that night.

The next day, May 14, was a flawless day. Washington had never looked more sparkling. But as we trudged up the steps of the Capitol, a shadow crossed our path—the long thin figure of Pat Nixon coming down the steps. (We also ran into I. F. Stone, who told us later, over lunch, what it was like covering Washington for his anti-cold war *Weekly*: every official and congressman fled at his approach to avoid "guilt by association.") Joe's inquisition chamber was the Senate's Old Caucus Room—a place that would become familiar to millions of TV viewers a year later when he met his Waterloo at the Army–McCarthy hearings, and again twenty-one years later when it was the scene of Senator Ervin's Watergate hearings. The spectator seats were filled with Americans come to the nation's capital to see the democratic process in action. The press seats held at least fifty reporters, many of whom I had known on newspapers where I had worked. Some were cordial, some embarrassed, others averted their gaze to avoid encounter.

Then the swinging doors burst open and Joe McCarthy entered, a pat on the back for the Capitol cop at the door, his double-breasted suit coat open to catch the cameras, a familiar wave to the Goon Squad (the reporters who covered him day to day). He took his seat at the center, buttoned his coat, and the smile vanished. The Grand Inquisitor was ready for the scourge of the day. Schine was present this time along with his gumshoe twin, Cohn, and with young Bobby Kennedy, counsel for the Democratic majority, who was learning the inquisitorial ropes. Magisterially flanking their chairman were Symington and Jackson and some other committee members who remained mute.

In retrospect, as Cedric and I have recalled our sessions with Joe and reenacted the scene for students and friends, there were moments of high hilarity. In actuality it was a nightmare. The full power and prejudice of government was arrayed against any possibility of reasonable exchange, and the intervening press tables, occupied by intimidated or compliant reporters, guaranteed that effective protest would be ignored or muffled. It may be difficult, because of the experiences of the 1960s, for newer generations to transplant themselves into the atmosphere of the time, and it may be a cliché to say that a blanket of fear was smothering the nation, but that was the case. This is not said defensively. History can be written accurately from the perspective of another day only if it countenances and absorbs the conditions of the time.

The questions put to me in private session were repeated with greater hostility in public: Germany (Joe wanted the record to show that I did not personally know Eisenhower, whose directives I insisted we had carried out diligently); my service on the New York *Herald Tribune,* the *Post* and the *Times* (with leers at the correspondents covering the hearings for those papers); the Rosenberg case (from Symington: Did I think an injustice had been done in the case? "Just a yes or no answer"); and of course my relationship with Cedric (did I know he was a Communist when we met in Germany?)

If my hour (which I have never been able to describe as my finest) before the committee was nightmarish, Cedric's, as it turned out, was only too real. When I stepped down, Joe noted the presence of a Mr. Noto of the Immigration Service and took the handwriting down off the wall by saying to Cedric: "I assume they will take the necessary action after your evidence has been reviewed." The chairman then excused himself to go to the floor of the Senate, where he was scheduled to denounce poor old Clement Attlee, Britain's Prime Minister, as a tool of the Communist conspiracy. He turned the chair over to Symington.

Almost immediately there was consternation at the committee table when Cohn put The Question to Cedric: "Now, between 1937 and 1953, that is, today, have you continuously been a member of the Communist Party?" Cedric replied: "Mr. Cohn, 'Thou sayest it' is a famous answer to a similar trick question." Symington was disconcerted and there was much gavel banging. I was sitting in the spectator seats with Jack, who almost fell off the bench with delight at Cedric's response. I had a general idea of what was going on, but being an Old Testament boy, I asked Jack, whose Catholic upbringing made him more conversant with the New, what the excitement was about. "That's what Jesus said to Pilate when he asked him whether he was King of the Jews," said Jack. "This is great stuff."

There followed more questions about the operation in Germany, espionage, violent overthrow, and then Cohn got down to business. "Mr. Chairman," he said, "we have Mr. Noto of the Immigration Service here today, and I wonder: Senator McCarthy had in mind requesting the Immigration Service to see if something cannot be done immediately about this man, who refuses to say whether or not he believes in the overthrow of our government, whether he is engaged in espionage against this country, and who has been staying in this country as a resident alien, and refusing to answer the questions as he does here. It seems like a highly unusual situation, to say the least."

Cedric sought to make a statement but Symington pursued the questioning; Mr. Noto was asked to comment on immigration law and procedure; Cohn and Symington made further speeches about alien corn, and finally Symington said: "I think we ought to look into the question of how this man got into the United States and what the questions were that he answered when he got in, and how he answered them." The hearing was recessed.

Symington's style is demonstrated in the following colloquy taken from the official record:

SYMINGTON: I asked this witness in executive session if he thought he was a good American and he said he did. I would like to ask you again: How can you be a good American and be afraid or ashamed to come before this committee and tell them whether or not you are a member of the Communist Party today?

ARONSON: I must decline to answer that question.

SYMINGTON: Do you think the Korean war is the fault of the United States or the fault of Soviet Russia?

ARONSON: I must decline to answer that question also.

SYMINGTON: Well, the presumption is, if you would not answer that question, is that you believe it is the fault of the United States, is it not?

ARONSON: No, sir; I don't think that is the assumption.

SYMINGTON: Then if you are a member of the Communist Party, you would be afraid to say in public that it was the fault of Soviet Russia, would you not?

ARONSON: I must decline to answer that question.

THE CHAIRMAN: I might say, Senator Symington, that if he were to say he were not a member of the Communist Party, we would promptly refer the question to the Justice Department for perjury action.

More precisely than anyone else, the chairman had explained why it was the course of wisdom in this situation to invoke the Fifth Amendment.

Immediately thereafter, Cohn had his opportunity to shine. In executive session I had been asked whether, when I worked for the general press, the Communist Party had advised or discussed with me what and how to write. I invoked the Fifth. In the public session the question was repeated and, annoyed by its absurdity, I replied: "No, sir; they did not." The thunder clouds broke. Counsel whispers to Chairman. Chairman simulates rage that the witness used a constitutional amendment in private as a subterfuge to avoid answering an embarrassing question. Speeches about being sick and tired of Fifth Amendment Communists abusing the courtesy of the committee. Threats of perjury and contempt. Witness asks that the testimony of the previous day prevail. Further threats and bombast. Storm subsides. Symington asks a last obscene question. Witness steps down under continuing subpoena.

Before the hearing opened I had told several reporters present that we would not answer certain questions, but that we would explain why if they would meet us outside the Caucus Room after our testimony. I asked those I spoke to to pass the word. Three came. We informed them that we were not Communists but that we felt it was our right—our duty—to remain silent before a committee of Congress which had no authority to inquire into our beliefs and associations. Only the New York *Times* printed the barest bones of these comments, adding in a New York "shirttail" the dates of my employment on the *Times* Sunday staff and carefully noting that I had resigned in 1948.

We spent almost the entire trip home in the bar car of the Pennsylvania Railroad train, reviving our spirits with Old Fitzgerald in honor of Anita Blaine. In New York our wives were waiting at my home, having prepared a touchingly splendid dinner which we were not much in the mood to enjoy. Grambs said to me: "I think you had better call your father." I pictured this gentle man, much more given to reading the classics than the news, sitting in my sister's home in Boston, probably at that moment with a book in his hand. I had been grateful that he rarely expressed to me his concern about the maverick tangents of my career. It would be a jarring intrusion. I made the call, having carefully rehearsed a speech about why I had to do what I did. After the inquiry about his health, I paused to present my case, and in that pause he said to me: "I just saw you on television." I made a similar call to my brother Earl, then bureau chief of the Associated Press in Albany, whose integrity as a journalist had been an early inspiration to me. He was as reasonably well informed about the day's proceedings as the Washington AP wire permitted. I said I hoped my situation would not affect his career. He said: "No matter what happens, you are always my brother." I felt better.

Next morning we arrived at the GUARDIAN and found in the little office we shared two vases of flowers from the staff, who gathered immediately to hear our story. Cedric was in mid-sentence when the elevator stopped at our floor and two beefy individuals emerged with the writing-on-the-wall in their paws—an Immigration Service warrant for his arrest as a "dangerous alien." No charge had been placed against him but they took him off to Ellis Island, the then Immigration detention center, to be held in custody without bail.

Almost as soon as the news broke we were besieged with letters, wires, phone calls, and money for a spontaneously organized Belfrage Fight-Back Fund. From Ellis Island, Cedric requested pipe-cleaners, a thesaurus, dictionary, carbon paper, and eraser, and the song score of Jay Gorney's irreverent revue "Meet the People." He wrote: "I feel our boys [the nine political detainees in the island cage] might have fun learning the chorus of the Bill of Rights to sing to the visitors as the ferry back to Manhattan pulls out of the Ellis Island slip."

Cedric continued to write for the paper from the island while Nat Dambroff and Blanch Freedman, counsel for the American Committee for Protection of Foreign Born, went to court on a writ of habeas corpus to get him released on bond. On June 10 Federal District Judge Edward Weinfeld, in a scathing rebuke to the government, ordered Cedric freed on $5,000 bond. The GUARDIAN's bank overdraft exceeded this amount at the time and a staunch "angel," Louise Berman, herself in deep trouble with the witch-hunters, put up the cash. Our attorneys in their brief had noted that years earlier Cedric had been "thoroughly investigated" by the FBI (Hoover would hardly deny it) and had appeared before a grand jury. In his opinion, Weinfeld wrote:

If for the long period of seven years following . . . the immigration and other government officials did not consider Belfrage's presence and activities inimical to the nation's welfare and a threat to its security, it is difficult to understand how, overnight, because of his assertion of a constitutional privilege, he has become such a menace to the nation's safety that it is now necessary to jail him without bail pending the determination of the charges as to which the government has the burden of proof. . . . The refusal to answer the congressional committee on a plea of constitutional privilege in and of itself in the circumstances of the case does not warrant holding Belfrage without bail pending a hearing on the deportation charges. . . . The privilege is for the innocent as well as the guilty and no inference can be drawn against the person claiming it. . . . The truth is that privilege exists for the sake of the innocent as well as the guilty—or at least for reasons irrespective of the guilt of the accused.

It was a splendid victory, however temporary, and Cedric came back to work.

But there was neither time nor desire to celebrate, for while we awaited Weinfeld's decision the Supreme Court for the third time refused to review the Rosenberg verdict. The lower courts meanwhile spurned the new evidence about the console table and other significant material that had come to light. The government set the new execution date for June 18, and Attorney General Brownell offered Ethel and Julius a grisly choice—confess to an act which they insisted they had not committed, or die.

Ethel and Julius wired Manny Bloch from Sing Sing what they had told Federal Prison Director Bennett, who had conveyed Brownell's message: WE BOTH REASSERTED OUR INNOCENCE AND SAID SINCE WE ARE NOT GUILTY WE CANNOT TELL THEM ANYTHING ABOUT ESPIONAGE. The efforts for clemency intensified as the days ticked away. In his first editorial upon release from Ellis Island, Cedric wrote on page 1: "Ethel and Julius have saved America's name. That is the tribute we pay them from our hearts. Let us save their lives."

The worldwide clamor against the death sentence became so loud that the media could no longer suppress it. In the last agonizing week the Rosenbergs were on page 1 everywhere. Manny Bloch, joined by attorney John F. Finerty, placed before the Supreme Court new motions for a stay of execution and for a rehearing of the court's denial of a review. The court, by a 5 to 4 decision, denied both motions. Then, thirty-six hours before the scheduled execution, attorneys Fyke Farmer and Daniel Marshall, acting on behalf of Irwin Edelman of Los Angeles, a tireless researcher in the case,* moved before Justice Douglas for a stay on different grounds. They contended that the impounding of the "scientific evidence" during the trial (an unheard-of "expert's" comments on Greenglass's ludicrous A-bomb sketches) had kept

---

* At the time and for years afterwards, Edelman inveighed obsessively (as we thought) against Bloch's conduct of the case. It was our view that, as the only attorney the Rosenbergs could find for the trial, and in a field of law in which he had no experience, Bloch did his very utmost from start to finish though he was far from being a Clarence Darrow. Our most compelling reason for not entering into Edelman's dispute with Bloch was that Ethel and Julius themselves had total confidence in Bloch and did not believe that, in the nakedly political nature of the case, even a Darrow could have saved them.

the matter from consideration in the courts; and that the Rosenbergs had been improperly tried under the Espionage Act of 1917, when the proper law was the Atomic Energy Act of 1948 which restricts the death penalty. The petition to a single justice was necessitated by the fact that the court had gone into summer recess after its last denial of a review.

Justice Douglas granted the stay, then left by car for his home in Washington State. As he arrived at a motel near Uniontown, Pa., he learned by radio that Chief Justice Fred Vinson, a Truman appointee, had convened a special court session for the next day, Thursday June 18, to consider Brownell's demand that the full court consider the issues underlying Douglas's stay. It was a rare step for a Chief Justice to take. Douglas proceeded to Pittsburgh airport for a flight back to Washington. Boarding the plane, he received a spontaneous ovation. The Supreme Court session on June 18 (the execution was postponed) was one of the stormiest in history, and the discomfort of several justices was evident. But at noon next day the court announced its decision: 6 to 3 in favor of vacating the stay. Justices Douglas, Frankfurter, and Black voted in the minority. At 2:15 P.M. President Eisenhower, repeating Judge Kaufman's murderous nonsense at the trial, rejected a final clemency appeal.

Once again we had delayed an issue of the GUARDIAN to wait for the news. Jack, Cedric, and I sat in Vic Levitt's office above our own, listening to the radio. I had prepared two headlines. One read, ROSENBERGS REPRIEVED; the other, ROSENBERGS EXECUTED.

Shortly after 8 P.M. Ethel and Julius were put to death by a compassionate government which, to avoid desecrating the Jewish sabbath, had hurried to complete its business before sundown. I picked up the second headline, waited for Jack to write the lead to the story, and we all took the elevator down to the composing room in the basement of the building. A skeleton crew of printers was waiting. The paper was complete except for holes for the headline and the lead. Murry Melvin, the foreman, looked at our faces, took the copy paper from my hand, and went to a linotype machine. No one said a word.

Outside the White House pickets seeking clemency lowered

their signs. In Union Square and at vigils throughout the world, hundreds of thousands of men, women, and children wept for Julius and Ethel and for the shame of America.

The funeral was held the following Sunday in Brooklyn. As the bodies were being lowered into the grave, W. E. B. DuBois said: "These people were killed because they would not lie." That was all he said. But the same issue of the GUARDIAN that reported the funeral also published some bitter truths about the history of the case, and particularly the role of the media. Bloch wrote:

I remember very well those first grim days in March 1951, following the trial and the sentence, when every avenue of information and publicity suddenly closed. With the slamming of the door of the Death House on the Rosenbergs, a conspiracy of silence settled on the press. Our great newspapers which, during the trial, had seized eagerly upon every propaganda release of the prosecution, closed their pages to all news about the victims. From the government point of view, and from the point of view of its ally, the press, the Rosenbergs were as good as dead. The next news item would be the news of their execution. . . . The deadly conspiracy to forget the Rosenbergs was shattered by the NATIONAL GUARDIAN. Its editors saw the meaning of this attack upon an obscure engineer and his wife. The Rosenberg Case, which had died in all the great papers, came alive in the NATIONAL GUARDIAN. To the GUARDIAN is due the credit of first showing to the world what the world now recognizes as a bare-faced political frame-up.

But for the narrower world of the law there was still no recognition. In January 1954, the Bar Association of the City of New York petitioned the Appellate Division of the New York State Court to take action against Manny for his characterization of the trial, at the victims' funeral, as "an act of cold, deliberate murder." On January 30 Manny was found dead in his Manhattan apartment, victim of an apparent heart attack. Rather, it could be said, his heart had given out in exhaustion and despair.

Messages of condolence came from all parts of the world. Editorials of tribute appeared in the press of Western Europe. In Paris hundreds of lawyers gathered at the Palais de Justice to lay a wreath in his honor at the memorial to the dead. But in the media in the United States there was nothing.

The conspiracy of silence held to the grave.

Postscript [**C.B.**] I concur in Jim's appraisal of our performance on McCarthy's trapeze as "not our finest hour." In fact you had to feel dirty afterwards although you weren't the one who really needed a bath. That it was the hour of abomination for all America seems to be recognized now even by "intellectuals" who, at the time, connived actively or passively with the inquisitors and their partner, the press. Among the crudest frauds perpetrated by this partnership was sticking the label "Fifth Amendment Communist" (read, "traitor") on people who stood up for the precious rights of the innocent before a Star Chamber. The media never attempted to explain to a befuddled public what the Fifth Amendment was and how it got into the Constitution, and any attempt by the victim to explain it was derisively spiked in newspaper offices.

Judges were of course supposed to know the Constitution, but to find one like Weinfeld, who would act on it, you had to travel far. Because the judge on the bench when I entered Ellis Island was not renowned as one of these, and Weinfeld was next in line, my lawyers dawdled with their habeas corpus writ. This ploy kept me on the island for a month but paid off, and I salute Weinfeld's "decent respect to the opinion of mankind."

Quoting Jesus to the McCarthy gang seems daft when read in the printed record, but I'm glad that Jack McManus enjoyed it. The notion entered my head, as I recall, just before I took the hot seat in the Senate Caucus Room. My Fifth Amendment incantations before HUAC had left me weak with frustration, and I was desperate for something I could say that would have a spark of originality without causing trouble for the GUARDIAN family. Had I not been gaveled down I would have added the rest of the Bible text: "And when he was accused of the chief priests and elders, he answered nothing." It wasn't a bad precedent, after all, if a bit presumptuous.

While I was aware of the stench emanating from McCarthy during my time in his presence, I am an incorrigible believer in giving the devil his due. With all credit to the skill of "historian" worldsmiths, I resent the apparently permanent attachment of Joe's name to the witch-hunting 1930s, '40s, and '50s. Not so much because Joe was only a brief phase of an inquisition sponsored from first to last by the Establishment, and by all branches of government except for one President, Roosevelt; but because, as the wordsmiths no doubt intended, the "McCarthyism" and "McCarthy Era" labels let so cozily off the hook his dozens of predecessors (e.g., Nixon), committee colleagues (e.g., Symington and Jackson), and rivals and successors (e.g., Eastland). Nixon became President with hardly a reminder to the electorate that it was he who taught McCarthy his tricks, not vice versa; Symington floats down the years as a "liberal"; nobody mentions that Eastland, chairman of the Senate Judiciary Committee for some two decades now, was an even more uncouth witch-hunter than Joe; in 1976 Jackson was a Democratic hopeful for the White House. And why not, after the brilliant career of Nixon, who was "found out" only after six years' tenancy as the man he always was? As for the experts in Salem law who tried and convicted Ethel and Julius, the survivors, like Hitler's surviving associates in West Germany, are all doing nicely as pillars of the community.

Those were times that tried men's souls with a farrago of tragedy and knockabout farce. From today's perspective one sees that the most appalling tragedies can have delayed happy endings; and to reach 70 is to know that if one lives long enough, one sees everything. The event that has given me most recent pleasure has been catching up again with two kids named Michael and Robby. I hadn't seen them since Manny Bloch and I drove them up the Hudson to Sing Sing prison for one of their last "family visits." Michael was 10, Robby 6, and the U.S. government was about to deprive them of their parents. Today, as Michael and Robert Meeropol (their foster parents' name), they are alive and well, as decent a pair of young Americans as you could find, and raising four beautiful Rosenberg grandchildren. Since I thought of Ethel and Julius as my sister and brother (though I never met them), the grandchildren seem like my own.

Michael and Robert are fighting to "rehabilitate" the two whose bodies we laid in that Brooklyn cemetery in June of 1953, a few days after I emerged from Ellis Island: that eerie "rehabilitation" of the dead which—on a far greater scale, and not by orphans but by governments—we have seen in socialist countries. Perhaps Michael and Robert can't succeed; the episode is still, we must suppose, somewhat embarrassing to the murderers and their successors in the administration of justice. But the "boys" have written a book, *We Are Your Sons,* which sold fairly well, and about which media attacks were warily oblique: the prose, for example, isn't all it might be. Morton Sobell has written *On Doing Time.* And two novels have been inspired by the Rosenberg case: E. L. Doctorow's *The Book of Daniel* and Robert Coover's *The Public Burning.* Quite a few Americans must have read these books and wondered. Even the media feels that "times have changed." In 1975 the Chicago *Tribune,* than which no newspaper howled louder for Ethel's and Julius' blood, published this about *We Are Your Sons:* "It eloquently emphasizes what was clear previously: that, guilty or innocent, the Rosenbergs were shamefully treated and their execution was a tragic scandal."

I would be more moved by these changes of heart about the shedding of "guilty or innocent" blood if our media would look at their back files and show a trace of remorse. In that way they could provide ground for hope that, next time, they might speak out before everybody was dead. I am thinking also of the late holocaust in Vietnam, which all now find so regrettable. But we are still in the prehistory of civilization, in which such candor and modesty cannot be expected from any press establishment in the world.

The reason I wanted a thesaurus on Ellis Island was that Jim wanted me to keep writing, and I couldn't think there of any words polite enough for publication.

Curtains

[**C.B.**] In the wake of the Rosenberg executions with their depressive effect on peacemongers and old-fashioned democrats, the Establishment in 1953–54 stepped up the cold war on all domestic and foreign fronts. It publicly disgraced Joe McCarthy late in 1954 for red-hunting in the U.S. Army, but his services had become an embarrassment throughout the Free World and the political terror ran more smoothly without him.

Stool-pigeoning for Hoover developed into a booming profession,* and Smith Act trials of Communists proliferated around the country along with federal, state, and local inquisitions of "suspects." A Smith Act sentence for Steve Nelson, Communist hero of the International Brigades in Spain who already faced twenty years for "sedition," gave him a total of a quarter-century in jail—a record topped only by Morton Sobell. The government put Sobell to serve his thirty years in the "hardened criminal" prison Alcatraz, and tried to seize the Rosenberg children from their foster parents.

Vincent Hallinan was returned to jail, the fifth attempt (out of six) to deport Harry Bridges was made, Corliss Lamont was in-

---

*The *Guardian* was among the few radical organizations of the period that didn't produce a single stool pigeon.

dicted for "contempt" of McCarthy, and the Presbyterian Church unfrocked Claude Williams—not officially for "communism" but for heretical views on the Virgin Birth. But inquisitors ranged far beyond committed radicals, intensifying their pursuit and humiliation of orientalist professor Owen Lattimore, clearly a "spy" (he had met Mao), and physicist Robert Oppenheimer, "father of the A-bomb" who once consorted with Communists. While the Supreme Court ordered desegregation of schools "with all deliberate speed" (meaning no hurry), legal lynchings of blacks continued at normal rhythm; Rosa Ingram and her sons (see chapter 7) were denied parole in their seventh year behind bars; and Louisville journalist Carl Braden got a twenty-year sentence for the "red plot" of buying a house in a white area for a black family. In a recurring obbligato to all this, sirens blew a jittery public into "shelters" and the press counted casualties from imaginary Soviet bombs. A "civil defense test edition" of Hearst's New York paper banner-headlined: 2 A-BOMBS HIT CITY: KILLED 1,104,814; INJURED 568,393; 1,690,000 HOMELESS. Only the Rosenbergs and Bloch had in fact been exterminated by the atomic hoax.

France's U.S.-financed war against self-determination and socialism in Indochina collapsed at Dienbienphu, and Washington and the media went all-out to sell the U.S. public on taking over the crusade. The GUARDIAN called it "beyond comparison the most lied-about conflict in which this country was ever involved." Citing a Dr. Virgil Jordan's outline of America's imperialist prospects at an Investment Bankers' convention back in 1940, we asked: "Is this what Americans must die for in Indochina?" The answer was to be Yes. Secretary Dulles had to make verbal agreements with Asian socialists at Geneva in 1954 but the GUARDIAN never expected him to keep them. On the eve of Dienbienphu and the Geneva conference, DuBois sounded a tocsin in the GUARDIAN for "this paralyzed nation" to stop and think: "Awake all cowards, scream all women, stand up and be counted all real men!"

Nearer home, the Free World found ominous the concern for their poorest citizens shown by the regimes of two small countries, surrounded by dictatorships in the Western Hemisphere. British

Guiana had an elected Prime Minister, Cheddi Jagan (with little substantial power since it was a colony), who was a socialist; Britain, by sending troops, could for the time being take care of his "communist plot." Guatemala had an elected President, Colonel Jacobo Arbenz, who thought that Guatemalans rather than America's United Fruit Company should own the country. The rumblings of "trouble" there reached us in March 1954, three months before the CIA overthrew Arbenz, causing me anguish for Manuel Cuevas Díaz.

Manuel, a Spaniard, was one of the nine from different countries with whom I had shared the "political" deportation quarters on Ellis Island. Altogether, America's historic vestibule for "wretched refuse" from "teeming shores" contained at the time some 400 bodies forcibly going the other way. Many had been U.S. residents for decades and most, like Manuel (and myself), had American-born children. There were those who, having been brought to America as babies, didn't even know the language of the country where they must reconstruct their lives; and some of the politicals faced torture and death at the other end of their impending journey.

The American Committee for Protection of Foreign Born, whose campaigns the GUARDIAN publicized, was the only organization resisting Washington's resolve to deport (for example) a pro-Peking Chinese laundryman to Chiang Kai-shek's Taiwan, and Manuel to Franco's Spain. While the committee struggled for their very lives Chen, the laundryman, tried to teach me Chinese in our quarters and Manuel sat all day knitting into sweaters the colors of the Spanish Republic. He had settled in America after fighting fascism with his Republic's navy and then, after two years in a North African concentration camp, with the Free French in World War II. Nine months after I got out, and two days before his scheduled shipment from the island to Spain, the committee won Manuel the right to go to Guatemala, where a job as cook awaited him. He had hardly reached there when U.S.-paid assassins replaced agrarian reformer Arbenz with the kind of tyranny that Dulles and Eisenhower thought appropriate for Latin America.

There was no further word of Manuel, the gentlest and most decent of men, and the GUARDIAN turned to the defense of Chung-soon and Choon Cha Kwak (see chapter 7). Other "cases" turned up almost every week. It was a big time for political deportations, especially of leftist newspaper editors whose parents had lacked the foresight to hatch them in America. The papers they edited were foreign-language ones mostly linked to the CP. One such editor, the Finn William Heikkinen, got a ten-year jail sentence for "willful failure to apply for travel documents" after a deportation order. These journalists were deportable for sharing the illusions of the Roosevelt-appointed Supreme Court Justice Frank Murphy, who had thus interpreted the Constitution:

> Once an alien lawfully enters and resides in this country, he becomes invested with the rights guaranteed by the Constitution to all people within our borders. Such rights include those protected by the First and Fifth Amendments and by the due process clause of the Fourteenth Amendment. None of these provisions acknowledges any distinction between citizens and resident aliens. They extend their inalienable privileges to all "persons" and guard against encroachments on these rights by Federal or State authority.

I cannot move on from Ellis Island without a word about Stuart Morris, a pink, cricket-blazered British churchman and pacifist with whom I used to chat in the yard facing the Statue of Liberty's backside. He had been nabbed and held for deportation on arrival from Britain to lecture on peace. At an Immigration "hearing" he had refused to omit American policies from his indictment of the cold war. Specifically, he proposed to criticize the invasion of North Korea, the rearming of Germany, and China's exclusion from the United Nations. His Oxford-accented comment to me echoes down the years: "That hearing chap said I couldn't enter America because I was 'a man who puts his conscience above the law.' Extraordinary, really!"

I brought out of Ellis Island many hundreds of letters from members of the GUARDIAN family, few of whom I had met. The uncensored, unrestricted mail had included gifts of pipes, home-killed meat, Florida mangoes, and Indian herbs with advice on "keeping regular." There were messages of good cheer invoking the Founding Fathers, the three standard versions of God, and Allah—many on postcards "because," as one wrote, "I want the authorities to read this too." My proudest acquisition on the island was a garish "shirt off my back" (not my size) from the proprietor of "Alex's Borscht Bowl" in Greenwich Village, a stubby immigrant from Russia. My most treasured letter was from 85-year-old DuBois in Brooklyn:

"I am beginning to feel that unless I get in jail soon I have not been doing my duty towards my nation and my times. Shirley [Ms. DuBois] says that deportation to almost any country just now does not seem to hurt or be so bad, but I am disposed to believe that one of our freedoms is to live where we will in the world so long as we do the needed work. This you have certainly done and I hope from my heart that we are not going to lose you."

Five days after Judge Weinfeld returned me to my desk the government began a series of appeals against his order, still relying solely on my invocation of the Fifth Amendment before Velde and McCarthy. For the Justice Department this by itself unmasked me as "a self-confessed betrayer of the country of his adoption" who was "dangerous" to allow "at large." Irritated by this approach, the Court of Appeals finally rejected the government's petition in December 1953, pointing out that I had blown nobody up in the six months since my imprisonment. I was to continue "at large," it ruled, until the deportation experts produced some evidence that I "was or had been."

"Large" hardly described the area in which my body might move under the bail terms: it comprised fragments of New York State and New Jersey and stopped dead at the Connecticut border. This Washington version of the "iron curtain" I shared with socialist country diplomats and spokesmen for certain UN-affiliated international organizations, whose circulation limits were often much narrower. The frontier for Dora (ex-Ms. Bertrand) Russell, for example, who came from London on UN business for the Women's International Democratic Federation, was the east side of Central Park West. She wanted to take her American grand-children to the Natural History Museum, and I to visit friends in Connecticut, but who could guarantee that we wouldn't overthrow the museum and the commonwealth by force and violence?

I also had to "report" every fortnight to an Immigration official, whose duty was to ask me: "Have you been seeing any Communists?" A bail condition was that I mustn't see any and could be hauled back to the island if I did, but my daily routine put me in the presence of people who might have been for all I knew (some of the GUARDIAN staff) or who certainly were. Once I was compelled in all honesty to answer: "Yes, last night—maybe two or three hundred, I didn't count." I was referring to diplomatic and other fellow guests at a Plaza Hotel party hosted by the Soviet ambassador. Abandoning hope for my better behavior, the Immigration man now stopped asking but left me at large while the clock ticked on toward my Hour.

It struck in August 1954 with an invitation to an Immigration Service "hearing" on the 10th. Between this and my final arrest, America's soul suffered irreparable losses with the deaths of Marc-antonio and Raymond Robins, and of Albert Einstein, one of the thimbleful of eminent intellectuals who had stood firm for peace and the Constitution. (Einstein and Thomas Mann, to whom New Deal America had given a haven from Hitlerism, did undying credit both to their adopted and their native countries.) The inquis-itors' prize informer, Harvey Matusow, confessed to being a liar and was sentenced to five years for "perjury" in at last telling the truth. Realization that a war against the Soviet Union was impossi-ble filtered into some higher circles (they never questioned its mo-rality or sanity) even as the media swelled their denunciations of those who "beat tomtoms of peace." The People's Republic of China (for the media, "Red China" or "Peiping") joined in the first gathering of "third world" ex-colonial nations at Bandoeng, Indonesia, and a year after Stalin's death Moscow absolved Anna Louise Strong.

I pointed out to GUARDIAN readers that for me, compared with threatened Spaniards, Greeks, and Koreans, deportation would be painless, but angry letters and extra "fight-back" dollars immediately poured in. All the essential questions at my "hearing" concerned 1937–38, that is, sixteen to seventeen years previously. Two slight acquaintances of those years, whose very existence I had forgotten, had been dug out and brought to New York to testify that they had known me as a Communist. This was enough to deport me under the Walter–McCarran immigration act of 1952, which provided (and still provides) that the Immigration Service's kangaroo court, not courts of law, had jurisdiction over deportable aliens. Since CP membership was and always had been legal, and I had for six years been making my position on that party clear in the GUARDIAN, the "hearing" was pure Lewis Carroll.

An Immigration man named Aaron Maltin presided over it as prosecutor, jury, and judge. On the advice of three "subversive" lawyers (Dambroff, Blanch Freedman, and Gloria Agrin) who defended me for bare expenses, I again remained silent to avoid a "contempt" indictment for rejecting questions about friends after answering about myself, or a "perjury" indictment for denying what the informers testified. (To "prove" the substance of their information the informers had been rehearsed in dates, places, and names, which were all false.) Such indictments could have meant a long stay in jail before deportation, and I didn't yet know that I could and would go there for nothing—that is, without being charged, let alone indicted, for any crime in the statute book.

The utmost my lawyers would approve was to swear an affidavit that I wasn't a Communist, and to rely on Claude Williams, the journalist Frank Scully, and a handwriting expert as defense witnesses. Claude toiled up from Alabama for the purpose but Maltin found the painstakingly truthful testimony of an unfrocked minister no more weighty than we expected. Frank—*Variety* columnist, papal knight, elected leader of Hollywood Democrats, and all-American record holder for time spent in hospitals—had taken his one leg and half of one lung into the desert in desperate flight from Los Angeles' poisoned air. He crutched himself into Los Angeles for two days of character witness testimony before a tribunal that Immigration set up there especially for him. As a former California official dealing with mental cases he testified to the "nuttiness" of one of the informers, and turned his ungovernable humor on the attribution of violent tendencies to me—"the sort," he exaggerated, "you would trust with your life." He suggested that Immigration "deport Belfrage to Hollywood and parole him in my care and I in his. The house next to ours has been empty for two years due, I suspect, to the smog, fog, grog, and hog-eat-hog that seem determined to make Los Angeles the Carthaginian ruins of the New World. I would like him to help in the fight to win back fresh, clean air for 4,000,000 people." (When Maltin came up with his "findings" on the 600-odd pages of testimony, in a long and solemn report after a long and solemn interval, he dealt with Scully effectively. He simply left Scully out, as if the special Los Angeles hearing had never been held.)

The performance in the Immigration Building on Columbus Avenue, New York, ran through several days in August and several more in September. It was astonishing what a time the inquisition could take to cook an already preroasted goose, and how much of the taxpayers' money—it must have run far into five figures—it could spend on so prosy an operation. Although nothing but the informers' testimony mattered for "conviction" purposes, scores of "questions" about other parts of my life were put while I sat silent. Did I publicly urge clemency for the Rosenbergs? (Yes.) Did I ask the editor of *Tribune des Nations* to publicize the Rosenberg case in France? (Yes; note the shamelessness about opening my mail.) Did I write a GUARDIAN article "rebutting the idea of an invasion of all Communist countries by spies to destroy communism"? (Odd way of putting it, but yes.) Did I speak for peace, for U.S.–Soviet friendship, for the Hollywood Ten, for CP leaders? (Absolutely.) Did I "advocate peace camps to instruct Americans who are afraid of the Soviet Union"? (Never thought of it, but why not?) Did I "have anything to do with placing three well-known Communists as editors" in Germany, and did I write a profile of Emil Carlebach for *Harper's* magazine? Did I (along with Hemingway, Steinbeck, and others) write for *New Masses* before the war? (Guilty, my lord—guilty as hell.)

The "fight-back" mobilized just about every American who heard about the case and would take the risks of guilt by association. Since the media were almost as silent as I was at the "hearing," these few tens of thousands consisted predominantly of GUARDIAN readers. The New York fight-backers looked and sounded good, though, at our post-"hearing" rally chaired by Jim in October. They jammed the shabby City Center Casino (the best hall we could get) to hear I. F. Stone, civil liberties lawyer Leonard Boudin, blacklisted movie actor Lionel Stander, Charles Collins (director of the "subversive" Liberty Book Club, himself threatened with deportation to Jamaica), and read-out messages from Claude and Frank. Stander submitted that "only an idiot" could believe I planned to overthrow the government. Boudin said: "We have become not a nation of doers but a nation of answerers of questions." (To such an audience of stubborn nonanswerers he might more aptly have said, "targets.") Stone, calling the attack on me "lawless, unconstitutional, disgraceful," flayed the press for "professing to be anti-McCarthy but refusing to speak up for any McCarthy victim below the rank of general." In effect, what the press was saying by its silence—in contrast with its wrath about editor Wechsler of the New York *Post,* who avoided McCarthy's trap by jumping into it with five dozen names—was that NATIONAL GUARDIAN wasn't a newspaper and hence I wasn't an editor. Thus there was nothing improper under the First Amendment even about the questions put to me about my work.

My own remarks at the rally appeared as a sixth anniversary Report to Readers. I recalled that the GUARDIAN had talked up about the Korean War, the Rosenbergs, the Trenton Six, the general gangsterism-piracy-provocation against socialist countries, and the humbug of Smith Act trials for "conspiracy to advocate violent overthrow." In return, the government had "started by conspiring to advocate, and proceeded to advocate" overthrow of the GUARDIAN, and finally, in the drive to deport me and other radical editors, arrived at the stage of actual overthrowing. It had left us no choice but to breast the waves or turn back and become trained pigeons for Hoover, McCarthy, & Co. Yet we had learned in six years that the United States had a progressive movement "including every age group from 10 to 90, every racial and national group, every religious or nonreligious philosophy, every intelligent view on the desirability or inevitability of some form of socialism for America. Every single man, woman, and child who is standing up against the terror is precious. Let us then do all we can to replace divisions within our movement in its broadest sense with a real attempt to understand and work out constructive unity on the great issues. We have to confound the Know-Nothings, but it can't be done by Know-It-Alls. Only after mastering the art of burying minor hatchets in our own circle can we speak with the voice of reason and morality, moderately and modestly, to all who will listen."

No believer in the White Queen philosophy of "sentence first, verdict afterwards," Maltin surfaced in December from his lucubrations to pronounce me guilty of my noncrime, adding in his decision: "It may be presumed that his [CP] membership continued." To explain the presumption, he quoted from a lawschool text: "An adulterous intercourse is presumed to continue. . . ."

By this time Ellis Island had been closed and regular jails were being used as receptacles for deportees. In a last effort to avoid my confinement in one of these, our lawyers appealed to the Immigration Appeals Board—the same judge-jury-prosecutor setup wearing another hat. While we awaited its verdict one newspaper, the Denver *Post,* published one reader's letter about the case. This evidence of the free-press tradition so startled us that we reprinted it in full:

The evil that men do [wrote John Blawis of Lakewood, Colo.] lives after them. . . . A 13-line item in the *Post,* headed "Red's Deportation Set," says that the government has ordered the deportation of Cedric Belfrage, editor of the NATIONAL GUARDIAN. That is all; evidently in the *Post*'s estimation this wraps up and disposes of the matter. But if Belfrage is deported, it will be, in addition to a body blow at the freedom of the press, a signal personal victory for the Appleton anthropoid [Joe McCarthy] and for the policy with which he is identified by name.

It was clear in 1953, when McCarthy rode much higher and Belfrage defied his inquisition one day, that many officials in executive departments were jumping when Joe gave the orders. That much has perhaps been corrected by now. But where is the victory, when mccarthyism is carried on without McCarthy? The *Post,* it seems, opposes not the principle, but only the man. McCarthyism is OK, just so long as McCarthy is not now connected with it. Let Brownell do it.

I define mccarthyism as a pretended anti-Communism, on false grounds, the true object of which is . . . to destroy by attrition the liberty of Americans, to force conformity on them and to make them the victims of despotism. Thus defined, the nature and the aim of mccarthyism are seen to fit like a pair of gloves the government's case for the deportation of Belfrage. They hope to deport him not because they know or care if he is or was a Communist, but because he edits a paper which opposes what it sees as the government's drive for world domination. The liberty to do this is dangerous, they fear—and you must begin trimming somewhere.

It will be ironic if, when the garbage collector named History has deposited Joe on the dump, his 'ism' is permitted this particular success, in which he can so truly claim to have made the first move.

In April I was still at large and the buds of spring smelled unusually sweet within my American "iron curtain." Vincent Hallinan, fresh from a California jail, came into town to help us commemorate the tenth anniversary of FDR's death and of the birth of the United Nations, in a "Fighting Rededication to the Principles of the New Deal." The media showered venom on FDR in "reappraising" his meeting at Yalta with Stalin and Churchill to organize peace. (The New York *Times*'s reappraisal was that FDR let Stalin, whose country fought and sacrificed most to destroy fascism, "emerge with loot beyond his wildest dreams.") In a recording titled "The Unforgotten Man" the GUARDIAN gathered American people's songs of the New Deal period with excerpts from FDR's talks and his report on Yalta.

As I walked from my brownstone floor-through on 65th Street one May morning, two men bundled me into a parked car beside which they had been lounging. Half an hour later I stood nude before the booking cop at West Street Federal House of Detention, who searched my orifices for weapons or drugs ("Lift 'em—

spread 'em''), took yet another set of my fingerprints, gave me prison clothing, and assigned me to a "maximum security" cell. Washington's political hoax extended even into the jail: over the booking-in desk hung a sign, FIGHT COMMUNISM WITH TRUTH DOLLARS. The jail was sprucely painted, to the last bar, in chartreuse. The "supreme kangaroo court" having rejected my appeal, here I must abide until we exhausted our pre-doomed appeals to courts of law, to consider whether Immigration had committed any improprieties under the Walter–McCarran law, which was one giant impropriety in itself.

Interviewed by one of our staff, Edward J. Shaughnessy, District Immigration Service Director, said I had earned jail-without-bail by being "actively engaged in advocating policies which we think involve national security." He couldn't have put it more plainly, since editing the GUARDIAN was my whole activity. He said Immigration now had "a spacious, cheerful room on Washington St." to replace Ellis Island as deportee deposit, but I was one of a half-dozen deemed unworthy of it because we either threatened "national security," or had "the worst police records," or "might disturb the routine of detention facilities."

I sent word to West Street's warden that I wouldn't eat until he widened my "curtain" (real iron this time) from the locked cell to the full amplitude of the jail, which included an exercise roof open to inmates for an hour a day. The hunger strike worked and, after a period in the jail "hospital," though I wasn't sick, I emerged to consort freely with my fellow criminals: good human beings for the most part, and an invaluable experience for me in retrospect. We were allowed to chat via a sort of telephone through a glass barrier with three predesignated visitors a week for a total of half an hour, and to send and receive censored mail to and from six predesignated correspondents. My requests to receive *The Nation,* the London *New Statesman,* and my own paper were rejected.

Our chartreuse home became a sweatbox as summer advanced, the sultry air throbbing with Hit Parade songs endlessly repeated, from a radio tuned to split the least sensitive ear. A permanent scar was left on my soul by Nat "King" Cole, the most popular moaner of the day. From time to time I was brought out (with orifice searches at each departure and return) for courtroom proceedings which could only extend my stay in the hoosegow, since deportees had no standing under the law. Aware as I was of this, I expatiated futilely before a bow-tied federal judge named Archie Dawson about the nature of the GUARDIAN and my political views; he listened inattentively and denied bail because I invoked the Fifth Amendment on other questions. Dawson and the other appeals echelons had only, of course, to read the GUARDIAN for a full exposition of where I stood: no one in America lived politically in a more transparent goldfish bowl than I. By late June we had come to the last stop before the New York port of embarkation—a single Justice (the court not being in session) of the U.S. Supreme Court.

After repeated nagging from Jim, who worked like a dog for any conceivable opening, the New York *Times* had published in mid-June a letter from him and an editorial. All his comments about press freedom were deleted from the letter (''for space''), leaving only his protest against my imprisonment without bail. The editorial, delicately omitting my name and function, deplored the detention of deportees in regular jails instead of ''appropriate places'' (the deportation law's term) and the denial of access to bond. Shaughnessy explained to the *Times* that I and the six other deportees were in West Street because we were ''rough tough criminal types and agitators.'' The GUARDIAN was able to reprint four protesting editorials about my ''case,'' all from ''subversive'' publications (*Iowa Union Farmer, The Nation,* I. F. Stone's *Weekly, Monthly Review*), but when I had sojourned six weeks in West Street a lone respectable voice was heard from St. Louis. Naming me and the GUARDIAN, the *Post-Dispatch* ''held no brief'' for my views (who would expect it to?) but saw ''a threat to our democratic institutions.'' Washington's top deportation man now entered the ring on a shrill note. He was a buddy of President Eisenhower named General Joseph Swing. I was imprisoned without bail or charges of crime, he said, because my ''political beliefs are allied to a worldwide conspiracy to destroy the Free World,'' and it was all my own fault because we were appealing. I was still capable of surprise that even this admission of government lawlessness drew no comment from the media.

This and the muffled New York *Times* rebuke had "no effect on Attorney General Brownell," the GUARDIAN editorialized, except that he "responded by bringing Harry Bridges to trial for the fifth time, by asking a compliant slatternly Congress to double the penalties under the Smith Act, and by holding Belfrage in prison in violation of every concept of Anglo-Saxon law." The GUARDIAN added that we seven in West St. had addressed a joint letter to the *Times* commenting on its editorial and describing our conditions, but that West Street wouldn't let it go out. (I hadn't included the editor of the *Times,* the jail authorities explained, in my list of correspondents.) Such nuggets of information from behind my curtain I could smuggle out through Jim and my lawyers who paid me regular, heartwarming visits. They in turn brightened my captivity with such nuggets as the American Civil Liberties Union's beef that we seven were jailed without having been sentenced for any crime. That was the size of the error for ACLU, but it did finally prod the *Times* into mentioning my name in a news item.

The days in the chartreuse sweatbox lengthened into three months of collapsing hope, of human interest and boredom and crossword puzzles and study: I read all the works of Mark Twain that are proper for jailbird consumption, reveled in Whitman, and established once and for all my distaste for Trollope. Months threaded with that note of wild absurdity which had persisted through all my "dramatic" experiences. I shared one cell with a pot-smoking philosopher who, in defense of his weed, proved that deprivation of it affected him less than alcoholic deprivation affected me; another with a 16-year-old Puerto Rican, a handsome and wonderful lad, who was beginning a two-year term because a package he agreed to carry for a dollar turned out to contain pot. My exchanges of political and criminal anti-Establishment talk in the jail library with a group of bank robbers, who had the best literary taste of any of the inmates, were mutually educational. The tales of a confidence man who was in for impersonating an American admiral (he wasn't even American) provided rich and rare entertainment as we walked up and down the roof in the exercise hour. I learned a lot about inquisitorial law from Gloria Agrin, the lawyer who visited me most frequently. She explained that the absence of any charge against me was the precise reason why I couldn't get out. "If you'd committed any crime," she said, "we could bail you out tomorrow."

"What about throwing a brick at the warden?" I asked her. "Then I'd be charged with assault and battery and we'd be off to the races."

"You could," she said, "but I don't advise it," and I didn't.

By all relative standards the mildness of my jail experience was, I realized, grotesque. In one cell I inherited a bunk from Julius Rosenberg, and this sharpened my awareness of the vast jail population all over the world who, mentally and physically tortured by professional sadists, would only emerge crippled or in a coffin.

In the second week of August Justice Harlan, acting for the Supreme Court, gave me the expected brush-off. For Ethel and Julius the Supreme Court's refusal to consider their case had meant a summons to the cemetery. For me it meant no more than dislocation of my life and a boat-ride to Britain, where the press was treating me sympathetically and questions had even been asked in Parliament. The one possibility of further delay was an appeal to the full Supreme Court when it reconvened. Since this might involve many more, and almost certainly futile, months in West St., Jim, Jack, the lawyers, and everyone agreed that we should give up. I liked Jim's GUARDIAN comment on this decision: I was "not replaceable" but "not indispensable—no man is."

After all, we thought, I could do the paper some good by becoming an "editor-in-exile." On the same grounds that made me deportable, no one else on the staff could get a passport to leave. But I would be able to travel to, and report with an American slant from, every country on earth except one.

My orifices inspected for the last time, I left with two Immigration guards for the Holland-America Line pier with my "luggage" (the contents of my pockets when I entered jail) in a paper bag.

My American wife joined me there with our worldly goods in thirty-four bags and boxes. There wasn't room in our cabin for the friends who brought flowers and champagne to enliven our voyage into exile. Some media reporters turned up and conducted an interview with a politeness I hadn't learned to expect from them. They took small notice of former Secretary of State Dean Acheson, who was our fellow-passenger. By becoming an exile I seemed also to be becoming quasi-respectable. One reporter took me aside to say he was jealous. He asked how one proceeded to get heaved out of America and I said, "As if you didn't know!" The basic essential, of course, was to have had a geographically non-prescient mother.

We embraced everyone and they formed a big crowd on the pier, waving and blowing kisses. We thanked my two guards, with whom we had soon got on first-name terms, for their considerateness to us. Theirs were the last hands we shook in America. They had done their duty of seeing that I was incontestably on the ship when she pulled out, and waiting to confirm that I didn't jump off and swim back. I thought they looked forlorn as they hunched back along the pier, to report for the next job of ejecting heretics from America.

Postscript [**J.A.**] "Congress shall make no law . . . abridging the freedom of the press . . ." No other country in the world has such a guarantee written into its Constitution; and when the founding fathers placed that provision in the First Amendment of the Bill of Rights they meant precisely what they said: no law on the books and no legislation proposed for the future could in any way tamper with the gathering, editing, or publication of news and comment in any newspaper, big or small, reactionary or radical.

When Cedric was picked up on the street and thrown into the federal prison on West Street, under the authority of the Walter–McCarran Immigration Act, we issued this statement:

"This question must be asked: Has Belfrage been hounded for two years because he is the editor of a weekly newspaper which has been highly critical of the Washington Administration's cold war policies and attack on civil liberties at home? If that is the case, then no American newspaper is safe from persecution. The First Amendment is in danger whether the attack is made on a small weekly or a great American daily."

The question of course had been answered several times in the affirmative by statements and actions of the inquisitors (Velde, McCarthy); of the Immigration authorities (Shaughnessy, Swing); and, by negation, of the court which yielded to the jurisdiction of a federal agency (the Immigration Service of the Department of Justice) as superseding its own—and therefore the Constitution. Belfrage was being hounded because he was the editor of a dissenting newspaper, and outside the protection of the cold war umbrella.

When New York *Post* editor Wechsler went through his hearing before McCarthy, just before our appearance, he repeatedly insisted that McCarthy was violating his First Amendment rights. The GUARDIAN supported him in that contention. The transcript of his hearing was sent to the American Society of Newspaper Editors, which appointed a special committee to study and comment on all relevant material in the case. The eleven members were unable to agree whether freedom of the press had been infringed in the Wechsler hearing, but four of them felt strongly enough to issue a supplementary report which included a splendid interpretation of the First Amendment and the responsibility of the press:

"Newspapermen, by the very choice of their profession, avail themselves of the privileges and immunities of a free press, guaranteed in the Constitution, and they assume at the same time certain obligations and duties, not the least among which is to defend the freedom of the press against all attack. Where such an invasion of freedom occurs, other citizens may speak or remain silent without being identified with trespass; but the silence of the press is invariably construed, and properly construed, as an indication that no trespass has occurred and its silence inevitably will be summoned in support of like trespasses in the future. In our opinion, therefore, whatever inconvenience results, whatever controversy ensues, we are compelled by every command of duty to brand this and every threat to freedom of the press, from whatever source, as a peril to American freedom."

With this ringing affirmation in mind, when Cedric was dumped into prison I wrote to Wechsler, whom I had known from my days on the *Post,* and to J. R. Wiggins, then managing editor of the Washington *Post,* who had chaired the ASNE committee sifting the Wechsler testimony. I outlined the Belfrage case, noted the obvious political differences between our papers, and said it was the very expression of these differences that the First Amendment guarantees for the press so zealously guarded. Neither editor responded—not even with an acknowledgment of my letter.

I wrote also to the St. Louis *Post-Dispatch.* Its editorial page was in the hands of Irving Dilliard, a Jeffersonian democrat whose dogged defense of the Bill of Rights matched that of two great Supreme Court justices about whom he would write at length—Hugo Black and William O. Douglas. The *Post-Dispatch* published an excellent editorial, as did the York *Gazette & Daily.* (It was unfortunate that the Court was not in session during the last stages of the Belfrage fight; but even if it had been, it is doubtful whether we would have fared better there—the Court majority was in thrall to Chief Justice Fred Vinson, a political crony appointee of President Truman.)

The story of my negotiations with the *Times* is instructive. My original letter to the editor emphasized that Cedric had not been convicted or even accused of any crime and that his detention without bail was outrageous. Beyond that, I wrote, the principle of freedom of the press was deeply involved since Cedric's persecution was clearly an attempt to silence the GUARDIAN. I urged that the letter be printed and that an editorial on these issues be considered.

A few days later a member of the *Times* editorial board phoned to say that the letter had been accepted for publication, and that an editorial also would appear in the same issue. But the letter was too long: would I agree to certain deletions? I asked what they were and the letter, as suggested for publication, was read to me. All the deletions concerned the freedom of the press issue. Thus I was confronted with a dilemma: if I stood on principle and demanded all or nothing, most likely neither the letter nor the editorial would appear. The important first step, I felt, was to get Cedric out of prison. If the double dose of the letter was too much for the *Times,* perhaps a single-dose dialectic approach on my part was indicated. I agreed to the deletions and both letter and editorial were published.

I well remember those Saturday mornings when I walked through the midsummer heat of Greenwich Village to the prison on West Street for my half-hour with Cedric. Each week he looked paler and more hollow-eyed, and invariably he wore a T-shirt with a hole in it, as though the commissary had singled him out for special ventilation. His mood was cheerfully resigned, even stoic. From the attitude of the other prisoners we could see that he was popular.

Sometimes, when we could get past the privileged-visitor regulations, Jack McManus would come with me, as he did on my last visit. Jack and I had discussed this occasion carefully and had come to the conclusion, in consultation with the lawyers, that we could not be accomplices to allowing Cedric to rot away in a cell. No one knew better than I that what oppressed Cedric most was not so much the lack of freedom as the lack of freedom to work. For if there was one quality about him that struck me from the beginning of our collaboration, it was his need for work. In idleness he withered.

So on this last visit, we pierced the plateglass curtain by asking how long he felt he could remain in prison. He said: "I'll stay here till hell freezes over, if it's necessary." We appreciate that, we said, "but we have made up your mind for you. We have decided that you should accept deportation, go to England, and continue working for the GUARDIAN." He protested, but the word "work" was the key, and he yielded.

As we left the prison, Jack said: "The dirty sons of bitches."

Jack wrote the lead to the Belfrage departure story in our issue of August 22, 1955: "America banished one of its most devoted sons last week in the person of Cedric Henning Belfrage, editor of this newspaper. With his wife, the GUARDIAN editor sailed at noon, Monday, August 15, on the Holland-America liner *Nieuw Amsterdam* for his native England under a deportation order demanded 27 months ago by Senator Joseph McCarthy.''

If the perpetrators (as the New York cops say) thought they were shutting Cedric up or crippling the GUARDIAN, they had another think coming. But if we thought we were free of the inquisitors, so did we.

Life Without Father

[**J.A.**] In the dog days of 1955 when Cedric sweltered in jail, a hound from the Mississippi bayou country came sniffing around Times Square. James O. Eastland, squire of Sunflower County, Defender of the White Christian Faith, was by ancient rite of seniority chairman of the Senate Judiciary Committee and of its Internal Security Subcommittee. The subcommittee was authorized to investigate "the extent and effect of subversive activities in the United States . . . including, but not limited to, espionage, sabotage, and infiltration by persons . . . seeking to overthrow the government by force and violence."

Eastland's chief counsel was an unpleasant fellow of uncertain vintage named Jay C. Sourwine. An intimate of Senator Pat McCarran, he had helped the Nevada troglodyte to shape the McCarran and McCarran–Walter acts. He shared McCarran's and Eastland's aversion for the New York *Times* which, by calling both acts undemocratic and by applauding the Supreme Court's school-desegregation decision a year earlier, had shown itself to be a command post for inkstained overthrowers.

That June, Eastland's subcommittee opened hearings on "subversion in the press." Its first witness was Winston Burdett, a CBS correspondent whose pear-shaped tones had for years mingled with

St. Peter's bells to convey the mood of Rome to America (and at this writing still do). Burdett testified to a career of inept espionage for the Soviet Union from European capitals—a tale of rendezvous in hotel rooms, on snow-swept street corners, and in movie houses in Sweden (where, he revealed, "Swedish movies" were shown). This third-rate thriller narrative set the stage for Burdett's confession that, in the late 1930s, he had belonged to a CP cell at the Brooklyn *Eagle* (now defunct). He named thirteen alleged cellmates and ten others who, he said, were Communists at the time, among them, some of the Newspaper Guild's most effective early leaders. One of the thirteen was Melvin Barnet, a bookish, witty Harvard classmate of mine, whom I would have nominated least likely to succeed in overthrowing Brooklyn's Borough Hall. Burdett had been best man at Barnet's wedding. Barnet, at the time a copy editor in the *Times* financial department, was one of eighteen newspapermen whom Eastland summoned as a result of Burdett's testimony. Asked by his employers what his "demeanor" would be before the committee, Barnet told them he had been a CP member, no longer was, and would "avail himself" of the Fifth Amendment for questions prior to 1942. Nothing was said on that occasion about the future of his job.

At the hearing in July in Washington, Barnet did just what he told his bosses he would do. As he left the stand he was handed a telegram from Arthur Hays Sulzberger, publisher of the *Times*. It said he had been discharged because his testimony (given after the telegram was prepared) had "caused the *Times* to lose confidence" in him. Thus the *Times,* having editorially defended the right of witnesses' to the Fifth Amendment, fired a staff member for invoking it.

Determined to save his job, Barnet went through a months-long series of charades with the *Times* and the Guild, protesting against his own colleagues' "apparent compulsion not only to kick me in the pants but to belabor me elsewhere below the belt." He kept his sense of humor but lost his job. The New York Guild leadership not only retreated from any legitimate battle, but polled its members for—and received—authorization to abandon any Fifth

Amendment-invoking member. It was the Guild's "irrevocable stand," said its president Joseph P. Murphy, that it would "have no part in the defense" of any member "proved to be" a Communist.

Barnet had company that summer. Fired for the same reason were a *Daily News* staff member, and a former *Daily Mirror* employee who had become publicity director of the National Municipal League. The Washington *Post* condoned the firings but worried that Eastland's circus would "endanger American principles . . . if [it] is now . . . to make the press the particular object of its investigations." At the same time the *Post,* exhorting all ex-Communists to confess and name others, took the view that exercising the Constitutional right to refuse to inform was un-American.

After firing Barnet ("for lack of candor," an amended explanation said) the *Times* resumed its defense of the First and Fifth amendments and rejected "a tightly controlled society in which every dissenter . . . is enchained in a futile attempt to ensure conformity in the name of security." This hybrid approach failed, however, to secure the *Times* against the hound dog: Eastland subpoenaed thirty-eight more journalists (mostly present or former *Times* employees) for the third week in November. When Sourwine discovered that that was Freedom of the Press Week, the hearings were set back.

Having once worked for the *Times,* and having become a potential embarrassment to it by our subsequent "demeanor," Jack McManus and I were among the thirty-eight. At the GUARDIAN, the subpoena servers got a cool reception; at the *Times,* management graciously installed them in a reception room to which it delivered the victims. Management also suggested that employees with scruples against informing should speak their piece in private to the FBI; then, after testifying fully to Eastland about themselves, they could be silent about their associates on the ground that they had already told all to Hoover. Some were advised to use the cadaver route to get off the hook—simply name one or two dead Communists. Two editorial staff members told management they would invoke the Fifth. They were given the opportunity to resign; one did, the other refused and was fired.

Press coverage of the hearings, finally held in January 1956, was wary. At first there had been a "gentleman's agreement" not to publish the witnesses' names—except for Jack and myself. We told reporters we wanted the public to know, but that agreement of course yielded to the "right to know" once the hearings were under way. In a typically righteous admonition that came too late (but hadn't come at all when Cedric was under McCarthy's fire), the New York *Post* said it would be tragic if "the pressure of the inquisition convinced the *Times* that men who invoke the historic protection of the Bill of Rights are disqualified from future service in our profession."

Clayton Knowles, one of the only two *Times* men who were fully cooperative, provided Eastland with a geyser of information about colleagues who had been pioneer Guild organizers. Three employees invoked the First Amendment, held their jobs, but ended with jail sentences for "contempt." (The convictions were upset after years of litigation, not on the free press issue but on technicalities.) A *Mirror* rewrite man who invoked the Fifth, and *Daily News* reporter William A. Price, who invoked the First, were both fired. (Price's "contempt" conviction for so doing would likewise be thrown out on technicalities. He later joined the GUARDIAN staff.)

Although Jack and I had been called as ex-*Times*men, Sourwine appreciated the extra bonus provided by the GUARDIAN. There was intense grilling on our publication of the Korean POWs' names and letters in 1951. Had we tried to check their authenticity? (The Defense Department had long since verified them.) Were the letters selected because they were critical of the United States? (Very few were; most were desperate pleas for a link with home.) There were implications of treason in our contact with John W. Powell, editor of the *China Monthly Review*, main source of the names. Jack suffered most of this line of questioning. I went through the litany of Germany as I had before Joe McCarthy, and my past newspaper history, stopping dead at questions about the GUARDIAN.

On the point of dismissing me Sourwine leaned over to confer with Senator William Jenner, a legendary tippler from Indiana, then addressed me: "Do you know William Hinton?" I asked the unflappable Nat Dambroff (always at our side in these ordeals) if I should answer that and he said: "Who the hell is Hinton?" There was time to tell Nat that Hinton had trained with me at Fort Benning in 1945, had gone to China when I went to Germany, and had later returned to China on his own as an agricultural expert.* Nat shrugged his permission and I missed the danger signal: both Powell and Hinton (as I should have remembered) had tangled with this same committee, amid cries of "treason," when they returned from China in 1953. In a transparently devious effort to escape the trap I tried to persuade the inquisitors that all Hinton and I talked about at our last meeting (dinner at my house) was the improvement of milch-cow breeds in Shansi province. What I did not disclose was the subversive menu on that evening—a Peking duck (Hinton insisted it was a Szechuan duck), which Grambs prepared for our guest. Apart from violating the privacy of the kitchen, this would have marked my wife as a Red Chinese agent—despite the fact that her hard-shell Baptist grandfather, like Eastland a Southern product, had labored as a missionary in China to convert the heathen to Eastland's brand of Christianity.

We only realized how close we had come to a new tangle with the authorities when, later that year, Powell and his *China Monthly Review* colleague, Julian Schuman, were indicted on a sedition charge stemming from their publication of the POW names. Thus was born another GUARDIAN cause—the Powell–Schuman case which, after thousands of dollars had been spent in legal fees, was thrown out of court for lack of serious evidence. The dismissal was barely noticed by the media, but the flood of publicity before and during the inquisitorial and indictment proceedings served as an effective damper on anyone seeking to report honestly on China. But such intimidation, after all, was what the inquisitorial committees were for.

The hearings generated little public controversy or interest.

---

*In 1966 Monthly Review Press published Hinton's *Fanshen, a Documentary of Revolution in a Chinese Village,* a widely praised narrative of rural life in the new China.

LIFE WITHOUT FATHER

America was getting sick of the circuses, and the repression had been so institutionalized that the government no longer encouraged the extravaganza approach. Eastland's own satisfied comment must have brought moans of despair from the catacombs holding the bones of John Peter Zenger and Elijah Parish Lovejoy: "We've gotten more cooperation from newspaper men than from any other group in the country, and we have had witnesses from most of the professions." The newspaper world, however, continued solemnly debating whether the *Times* was being singled out and whether Eastland was violating the First Amendment guarantee of a free press. The *Times* made its own position clear on the last day of the hearings: the press was not sacrosanct so long as an inquiry into it was "conducted in good faith and not motivated by ulterior purpose"; the *Times,* "so far as we are aware," was 100 percent Communist-free. (I could not help thinking of the Nazi phrase *Judenrein,* cleansed of Jews, and the fact that no management ever showed concern about fascists on its staff.) The *Times* would judge cases of former Communists on individual merits: it did not subscribe to the "irremediable sin" doctrine and would acknowledge atonement "through good performance for past error."

On the other hand it did believe that Eastland had "aimed with particular emphasis at the New York *Times . . .* because of its opposition to many of the things for which [Eastland, Jenner, and Sourwine] stand." And "if this is the tactic," and "if further evidence reveals that the real purpose of the present inquiry is to demonstrate that a free newspaper's policies can be swayed by Congressional pressure, then we say to Mr. Eastland . . . this newspaper will continue to determine its own policies."

The paper, flinging down this iffy gauntlet, proclaiming that it would not yield to Eastland, had already done just that (whether under pressure or voluntarily, and if voluntarily then all the more reprehensibly), by firing the three "Fifth Amendment" employees. In any case the *Times* was pleased with itself, and editorials appearing elsewhere (although many papers remained silent) indicated that the media could by and large live with the *Times*'s position. Against the tampering with freedom of the press, which was already far advanced, the dominant counterblast was, Don't let us catch anyone tampering. The GUARDIAN responded differently after the hearings:

We take with a grain of salt—not to mention aspirin—all the press protestations which fail to countenance the real menace in the situation: the fact that the press of this country which disputes the McCarran Act thesis of the "Communist conspiracy" is under constant harassment and has been for at least seven years. The government has conducted a thousand or more legal actions designed to prove the existence of such a conspiracy. And with all its informers, liars, and parrots, it has never succeeded in producing a jot of evidence—although it has executed two people, jailed dozens, and deported hundreds for this alleged crime. Press freedom to support the Cold War and the Big Lie on which it has been based has never been in jeopardy; what is at stake is freedom to oppose.

We ended with a Nazarene warning: "Inasmuch as ye have done it unto one of the least of my brethren, ye have done it unto me." We expected our biggest brother to ignore the warning, and later in 1956 it was done unto him again: the Solvay Board of Education in Onondaga County, N.Y., forced the town's high school senior class to cancel a subscription to the *Times* because of its "Communist slant." The instigating board member was also auditor of the Syracuse *Post-Standard,* which was then serializing a 100-page handbook on communism, prepared by the Eastland committee. Even after purging its financial copy editor Barnet, the *Times* was still suspect.

All this inquisitorial hoopla took place more than a year after Cedric had gone over the horizon. The triumvirate on the home grounds had become a duumvirate. I succeeded to the title of editor-in-residence, while Cedric became editor-in-exile. Jack remained intact as general manager. On advice of lawyer and business consultants, Cedric turned over to us his nonproductive $100 share in Weekly Guardian Associates Inc., and Jack and I, with $150 each of nonproductive stock, became partners in ownership of the GUARDIAN. Cedric said he felt no pain in surrendering his "share of the ill will" provided that he retained, as he felt he did, and did, his share of the good will. We continued the practice of including the staff in all decisions affecting the contents and life of the paper.

There were attending tensions—Cedric and I had become so accustomed to working in harness that we could almost read each other's minds, and whatever differences we had were easily resolved. Temperamentally, Jack and I tended to clash more—not so much on basic issues as on the approach to these issues. For example, when Polish Jewish Communists presented disturbing evidence of antisemitism in the Soviet Union, I felt we must examine and comment on it. Jack was insistent that we wait until all possible evidence was in. Adamant, I wrote an editorial to which Jack took exception as too strong. I suggested, somewhat acidly, that he try his hand. It was typical of Jack's devil's-advocate approach that he argued his adversary up the wall and then conceded beyond the position confronting him: he wrote an editorial stronger than mine. I worked over both drafts and achieved a fully acceptable compromise.

At this time also staff fissures appeared and there were attempts to pit Jack and me against each other. They stemmed partly from the upheaval in the American left caused by Khrushchev's indictment of Stalin, and partly from the formation of internal power blocs believing they had the key to circulation growth. Here Jack and I held firm: we insisted on open argument and decision making, persuaded that our model of democratic operation had yet to be proved faulty. These divisive efforts failed and the alliance remained unbroken.

In the adversity of Cedric's eviction there were benefits too. Washington's denial of passports to all who wouldn't answer its unconstitutional "Are you or have you ever been?" questionnaire had forced upon us a tendency to parochialism, and Cedric's outside-looking-in viewpoint, now that he could roam the world with access to non-American minds and experiences, provided a positive balance. A correspondence began between him and myself which, over the next dozen years, filled two massive folders (an invaluable source for writing this book). With the frankness of long habit we ranged from the smallest problems of the GUARDIAN and of Cedric's "exile" functions to the great political issues of the day, with all their interconnecting implications.

While we were still combing Eastland out of our hair and adjusting to remote-control connection with the triumvirate's third member, the fiercest political gale from the east struck us amidships. The first blast was Khrushchev's sensational speech, at the Twentieth Soviet CP Congress in February 1956, about Stalin and his era.

According to a GUARDIAN report later that year from Ralph Parker in Moscow, delegates fainted and Khrushchev sobbed as he depicted the horrors of the "cult of personality" years: the sacrifice of millions of the Soviet Union's best lives, the stifling of its people's creative force, the appalling military and political blunders. Communists all over the world were thrown into anguish and turmoil. Speaking for Soviet writers, Alexander Fadeyev said they had "made ideology a cross-grained shrew" by their "excesses and stiffness," and then killed himself. In Peking Liu Ting-yi, head of the CP propaganda department, said: "Let flowers of all seasons bloom together and let diverse schools of thought contend."

In our pages thousands of words sprouted about the "revelations," as they were called. We sought information wherever we could find it. When the *Times* obtained an obviously authentic version of Khrushchev's speech, we published major portions of it. We reported world reactions and our Mailbag brimmed over with pros and cons about Stalin. As the full story seeped out the pros became fewer, but they never disappeared.

From Poland Ursula Wassermann reported on a new spirit of freedom and independence, to be demonstrated not long thereafter in the new Gomulka government's defiance of Khrushchev. From there she went to Hungary, where the despised Matyas Rakosi had been deposed the previous summer and moved into sanctuary in the Soviet Union. A new regime (tarred with the same brush) was temporizing. There was great restlessness in the country. A meeting of the Petöfi Circle, originally founded by Hungary's youth movement, in late June 1956 drew an audience of 8,000 to discuss freedom of the press. The writer Tibor Dery spoke of the blindness of the regime:

"They underestimate the people's sense of honor and its moral force; its capacity to think and create. But we who have always believed in our people . . . have the duty to create conditions under which love of life and love of work can once again function normally. The prerequisite for such conditions is honest thinking."

As Dery finished, the audience went wild. The Party's answer was expulsion. When Ursula spoke with Dery in September, he was unrehabilitated and unrepentant. He told her: "The fight today is concerned with the concept of socialist democracy. The fight is hard and all the harder because we ourselves have not yet completely clarified this concept. I trust that we will reach our goal in the best and, I believe, the only possible way: through the closest contact with the realities of life."

The realities exploded a month later with the ouster of the government, installation of Imre Nagy (long an opponent of Rakosi) as the new leader, eruption of counterrevolutionary mayhem by Hungarian fascists, and Soviet occupation of Budapest and major Hungarian centers. The components of the explosion, including manipulation by the CIA, would emerge later, but a decisive factor was clear from the start: the yearning of rank-and-file Hungarian Communists for a genuine socialist society in which people would be participating human beings rather than "norms."

We kept on publishing everything we believed factual and pertinent. In January 1957, Anna Louise Strong wrote: "The Hungarian tragedy grew from old enmities, inflamed by Communist stupidities and American agents' plots. Moscow bears heavy blame, not for the final intervention but for eleven years of bad policies which in the end made intervention necessary. . . . The Hungarian tragedy destroyed socialism as 'man's dream.' But it is still man's tool for a third of the earth's people. If we of the West can keep our spies, provocateurs, and H-bombs off them, they will remodel it to whatever ends men desire. That is what we owe the dead in Hungary . . . that they may not have died in vain."

Anna Louise expressed our position well. Our sympathies in the situation were consistent with the point of view represented by Dery, who went to prison soon after the Soviet occupation (he was released when common sense was restored). At the same time it was plain that the stupidities of Soviet leaders and the Rakosi regime had paved the way—with a strong assist from Western intelligence—for a revival of the religious/fascist centers of power. Whether they would have taken over if the Soviet army had not, no one could know. But if they had, the Budapest bloodletting in October 1956 would have paled in comparison with the butchery that would have ensued. In any case, the Hungarian story was far from finished, and we maintained the watch.

These tumultuous events had a profound effect upon what most concerned the GUARDIAN—left politics in America.

In customary fashion the presidential campaign of 1956 began more than a year before the election. Among the Democrats, cold war architect Averell Harriman was competing with Adlai Stevenson to dislodge President-General Eisenhower who, putt by putt, was working his way to the Great Eighteenth Hole of immortality. The Democrats ensured their defeat by agreeing with the Republicans to remove foreign policy as a campaign issue. For us there was no "lesser evil" and we documented the reasons week by week.

To underscore our disagreement with the CP's "mainstream theory" we took a text from Thoreau. For seven years, we said, we had been reporting great victories by the people of half the world while at home there was little but retreat and frustration. This could be attributed in part to our being forced to play on the enemy's ground, to accept premises in which we did not believe, to argue with tyranny according to the rules of the tyrants.

The American left, we said, had not always acted politically but rather played politics, concentrating on elections and conventions—the trappings of politics which most Americans had long known to be false reflections of American life. "In a passion for conformity with what it conceives to be the American way, the left

LIFE WITHOUT FATHER

in our country does reverence to the two party system and has come to look with hopelessness on the status of a minority party. Those on the left who have taken this hopeless course are perhaps the best and the bravest radicals and, as such, have grown lonely. We might well exhume that nature-loving, freedom-loving revolutionary Henry David Thoreau from his shrine and listen to him: 'A minority is powerless while it conforms to the majority; it is not even a minority then; but it is irresistible when it clogs by its whole weight.' ''

Thoreau wrote those words in *Civil Disobedience* in 1849, when the United States was engaged in a monstrous war against Mexico, when it had four million slaves, and when citizens who fought too openly against the slave-holders were hanged or imprisoned. ''How does it become a man to behave toward this American government today?'' Thoreau asked. ''I answer that he cannot without disgrace be associated with it. I cannot for an instant recognize that political organization as my government which is the *slave's* government also.''

And in 1956, we wrote, ''we are to be presented with Republican and Democratic candidates, and no one expects them to have many more qualifications beyond their availability. Is the choice between such candidates really the decisive one? Will it determine the future of American liberties and the peace of the world? 'Cast your whole vote,' Thoreau said, 'not a strip of paper merely, but your whole influence.' Perhaps the turning point will come in our times when we will discover how to cast our whole influence, when we will not measure victories and defeats by the tallies of available candidates, when we will not build, or dismantle, organizations according to election returns. Perhaps one day we will build an organization that is unashamedly a minority—but a minority untrammeled by ground rules. We must assert the right to vigorous dissent, to battle every injustice and to fight for peace without the sanction of any tribunal. Where we can talk through the ballot, let us talk—and where we cannot, let us find better means to talk to the people.''

The response from the Communists came in two cautiously respectful *Worker* articles elaborating their mainstream theory, insisting that progressives could better advance a third party if at that stage they helped organize "that kind of independent activity within the major parties, than by remaining aloof, waiting majestically for the workers eventually to come to them and priding themselves on being true to principle. . . . The GUARDIAN," said the *Worker,* "charges the left with sowing illusions in the major parties. The contrary is true. The illusions are there. It is our view that the way to dispel them is in practice, in activity directed toward advancing the program and nature of the candidates of the Democratic Party against the resistance of the politicians of that party. The GUARDIAN would leave the masses with their illusions and withdraw to Walden."

How Democratic candidates could be separated from Democratic politicians (almost invariably identical twins) the *Worker* did not say. In any case, we neither supported the Democrats in 1956 (it was a landslide for Ike over Adlai) nor retired to Walden. We plowed ahead on our course and helped into being in 1957 the American Forum for Socialist Education, whose title I had suggested. It was led by A. J. Muste, pacifist leader of the Fellowship of Reconciliation, and had a national committee including educators, trade union officials, and individuals of widely divergent tendencies—Communists, Socialists, Trotskyists. This small miracle resulted from the patient efforts of Jack McManus, who became a vice-president along with Mulford Q. Sibley of the University of Minnesota, Bayard Rustin of the War Resisters League, Kermit Eby of the University of Chicago, and others.

The purpose of the Forum was to promote "study and serious untrammeled political discussion among all elements that think of themselves as related to historic socialist and labor traditions, values and objectives, however deep and bitter their differences may have been." The plan was for branches on a national scale. Some were established, and some polite public forums were held, but the organization as a whole did not flourish. The varying political factions were civil but not compromising, and lack of funds and communications apparatus worked against a continuing effort. The American Forum simply petered out.

LIFE WITHOUT FATHER

One outgrowth, however, was the formation in 1957–58 of the Independent–Socialist ticket for the New York State elections of 1958, with Jack making his third race for governor, Annette T. Rubinstein, author and educator, as candidate for lieutenant governor, and Corliss Lamont for U.S. senator. Simultaneous opposition came from the cobwebbed Socialist Party-Social Democratic Federation (warning that the new group was dominated by "pro-Soviet" elements) and the Communist Party (the independent movement was controlled by "anti-Soviet" elements). We said editorially:

"The new group can't be both and if the silly argument must be countenanced, it should be said of course that it is neither. It is an attempt to place on the ballot and into the area of free and open discussion the possibility of a socialist alternative for America. . . . The people who placed this ticket in the field are sincere and honest people who want above all to put peace on the ballot. They arrived at their decision in open and democratic conference. This is the fact of the matter, no matter how many scoffing quotation marks the *Worker* puts fore and aft the word socialist, and no matter how many advertisements it refuses to print." The CP leadership had a right to its views, "but it should also be the right of a new group to have its position and its candidates presented without distortion and censorship in any medium of communication—left, right, or center—and that, unfortunately, has not been the case."

Three months before the 1958 election the CP made a curious proposal: as a condition for CP support, all candidates on the Independent–Socialist ticket, except Lamont, should withdraw from the race. The proposal was rejected; Lamont was its most vocal opponent.

Opposition to the I–S ticket also came from Carmine DeSapio, Democratic Party boss, who sought to bar it from the ballot. DeSapio had some initial success but was overruled by the courts. The legal battle took up much of the candidates' time, and the press for the most part blacked out the I–S campaign: most voters were hardly aware of the ticket's existence until they entered the polling booths. Lamont drew close to 50,000 votes and McManus 35,000.

The combined hostility of the machine politicians and of some leaders of the left made the effort a failure in the non-Thoreau sense. For us it seemed to prove the validity of Thoreau's position. While we were not going to settle on Walden Pond (it was a great place to visit), neither were we going to dive into a mainstream flowing only to the bottomless ocean of big party politics. The major lesson was that developing a political alternative for America was tougher than any of us knew, but that there was no alternative to the alternative.

In the cataclysmic fall of 1956 we took time out to mourn a very personal loss—Vic Levitt, our devoted and bombastic landlord, printer, friend. For two years he had known he had cancer, but kept on with hardly a word to anyone until he went into the hospital that April. He never came out.

Vic was that rare bird in the modern world of newspaper specialists: a reporter and editor of great ability equally at home in every phase of journalism, from the perches of editorial policy making to the bowels of a press room. He loved newsprint as much as he disliked slick paper. He was a people's journalist, and that's why he called a short-lived Depression-time paper he had started *The People's Press*.

When Cedric came to see him one hot summer afternoon in 1948 (they had never met) and outlined the GUARDIAN's aspirations, Vic reached down into the recesses of his desk, hauled out a dusty bottle of brandy and two equally dusty pony glasses, and poured into each a generous portion. Thus was sealed the pact that brought the GUARDIAN into physical being. From that time on Vic was elbows deep in GUARDIAN affairs—perhaps bellows deep would be more accurate. Caustic he was, but with great humor too. He kept Fowler's *English Usage* within arm's reach to settle all questions of style. He read voraciously and stored up knowledge for three lifetimes. Often his command-performance chess or pinochle games at the end of a day turned into evening-long disquisitions on subjects ranging from Karl Marx to Izaak Walton.

We saw him regularly during his hospital stay. He was forbid-

LIFE WITHOUT FATHER

den liquor but was not the kind of man to accept any taboos. I recall his joy when Jack and I brought him an ancient leather-covered volume (Jack's inspiration), and he opened it to find a pint of Old Fitzgerald nestling in a cut-out of the pages.

On my workshop wall is framed the first check ever issued by Weekly Guardian Associates Inc. Dated October 18, 1948, the date of Volume 1 Number 1, it is in the sum of one dollar payable to the order of Victor Levitt. In the lower left-hand corner, on the line explaining the expenditure, is the legend: "For invaluable services rendered."

Postscript [**C.B.**] When I was a lad my father tried to convey to me his and his friends' anguish during the Boer siege of Mafeking—an event five years before I existed that shook their faith in Britain's imperial power.

The Soviet–Hungarian convulsions of 1956 shook a different kind of faith in socialists around the world—faith not in the past but in the future. So much greater the anguish, but no less futile the attempt to convey it to a generation born after or just before Khrushchev's "revelations" and the uprising in Hungary. One can only state it and hope that the experience of each generation may add a little to the wisdom of its successors.

The hope seems valid again in 1977 although it has flickered in the interim. In the 1950s our generation was learning the hard way the folly of "instant" illusions (as history measures time) about socialism. In the 1960s, the folly was compounded by a "new left" proclaiming even more instant revolution through massive demonstration and confrontation, not only spurning our experience and lesson but dismissing Marxism altogether. It seemed that this further disillusion was needed to produce the young radicals of the 1970s, with their greater capacity to reflect on lessons of the past. A generation beginning to appreciate as perhaps none did before that changing Man is a very long and hard process, and that changing Man's economy only lays the foundation stone.

For us at the GUARDIAN the anguish in 1956 was eased by an educational process that the Anna Louise Strong–Noel Field–

Konni Zilliacus "cases" had begun seven years earlier. While the faith of some socialists in America and elsewhere couldn't weather the shocks of that year, ours remained intact if battered and somewhat modified. We continued to believe that socialism was the only alternative to genocide of the human species. The fact that the struggle for it would be more agonizing than we once thought couldn't alter its inevitability. But basic change in America was the GUARDIAN's concern, and the time was past (would it ever come again?) when the gospel could be spread in America by pointing to the socialist "bloc" or any country in it as a model. The atomic stalemate removed what had been the very real justification for leaning over backward in the Soviet Union's defense. Indeed such absolutist defense had become as plainly counterproductive as Zilliacus thought it was in 1950.

Thus in 1956, when both Tabitha Petran and I visited Moscow and were told by Soviet spokesmen that executions of Jews without trial were "an internal matter", the GUARDIAN declined editorially to regard them "and resulting terrorization as in any way different from legal lynchings" or from the Rosenberg executions in America—except that black Americans and the Rosenbergs did get "trials." "All humanely concerned Americans await full reassurance" about "the Jewish question" in the USSR, the GUARDIAN said—despite the insistence of Moscow's Chief Rabbi Schliffer that it didn't exist.

The problems we faced in my early exile period, as journalists persuaded to the socialist cause, were extraordinarily tough; and since I could only be (but always was) brought in on them by correspondence, there were occasions when the decision might have been different had I been present and voting at deadline time. But our triumviral unanimity on the handling and selection of news, and on viewpoint about it, stood up overwhelmingly across the ocean.

When innocent Hungarians met death again in the summer of 1958, presenting the enemies of socialism with propaganda grist on a platter, the GUARDIAN went all-out in firm fraternal criticism. Zilliacus, reporting the executions of "revisionist" Prime Minister

LIFE WITHOUT FATHER

Nagy and others after a secret trial, wrote that they had "spread bewilderment and dismay among all those in the West fighting for a sane and civilized attitude toward the Soviet Union." Jim and Jack again used the Rosenberg parallel in a condemnatory editorial ending: "Let us have an end of blood and a beginning of reason." Elmer Bendiner recalled that "Communists died to teach an old order" the lesson that "ideas cannot be hanged or shot"; the executions "seemed to shatter the hopes of those for whom socialism means not only material benefits but social justice as well." I wrote from London deploring *Ta Kung Pao*'s (Peking) approval of the executions as "correct and necessary" and its denunciation as "imperialist henchmen, renegades, slanderers" of all who protested. "If the socialist world leaders fail to recognize in such protests the voices of their true friends it will be perhaps the greatest tragedy of all. The voice is saying that socialists in the capitalist world have made sacrifices too for the cause, and will not stand silent while that cause is again dragged through a mire of terror where socialism reigns and torn to pieces where the fight remains to be won. It is reminding the socialist world that the movement is universal and that if its less advanced forces have a responsibility toward the more advanced, that goes in the other direction too."

All this while recognizing (as I put it and the GUARDIAN ceaselessly documented) that "in the few years since the Soviet Union halted its Stalin-era bloodbath, the ghosts created by imperialism run into tens of thousands in Africa alone." These were among the contributions in 1957–58 to Free World civilization: Washington sent the army to control mob violence against black schoolchildren in the South, and Marines to Lebanon to quell popular upsurges in Iraq and the Middle East, and deepened preparatory talks with its Vietnam puppets for the Indochina bloodbath. Spanish, Greek, Korean, and Taiwanese patriots slowly expired in the hell-holes of U.S.-sponsored fascists, and a gallant general's attempt to end thirty-two years of fascism in Free World Portugal was strangled in post-"election" torture chambers. France and Britain committed unmentionable atrocities upon Algerians, Cypriots, etc., struggling for freedom.

But in the purgatories of Latin America Fidel Castro's men were fighting their way toward dictator Batista's citadel in Havana (GUARDIAN reports beginning in 1956–57); and Uruguayans, Argentines, Peruvians, and Venezuelans greeted Vice President Nixon with rocks, orange peel, eggs, bottles, and spittle. ("Can the oldest resident," Jim had wondered in the GUARDIAN in 1956, "recall when the American scene was graced with as unpleasant a piece of political baggage as Slippery Dick Nixon?") Yes, there were always grounds for the conviction that the human spirit is unconquerable.

Editor-in-Exile

[**C.B.**] Counting back over the years since I was 23, I had landed in Britain from transatlantic liners wearing seven different hats: as a movie-fan journalist (1927, 1929), Sam Goldwyn press agent (1930), London *Express* film and theater critic (1932), world-travel correspondent (1934), book author and embryo U.S. citizen (1939), wartime spy (1942), recruit for the press-purge in Nazi Germany (1944). My eighth landing, as a U.S. jail graduate and editor-in-exile, was naturally enough the first to draw attention—but not much. Since all hopes of rescuing and perpetuating world capitalism had come to rest in America, its "McCarthyist" hysteria had provoked in the British establishment a politely bewildered mood—a tendency to laugh nervously and turn to some pleasanter topic. It was a relief, though, that the British had retained their sense of humor while Americans were losing theirs.

In British left circles, so much broader where the Munich-to-Nuremberg decade's wounds and political lessons were still fresh, the NATIONAL GUARDIAN's resistance to the new imperial monster from within its entrails had won recognition. The paper was known for its championship of the UN Charter against atomic "diplomacy" and against America's re-play of the disastrous post-World War I serenade to Germany, and for its defense of Ameri-

233

cans whom the outside world respected. This applied especially to our Rosenberg campaign, which had touched off the anger of millions in the Free World satellites.

Now I was to spend five years headquartered in London with forays into continental Europe, Asia, and Africa. My MP friends Zilliacus and Tom Driberg (an old drinking companion of *Express* days later endowed with a peerage) urged me to join the Labour Party, whose genuinely socialist minority needed every recruit it could get. Infected with the witch-hunt virus by CIA agents billed as AFL–CIO "fraternal delegates," the party would accept me only on the basis of abjuring all red-tinged organizations. I refused on principle (though my sole affiliation was the National Union of Journalists) and that ended the possibilities, as I saw them, of activity within any British party.

My hands were full, anyhow, with chores for "the other America." My London flat became a kind of embassy for Americans trapped within their frontiers by the passport ban, a liaison center with like-minded Europeans who, once little concerned about America, were realizing how much its fate now dominated their own. I developed an overseas committee of correspondence to help American heretics under the gun, who struggled against their own country's conspiracy of lies or silence.

The cold war had begun on Churchill's rallying call to "the great English-speaking peoples," and British public opinion counted somewhat in Washington. Liberals and even Tories, when canvassed in behalf of left causes, showed less reluctance than their American counterparts to defend Anglo-Saxon traditions of justice; and there were still "famous" people, like Bertrand Russell and Sean O'Casey, who would speak out without reservations. When Rose Russell sought literary/scholastic support for her witch-hunted (and eventually destroyed) New York Teachers Union, O'Casey of the great but ailing heart wrote me from Devonshire:

Of course my sympathy and good wishes go with Rose Russell and her union. And I could wish that the Teachers Union of Ireland had half the fighting spirit of their American brothers and sisters; for they are facing finely the informers who would be ready to swear that a prayer to God threatens His throne; while my Irish comrades wouldn't dare to say boo to a Roman Catholic school-manager on the one hand, or a Protestant school-manager on the other.

In a way, it's amusing to think of the manner innocent people are harried while the great sub-vertionist has to go free forever; for the greatest sub-vertionist is life itself, changing everything as she goes through Time, cuckolding the McCarthies and McCarthy's stooges; at times, even, turning things all tapsalteerie O!

Life in Time will pull the McCarthies and the stooges into forgotten graves; as she has carried the Great into the grave too; but these are about us still: Jefferson and Lincoln speak still within the minds and hearts of America's people, and Whitman sings his songs still in Manhattan, and not only there, but everywhere all the world over.

Adjustment came slowly to the odd sensation of moving about freely on my journalistic and ambassadorial errands. No one seemed to care where I went, whom I saw, what I said in private or in public. My passport read, as British passports always did, "Valid for All Countries." Routinely summoned for jury duty at the Old Bailey, I thought it prudent to mention that I was a recent jailbird and was told: "Quite irrelevant, my dear sir." In time I was chatting with notorious Communists and entering the Soviet and other socialist embassies without looking over my shoulder. Two cheery diplomats from Bulgaria, the first socialist country I visited, were favorite guests at our flat, always armed with bottles of their native wine. Hoover wouldn't have had to look twice to identify my circle of old and new friends as a fearful conspiracy against all he held dear. But if British hawkshaws watched me, tapped my phone, or opened my mail, they did so with their traditional discretion.

I wrote more than in any equivalent period of my life, casting a transatlantic eye mainly on the lives of ordinary peace-minded folk and resistance movements to neo-imperialist obscenities, with an occasional "celebrity" interview: the Dean of Canterbury, Bertrand Russell, Kwame Nkrumah in Ghana, Moshe Sharett in Israel, Jawaharlal Nehru in India, Charles Chaplin in Switzerland.* In London, through the Movement for Colonial Freedom, in which many young radicals were active, I met and publicized obscure, threadbare Africans dedicated to winning freedom for their peoples. One of these, Rhodesia's Joshua Nkomo, was for some time my house guest. Almost everywhere on my first travels—France, Switzerland, Czechoslovakia, Bulgaria, Germany, Poland, Scandinavia, the USSR—I found former American residents whom the inquisition had dumped "back where they came from." There were comradely reunions with Ellis Island alumni who, though the adjustment had sometimes been relatively painless, all thought of America as home. Missing my American circle and activity as much as they did, I was lucky in the constant, direct, and active contact I maintained with it and in the fact that all my American children were in Europe too. Jim asked me for taped messages to be read at the GUARDIAN's annual fund-raising dinners, and these further stimulated correspondence from members of our newspaper family.

My journeyings through these years yielded outlets for my GUARDIAN and other articles, and for a few translations of my books, in New Delhi, Tel Aviv, Rome, Cairo, Duesseldorf, and New Zealand (mostly unpaid) as well as in Prague, Sofia, East Berlin, Peking, and Moscow (paid for in not-always-blocked currencies). The blocked currencies came in handy for travel expenses which the GUARDIAN couldn't afford. When I went to my London bank, the staff greeted me with winks and smiles. The manager finally overcame his reserve to explain that I was the only customer depositing both dollars and rubles. ("A bit unusual, wouldn't you

---

*Chaplin invited me to interview him at his home and stay overnight, and talked with humor, pathos, and startling frankness about the American inquisition from which he was a voluntary refugee. After the interview (which I checked with him by phone) appeared, *Time* phoned him and he told them my quotes were unauthorized. *Time* then reported: "A newswolf in house guest's clothing, Britain's deep pink Cedric Belfrage . . . without leave from Leftist Chaplin, tattled on Charlie in the fellow-traveling *National Guardian*." Having told me he "wouldn't return to America if Jesus Christ was President," he returned years later when Richard Nixon was President to accept, without an admonitory word, the plaudits of those who had stomped on him. Such are a journalist's hazards when dealing with prima donnas, for all their charm and genius.

say, sir?'') A London firm published my book, *The Frightened Giant,* about the inquisitorial experience. Since even submitting it to a U.S. publisher was futile in the stifling climate there, I cast around for a hygienic American theme and embarked on a novel about the man who started it all, Christopher Columbus, suggesting how the ''discoverers'' looked to the ''discovered.'' I called it *The Pink People* and the New York firm that accepted it wrote: ''You'll have to change the title, otherwise your name as author will make people think it's political.'' They decided on a prosaic *My Master Columbus.*

A decade had passed since the short-lived ''victory'' euphoria in Britain, when the people rejected Churchill for radical change and the ''radical'' Labour government invited American troop occupation. The advantages of the Free World arrangement were measurable by the fact that, while Germans gluttonized, meat had just ''come off the ration'' in Britain for the first time in fifteen years. Yet it was a time of gleams of hope for ordinary Britons. The empire, which had never benefited anyone but a few millionaires and foreign-service officials who couldn't stand the British climate, was fast disintegrating. It was pronounced dead in 1956 after the fiasco of British armed intervention in Egypt—coinciding with Soviet armed intervention in Hungary.

The Tory government squandered the backbreaking taxes on its ''own'' (exceptionally futile) atom bombs, but at the same time gingerly thawed relations with the socialist world. With world trade falling into the hands of American monopolies and their German and Japanese colleagues, Britain desperately needed new commercial outlets. The thaw began with the arrival of the Moisseyev dancers, the Bolshoi ballet, and the new Soviet leaders, Bulganin and Khrushchev, whom the Queen invited to tea. I stood with elegant, respectful theater audiences while orchestras followed ''God Save the Queen'' with the Soviet national anthem—a weird but wonderful rite to participate in, even if one sorrowed for the ''Internationale.''

''B. and K.'s'' unpretentious frankness with the press drew comparisons with the cold war's Saint Paul, John Foster Dulles, who kept flying in and out on the business of defending us against socialism. The only rudeness they encountered was from some of their hosts at a Labour Party dinner. A sight for sore socialist eyes was Bulganin publicly apologizing to Zilliacus, outside the House of Commons, for the bloody "spy" nonsense of Stalin days (see chapter 5). Meanwhile in New York, undaunted inquisitors were raiding the *Daily Worker* to seize its battered equipment for "unpaid taxes." Hoover, Nixon, Eastland, and the media spared no effort to maintain hysteria at a McCarthy pitch. Yet the whole troupe—Moisseyev, Khrushchev, Bolshoi, and anthem—would soon be there too, spreading their coexistence gospel. The facts of life which the GUARDIAN had sustained were painfully but remorselessly asserting themselves.

Of all the thousands of Americans whose politics barred them either from earning a livelihood at home or doing so elsewhere, Paul Robeson was the best known and loved in Britain, where he had often performed—the ideal symbol through which to attack Secretary Dulles' passport curtain. A year after my deportation an appeals court confirmed Dulles' right to padlock Robeson and his wife Eslanda, and HUAC summoned both for an "investigation of the use of passports in furtherance of the international Communist conspiracy." Paul denounced the inquisitors; their chairman, Francis Walter (of the Walter–McCarran Act), roared: "I've stood about as much of this as I can—session adjourned"; and Paul roared back, "You should adjourn this forever."

I was joined in a "Let Robeson Go" campaign by Peggy Middleton, member for Greenwich of the London County Council, and Franz Loeser, a young German orphaned by Hitler and living in Manchester. They knew little more about America than about Tibet but learned a lot fast; for them Paul was "America singing" and they resented anyone trying to stop him. As the NATIONAL GUARDIAN reported our campaign's progress, they and my tribe over the waters achieved mutual familiarity. We held meetings across the land and pursued MPs, labor leaders, lords and ladies, and bishops until two columns of "names" adorned our stationery. The historian Sir Arthur Bryant did a foreword for Paul's book *Here I Stand,* whose publication we arranged, and we persuaded Stratford-on-Avon to invite him to play Othello. Soon 150 British organizations were participating in our plot against the State Department, and I was on a board of directors chaired by a Lord. Unable to produce Robeson in the flesh, we presented him as a ghost in a series of taped concerts. In London we filled a hall to bursting for a transatlantic telephone recital, the first and (we hoped) last of its kind. A Welsh miners' choir sharing the program sang to him and he to them. We on the stage chatted with him in our final minute on the wire. His well-remembered voice moistened the eyes of the audience he couldn't see, and broke a little at the sound of our boisterous greeting.

During my first three exiled years only two Americans in my orbit turned up in London: the fake admiral from West Street prison (as a deportee), and Rose Sobell, whom Dulles thought it prudent not to prevent from coming to discuss with Bertrand Russell the fate of her son Morton. When the Rev. (later Canon) Stanley Evans commemorated the fourth anniversary of the Rosenbergs' execution at Holy Trinity, Dalston, only Britons were present to hear him say:

"Julius and Ethel with a quite simple 'No' held together against iniquity in a society where, as in Bunyan's Vanity Fair, everything seemed to be for sale. They refused, as Ethel wrote, to play the role of harlot to political procurers. When the masses of the people are like that, the end to the beginning will come and the real future of humankind will begin."

In 1958 the dam burst. After even the *Wall Street Journal* had joined in mocking Dulles' leash on Robeson, the day came that every American with the price of a plane ticket had yearned for. In a "right to travel" test case brought against Dulles by psychiatrist Walter Briehl and artist Rockwell Kent, the Supreme Court found against Dulles. From July on, with their first passports in up to a decade, known and unknown GUARDIAN readers poured into town and kept my phone ringing with delirious calls. Those who came at Easter-time in 1959 and 1960 formed with me a NATIONAL GUARDIAN contingent in the spectacular three-day "Aldermaston marches" organized by Bertrand Russell's Campaign for Nuclear Disarmament.

The invasion turned me into a meet-all-planes Toonerville Trolley. My second airport meeting with Anna Louise Strong, en route to her long-delayed "rehabilitation" welcome in Moscow, was an exhilarating contrast to my first. MPs and nobodies of our Let Robeson Go committee, Asians and Africans, a Prime Minister (Jagan of British Guiana), a viscount (but no bishops) formed a small bouquet-laden mob to welcome Paul and Eslanda. Reporters from the more indecent journals were primed to heckle them about "communism" but subsided before his firm, gentle humor. The *Manchester Guardian,* which had been spiteful, recovered its liberalism in a long straight report. Apparently Paul abashed its interviewer by speaking "without bitterness" of being a slave's son and of "a hundred million Africans sacrificed on slave ships." We took Paul and Eslanda by taxi to the flat we'd rented for them and the driver said:

"I wouldn't take no fare from you, Mr. Robeson. The pleasure was mine."

So many Londoners recognized the black peacemonger with the heft of a bull and the voice of a god, that even on his early morning walks there were hands to shake on every block. Within days he had been booked for three TV half-hours at £1,000 each and received cable offers from around the world, and a date had been set for *Othello* rehearsals at Stratford. Luxuriating in his recovered freedom and dignity, Paul was at his best vocally and spiritually at an informal concert in Peggy Middleton's backyard, where a Ghanaian gave him an African drum welcome and the guests were the local dustman, postman and union shop stewards, teenagers and orphanage kids.

Jim and Grambs were there too, having flown in for our first reunion in three years, and we were all soaring for two weeks. On their last night, every inch of Albert Hall's standing room was sold out for Paul's first recital. His old friend and accompanist, Larry Brown, flew over from Harlem to be on stage with him. The audience got eight encores ending with *Joe Hill,* and wept a little as people did when Paul sang. On the next Sunday a program of spirituals drew ten times the normal congregation to a service in St. Paul's Cathedral, with a collection for the South African "treason trial" fund. Paul was no stranger to singing in churches (his brother was a Methodist minister), but was the first black man to stand at the cathedral lectern, on the spot where the fourteenth-century British establishment tried Wycliffe for heresy.

In the 1930s when politics was only beginning to bother me, I had taken lightly the tasks of a world-traveling correspondent— even in the Soviet Union, which I'd visited in 1936 for London's liberal *News Chronicle* (picking up some primitive Russian). Twenty years later, in a far more tumultuous and perplexing time, I was called upon to appraise the progress of "the hope of mankind" on the basis of brief visits to socialist and emerging third-world countries of strange tongues and cultures. This would have been onerous indeed had not the GUARDIAN set its more modest tradition of socialist reporting.

My first Soviet re-visit was an extension from a week in Helsinki at the congress of the International Organization of Journalists (IOJ), the left-wing half of the originally global journalists' organization, split by the cold war. It was July of 1956. The IOJ was glad to have a delegate whom, by courtesy of our inquisitors, it could label "U.S.A." I reported on the NATIONAL GUARDIAN'S struggles and on American journalists forced out of their craft or into whoredom within it. The reception was cordial, though I tried to persuade my "Iron Curtain" colleagues that they had much to learn from as well as teach to capitalist country journalists. In fact, later travels deepened my belief that no establishment press had much to be proud of. Socialist country newspapers had earned honest journalists' gratitude by eliminating lowest-common-denominator sensationalism. At the same time they committed the very sins against which Lenin fumed: parochialism, long-windedness, jargon—adding up to dullness. Politically they could be no better than their governments, which controlled them as effectively as advertisers controlled the capitalist press.

The congress was memorable for bringing me together with two English-language journalists whom I admired, Wilfred Burchett and John Peet. Fed up like Burchett with editorial doctoring of his copy for cold war purposes, Peet had quit as Reuters' man in West Germany and launched in East Berlin the *Democratic German Report,* the socialist world's only English-language journal with a sense of humor. Presumably he felt that if he must submit to a political blue-pencil, socialists should hold the pencil. Burchett, for one who had supped so full of the horrors of dirty wars, astonished me with his zest for the joys of living. Australia having canceled his passport, he traveled with a document that looked like a Chinese restaurant menu, issued in Hanoi where he lived with his family. All socialist countries published his articles and books, making him "wealthy" in blocked currencies. We had a lively beer-and-schnitzel journey together on the Helsinki–Leningrad express as far as Viborg, where Soviet authorities made him get off for an overnight check of his menu.

On the sunny day of my arrival in Moscow, bands played and loudspeakers roared adulations for the latest state guest symbolizing the "thaw." It was Yugoslavia's Tito, who since 1948 had vied with Stalin for vituperation suitable to characterize each other. As a house guest of Ralph Parker, a veteran Moscow correspondent with a Soviet wife and kids, I established immediate contact with Soviet citizens. Three months after Khrushchev's "Report on the Cult of Personality," no conversation long avoided that subject. The talk was more frank than in 1936, when Stalin's pall had yet to hang most fearfully over the scene. People back from camps and jails described how Stalin's police, with "a vested interest in keeping him convinced of plots," practiced unimaginable degradations on their victims, on each other and on socialism. Yet the victims, including the flower of the revolution, had consoled themselves with the thought: "It must be a mistake, Stalin will put it right." Few could believe in the personal responsibility of the man who led the victory against fascism. Years later in Budapest I would hear the same thing from the lips of Noel and Herta Field (see chapter 5). Noel went further: cut off from all news during his jail years, he had, when apologetically released, been told that

Stalin was dead. "I burst into tears," he said, "—and then they told me . . ." *Pravda* had written after the Khrushchev report that the worst of the paranoid Stalin era wasn't its cruelty but "toadies and sycophants, brought up in a spirit of servility and subservience." Unfortunately, the cap fitted *Pravda* better than ordinary citizens without access to the seats of power.

One could only try to understand Soviet citizens' thinking about these horrors in the perspective of the nightmares (which they considered far worse) that the capitalist world had visited on them in the post-revolution and German occupation years. An outsider might think suffering would be easier to take when inflicted by an enemy, but they didn't seem to find it so. They wanted no sympathy from kindly Westerners who had experienced almost nothing. A critic–editor in Leningrad named Garelov, a Communist for thirty years who had spent seventeen of them in Stalinian hells, said to me in a mild tone: "These things have happened; we who are dedicated to socialism don't want to rub salt in the wounds."

The prevailing sentiment was that now it would be full steam ahead for the real thing, a socialist beacon to the world. This shining optimism reached its peak at Moscow's World Youth Congress which I covered in August of 1957 along with 2,000 other journalists. Conspicuous among the youth delegations from 127 lands was an American contingent including my daughter Sally (presumably consisting of people too young to have FBI dossiers), with the normal quota of police spies. Young Russians poured forth for free-for-all palavers with their guests, continuing all night in the great square beneath my hotel room window. In the university's marble halls loudspeakers blared songs from *South Pacific* while lecture rooms buzzed with inter-people discussions on every learned theme. The guests found the Muscovites monolithically loyal but beginning to exercise group protest, impatient for faster movement toward democracy, and surprisingly critical of Khrushchev. A young American lawyer of dubious political complexion read aloud in the street the UN report on the Soviets' Hungarian intervention; perhaps hoping to be arrested, he merely started another hot discussion.

With the privileged few I had attended lavish Kremlin receptions for "thaw" guests—Tito, the Shah of Iran, Cambodia's Prince Sihanouk—which, contrasting uncomfortably with the hard lives of the masses, one hoped did not presage the rise of a new "elite." But now the Kremlin flung open its gates for a party to which all Toms, Dicks, and Marys of the youth delegations were invited, and which they took over. Fireworks burst from the "grim" towers, Egyptian women bellydanced, Americans rock-and-rolled beneath Stalin's old windows. East met West not only in the new sense but in the old, as "colonials" discussed freedom plans with black, brown, and yellow fellow-sufferers from other continents. One evening half a million youths marched into the square crying "No More Hiroshimas!" in a hundred tongues, multicolored searchlights playing over their faces and uplifted arms. Watching them with Burchett (by then installed as the NATIONAL GUARDIAN's permanent man in Moscow), an unseasonable thought came to me. These beautiful young people, some of the cream of the world's crop, were in target dead-center of American H-bombs aimed from all directions. Five thousand miles away an aging and never very bright general,* and his Secretary of State whose bigotry would have shamed Cotton Mather, had their fingers on the button. But the Armenian brandy was excellent and one could but hope that something would keep them distracted from their toy.

Between Congress events I wrote madly to earn enough rubles for a ticket to China, and was wined and dined by Soviet journalists and by a government official named Gorokhov. I put it to Gorokhov that the thaw had surely gone far enough for foreign-language journals other than CP organs to be offered on Soviet newsstands, and why not start with our paper? In Warsaw I had reached down a London *Times* and a NATIONAL GUARDIAN from a peg on a cafe wall. Gorokhov refilled my champagne glass in fervent agreement; only currency regulations, which could surely be overcome, stood in the way of this splendid idea.

To this day, so far as I know, CP organs are the only foreign-language publications sold in the Soviet Union. And, with the in-

* In retrospect, a lot more human than his successors—J.A.   Agreed—C.B.

The NATIONAL GUARDIAN revived the great tradition of humor and satire in line drawing.

Are you now or have you ever been a member of any one of these subversive organizations?"

FACELESS INFORMERS AND OUR SCHOOLS

SEE PAGE 4

THE DENVER POST CRIES A WARNING
The faceless informer in the classroom—this is your FBI

Victory! 4 of Trenton 6 fre

Fight goes on to free two sentenced to life in prison

By William A. Reuben
GUARDIAN Special Correspondent

TRENTON, N. J.

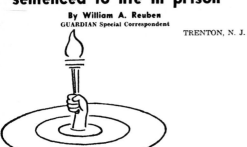

NATIONAL

5 cents

GUARDIAN

the progressive newsweekly

Vol. 3, No. 35   **NEW YORK, N. Y., JUNE 20,**

A target from the beginning was the witch
hunt and the institution of repression.

THIS IS NEW YORK . . .

Shame of the city:
What befalls those
who tell the story

By James Aronson

ROSENBERGS EXECUTED!

Ethel and Julius Rosenberg leaving court in
a patrol van.   cr. International News Photo

THIRTEEN ANNIVERSARY OF THE EXECUTION

Quest goes on for vindication of the Rosenberg

Vol. 5, No. 35   NEW YORK, N. Y., JUNE 22, 1953

Rosenberg Case   NEW YORK EDITION

Eisenhower refuses clemency
In face of a horrified world

January 29, 1953

Dear Mr. President : About the Rosenbergs . . .

A Rosenberg defender's 14-year crusade

The Rosenberg children, Robert and Michael
with defense attorney Emanuel Bloch.
cr. International News Phot

THE POISONED PEN AND THE ROSENBERGS

The rotten role of the U.S. press

By James Aronson

Last evening Julius and Ethel Rosenberg died in the electric chair. . . . They were tried in open court by a jury of their peers and were found guilty. . . . Meanwhile every facility for petitioning for clemency was granted to the supporters of the defendants. They had access to the press. . . .
N.Y. Herald Tribune editorial Saturday, June 20, 1953

ACCESS to the press. . . . The editor of the N.Y. Herald Tribune refused to see a delegation from the Natl. Committee to Secure Justice in the Rosenberg Case; the paper had adequate information on the case, he said. The Herald Tribune, along with every other newspaper in New York, and most papers throughout the country, consistently spiked committee releases reporting that distinguished persons all over

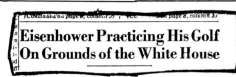

NEW YORK
Herald Tribune
Early Bird

Eisenhower Rules Rosenbergs Must Die,
Got 'Full Justice' for 'Most Serious Crime'

(Continued on page 9, column 3)

Eisenhower Practicing His Golf
On Grounds of the White House

Same paper, same day, same page.

of news was the almost total of the news that Pope Pius made three intercessions in t Even the Catholic press proscr Pope.

When the GUARDIAN broke of new evidence (the missin its editors sent copies of th photostats and glossy prints paper in New York and to services. There was thundering Abroad the news was Page On

A CHANGE COMES: In the before the execution, the change. News flooded into the There were press vigils in Wa and at Sing Sing. Top-name were assigned. The story almos ed the shocking news from K of the headlines.

There was a change in the of the coverage too. Aside obscenities that appeared us bylines of the bought-and columnists and pundits, the the working press were full and sober. They reflected the of the events being covered. T

Carthy in Whitaker Chambers' pumpkin
ch? A GUARDIAN montage.

"Everywhere I go I see pumpkins, Doc."

Senator Joseph McCarthy enjoyed any and
all publicity.   cr. International News Photo

Fight to free Belfrage from Ellis Island — Arrest riles Britain; U.S. press silent

Belfrage, leaning on bookcase (upper left), tells the staff of his McCarthy ordeal. McManus stands in doorway.

Minutes later the Immigration boys walk in and Belfrage is arrested.

2-DAY HUNGER STRIKE

Belfrage jailed after he loses deportation plea

Belfrage (center) leaving Foley Square courthouse, Aronson (left) and McManus (right).

Belfrage captions this "The DA, The FBI Man, and The Cop."

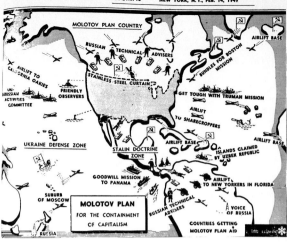

Vol. I, No. 18   NEW YORK, N.Y., FEB. 14, 1949

Paul Robeson visits the GUARDIAN Office.

Paul Robeson with Larry Brown, his long time accompanist.

Two exiles—Belfrage with Charlie Chaplin.

Belfrage visits a Moscow synagogue in 1956.

Louis E. Burnham represented the bridge between past and future, and between the races.

Wilfred Burchett as Our Man in Vietr

Wilfred Burchett in

THE WARNING SIGN'S UP

The undeclared war in Vietnam: We're getting very deep

WAR & PEACE

U.S. on brink of war in Indo-China on eve of Geneva talks on Asia

Southeast Asia was a focus of prime concern even before the Geneva Conference of 1954.

ANOTHER WARNING FROM CHINA

U. S. presses 'war' in South Vietnam, risks a 'new Korea'

THE WHITE PAPER AND THE COUNCIL

Washington assists Cuban exile scheme to overthrow Castro

FREEDOMS

McCarthy taps N. G. editors; renews deportation threat

NEW YORK EDITION

January 12, 1959

WASHINGTON CONFERENCE MAPS ACTION

Women seek equal opportunity in science

The headlines in the 1950s were prophetic —and the perils for the "prophets" implicit.

dependence stirrings that characterize the world CP scene in 1977, probably not all of them.

Three years after the Supreme Court's school integration decision, America began moving ponderously into the global renaissance of colored peoples: token black children entered Southern white schools under a hail of jeers and stones. And as the 1957 school year opened, the trans-Siberian plane was depositing me in the capital of the greatest revolution against white overlordship, Peking. Apart from the Baltimore *Afro-American*'s William Worthy, who had defied Dulles's five-year jail threat for anyone going to China, I was the only journalist from America who'd been there for years.

China for me was six weeks of challenge and excitement, with one outstanding moment. A train drew into Peking station with young Americans—China's guests from the Youth Congress—in a special car. First out was a blond lad with a grin as radiant as a page of *Leaves of Grass*. A mass of young Chinese surged forward with bouquets; he raised a parade-size Stars and Stripes over their heads and they broke into cheers. I pushed through somehow to embrace Sally, whom I'd last seen on Gorky Street with her handsome Russian friend Vladimir. Never, I thought, was a flag more honorably unfurled. Never had I felt such pride in my American daughter.

I have only two gray memories of that visit. One was my futile attempt (see chapter 6) to get word of the Kwaks through the North Korean embassy. The other, the simplistic misconceptions which I found to prevail about aspects of America—almost as great as America's about China. In 1957 the Chinese seemed to grasp the American establishment's determination to destroy socialism wherever this might be possible and by whatever means, however pitiless, but they grossly misinterpreted and exaggerated the domestic American counterforces. In 1977 they believe that the Soviet Union is a greater menace to socialism, to be countered everywhere in the world, basing on this a series of foreign policy errors which may indeed threaten the international socialist cause.

(Perhaps Mao could have convinced me that this belief isn't another dangerous oversimplification, but so far as I know he never really explained it.) Not that the Soviets didn't behave unpardonably toward China in 1960, nor that China's charges of Soviet "revisionism" are unfounded; but where is the detached Marxist analysis, where the "Workers of the world, unite!" spirit, in the behavior of either?

It seems like fiction to recall now the heartfelt gratitude toward the Soviet Union which I found throughout China in 1957. From Shanghai to Lanchow Soviet buses and trucks, giant excavators, planes, and whole factories were part of the scene along with Chinese bicycles, mule carts, barrows, and "ants" (the West's favorite word for Chinese workers) moving mountains in shoulder-pole baskets. Soviet engineering experts were the honored guests at every hotel, to the point of providing special restaurants for them. Chinese were fast learning the know-how to step into their shoes but were very discreet about it.

"How is it possible," I asked my interpreter and good companion Tsai Shen-ling, "for them not to like your magnificent Chinese food?"

"How is it possible," said Tsai, "for us to say they're wrong? Aren't they our best and truest friends?"

The big bogey word mined by American propagandists out of the Korean War, via the camps in China for American POWs, was "brainwashing." For the Chinese it was a perfectly good word: why, they said, spend so much time washing the body and leave out the brain? Indeed, after generations of capitalist and imperialist corruption, nothing in man's equipment stood in more urgent need of a bath. No one in that vast land was excluded from the campaign to "rectify" people's thinking: a parading of contradictions, an open-to-the-public testing of everyone and everything in China.

The Chinese saw this national group therapy as coessential with economic change to the success of socialism, and expected it to continue for the foreseeable future. Socialism, they believed, could only be won by honest and responsible people who would really live by what religions had always talked about: putting the good of "the brethren" or society first, their own desires second.

(As a recent student of child-rearing in China puts it: not "selfless-ness" but "selfish-lessness" . . . . "The development of the 'indi-vidual self' and the 'social self' are not mutually exclusive, it is more a matter of emphasis.") As part of this serious effort to pass from words to deeds, leading people and intellectuals had to de-scend weekly from their towers and wield a shovel or otherwise dirty their hands with the rest of the people. Thus China hoped to do away with prima donnas as it had already done away with beggars, prostitutes, and houseflies.

It was with deep respect for the undertaking of this task, on so immense a scale, that I moved by train and plane through what the Free World called a "blue antheap." Whether it could be achieved was hard to judge across the cultural/linguistic gap that made all but rare Westerners more helpless than Chinese babies. Yet I felt that my nursemaid, university graduate Tsai, was telling me as nearly as possible what people said—hundreds and hundreds of talkative people. He went easy on Marxist jargon and slogans, but the word "imperialism" (always equipped with derisive quotation marks in Free World counterpropaganda) cropped up as often as "before liberation," "after liberation" in the life-stories people told us. I had seen enough on my brief Chinese visit in 1936 to ap-preciate the word's meaning for every Chinese: massacre, famine, rape, filth, slavery, opium, corruption, cultural vandalism, and pillage—all for the benefit of Western civilization and its native parasites. The "Damn the Imperialists!" signs over the smashed Loyang Cave Buddhas—masterpieces of art, intact a century ago, now reposing in fragments in Western museums—put Chinese sen-timents mildly. .

Nor did Tsai need to glut me with statistics about the material transformation since the revolution. The blossoming of the land and its millennially ravaged resources, to which every Chinese with a bit of sense was contributing sweat and thought, was before my eyes. It was greater than any socialist could have imagined, and enough to daze any honest capitalist—as it has been doing ever since Nixon's visit to China opened the door to Americans in 1971.

From peasants to philosophers, everyone talked about "rec-

tification." Some laid on indigestibly thick their contrition for
"old" attitudes, their insistence that they had yet to overcome
them. Some indicated without saying so that they submitted resent-
fully. Some still held out against cooperation, which was what the
washing of brains was all about. Businessmen/employers had had
the choice of staying in China with brainwashing or getting out if
they rejected it. It had been tough, confessed Cambridge-educated
N. N. Lieu, the only member of a "match king" family who
hadn't decamped to Hong Kong, but he impressed me as either a
happy man or a very good actor. He said he visited the family
once or twice a year in Hong Kong and couldn't wait to get back.
His brain had been washed into an attitude of boredom with the
"night life" they claimed to enjoy, and he felt that his new way of
working and living guaranteed him against the stomach ulcers of
which they complained. Instead of ordering "his" workers around
he listened to them and found they often knew more about efficient
match production than he did. He lived quietly, pleasantly, and
securely on an adequate state salary, shorn of all "labor troubles"
and worries about fluctuating markets and currencies, interest
rates, and exactions by warlords and official crooks.

But the "loss of face" involved in the brainwashing process—
endless tea-sipping huddles where everyone's behavior with subordinates was ruthlessly examined—was too much for many people
like Lieu. And I have had to wonder since how Lieu and two "rec-
tified" intellectuals, King Yo-ling and Liang Sze-chen, stood up to
the even tougher ordeal of the Cultural Revolution in the 60s.

Over a Peking duck dinner King and Liang, both Western academic products, traced for me their ideological Long March. For
Columbia graduate philosopher King, the departure point had been
"pure" Kant–Hegel–Bertrand Russell liberty; it had been "gradually knocked into his head" that this was a treasure of which peasants earning 1/700th of his salary didn't have much. Liang had
been an architect "caring only for outside appearance" who
thought "socialism meant your pipe and my teapot would be made
public property." With Chiang's downfall they had "waited passively to be brainwashed," but "found it had already started be-

fore we knew it" due to "events we saw and experienced." The Communist army's behavior was exemplary, everything moved ahead because everyone worked, and they had been invited to contribute to a twelve-year plan "for China's material, spiritual and cultural reconstruction."

All this they told me with humor and a certain relish. "In my case," said Liang, "I wondered at first how much brain I had to wash." He had been involved in a group to reconstruct Peking, and was able to explain what happened to the mountains of garbage I saw and smelled there in 1936, swarming with naked children in search of something to eat.

"No wonder you remember it. It had been accumulating ever since the Ming dynasty. In the first liberation year we carted off 349,000 tons of the stuff. In eighteen months we removed 610,000 tons of human manure and sent it to the farmers. Yet the party took two years to convince me that my ornamented building designs were an unforgivable waste of money."

King was amused to hear that his old liberal guru Bertrand Russell had invited me to tea, for an interview after his talk with Rose Sobell. Russell had read the Rosenberg–Sobell trial record left by Ms. Sobell and responded with outrage in a letter to the press.

"Good for him," said King. "But what about that lunacy of his not so long ago, calling for an atomic ultimatum to Moscow if it rejected American atom control?"

"I asked him about that and he told me, 'That was the worst thing I ever said and I'm sorry I said it.' "

"So the pure liberal species isn't extinct after all. But of course he always loathed the Soviet Union. An incurable intellectual aristocrat."

"Lately he's been reading about the political police in America and seems to be concluding that it's worse. Anyway he refuses to recognize the right of either of them to blow the rest of us up, and he's doing something about it."

"The courage of his convictions—fine. But the trouble is . . . I've attended an international conference or two and the same words no longer mean the same on both sides. One can't change one's ideas simply by staying in the academic atmosphere and exchanging discussions. *With* all that's been happening here we've come to see it isn't what people think that changes things. It's life and experience that change what we think.''

I thought dejectedly of the puny contribution I could make (or a thousand other journalists, if Dulles would let them come) to demolishing the rampart of humbug about China. How long, for example, before most of us would even begin thinking of China's exquisite children as we thought of our own, rather than as bomb-fodder for the security and glory of our "way of life"? Probably only when America found its way to socialism, as it surely would. And China convinced me that we'd all have to pass through the rectification tunnel to get there. We all needed our brains washed to restore our societies to health. It was a process with many possible pitfalls, should it get into the hands of closers rather than openers of minds. The Chinese saw at least that it was a long process of trial and error, really beginning not with the adults but with the kids. Elimination of "elite" notions to equalize educational opportunity, and determination of just what education is, would likely take generations. Rooting out the last of the anti-brotherhood poisons, handed down from parents to children since the mists of time, might take a century.

I left some flowers on Agnes Smedley's grave in the "heroes' cemetery" outside Peking, and flew home. For weeks capitalism had faded for me into a haze of space and time. From beyond the range of its baubles and artificial enticements, it looked like a folly in a history book or on cloud minus-nine. Then, back in the Kafka ambiance, China hazed over. But even if you'd only dreamed it, it made you feel oddly detached from those who hadn't.

Ever since deportation I had acted as forwarding agent between DuBois and the socialist countries, since "my mail," as he wrote to me, "is so tampered with that I am afraid it may not reach." On the heels of the Robesons in 1958, he and Shirley arrived in Britain by ship. I drove them through the New Forest to London and the "darlin' man" (how well O'Casey's phrase fitted him) was in the gayest of moods. He knew much of the world from pre-Dulles travels and had never doubted he would see the old haunts again. His escorts in the countries he would now revisit were fascinated by the anecdotes he threw off in conversational lulls: "When I was last here in 1894 . . ." I took him and Shirley to my favorite unaffordable restaurant, the Ivy, where he downed a cocktail, three-course dinner, wine and cognac with relish and digestive impunity.

In the course of his resumed travels he received various university doctorates, attended the World Peace Council in Stockholm, was nominated in Moscow for the Lenin Peace Prize, and gave lectures and interviews mainly about Africa. He thought the American inquisition too infantile to deserve much comment. I caught up with him that fall in Tashkent, at a congress of writers from thirty-six Afro-Asian countries. As the congress's special guest, he strode into the hall to the only standing ovation. In Tashkent's main square, turned into a book fair with translations of Afro-Asian and white writers into countless languages, pigtailed Uzbek girls in beanies and bright-striped nightshirts mobbed DuBois and the other literary "stars" for autographs. In my white innocence/arrogance I didn't even know the names of most of the authors, whose works were familiar to a multilingual Soviet multitude. The extent of this cultural operation was among my very positive impressions of Soviet Asia, which I toured after the congress. A poet from Daghestan (pop. 1,000,000) told the congress that many Russian, Western, and Afro-Asian authors had been translated into nine of his Soviet republic's languages. He concluded, turning toward DuBois:

"We mustn't confuse colonialism with culture and Dreiser with Dulles. Do we burn a lovely carpet because it has dirty marks? Culture isn't a muskmelon to be divided into parts. In our country they say the most beautiful thing in the world is the back of an enemy. The face of a friend is more beautiful."

DuBois hadn't come there to look beautiful, but he did: to everyone he was like a brother and a father. He urged liberated colonies to pass directly into socialism if they could, and warned of the new economic imperialism if they didn't. He was thinking particularly of Ghana, where his days were destined to end shortly before capitalist-minded militarists deposed his disciple Kwame Nkrumah. I had covered Ghana's freedom celebrations in 1957 and had hoped to see DuBois, Nkrumah's choice to represent America, there. Instead, Eisenhower and Dulles had sent Nixon.

In March 1959 DuBois' American alma mater, Fisk, cabled imploring me to locate him to dedicate in April a DuBois dormitory and launch a series of DuBois lectures. He cabled back through me: NOW IN CHINA RETURNING JULY THANKS. He had spent his 91st birthday in Peking, dining with Chou En-lai, visiting Mao, and being honored at a banquet before touring the country with a trained nurse assigned to stay at his side. From Peking University he spoke on a broadcast beamed to Africa:

"I speak with no authority," he said, "no assumption of age nor rank; I hold no position, I have no wealth. One thing alone I own and that is my soul. Ownership of that I have even while in my own country for near a century I have been nothing but a 'nigger.' On this basis and this alone I dare speak, I dare advise. . . . China after long centuries has risen to her feet and leapt forward. Africa, arise, and stand straight, speak and think! Act! Turn from the West and your slavery and humiliation for the last 500 years and face the rising sun . . . Speak, China, and tell your truth to Africa and to the world!"

On his way home through London my friend Laurence Bradshaw, sculptor of the bust over Karl Marx's grave at Highgate, made a DuBois head which we formally presented "to the Chinese people" at their embassy. For this GUARDIAN readers across America contributed funds. When DuBois was 92, Nkrumah invited him to organize an *Encyclopedia Africana,* symbolizing united Africa's redemption of its history and culture. He saw this as his life's final challenge and fulfillment. Typically, he circulated among his farflung friends his first encyclopedia plan: "Kindly read it over," he wrote to me, "and at your convenience give me a word of advice." Shirley wrote me of their landing in Accra:

"We were received by a full military guard and band. W. E. B.

spoke to a great multitude and when he finished women danced around the platform and up and down the aisles in a demonstration such as I've never seen. You should have seen him, beaming with sheer joy, waving his hands. Years have literally dropped from him.''

But, settled in a fine Accra house with tropical garden chosen by Nkrumah, DuBois' health wavered. On his 94th birthday he was being told, at Dr. Aslan's clinic in Bucharest, that he needed risky surgery. A London surgeon performed it successfully and, as the best place for physical and spiritual recuperation, DuBois chose— China. Of that land he had written in the NATIONAL GUARDIAN:

''I have seen much of the world but never seen a nation which so amazed and touched me. I have seen more impressive buildings, greater display of wealth, more massive power, better equipped railways, more showy automobiles, but never a nation where human nature was so abreast of scientific knowledge; where daily life of everyday people was so outstripping mechanical power, and love of life so triumphing over human greed and selfishness. . . . A sense of human nature free of its most hurtful and terrible meannesses. . . . No utopia but the saving nation of this stumbling, murdering, hating world.''

Back in Accra, a school choir in the garden wakened him on his 95th birthday; he became a Ghanaian citizen and was loaded with honors throughout the day. A week later Shirley wrote that ''his body seems to be slowly but surely fading away.'' His life ended a few hours after Nkrumah's last bedside visit.

His millions of friends had cause for gratitude to death for visiting him when it did. He was still able to believe, with so many of us then, that Moscow's conflict with Peking would be healed as its vendetta with Tito had been. As for Africa, a sickening smog was soon to poison the air that had so invigorated DuBois. In a series of coups—with sometimes more, sometimes less trace of Washington's hand—military dictators took over most of the ''liberated'' continent.

Proud and undismayed, Shirley wrote on the title page of her memoir: ''His Day Is Marching On!'' And how could I weep when

I heard of his death? I rejoiced that he had existed. And when American intellectuals began paying tribute to his corpse, I laughed with him, thinking of the days when they pretended he wasn't there and he was ours alone.

"Happy is the man who may mention his name without blushing! Woe to the many who dare to mention his name because they are no longer able to blush!"*

Postscript [**J.A.**] The Soviet Union, the People's Republic of China, Paul Robeson, W. E. B. DuBois. These became the four cornerstones of Cedric's first editor-in-exile years, as they were also governing factors in the life and times of the NATIONAL GUARDIAN and of the other men and women who produced it. Two great nations that rose in revolt against the oppression of external colonialism and internal imperialism, to offer to the peoples of the world an alternative social system. And two great men who embodied in their lives and work the concept of freedom for people of any color, particularly for the black people of America. Each of these men looked to each of these countries for hope and nourishment of the freedom concept. So did we.

The restoration of my passport in 1958 validated the nonparochial truism that travel broadens. For a journalist it is the blood and ink of the craft. London was gloriously bright and clear that August and the Royal Albert Hall, the night of the Robeson concert, our liberating journey's crowning glory. The pride we felt in Paul and the joy over his own liberation were boundless. The great bear hug in his dressing room after the concert was an all-embracing act of love and comradeship.

These memories flooded through on a day in January 1976 in Hong Kong when I read of Paul's death—tucked away in the *South China Morning Post* amid reams of copy about the condition of the pound sterling and the fluctuating value of gold on the Crown Colony exchange. Grambs and I had just emerged from three weeks in China—her first trip "home" since she left in 1934

*From an obit of Joseph Schoeffel, relentless foe of Vienna's "whoring" press in the 1900s, in Karl Kraus's heretical journal *The Torch*.

at age 17 to come to New York as an art student; my first visit. Cedric's cornerstones were prominent for us in China because the talk had often turned to Robeson and DuBois, both revered there, and inevitably and invariably to the Soviet Union. Our visit sadly coincided with the passing of another great figure of our political maturation: the night we arrived in Peking the death of Premier Chou En-lai was announced.

Thus in the same month on two continents there was an outpouring of sorrow and love for two irreplaceable human beings. The watchword in China—"Turn grief into strength"—which we saw put in practice before our eyes, was applicable for Robeson and the struggle in America as well. China wept but never stopped working. For some the only breaks were the processions to the memorial for the revolutionary heroes in Tien An Men to place wreaths of white chrysanthemum in Chou's memory.

The year 1958 witnessed developments in relations between China and the United States which concerned us deeply at the GUARDIAN. The first Washington–Peking confrontation since the Korean War came that summer over Secretary Dulles' renewed promise to Chiang on Taiwan to bring about the "passing" of the heathen People's Republic. The Presbyterian pledge came in the context of Peking's determination to break the blockade of Amoy and Foochow by Chiang's troops (one fourth of his forces) on Quemoy and Matsu islands five miles off the China coast. Following Dulles' threat, Peking reiterated its determination to liberate Taiwan, and there was a mobilization in China. Eisenhower ordered the Seventh Fleet into Taiwan Strait, and Dulles raised the specter of nuclear weapons to thwart the "takeover" of territory which even Chiang insisted was Chinese.

Peking turned for support to Moscow, the other great nuclear power and its closest ally, to counteract the American blackmail. Premier Khrushchev, in an exchange with Eisenhower, said that an attack on China would be considered an attack on the Soviet Union; but he made it clear that Soviet power, including nuclear weapons, would be used only to help China defend itself against attack. Chinese policy before and since Quemoy and Matsu suggests that Peking would not even consider first-strike action, so the Soviet messages to Eisenhower seemed to Peking to be an unnecessary warning not to rock the battleships in Taiwan Strait. In public the Chinese kept their counsel and the crisis abated without serious consequence. But cracks were beginning to show for the first time in the Chinese–Soviet alliance.

Watching these events closely in the GUARDIAN, we gradually were becoming aware of a turn which socialists and their friends throughout the world felt could never happen—a division between the two great socialist countries. Anna Louise Strong was in China again, as our correspondent, and I cabled her for news. None came. After repeated requests, she finally cabled: "Our Chinese friends say now is not the time to create public debate." Even two years later, when Khrushchev abruptly ordered all Soviet technicians, equipment, supplies, and blueprints out of China, the Chinese were still reluctant to make the issue public.

In the course of the argument, when it finally became public, we sought to present both sides as fully as we were able, with background material on Mao's relations with Stalin, documents of discussions in Moscow and Peking, and commentaries by experts who could only speculate upon an unprecedented situation. Inevitably the tensions turned inward, with Communist Party partisans on the staff pressing for support of the Soviet position. Much of the internal storm centered on our India-born foreign affairs editor, Kumar Goshal, whose loyalties to his motherland kept pace with the increasing border tensions between Peking and New Delhi. Our advice to our readers was to keep their shirts and chemises in place until more was known and, in the last analysis, not to be diverted from an inspection of the main source of world discontent—Washington policy.

I resisted all efforts, internal and external, to "take sides." In this policy I was guided by Anna Louise, now writing bountifully, if discreetly, about the debate. In December 1962 she quoted a Chinese official: "The whole world is now going to school and must study hard, because the lessons are difficult but vital for mankind's future." In an editorial published on July 13, 1963,

EDITOR-IN-EXILE

under the headline, "The Great Debate and what it means for American progressives," I wrote:

"To suggest that radicals and progressives in the West can stay aloof from the content of the struggle would be an illusion; by the same token, it would be stretching reality across too many oceans and too many problems at home to suggest that radicals and progressives in the West, and particularly in the United States, must engage in divisive fashion in a debate which is bound to go on for a good long time and will ultimately be decided by the impact of events on the basic Marxist-Leninist theory which the Soviet Union and China hold in common. It is the interpretation of this theory, and the tactical approach to put it in practice, which is the main issue in the debate.

"For progressives in the West it hurts nothing to be reminded that for a third of the world living under it, socialism is not a dirty word, and for another third of the world it is a goal which is openly striven for. If a restoration of this knowledge reawakens an interest in and a study of the works of socialism, the debate will have made a notable achievement. But there is a danger, in the course of such a study, of restoring also a dogma which has plagued radicals in the West, and elsewhere, for generations. It is the dogma of absolutism, the espousal of a point of view as being 100 percent correct, and the rejection of all other points of view. None of us, East or West, is so all-wise that we can judge ourselves as anointed with perfect wisdom."

People the world over did go and are still going to school. There have been many dropouts. Whether fundamental answers have been achieved, it is still impossible to judge; but some fundamental positions have been put forward, especially in China, as I discovered in January 1976 in a 2,000-mile journey to seven cities and in innumerable conversations with Chinese hosts in all walks of life. One basic position was a core disagreement with the road the Soviet Union has taken as a betrayal of socialist principles. The memory of the Great Pullout of 1960 was bitterly apparent. "We have much to thank the Russians for," said one Foreign Office official. "They taught us how to be self-reliant."

Self-reliance was indeed the mark of China in the twenty-seventh year of liberation—and confidence, a confidence that they as a people held their destiny finally in their own hands and would never let it be torn from them. In this mood perhaps the most impressive elements were their sense of the dignity of work and the steady eradication of privilege. Again there comes to mind a theme from one of Cedric's cornerstones, W. E. B. DuBois, in the Credo of his novel *Darkwater*:

"I believe in Service—humble, reverent Service, from the blackening of boots to the whitening of souls; for Work is Heaven and Idleness Hell, and Wage is the 'Well done!' of the Master, who summoned all of them that labor and are heavily laden, making no distinction between the black, sweating cotton hands of Georgia and the first families of Virginia, since all distinction not based on deed is devilish and not divine."

While DuBois' reference was to another country in another continent, his message is universal. The "service" in China is to the people, and the "Master" who summoned all to labor was without question Mao Tse-tung—to the Chinese the embodiment of the struggle that "carries the hope of mankind," as Anna Louise Strong once characterized the effort to achieve socialism in the Soviet Union. I do not believe Mao's inspiration will disappear with his death.

Cedric's description of what he saw in China was confirmed for me almost two decades later when I retraced many of his steps there. I can amend his description only in positive degree. His concern over what he sees as China's foreign policy errors stemming from their conviction of the menace of the Soviet leadership gives me pause. Yet puzzled as I am by some aspects of this foreign policy, I foresee clarification in the developing situation following the great internal upheavals in China in the years 1976–77. Not a change in attitude toward Soviet policy, but a separation of that attitude from China's approach to nations and peoples struggling to be free.

Heavily laden the Chinese people are indeed as they patiently continue the Long March after the passing of Mao, Chou En-lai, and Chu Teh—the revolutionaries who signaled the beginning of the journey. Whether they ever will be able permanently to lay down their burden with a ''Well done!'' from the Master, I cannot say. But I believe they are on a course which, allowing for correction of errors, will one day lead socialism back to the road of *Zusammenarbeit*.

"Sorry, Not Interested"

[C.B.] Every journalist is supposed to dream of the day when he will be the only man on the spot at some historic occurrence; but two occasions in my career illustrate the vagaries of editors as to what is historic. The first was during my gilded bondage with the London *Express* in the 1930s, when fascism was creeping across Europe but the *Express* barely noticed it. The film companies, exasperated by my bleak views of their product, had refused to advertise any more while I remained as movie critic, and I had been switched to meeting ships at Southampton and interviewing their noteworthy passengers. One day the *Queen Mary* stuck placidly on a sandbank near the Isle of Wight and, since the tugs would take hours to free her, I wrote off my mission as unaccomplished and went home. I never heard the last from my editor of my failure to hire a launch and get what, by *Express* standards, would have been a screaming sensation. If duchesses and movie stars were not screaming in panic on the *Queen Mary,* and of course they weren't—merely drowning their irritation at the bars—as the only reporter present it was up to me to invent it.

In March 1961, I was the only Anglo-American weekly or daily reporter in Cuba when Washington sent bombing planes and

Cuban mercenaries to overthrow Fidel Castro.* I cabled *The Observer,* one of London's two "serious" Sunday papers, offering an eye-witness exclusive on the most historic Western Hemisphere event since Cuba cut off the tentacles of "Tío Sam." The reply came with British promptitude, and I appreciated the extra half-crown's worth in the first word: SORRY NOT INTERESTED.

With all allowance for editorial shudders about the by-line, this was a prize sample of the Great English-Speaking Peoples' indifference to their 200 million cousins between Texas and Cape Horn. Five centuries after Columbus, Latin America was still an undiscovered continent except as an object of white plunder and (when it couldn't be ignored) lies. Only readers of the GUARDIAN, of my other scattered "syndicate" journals and of Britain's left-wing *Tribune,* got my report on the Playa Girón (Bay of Pigs) fiasco. In the United States, while I watched the counterrevolutionaries being herded sheepishly into beach-resort dressing rooms, the media regaled the public with Adlai Stevenson's vows of American innocence and Miami-datelined rumors of Fidel and Che Guevara committing suicide. And this despite the fact that Cuba–U.S. phone lines remained open.

I had had an extra motive for going to Cuba, apart from reporting a unique kind of revolution ninety miles from Florida. Cubans at the United Nations had told Jack McManus that the Havana regime planned an English-language newspaper and that, if I was there, I could be first in line to edit it. In the slow course of absorbing the enthusiastic Latin American temperament, I would find that this "plan" was never more than somebody's bright idea. But I let myself dream of creating the first "human" (in our terms) socialist-country paper in a land close to "our" journalistic tradition. Linguistically I was even dreamier. The rudiments of Castillian taught me by a Spaniard in London hardly served, on arrival in Havana, to make a word comprehensible in the Cuban dialect.

But getting there was a long ride. Even Pan American Airways

---

*Except for my notorious lunch companion, Joe North of the New York *Worker,* whose bad luck it was to be hospitalized at the time. Leo Huberman of the *Monthly Review* was the other American journalist at the scene.

underestimated the edginess of Washington's nerves. Brushing aside my warning that I was a banned banshee in America, they sold me a ticket to Havana via New York (the then standard route from London) on the basis that no political litmus test was needed to move through Idlewild (later renamed Kennedy) from one plane to another. Instead, U.S. Immigration held me in an airport office while disposal of this human bomb was pondered at high Washington levels; and after six hours I was again airborne—back "for free" to London, where officials claimed I had broken the round-trip transatlantic record. As a veteran General Franco-phobe I had flinched at taking the other route to Cuba, via Madrid, and the more so now that the press, in reporting my second deportation, had resurrected the details of my first; but there was no help for it. The Spanish butcher's officials proved impressively immune to their American colleagues' fear that I would overthrow their airport. They treated me affably and sped me on my way. The GUARDIAN's December 12, 1960, issue headlined: OUR MAN'S IN HAVANA, NO THANKS TO THE FRIGHTENED GIANT.

A week later Jack flew in from New York with a tour of GUARDIAN readers, and we were all together at a government reception when Washington's break with Havana (no surprise to us, but complicating their trip home) was announced. It was a euphoric setting for my last reunion with Jack.

As in London under Dr. Wernher von Braun's hail of V-1's and V-2's in 1944, I adjusted to sudden explosions and fires lighting up the night sky—a scourge which Havana took with equal calm. Fidel's intelligent policy with pro-U.S. Cubans (about a tenth of the population) was to let them go where they felt they belonged as fast as transportation became available. A realist about Tío Sam, he expected some of them to be sent back to cooperate with the still-unevacuated remnant in dynamitings, arson, and assassinations. By prudently infiltrating them with agents, who alerted him to sabotage and invasion plans, he kept the upper hand for the revolution and thwarted the assassins whose chief target he was. While the truth about the Bay of Pigs couldn't long be concealed, the U.S. government's missions to shoot, poison, or otherwise

"SORRY, NOT INTERESTED"

obliterate Fidel were "revealed" only in 1975 by apparently startled congressmen. At the time there was no proof of U.S. sponsorship that 99 percent of Americans would accept, but three considerations left me in no doubt: 1) the history of intervention in Russia after 1917; 2) the nature of the CIA, the arm of Washington responsible for such exploits; 3) the nature of Fidel as I studied his actions and words from day to day.

Classical revolutionary theory holds that the masses, when conditions are ripe, will inevitably throw up men with all the diverse qualities needed to lead and consolidate. They haven't always done so, and it isn't espousing the Great Man theory of history to doubt the outcome in Cuba had Fidel not been born just when he was, with the natural endowments to become what he did. After his abortive revolt in 1953 against Washington's stooge dictator Batista, he had denounced Batista's regime before his judges and outlined the first steps he would recommend to cleanse and advance his country. He was taking these steps in 1960 and they were leading naturally, as Washington had failed to detect in time, to socialism. (The sure sign was the gradual disappearance of prostitutes and artificial sex stimulants, turning "fun-filled" Havana into another "drab" capital.) But over two years in the island we detected no other Cuban who combined the necessary self-confidence, personal magnetism, and stamina with the wit and wisdom to learn the new trade of socialist government. The Cuban masses, an amalgam of Spanish conquistadores and African slaves, were an essentially volatile, live-for-the-day people long exposed to (but never sharing) the material enticements of "the American way of life." They had to be steeled in battle against almost hopeless odds, and held with higher work-incentives through years of stress.

The traditional Latin American "savior" never took long to show whom he was concerned to save: he shut himself up in a palace counting his loot in Swiss bank accounts, and strutted forth occasionally in a fancy uniform surrounded by bodyguards. Fidel went about talking to ordinary people as modestly as he lived and as casually as he dressed, so that everyone fell into the habit of calling him by his first name, a style that would wreck the dignity of most wielders of power but only enhanced his. As a statesman he faced extraordinary problems, among them the split in the socialist camp while Cuba's dependence on the Soviet bloc, strange and remote cultures for Cubans, was an unarguable fact. At home, the exodus of pro-U.S. Cubans deprived him of thousands of doctors and educators and of nearly all trained administrators. Men and women who had shone as guerrilleros weren't necessarily, and indeed not often, paragons at running an industry or government bureau. Fidel made serious errors of judgment but, in contrast to the "we all make mistakes" line that familiarly passes for self-criticism, spelled them out in his candid and cant-free talks to the people about the nation's problems.* Thus he anchored himself in scores of millions of hearts beyond Cuba to Latin America's darkest confines, and made himself a top priority for Washington's murder details.

His Argentine compañero Che Guevara was also worth assassinating regardless of cost, but when Washington succeeded in that enterprise he was shown to be a great but not decisive loss to the revolution. As Minister of Industry (a job for which he admitted his poor qualifications, but there was no one else) he gave me an after-work interview lasting from midnight till nearly 3 A.M. He was dynamic and magnetic, intelligent and totally honest; but the purity of his courage, which would make him a legend, was too unbalanced by maturing wisdom to save him from foolhardiness. His global perception of a revolution needed and craved throughout Latin America and the third world was his enduring legacy. But Washington was not again going to let a small rebel band, whom it could not rely on corrupting, repeat the Cuban experience.

* In these talks Fidel gave the impression of greater concern than any other national leader, including China's, about the toughest of all democratic problems—bringing democracy into the field of foreign policy, where decisions are almost always and everywhere made by a small group at the top. There were of course aspects of foreign policy which couldn't be publicly discussed when it was in process of negotiation and development. But in such cases Fidel frankly said so, sharing the problems with the people to the extent that the national interest made possible at any given moment. Thus the people could and did feel that he never lied to them.

"SORRY, NOT INTERESTED"

The Cubans needed everything dramatized and, when that was done as Fidel knew how, they plunged with delight into the attempt to perform miracles—the more impossible, the better. When he called for the liquidation of illiteracy, 100,000 youngsters from the age of 12 up swarmed into the countryside to teach a million older folk how to read and write. At the same time rural kids, who never had milk or shoes, poured into Havana on scholarships and were quartered in capitalists' abandoned homes. These and similar mass mobilizations caused dislocations to appall any economist or efficiency expert, and their success in their own terms was limited; but they were decisive in the area of morale and of liquidating the curses of rural isolation and urban snobbery.

At harvest time truckloads of men and women bellowing the "Internationale" moved out to cut cane, leaving Havana's factories and offices semideserted. The "Internationale" truly reflected the spirit of a revolution which all the "brother countries" across the world nourished with food, machinery, weapons, and technical and cultural brothers.* One of the latter was the Soviet cellist Rostropovich. He arrived fresh from a New York recital where $12 tickets had been at a premium. The middle-class exodus had left too few musical cognoscenti in Cuba even to fill the hall at a few pesos a head. Rostropovich decided that if the people wouldn't come to him because they'd never heard of him, he would go to them. A truck took him and his cello to the sugar plantations and, as the cane-cutters sweated with their machetes, he sat among the stalks playing Bach.

Nothing impressed us (and everyone in Cuba) more than Fidel's method with the captured Playa Girón mercenaries. He put them in a televised theater and strode in among them for a confrontation seen by every last person in the island. Out of their own mouths he

---

* Apart from the gay lilt that Cubans gave to the "Internationale"—they sang it as if they meant it, not like a dirge—the abiding musical memory of Cuba is the signature tune constantly repeated by the government radio. No one had told them it was the theme song of British imperialism, "Land of Hope and Glory," and when I did so, they expressed due amazement but never faltered in playing it. One can also not forget the "Music by Muzak" which continually syruped the air of offices and banks. This and a pirated version of Coca-Cola were enduring footprints left by the Americans in the island's subversive soil.

showed what interests they represented: all the U.S.-controlled exploiting enterprises of the old regime. He challenged them to produce before the Cuban people an honorable defense of their behavior, as he had defended his before Batista's hangmen in 1953. None was forthcoming: their servile excuses of having been "tricked" by the Americans were nauseously reminiscent of the journalists "tricked" by Hitler who paraded before me in Germany in 1945. The audience of 7,000,000 Cubans had been alerted to notify the authorities if, as the cameras panned over the mercenary faces, they recognized any of Batista's torturers and assassins. Now before the court of the whole nation there were confrontations between these and people whom they had tortured or raped in jail, or whose children they had killed. Regular courts reviewed the evidence and the guilty were executed. The rest were eventually exchanged for medicines, bulldozers, and other useful U.S. products. Their sponsor, President Kennedy, greeted them as heroes and his wife wept over the obviously phony flag which they claimed to have led them into "battle" at Playa Girón. (As Fidel commented, "They left behind everything including their underwear.") The battle had consisted mainly of mercenaries throwing up their hands before the spectacle of overwhelming loyalty to Fidel and the revolution.

A number of Americans and other foreigners had "settled" in Cuba, some belonging to the tribe of "revolutionary free-loaders" whom I had met throughout eastern Europe, some aspiring to share the revolutionary experience with a positive contribution. I think all of us in the latter category would say, as socialists, that Cuba provided the most useful and durable education of our lives. What we could directly share were the frustrations and some of the privations of building socialism—a hard lesson that only day-to-day living in such a country could teach. The frustration was deepened for us by the ingrained characteristics of Latin Americans: their different wavelength on such trivia as time and death, their ardent agreement, as a matter of politeness, with whatever one said. In the minds of Cubans, "No" and "I don't know" existed in normal abundance; in their vocabulary, not at all.

"SORRY, NOT INTERESTED"

The excitement we could but share indirectly, for it wasn't our country and culture, and our destinies weren't inextricably bound up with it. The positive contribution most of us could make with whatever expertise we had was small: my ex-schoolteacher wife's at the Ministry of Education, mine as a chronicler for the outside world and foreign affairs columnist for *El Mundo*. (This non-party Havana daily later disappeared and the press, to my disappointment, narrowed down according to the Soviet model.) The Cubans insisted on making their own mistakes in their own revolution, and maddened us by the speed with which our purely technical arguments went in one apparently receptive ear and out the other. The more obstinately they pursued the "wrong" way of doing things until they had tested it for themselves, the more we had to love them. To this there were of course exceptions: officials whose petty power went to their heads and made them arrogant to their subordinates and servile to their superiors, and writers and artists who disdained the challenge of the cultural awakening of the masses. But passing guests from abroad at our house invariably left with a new kind of glow.* One of these was my daughter, who also left with a stitched and bandaged wound over her eye: innocently dining with the Cuban who was detailed to show her around, she had been struck with a Coca-Cola bottle by his hot-blooded girl friend. Sally had the right approach: "Oh for a revolution," she said, "in a country we know and belong to!"

In late spring of 1961 we set off, on the proceeds of a small legacy from my mother, to discover the rest of the undiscovered subcontinent, which was still Tío Sam's banana patch. We had trouble enough disentangling what was socialist from what was Latin American in Cuba. Now we proposed to savor, if hardly to

---

*Among them Queens Counsel D. N. Pritt, economist Joan Robinson, historian Eric Hobsbawm, businessman Jack Perry from Britain, and the New Zealand writer and Turkish poet, Rewi Alley and Nazim Hikmet, whom I had met respectively in Peking and Tashkent. Gen. Hugh B. Hester and authors Harvey and Jessie Lloyd O'Connor were among many Americans who defied the State Department's threats to come. The Americans were especially impressed by the safety with which one could walk the streets—policed by young militias, i.e., the people themselves—at any hour.

digest in our time-limit of some two weeks each, a dozen kindred lands in light of the effect upon them of their hemisphere's first socialist revolution. The journey opened up for us a vein of human culture whose richness we hadn't suspected, while imprinting on us the crimes which the U.S. government had committed—and was still committing—against it.

Haitians began our enlightenment with ghastly accounts of the terror under "Papa Doc" Duvalier. Washington viewed this with comparative benevolence as it had the even bloodier terror in the Dominican Republic, the other half of Columbus' first island stop. The recent murder of the Dominican monster Trujillo, an ungrateful puppet who had simply appropriated everything in his country for himself, had shown that one didn't have to be a socialist to inconvenience Washington and become a target for its assassins. But although this had brought the dawn of "democracy" there under a military junta, the long inquisitorial arm reached out from the banks of the Potomac. We pressed through the U.S. army men who swarmed over Santo Domingo airport, presented our passports, and were ordered back on the plane, whose embarrassing destination was the U.S. "associated commonwealth" (colony), Puerto Rico. My plea for a quick tour of the places I'd written about in my Columbus novel was cut short with a curt: "There will be no explanation."

I spent a fidgety airborne hour thinking of all the Cuban letters of introduction, in my checked suitcase, to revolutionaries in countries beyond. At San Juan (Puerto Rico) airport the separation of admissible sheep from inadmissible goats was in the hands of palefaces armed, as we expected, with the same Black Book they had at New York's Idlewild. The damning hieroglyphics against my name in the book turned them a shade whiter.

"What shall we do with you?" they said on a helpless note which didn't escape my wife Mary's finely tuned instinct.

"Put us on that," she said, pointing to a Trinidad-bound plane, the last of the day, from which the ramp was already being drawn away. Apparently grateful to escape involvement in the inquisitorial labyrinth, they had our tickets hurriedly rewritten, rushed us

"SORRY, NOT INTERESTED"

and our incriminating baggage on to the tarmac, and stood waving a pale good-bye as we soared above the coco palms.

Thousands of state-siders were "doing" Latin America in a series of planes, taxis, sightseeing buses, hotels, boutiques, casinos, and whorehouses so identical that only dates on tickets told them which country they were in. We were constantly exposed to their conversation, which dealt preeminently with the cost of their useless activities and purchases; when they could obtain something for less than its maker's family bean bill while working on it, they were triumphant. Through the language wall which they had no intention of trying to break, they saw just enough of the misery to rouse some pity, contempt for the government in question or, more often, fear. Both its absurdity and its criminality escaped them and their minds were closed to any awareness of guilt. Meanwhile American Ph.D.'s roamed the subcontinent meticulously studying every aspect of its misery, detached in the purest scientific spirit from any curative aim. Our aim was to learn how the victims hoped to throw off the incubus, in countries which had two common denominators, cultural history and the effective condition of colonies, but otherwise varied greatly. The frontiers between them were real in the classic British imperialist style, with the United States as interhemispheric hub for communications and source of "news" and official ideology. Washington's answer to Cuba had been an Alliance for Progress, guaranteeing for all the countries' common folk further impoverishment and desperation while the United States tightened economic and military control. But the "progress" façade spared us any more Santo Domingos and San Juans.

In the ever-swelling slums of Caracas–Rio–Buenos Aires–Santiago–Lima, the port area of Recife patrolled by an army of juvenile prostitutes, the desolate mining camps of Bolivia, the starving backlands of Ecuador, one asked oneself how people could live under such conditions and such ruthless repression. The answer was that most of them existed briefly and died anonymously, but everywhere we visited with subversively disposed peasants, urban workers, miners, journalists, students, politicians, and priests.

Some of them seemed more brave than realistic, especially those pinning their hopes to "the barrel of a gun" on a scale no larger than had brought victory to the Cubans. Tío Sam was in fact about to show his military and corruptive potency in presiding over the extermination of all Latin America's guerrilla forces and of such democracy as existed in the biggest country, Brazil. Others who talked to us were more sober about the formidable obstacles, not least of which were the antagonisms, now broadened and sharpened by the Moscow–Peking split and massive infiltration by CIA provocateurs, within left movements.

Chile, where both Socialists and Communists enjoyed the right to exist and contend in the political arena, was the one country where the majority of progressives believed in the honesty of the ballot and its viability as a means of change. So much so that Socialists, the main left party, had joined in a united front with Communists. We spent several hours, at the Senate and at his modestly tasteful home hung with autographed Fidel and Che photos, with the Socialist leader and united front presidential candidate, Senator Salvador Allende.

"The reason we stopped fighting the Communists," he said, "is that we really are socialists. We learned by bitter experience that ideological issues are the common enemy's weapon to divide us. Our disagreements on the Soviet Union are secondary beside our joint need to defeat imperialism. With all their money and propaganda the Americans, who always corrupted Chilean politics, can't succeed in breaking us up because anti-imperialism is our reason for being. Of course they understand that their worst possible kind of defeat is a legal one." He saw a socialist Chile as a "southern pivot of the second Latin American revolution" with Cuba in the north.

A honeymoon with Marxism, followed by repentance for this error of "youthful zeal," had in the 1940s and '50s been a prime formula for success in Latin American politics. As a Latin American saying put it, "our Presidencies are like the violin: you take it with the left and play it with the right." On the record, some Chileans were understandably cynical about the chances of Allende, a prosperous physician, continuing to "betray his class" when the chips were down. He impressed us strongly as a mature and honest socialist. He had known personally all of Latin America's repentant Marxist leaders and dismissed them with pithy professional diagnoses: "a clear case of arteriosclerosis," "the most psychotic anti-communists are always former Communists." Years later Allende as elected President would nobly bear out, as all but the most ultra-left critics of his specific measures agree, our impression of him. But Washington would not long permit this "worst kind of defeat" for capitalism to gather strength, and connived in his extermination and replacement by a replica of Nazism.

And this had been easily predictable ever since Tío Sam's response in the 1960s to the election of a socialist prime minister (Jagan) in Guyana and of a "moderate" progressive (Bosch) in the Dominican Republic. In Guyana the CIA's corruptive mechanism (again "revealed" by the U.S. press in 1976), brought to bear through a pauper labor movement and the stimulation of racist violence by *Lumpen,* took care of the situation.* In the Dominican Republic, the Johnson regime in Washington emulated the Tom Lehrer song with the refrain: "When in doubt—send the Marines."

In the Panama Canal Zone I stood again on "U.S. soil"—a nostalgic few hours despite my awareness of the quotation marks. The Black Book-less American in charge of the canal-viewing installation couldn't know whom he was welcoming to the most strategic of all sabotage targets, and in deference to his cordiality I restrained the impulse to toss a bomb. Only a street separated the Zone, with its Beverly Hills-like residential area and its camps where Latin Americans were trained to kill and torture their starving countrymen, from a Panama slum which was like a theatrical

---

* When we visited Guyana the second time in 1963, it was blockaded and accessible only by hired Cessna from Surinam. America's hand in the "destabilization" (the term later used about Chile) of Jagan's regime was obvious but then unprovable, and my dispatches to this effect produced the expected sneers. The sequel has been ironical: the Guyanese are so sold on socialism as their salvation that Forbes Burnham, the CIA's replacement for Jagan via faked elections, has ended up further to the left than his predecessor.

exaggeration by Gorky or Brecht. The resident Americans went about their work and play in normal oblivion to the crime their presence represented.

The New York *Times* we bought in Mexico City painted the picture of an America in the fall of 1962 gripped by panic. The Soviets had been caught installing rockets in Cuba at Cuba's request for its defense—popguns by comparison with America's press-button power to blow up the planet—and Kennedy was threatening Khrushchev and pressuring the whole Free World to join in a blockade of the island. Cuba had recently offered to disarm completely if the Americans would pledge not to attack (which of course they wouldn't); but without consulting the Cubans, Khrushchev removed the rockets rather than risk global war over them. Jim flew down to Mexico, notably un-panicked, and we agreed that I should return to Havana by the first plane out. Mexico had suspended the twice-weekly service but, as the one hemisphere country never joining the blockade, was about to resume it.

The passengers were mostly journalists, and at Havana airport militia men and women entertained us with revolutionary songs and congas until the "problem" we represented was "resolved" by taking us all under arrest to a luxury hotel. The hotel lobby throbbed with the Caribbean beat of "Somos Leninistas," to which dancers were kicking up their legs in the adjacent nightclub. In the morning some of the American ships and planes, surrounding the island with the latest lethal and radar devices, could be seen from the lofty suites that were our cells. I had passed a restless night haunted by thoughts of Stalin's "errors" in the first socialist country, but the friendliness of the guard at our door returned me to Cuban reality. "Paciencia, compañero," he said, "this is a new revolution and we have a crisis." The waiter was just wheeling a white-tableclothed lunch trolley into our cell when the error was recognized, with great hilarity by all concerned, and we were escorted to the house we shared with an American couple and their new baby.

The Cubans could no longer surprise us by their response to a crisis—far from panicking them, it was just what they needed to galvanize them into super-performance. Half of Havana's people were out on militia duty; those assigned to stay in the city queued up after work to relax with the Soviet circus or Chaplin's *Gold Rush* and *Modern Times*. Shabbier for its six more months without paint, Havana was stripped for action. Militias manning anti-aircraft guns out in the country, beneath pleasant groves of palms, told us they were ready to die but excited about living, and were equally convincing in both. While they waited, they studied philosophy and socialist theory and helped local farmers in the fields. Our poet friend Rosahilda, who had repeatedly risked her life in the anti-Batista underground, complained of the mosquitos but said of the crisis: "Oh, that! That's just *patria o muerte.*" However they felt about removal of the rockets, all were as grateful for their Soviet ally as the British in a similar crisis in 1941, and were no more de-nationalized thereby. Meanwhile they were versed enough in counterrevolutionary history, from the Paris Commune to Spain in 1939, to know what they must expect if they yielded. With what weapons they had they would clearly make any invasion a nightmare for the invader, so that all he could ever capture would be a cemetery.

We had intended to spend a week in Cuba but the blockade spun it out into three months. We left more than ever convinced of two things. That mismanagement would long continue in almost every area except defense, which fell into disciplined shape by a kind of spontaneous combustion. And that things would continue to get done by the effort of an indomitable, nameless multitude who asked no recognition—under the leadership of Fidel and of new-model Cubans whom the revolutionary generation, no longer "growing up absurd," must surely produce. The brainwashing process was making its slow, healthy transformation.

We were bound for Mexico, whose coast was 100 miles away, but again it was a long ride. In return for Tío Sam's "permission" not to break with Cuba, Mexico had agreed to let him (i.e., FBI and CIA) monitor its airport immigration when planes arrived from or left for Havana; and since he had declared all visitors to Cuba to be dangerous overthrowers, the Mexicans must put on a performance in that spirit. Thus all passengers from Havana were required to have through bookings to another country by an immediate connection, although Mexico would let them return, washed clean by the departure-point on their new tickets.

In our case the "destination" for this lunacy had to be Canada, there being no immediate connection to any nearer country where I was pure enough to land. Flying over my no-longer "home" state of New York, watching the caterpillars of headlights along familiar highways, we drank toasts to the GUARDIAN and to the continued freedom of the upper air. A few days later we re-crossed the Frightened Giant's territory and were welcomed with a cordiality which made us feel at home. The Mexicans needed no explanation of our peculiar and costly detour: they were far more familiar with the giant's paranoias than we would ever be.

The arrangement was that I would write the Latin American revolutionary primer for gringos which I had in mind,* and, using all the contacts I had made, establish myself as a correspondent for the whole subcontinent. Mexico's advantage for our personal lives was that, while we were barred from visiting our closest friends who lived north of the frontier, it was convenient for them to visit us. After my book was finished we made one more trip, as far as Guyana, to get acquainted with the Caribbean islands. At our first stop, Jamaica, we were house guests of the island's most active socialist—a fact evidently noted by the giant's busy agents and local collaborators. We were nowhere refused entry but at several islands the police had been warned of our arrival: they interviewed us gravely, limited the time we could stay, and were on hand to see us off. Like most Caribbean routes our return flight passed through Puerto Rico where an improvement in the giant's neurasthenia was manifested. A bare room had been provided where through passengers, including overthrow suspects, could stare at a wall while their plane refueled.

Back in Mexico I was soon confronted by the special problem of setting up a Latin American news service. One by one my corre-

*The Man at the Door with the Gun (New York: Monthly Review Press, 1963).

"SORRY, NOT INTERESTED"

spondents to the south, some of whom we already thought of as friends, fell silent in the various ways that Latin American socialists are silenced. Some were in jail. Some, like Brazil's peasant leader Francisco Juliao, were "allowed" after military coups to leave jail for exile and turned up in Mexico with nothing but the clothes they wore. Juliao brought word that Mario, the sensitive young journalist who escorted us around Rio, had been slowly tortured to death under the auspices of Tío Sam's cooperative generals.

Nobody much was interested. Mario was only one victim of a U.S.-sponsored "system of government" now too routine to be newsworthy.

Postscript [**J. A.**] Shortly after Thanksgiving 1960 a cable arrived from Cedric announcing his Pan Am stop-over in New York en route from London to Havana. Assurances of his "toleration" by U.S. officials had been given. Mindful, however, of his federal kidnap on a Third Avenue street corner five years earlier, we decided to fortify this assurance with the presence at the airport of Blanch Freedman, the no-funny-business lawyer who had anguished with us through the two-and-a-half-year battle to keep Cedric on U.S. soil.

Earlier than need be on the appointed day, Jack, Blanch, and I went out to Idlewild, tinkered with an uneasy and unpalatable airport lunch, then made our way up to the terrace walkway overlooking the international landing field. Security was not so stringent in those pre-hijack days. We were watching some black-backed gulls soar gracefully overhead when the Pan Am arrival was announced. The plane came in and settled on the field a few hundred yards from where we stood. Jack began sprinting toward the point closest to the plane with us close behind. He stopped in mid-journey and clutched a rail, face pale and shoulders constricted. I stopped with him. "You all right?" I said. "I'm fine," he said. "Just give me a moment." It was a sign of the heart condition he had until then concealed from us, which would carry him off a year later.

We saw Cedric debark in a cluster of passengers, wearing the same hand-me-down rain hat and trench coat he had worn the day we got him sprung from Ellis Island. There was an omen in that too. We shouted and waved, but the noise and distance kept him from noting our presence. He disappeared into the building.

We hurried downstairs to the waiting area outside the Customs gates and watched the Pan Am passengers come through. No Cedric. I dashed back upstairs to the observation deck looking onto the Customs lines. Still no Cedric. Back downstairs for a strategy huddle. Jack confronted a Customs official for an explanation. He got a stone-faced shrug. He demanded to see an Immigration official. Call Immigration in New York, said Stoneface: he knew "nothing."

Blanch called Immigration. Through the glass of the booth we saw her neck muscles tighten as she hissed into the mouthpiece. "They won't tell me a thing," she said. "I have to call Washington." After an hour's effort, Washington told her Cedric had been "separated" from the rest of the passengers for "special consideration." Would he be allowed to keep to his schedule? No one knew. What was wrong with escorting him to the Cubana Airlines waiting room a few hundred yards from where we stood? Well, he would have to enter U.S. territory en route and he was excluded by the terms of the Immigration and Naturalization Act of 1952 from setting foot on this sacred cement. But please be assured, Mrs. Freedman, he is receiving every consideration and we will inform you of developments.

Dozens of calls followed—to Immigration New York and Washington, to the Justice Department, to other lawyers for counsel. Much badgering of irritated airport personnel. No one knew anything. After three hours of this frustration, I detached myself from our little group, took out my New York Police Department press card, went through the swinging doors to the interior Customs turnstiles (a new crew had come on), and sailed through saying "Press" whenever anyone seemed to question my mission. Smiles, tipping of caps; it was criminally easy. I barged through Customs and Immigration (no one at the gate) down into a long deserted corridor in the bowels of Uncle Sam's purgatory. Many doors with little windows at the top. I peered into all of them. No Cedric. Finally, at the end of the corridor, an open door revealing a large square room lined on four sides with empty wooden folding chairs. All empty, that is, except the one containing a contemplative Cedric, still coated and hatted, puffing on pipe, staring at the opposite blank wall.

Framed in the door, I yelled his name. He looked at me and said: "My God, how did *you* get in here?" I said: "My God, how did *you* get in here?" We burst into laughter and hugged in the middle of the room. I had barely time to tell him of Blanch's and Jack's activities when we were joined by a third party—an Immigration guard, florid of face and menacing of manner. His question to me was more infernal than divine. "How the hell did *you* get in here?" he said. "Press," I said importantly. "I don't give a goddam what you are," he said joining heaven and hell: *"out!"* He moved toward me and I moved in an arc toward the door behind him, meanwhile muttering to Cedric assurances in which I had no faith. Back down the hall I went, my backside prodded by a glare extending the length of the escape corridor.

I reported my Stanley–Livingstone encounter to Blanch and Jack and the vigil and calls proceeded for three hours more. We knew at least that there was a body even if we did not have it. Finally, at the seventh hour of Cedric's arrival, Blanch was summoned to the phone. Immigration calling from Washington: Cedric had been put on a plane back to London one hour earlier.

President Kennedy chose United Nations Week in October 1962 to violate the Charter of the United Nations with the unilateral imposition by the United States of an armed blockade of Cuba. The apparent motivation for this progress from brinkmanship to atomic cliff-hanging was the emplacement on Cuban soil at Cuban request of ballistic missiles to guard the Cubans from a more sophisticated replay of the Bay of Pigs invasion. Premier Khrushchev diverted Soviet vessels from an encounter with U.S. warships off the Cuban coast in the third week of October, but before this decision the world went through a convulsion of fear of doomsday.

Some families fled the cities of America for the dubious refuge of the mountains against anticipated atomic incineration. In the schools of Los Angeles, children broke down and cried: "I don't want to die." In some schools the situation became so bad that principals went on the public address system to calm the students "with fact and common sense," as the Los Angeles *Times* reported. Where the principals unearthed these two staples was hard to say in light of the near-unanimous rally round the flag by Congress and press. The New York *Times* and the Washington *Post* had obligingly withheld—at the President's request—information in their possession that a major portion of the U.S. armed forces had been mobilized, and Kennedy planned to announce the blockade and an ultimatum to the Soviet Union to withdraw the missiles. The stage had been carefully set for a television broadcast by Kennedy on the night of October 22. The strategy was to maintain secrecy until then to prevent an emergency session of the UN Security Council, which might head off the blockade and the ultimatum.

I had scheduled a flight to Mexico City for the evening of October 23 to meet with Cedric and discuss his future plans. Except for that aborted moment at Idlewild we had not met since London in 1958. The GUARDIAN was ready to go to press with space held open for an editorial I would write about the Kennedy address.

That Monday night I watched the Kennedy telecast, listened to the portentous commentators whose scripts were predictable, gathered the first editions of the morning papers (same predictable portentousness), and spent half the night on the editorial. I brought it in early the next morning, passed it around and, while it was being set, called an emergency session of the staff. They were amazingly calm. No one had fled to the hills, families were all in place, and the place for many was picket lines and demonstrations in Hammarskjold Plaza outside the UN. There was some nervous joking. Should I proceed to Mexico City or sit tight? "You might as well go," said Bob Light, "you can be burned to a crisp down there as well as here."

With that reassurance endorsed generally, I decided to keep to the plan. Grambs accompanied me: while we never talked about it, there seemed to be a tacit agreement that if we were going to end up crisp, it might be easier together than separately. At the airport we were surprised by the unaccustomed sight of luggage being opened on tables set up in front of the ticket counters by uniformed inspectors. The crisis had invaded the airport. Would there be a search of bodies too? Abruptly I left a somewhat bewildered wife with our luggage in the center of the lounge. Be right back, I said, emergency call. It was not nervous stomach, however, but nervous notebook. I had tucked in my address book a list of Americans and Cubans in Havana who might be good news sources for Cedric if we decided that he should proceed to Cuba. A personal search yielding such a list, however innocent, might place me in a first-class seat at a federal inquisition rather than in an economy-class seat on a Mexico-bound plane. I went into a toilet booth, shredded the list and flushed it down the drain. I have rarely felt so self-degraded. As it turned out, there was no body search.

Cedric was at the airport in Mexico. It was close to midnight and we were exhausted by the tensions of the crisis week. "I know you'd prefer to go right to the house and bed," he said, "but there's a group of American and Mexican friends who feel isolated and worried sick about the situation. They're gathered at a house in San Angel and were hoping that you'd stop by and give them something from the horse's mouth. Would you mind terribly?"

We drove through the soft night to a lovely section of the city with cobblestone streets to a small brightly lighted house. A knock on the door drew a warm "Buenas noches" from the housekeeper. Beyond her was a living room ringed with worried faces, some familiar, others not, all of them precious. What possessed me, I do not know (although I was light in the head with fatigue), but as I walked into the living room I heard myself say: "There will be no war."

If there had been, it is unlikely anyone would have been around to offer recrimination to a false prophet.

Cold Journeys and Hot Wars

[J. A.] John Foster Dulles' death in the spring of 1959 seemed to signal the end of an era in American foreign policy. Since the two super-powers were lockstepped in the production of atomic weapons and missiles, and nothing could be done about that, it was time for a show of benignity. The show, with loud noises off, began in August when President Eisenhower announced a September visit to the United States by Soviet Premier Khrushchev.

Almost immediately the newspapers blossomed with full-page ads urging a "National Day of Mourning." HUAC launched a full-dress investigation of Khrushchev's un-American "crimes." The advertising firm of Erwin, Wasey, Ruthrauf, and Ryan called on Americans to ask Khrushchev "WHY THERE'S NO MADISON AVE. IN MOSCOW." The American Dental Association refused to give up the ballroom of the Waldorf-Astoria for a reception for the visitor. The State Department announced that it would fly the Hammer and Sickle at the airport and at the President's guest house, but not in the streets of Washington.

The New York *Times,* manfully proposing a courteous and correct reception, echoed the Washington *Post*'s plea to Khrushchev not to "disappoint or profane" the hope for fuller understanding

280

by regarding his trip "merely as an opportunity to make propaganda and sow division."

The division sowers, as it turned out, came largely from newspaper row. I bore personal witness to this as one of three hundred American journalists accredited by the State Department to accompany Khrushchev on his cross-country journey—from Washington to New York to Los Angeles to San Francisco to Des Moines to Pittsburgh and back to Washington. There were in addition forty correspondents from various parts of the world, not including the People's Republic of China and the German Democratic Republic, countries whose existence Washington denied. The press arrangements required the services of the State Department, Army, Navy, and Air Force, six commercial airlines, two railroads, dozens of hotels, and hundreds of local officials. Western Union alone set up 260 special telegraphic circuits to handle 400,000 words a day— the equivalent of a half dozen full-length books. Scores of reporters and photographers from local newspapers and radio and TV personnel augmented the international press horde at every city on the itinerary. The story, said the *Times*'s James Reston (who kept a princely distance from the horde), was more nearly smothered than covered. Presumably Reston hoped to throw a blanket of doubt on the reportage, but it missed: what the press smothered was mainly itself.

There was little benignity in the first front-line dispatches. Khrushchev did not walk; he waddled. His tailoring got flunking marks; Ms. Khrushchev wore a skirt which "hung lower in front than in the rear," and applicants for jobs as chambermaids, Dorothy Kilgallen reported for the Hearst press (she covered the Washington–New York sector of the trip in a $27,500 silver-grey Rolls-Royce), "are usually far more *à la mode* than Russia's First Lady." Syndicated columnist Jim Bishop offered an unsubtle hint at assassination possibilities.

At the National Press Club in Washington, then still a male bastion, there was a neanderthal vignette starring the club's president, William Lawrence of the New York *Times*. When a woman reporter, protesting discrimination, sought admission to the bar,

Lawrence himself physically ejected her, saying: "We don't even allow *ladies* in here." More than five hundred inquiring reporters were on hand for Khrushchev's speech—the awesome by-lines and the unknown reporters from Copenhagen, Jakarta, and Lowell, Mass., all standing in line to get into the dining room. The Soviet reporters had been let in the back door and were seated at front tables. Photographers climbed onto every vantage point. At the head table were the Khrushchev family, the editors of *Pravda* and *Izvestia* and the author Sholokhov and his wife. Khrushchev said:

"I beg you, gentlemen, to try to understand me aright and to convey correctly all that I say . . . for it depends on you correspondents to a large extent to provide people with truthful information about our stay in the United States."

Information there was—to the over-saturation point. From Andrews Air Force Base to the United Nations, from the Pacific Coast to the Catoctin Mountains of Maryland, where the "Spirit of Camp David" flickered briefly. The famous can-can performance on the set in Hollywood where Shirley MacLaine and the chorus line threw their bottoms up at the dumbfounded Khrushchevs perched on a makeshift balcony. The visit to Roswell Garst's farm in Coon Rapids, Iowa, where Khrushchev invited his traveling host, Henry Cabot Lodge, to get his patrician nose close to a live pig for the first time. The "welcome" to New York in the boiler room under Grand Central Terminal (for security reasons, they said), where speeches mingled with hissing steam. The inspection of a supermarket in San Francisco, where bulky photographers swept children off shelves with such remarks as: "What's the matter with you kids—don't you know the baked bean section is reserved for the press?"

There were the placard-holding peace demonstrators at the railroad stations at Santa Barbara and San Luis Obispo in California, who altered the character of the journey after the rudeness of Los Angeles officials and the visitor's anger. Khrushchev's speech to the Chamber of Commerce at Des Moines where, to a standing ovation, he discarded a prepared text with master showmanship and talked to his audience as "one businessman to another." The "debate" with the leaders of labor in San Francisco in which the Premier sounded like a trade union organizer and Walter Reuther of the United Auto Workers assumed the guise of Secretary of State. The "displaced persons" of Eastern Europe parading the streets of Pittsburgh as Secret Service men patroled the urinals in the hotels.

How closely did the assembled journalists adhere to Khrushchev's admonition at the National Press Club? In a Report to Readers, I wrote:

"Newspapermen have always been noted for their cynicism and skepticism—much of it warranted—but on the Khrushchev trip many of them ranged from unbalanced objectivity to active opposition, in person and in print. They made no effort to conceal their hostility, and yet there was a curious quality to their mood: it was as if they were adopting this conforming attitude because each thought the other expected it of him. For this observer, perhaps the most appalling aspect of the tour with Mr. K has been a firsthand appreciation of the extent to which the people who write and shape news and opinion in America have brainwashed themselves into frozen attitudes."

There was, however, a new element in the coverage: live television. For the first time in their own country—except for United Nations events—Americans by the millions were spectators at a "live" international occasion whose potential was overwhelming, and they sensed it instinctively. Despite years of conditioning and warning against the "international communist conspiracy," the public was curious about this man from Moscow (synonymous for many with Mars); and what they saw of him, his family, and his colleagues roused indignation against newspapers reporting the visit in a manner which bore little resemblance to what they were seeing. This spirit was reflected in a flood of letters to the editor in newspapers across the country, and its impact on the working press was manifest in the changing quality of their reports as the trip proceeded.

It was not a matter of Americans becoming captivated by an encounter with a representative of socialism. It was an expression of their yearning for an end to bitterness and hostility in the world, their hunger for peace. The wounds of Korea were still raw, and there were ominous rumblings of impending American involvement in Southeast Asia. While the editors of the New York *Times* and the Washington *Post* would protest indignantly if they were charged with seeking to dampen these hopes, it was clear that they were committed to the cold war, and sought to enlist the public in this commitment.

America's prevailing mood was underscored by a Gallup poll taken September 28, 1959, immediately after the "Spirit of Camp David" had been let out of the bottle at the final meeting of President and Premier, and an Eisenhower visit to Moscow in 1960 had been announced. The question asked was: "All things considered, do you think Khrushchev's visit to the U.S. has been a good thing or a bad thing?" The answers: good thing, 52 percent; bad thing, 19 percent; neutral or no opinion, 29 percent.

The Premier's plane for his flight home was hardly off the ground before press and radio–TV commentators went to work on the 52 percent. No aspect of the tour was too small for disparagement. The urgency of the counterattack reflected the concern of government that questions about Dullesian foreign policy would lead to a demand for radical change.

There was no such demand. Men and events conspired to keep the nation on the cold war track. In Paris in May 1960, just before a conference during which Eisenhower and Khrushchev would advance the Spirit of Camp David, the Soviet Premier charged Washington with conducting U-2 spy flights over the Soviet Union. Eisenhower denied the charge and the New York *Times* said Khrushchev had concocted it because he did not want to talk peace anyway. Khrushchev produced pictures of the captive U-2 pilot, Gary Powers, and the downed plane; the Paris conference was called off, and the Eisenhower trip to the Soviet Union was canceled. Several editors of the *Times* (including Reston) conceded later that they had long known about the U-2 flights but "in the national interest" had published nothing about them. In the same interest they objectively published Eisenhower's lies and supported them with their own. The *Times,* and the press in general, were accomplices before and after the fact.

In September 1960, Khrushchev returned to New York to head the Soviet delegation in the UN Assembly. The auspices were quite different. Instead of being saluted by spirited bands at Andrews Air Force Base, he debarked from a Soviet motor ship to be met at a shabby and rotting pier on the East River by pickets of the International Longshoremen's Union. They carried banners of greeting, one of which read: "Roses Are Red, Violets Are Blue; Stalin Dropped Dead, How About You?"

A few days later, at the conclusion of a UN speech by the U.S. delegate, Khrushchev took off a shoe and banged it on the table in mock accompaniment to the applause that greeted the speech. There were innumerable editorials in the press about decorum and manners at international assemblies; I do not recall a single adverse press comment about those East River picket banners.

Travel with a Soviet Premier was an extraordinary departure from the generally desk-bound routine of a GUARDIAN editor. More ordinary travel involved periodic visits with the GUARDIAN family and lectures at universities in various parts of the country. And while the journeys were almost equally arduous, the camaraderie and warmth of the visits more than compensated for the fatigue. Such travels made me acutely conscious of how little East Coast clingers knew about the people of the heartland. The phrase "Middle America," uttered with derision by most liberals, had no such connotation for me. At the GUARDIAN, we knew from firsthand experience that Middle America in their sense could be found as readily in mid-Manhattan as in Manhattan, Kansas. One trip and one person in particular have stayed with me.

On January 21, 1961, I left blizzard-ridden New York for a series of meetings with GUARDIAN readers and with students at universities in a dozen cities. I followed what can only be described as the polar arc. As the arc extended into the North Central states it got colder and colder. The blizzard had grounded planes and a harbor strike had halted trains in New York January 20, so I missed the first meeting scheduled for that night in Chicago. William Davidon, a brilliant physicist at the Argonne National Laboratories and then a compelling voice for peace, pinch-hit for me before 100 persons who had come to the South Side in zero weather. I got to the North Side for a meeting the next night.

Then on to Milwaukee, bleak and cold in the twilight, but a bright and warm room in the Hotel Wisconsin, filled with Progressive Party veterans, Unitarians, members of the Fellowship of Reconciliation, representatives of all groupings on the political left, and one self-confessed existentialist. Most impressive was the fact that people had come from Fond du Lac, Campbellsport, and Racine, some traveling 130 miles for the round trip in weather that called for rallying round the fireplace.

In Minneapolis it was 28° below: amazingly there were 150 people at the Andrews Hotel. Familiar names and postmarks came to life: George Vikingstad from Blue Earth, Harry Haugland from Watson, and Fred Stover, editor of *U.S. Farm News,* who had driven in from Des Moines to speak, introducing from the audience members of the U.S. Farm Association from Illinois, Iowa, and Nebraska. "It is easier," he said, "to get farmers to come to a GUARDIAN meeting than it is to get a farmer into the Department of Agriculture." That brought north country whoops and hollers from the audience. Ted Ptashne, a former member of the Minneapolis Symphony Orchestra (his businessman brother Fred was chairman) and a violinist with the Casals Festival Symphony, played with composer Lionel Davis at the piano. They were not hired musicians; they were GUARDIAN readers.

But the audience was the evening for me. The Scandinavian faces, the radical farmer–labor heritage alive in that room—lumbermen and trainmen, teachers and social workers—and a young Englishman doing special studies at the University of Minnesota. He watched the people as they greeted and fraternized before bundling up for the trip home, and said turning to me: "I feel as though I am meeting America for the first time." And there was Susie Stageberg, who had come 90 miles by bus from Red Wing.

Susie—no one ever called her anything else—was 84, handsome, square-faced, gentle in manner, firm in opinion, boundless in energy. To newer generations her name was a pleasant alliterative, but to those who knew the history of the North Central Plains it was synonymous with woman's suffrage, the Christian Temperance Union, grass-roots journalism, and the farmer–labor movement. She got into politics as the young wife of a professor at the Red Wing Seminary and was roundly criticized for it. To her critics she said she did indeed believe that woman's place was in the home, but that her home was every place children went. She said: "To me, an understanding of political issues has the same bearing to daily life as the Bible to eternal life. It brings direction."

She became active in the Non-Partisan League and with Magnus Johnson and Charles Lindbergh Sr. was present at the founding meeting of the Farmer–Labor Party in 1922. She was a columnist for the Minneapolis *Daily Star* and editor for some years of the *Organized Farmer,* publication of the Farmer–Labor Party. In 1943 she opposed the merger of the party with the Democrats, foreseeing accurately that the move would destroy the populist character of the party which had given the state the best leadership in its history. The administration of Governor Elmer Benson in the late 1930s comes to mind.

When the Progressive Party was founded in 1948, Susie was there, and later became the party's candidate for lieutenant governor of Minnesota. Once she arrived late for a party dinner-meeting in Chicago, to find Benson, Vito Marcantonio, the GUARDIAN's John McManus, and others already seated around a table laden with bottles of bourbon. Her great friend Benson sang out: "Well, Susie, what do you think of all this whiskey here?" "Now, Elmer," Susie said, "you know what we used to say in the Temperance movement: Hate the sin but love the sinner."

A couple of years later, when Susie was off on some travels and let her GUARDIAN sub lapse, she came home to find a note from Jack McManus telling her the GUARDIAN too loved the sinner but hated the sin of losing a valuable reader. The sub came tumbling in with an outpouring of apology to an impertinent letter writer who dared use an elderly woman's words to plague her.

Susie recalled that incident with high good humor that cold

night in Minneapolis. It was our first meeting, although we had corresponded frequently. Writing about it in her column (This 'n' That) in the Minneapolis *Posten,* a lively weekly newspaper with stories in Norwegian and English intermixed, she said:

"I am afraid that I shocked Jim Aronson deeply as I greeted him and said, 'Pardon me, but from reading your editorials I had expected to find you with long grey hair and a great solemn-looking forehead. And instead I find you young and cheerful and I am so glad because we will need you for a long time!' "

She wrote of the GUARDIAN's "ferreting out the truth on unimpeachable authority and getting it out to thousands of readers. . . . Some of us have known of this tremendous problem from the days of Ignatius Donnelly, who published his own *Monopolist,* and the Non-Partisan League with all their small papers dotting the countryside in the Dakotas and Minnesota, where it could also be said that 'truth was dangerous' to tell."

Two months after our meeting, Susie was dead of cancer in Red Wing. The *Minnesota Labor Review* said of her: "When the real history of Minnesota is written, the name of Susie Stageberg will be among the most illustrious and the most devoted to making and keeping Minnesota a land of the free in the best sense of the word."

Her friend Emma Carlson wrote from Minneapolis: "Susie called the GUARDIAN a newspaper with a heart."

The heart's blood came from people like Susie Stageberg; and it sustained the steady beat of our newspaper in perhaps its greatest and longest crusade of all: the protest against the war in Southeast Asia.

In the election campaign of 1960, the "fresh new voice" of John Fitzgerald Kennedy, when it was not flagellating the revolution in "Cuber," took up a tired old cry: Laos was "going Communist," and it was the job of the United States to preserve it for the Free World. Washington had already poured $300 million into Laos (under the umbrella of the Southeast Asia Treaty Organization) to build an army to crush the patriotic Neo Lao Hasket front (commonly known as the Pathet Lao) led by Prince Souphanouvong. The Front had ceaselessly fought the Japanese occupation and, since 1946, had been engaged in a struggle with Laotian rightists to establish an independent neutralist country.

In the interim between his exit and Kennedy's entrance as President, Eisenhower had alerted the Seventh Fleet in the South China Seas and stepped up military aid to Laotian reactionaries. The so-called Secret War in Laos was no secret to anyone but the American people. In an editorial in the NATIONAL GUARDIAN, January 9, 1961, ten days before the Kennedy inauguration, we wrote: "The peace of the world is in danger in Laos and the threat comes not from any reported intervention from China or from the Democratic Republic of Vietnam [North Vietnam], but by intervention of the government of the United States."

Four months later Anna Louise Strong left Peking for a GUARDIAN reportorial tour of Southeast Asia. On May 1 she interviewed Prince Souphanouvong and asked him why the United States was seeking a cease-fire in the Laotian civil war. "You are a journalist," he replied, "and to you the reason must be clear. Our patriotic forces are winning while the enemy forces are demoralized and even disintegrating. So those who are losing want to negotiate."

"As the Prince saw it," Anna Louise wrote, "the question was not even whether or not the U.S. forces would invade. In his view they had already invaded, in December 1960, together with several thousand troops from Thailand, from Chiang Kai-shek, from South Vietnam, and several hundred Filipinos and Americans, the latter as 'advisers.' The question, therefore, as the Prince expressed it, was: 'Will the U.S. widen the present invasion into a large-scale war?' "

Three weeks later Anna Louise was in Hanoi asking further questions of a man whose name in Southeast Asia had become synonymous with freedom: Ho Chi Minh. En route to her appointment at the presidential palace she passed through the wide, tree-lined streets of the former French colonial section of Hanoi, "with houses all massive and swank and painted the stucco-like yellow of a shopworn Beverly Hills." The huge yellow palace was circled by acres of lawn fenced in by ornamental spikes ten feet high. Into the reception room "there came a tall sturdy man in cream-colored khaki and sandals with stride effortless and smooth. He greeted me with both hands in a gesture so all-inclusive that it embraced the room from the blowing window drapes to the chocolate cakes on the coffee table." It was Uncle Ho's way of saying, "Be at home!" He said: "You are the first citizen from the United States who has come to our country."

The talk quickly turned political. "We have two tasks now," he said. "First, to make the life of our people better and better . . . Socialism, of course. And next, how can our country be peacefully reunified?" How did he expect reunification to come about? Anna Louise asked. He responded:

"It is complex. Your American imperialism spends so much money to keep Ngo Dinh Diem in power. . . . In history, when people are oppressed too hard, they make a revolution. Our people in the South are oppressed too hard by Diem. So Diem will fall, as did Chiang Kai-shek and Syngman Rhee and Batista. . . . All the money America spends on Diem is lost money. It buys only more anti-American sentiments."

Did he have any idea how long it would take? He spread his hands: "I am no fortune teller, but I know how it happens in history. If you in America struggle, and our people in the South struggle, and our people in the North also struggle to build a strong economic base for a united country, the liberation will come."

Anna Louise looked about at the ornate mosaic designs and heavy fixtures and asked him, in her inimitable fashion, whether the air did not smell bad from the previous occupants—the French, the Japanese, Chiang's generals, and the French puppet emperor, Bao Dai. "We've aired it well," said Ho, and then, as though sensing her unasked question, added almost abruptly: "I don't live here. I live in a small house with two rooms. We use the palace for the President to receive people." As Anna Louise rose to leave, Ho scooped the flowers from a vase on the table and gave them to her.

Some days later, Anna Louise wrote: "Back in Peking now. I wake at night and know that I am homesick. Not for Vietnam: the damp of the tropic land bites into my bones. I am homesick for a world where the presidents will be like Uncle Ho. Liberators and leaders of the people unshackled by forms of state. A world I never saw, but it must be one where our caravans go. And Ho, I think, has his house built there already."

Uncle Ho spoke his prophetic words to Anna Louise seven years after that historic spring when the Viet Minh forces he directed laid siege to the French fortress at Dienbienphu and signaled the end of French colonial rule in Southeast Asia. At the GUARDIAN we had recorded that struggle from the postwar French betrayal of the promise of freedom, through the humiliation of the French armies, and down to Vice-President Nixon's call in 1954 "to take the risk now by putting our boys in," as the brothers Dulles and Admiral Arthur Radford, chairman of the Joint Chiefs of Staff, applauded. British resistance, French exhaustion, and a native caution moved President Eisenhower to overrule the hawks. The United States "came close to using nuclear weapons there," said Chalmers Roberts in a retrospective look ten years later (Washington *Post,* February 2, 1964).

By 1961 Washington had spent more than $1 billion to shore up Diem in South Vietnam and equip his army. For the next two years a stream of American "advisers" flowed steadily in as the White House and Pentagon sought by directive, threat and blandishment to keep the press from telling the truth to the American people about our involvement. They had no serious problem: except for a small band of "young Turks" among the Saigon press corps—and a middle-aged one named Homer Bigart of the New York *Times*—the press was generally a willing accomplice in the deception, about both the extent and purpose of American involvement.

After the Cuban crises had settled into a bristling stalemate, the GUARDIAN turned its attention fully to Southeast Asia. Week-in, week-out, we recorded the "background to disaster," as we called it. And each week the headlines became more ominous:

U.S. TOLL MOUNTS IN UNDECLARED WAR IN SOUTH VIETNAM (March 21, 1963)

U.S. Image Of Vietnam Masks A Corrupt Police State
(April 4, 1963)
Is The War In Vietnam America's 'Spain'?
(April 11, 1963)

In mid-April 1963, we used the term "The Dirty War" for the first time. We kept our eye on Laos, commented accurately on the fraud of U.S. agreement in Geneva in 1962 to keep the peace in Laos, charted the virtual takeover of Thailand as a massive base for aggression, and warned about the future of Cambodia. We detailed the origins and composition of the National Liberation Front of South Vietnam and documented the oppressive reality of life in South Vietnam behind the press-created smokescreen of the "Miracle of Vietnam" under Diem. As *Time*'s "doughty little Diem" became Vice-President Lyndon Johnson's "Winston Churchill of Asia," we recorded the steady progress of the Liberation Front and the deterioration of the Saigon regime with on-the-spot reports from Wilfred Burchett.

Burchett had set up a home base in Pnompenh, Cambodia, and traveled widely throughout Southeast Asia. He was a frequent visitor to North Vietnam and one of very few Western correspondents permitted in the areas of South Vietnam controlled by the Liberation Front. His cabled and airmailed dispatches appeared regularly in the GUARDIAN. Often I had extra proofs of his articles run off and sent, with covering release, to the daily newspapers and wire services in New York. They were ignored. The unwritten code of American journalism was in force: the only "reliable" sources of information about the war in Indo-China were untainted Free World sources, and the center of the Free World was official Washington. Sources of information outside government were suspect and radical sources rejected altogether—no matter how obviously accurate the reportage and documentation. This code was scrupulously observed except in rare instances when the material had been "washed" through respectable channels. For example:

Burchett wrote also for *Mainichi Shimbun* of Tokyo (circulation 5 million) which published an English-language edition. Occasionally a Burchett *Mainichi* report was picked up by an American wire service reporter in Tokyo and relayed back to the United States where it appeared in abbreviated form in a few newspapers. *Mainichi* was the cleansing agent. Later, when the war admittedly was going badly for the United States, and when it was clear Burchett had access to authoritative information not available to American reporters, the Associated Press requested articles from him directly. These articles appeared with an italic introduction warning that they presented a "Communist viewpoint and should be read in that light." With cabled authorization from an exasperated Burchett I protested to the AP which graciously altered the description to note Burchett's "easy access to Communist leaders," or some such variant. No Burchett article was ever published unencumbered by this trade mark.

Others went much further. As late as 1967, when the New York *Times* and other leading American newspapers were beginning to anguish editorially about the Indo-China war, the Los Angeles *Times* published a four-column article (February 26, 1967) by Tom Lambert, a foreign correspondent than attached to the *Times*'s Washington bureau. Lambert characterized Burchett as "perhaps one of the most suspect, perhaps one of the most dangerous" of a new type of reporter that had come into being "with the inception of communism and its deliberate subjection of journalism to ideology . . . the journalistic political agent." As far as is known, wrote Lambert, burying a negative axe in Burchett's skull, "Burchett never acted as an outright intelligence agent for the Soviet Union, although he probably has passed along to Russian intelligence authorities any military information acquired in his travels through Asia." Actually, the sinister deed that provoked the Lambert profile was an article by Burchett, requested by the Associated Press earlier in February, indicating that Hanoi would be willing to discuss peace terms with the United States if Washington would halt the bombings in the North. That information of course placed Washington in an embarrassing position, so journalist-agent Lambert swiveled his typewriter into action to discredit the source.

The hypocrisy of Lambert's charges against Burchett became even more flagrant with the revelations in the 1970s that dozens of American journalists were cooperating with the Central Intelligence Agency, either as paid agents or voluntary patriots. Even in the 1960s the cronyism of the U.S. correspondents with embassy officials, many of them CIA representatives operating with embassy cover, made clear the willingness of these correspondents to act as political journalists. Yet there was no intimation that "this type of reporter" had come into being "with the inception" of capitalism.

Elsewhere, reprinting Burchett's articles had more immediate repercussion. In South Korea, the managing editor of *Pusan Ilbo* in 1965 published excerpts of a Burchett report in the GUARDIAN just after the government in Seoul had announced it was sending 2,000 troops to South Vietnam to join the South Vietnamese–American forces. The editor was hauled from a sickbed and jailed along with the newspaper's librarian.

The Game of Death

[J.A.] The curtain was rung down on the Miracle of Vietnam when, on November 2, 1963, a group of highly placed former miracle makers murdered Ngo Dinh Diem and his brother Ngo Dinh Nhu. It did not matter that the generals who took over would serve their allotted time and then be replaced: the heavy hand of the Diem autocracy had smashed the glass in the "showcase of democracy" in Southeast Asia, and its time was up. The decision to remove the brothers Diem was sanctioned, as the Pentagon Papers would reveal, by the White House, and without doubt by President Kennedy. Three weeks later the man who made the decision was himself assassinated in Dallas. The curtain had come down on Camelot too.

Then Lee Harvey Oswald, arrested as the assassin, was murdered in the basement of a police station by a flabby night club operator named Jack Ruby. America's state of shock deepened into stupefaction. On the Sunday night after the Oswald murder I was home seeking to piece together the coverage of the incredible events when the phone rang. It was a reporter from the New York *Times,* an old and respected friend. From the background clatter I knew he was calling from the newsroom and instinctively that the call was assassination-connected.

He fumbled a bit making small talk until I cleared the way for him: what was up? Well, he had been assigned to an angle of the Oswald story, seeking to track down his political affiliations. It seemed that Oswald, a reputed member of the Fair Play for Cuba Committee in New Orleans (where there was no such committee), had been a subscriber to the *Militant,* the weekly newspaper of the Socialist Workers Party (Trotskyist), and the *Times* was curious whether he had also subscribed to the GUARDIAN. We had anticipated such a query, I told my friend, and could report that we were "clean"—no record of an Oswald subscription.

I took advantage of the call to air my doubts about the "lone assassin" theory already being fixed in the public mind. What was the *Times* doing to validate or disprove this theory? "Look, Jim," said the reporter, "you worked here and you know the answer: don't look this way—they won't do it."

Of course they didn't do it. But, as with the Trenton Six story, the Rosenberg Case, and the Korean War, we knew that someone would have to do it, and almost inevitably that someone would be us. In the first issue of the GUARDIAN following the assassination, page 1 was dominated by the "change in command," with another accidental President taking over: Lyndon Johnson's record was carefully dissected. The rest of the page concerned the murders: "The Assassination Mystery," the headline read: "Kennedy and Oswald Killings Puzzle the Nation." Beginning with that issue, we sifted every piece of evidence and every contradiction that presented itself, and the paper soon became a clearing house for amateur Sherlock Holmeses, some sound, some wild, who flocked to the cause.

Soon after the Commission of Inquiry had been named and Chief Justice Warren announced ominously that the facts in the case might never be disclosed "in our lifetime," I heard that a maverick New York lawyer named Mark Lane had done some careful leg and brain work to produce a thesis casting doubt on the lone-assassin theory—and even whether Oswald had actually been involved in the crime. I called Lane, who told me that his article had been rejected by thirteen publications. "We'd like to take a look," I said. "It's 10,000 words," he said. "You wouldn't want to print all of it." "If it's warranted, we will," I said. He asked to think about it overnight—he had two final publications to hear from. "All right," I said, "but I can tell you now none of them will touch it. We may."

Early the next morning Lane called me at home: "It's yours," he said. We arranged a pickup and several of us read it through. There was no dissent to printing it even though we knew it would take half the issue. Thus on December 19, 1963, the GUARDIAN published the longest story in its fifteen-year history. It was presented as a lawyer's report to the Warren Commission and titled: "A Brief for Lee Harvey Oswald." In an introduction, we wrote:

> In an analysis of the civil liberties aspects of the assassination of Lee Harvey Oswald, the American Civil Liberties Union said the "public interest" would be served if the commission named by President Johnson were to make "a thorough examination of the treatment accorded Oswald." The GUARDIAN's publication of Lane's brief presumes only one thing: a man's innocence, under U.S. law, unless or until proved guilty. It is the right of any accused. . . . A presumption of innocence is the rock upon which American jurisprudence rests. Surely it ought to apply in the "crime of the century" as in the meanest back-alley felony. We ask all our readers to study this document. . . . Any information or analysis based on fact that can assist the Warren Commission is in the public interest—an interest which demands that everything possible be done to establish the facts in this case.

Few issues of the GUARDIAN created such a stir. Anticipating greater interest we had increased the press run by 5,000, but an article in the New York *Times* about our story brought a heavy demand at the newsstands and dealers were calling for additional copies. Before the month was out we had orders for 50,000 reprints.

Press reaction in the United States was uneasy. Except for the *Times* no New York newspaper printed a line about the Lane brief. United Press International was given proof-sheets in advance and announced it "wouldn't touch it." The Associated Press was not interested in advance proofs; after the *Times* story appeared, it became interested. The Philadelphia *Inquirer* published a story about Lane without mentioning the GUARDIAN. Our readers in Philadelphia rushed letters to the editor to provide the link.

Abroad the reaction was remarkable. Rome's largest evening newspaper, *Paese Sera,* and the magazine *Oggi,* circulation 1 million, reprinted the article in full, as did *Libération* in Paris. There were long news stories and commentaries in the Japanese press; in Mexico, *El Día* published the brief as "El Caso Oswald," and in *Izvestia* the title was: "Who Killed Kennedy?"

The "sowers of doubt," as *Newsweek* called them, spread their seeds in the London *Spectator, L'Express* in Paris, Milan's *Tempo* and newspapers in Iceland and Canada. In London the *Times* described Lane as a "left-winger" and cited as evidence that his brief had been published in the "left-wing" GUARDIAN. That brought a letter from Penrhyndeudraeth, Merioneth, Wales, signed by Bertrand Russell:

"Mr. Lane is no more a left-winger than was President Kennedy. He attempted to publish his evidence . . . in virtually every established American publication but was unsuccessful. Only the NATIONAL GUARDIAN was prepared to print his scrupulously documented material. . . . I think it important that no unnecessary prejudice against the valuable work of Mr. Lane should be aroused, so that his data concerning a vital event may be viewed with an open mind by people of all political persuasions."

Our experience with the Lane brief led us to conclude that there was widespread incredulity, both at home and abroad, over the assassination and its aftermath. Others expressed their incredulity standing on their heads. The Hearst press's chief incumbent redhunter, Jack Lotto, took off after Lane and us. Walter Winchell, J. Edgar Hoover's great friend, led a column in January 1964 with the characterization of the GUARDIAN, by then standard in the U.S. press, as "a virtual propaganda arm of Soviet Russia." He singled Lane out as an "agitator" seeking to abolish the Un-American Activities Committee which had inspired the GUARDIAN's label.

In mid-January we hired New York's citadel of free speech, Town Hall, owned by New York University, for a meeting on the

THE GAME OF DEATH

night of February 18 to air the doubts, with Lane and others as speakers. When we were finally able to reach her, we added Ms. Marguerite Oswald, Lee Harvey's mother, whose doubts about her son's complicity were increasingly vocal. On January 28, Town Hall's director Ormond Drake, an NYU dean, refused to sign the lease form. He wrote: "In our opinion Ms. Oswald's appearance could be incendiary. . . . Town Hall does not choose to be a party to an airing of a case that is presently being studied by the Presidential Commission." He returned the rent check.

To our statement that NYU ought to oppose suppression of any aspect of such a vital inquiry, Drake said the decision had been made on the highest university level and referred us to NYU's President James Hester, who of course was not available. Our attorney, I. G. Needleman, reached Edward J. Ennis, general counsel of the ACLU, who agreed to represent the GUARDIAN without fee. A man of some persuasion, he convinced NYU that it would look naked indeed in the glare of publicity of a free-speech suit.

NYU conceded, but with a tight fist: it agreed to the meeting as scheduled, but demanded a $25,000 bond "to protect the physical property at Town Hall in the event of material damage." Ennis protested that such an "unconstitutional condition penalized proponents of a peaceable assembly" rather than any possible opponents, and would scare away commercial surety companies. On February 7, Drake responded: no bond, no meeting. The demand for the bond, he said, had been determined "following conferences with other interests and thus it reflects a concern of more than this institution." That confirmed our feeling that the "other interests" included a three-letter federal organization or two.

With time growing short and aware that legal action might carry past the meeting date, the GUARDIAN at considerable cost obtained a one-day $25,000 insurance policy and submitted it on Lincoln's birthday. NYU was adamant; only a bond, or $25,000 in cash in escrow in a bank, would be acceptable. We appealed privately to a group of supporters, and the first four persons approached agreed to supply the necessary funds in bonds and cashier's checks. The arrangements were completed on February 17, one day before the meeting, and that afternoon Town Hall turned over the signed lease. Up to that time it had instructed its box office to inform callers it had no listing for an event the following evening.

Town Hall on the night of February 18 was filled to overflowing. The audience was engrossed, and the meeting was entirely peaceable.

During the months in which the Warren Commission met, the GUARDIAN pursued every plausible lead that might shed light on the double murder. On September 27 the Commission delivered its findings: the assassination could be regarded as a closed chapter, except for the necessity of protecting Presidents more closely in the future. The murderer was no longer among us, and since he had no accomplices, we could all breathe more easily despite the pain and sadness induced by the events in Dallas on November 22, 1963.

With unanimity, the press supported the Commission. "A tremendous service," said the Boston *Herald*. "A comprehensive and convincing account," said the New York *Times*. "Deserving acceptance as the whole truth," said the Washington *Post*. Even I. F. Stone, in an exasperated comment in his weekly about critics of the Commission report, denounced them as a "lunatic fringe" in the press and elsewhere who would not let the issue die with Kennedy and Oswald. The press reference, without name, was clearly to the GUARDIAN. It was not the last time we would disagree with Stone on major issues.

In the last week of November 1964, a year after the assassination, Lane was an honored guest at the GUARDIAN's sixteenth anniversary dinner. Reviewing the history of the investigation, he said:

"The GUARDIAN is the one publication which has so honestly and courageously raised the questions which the public is entitled to hear about the assassination of President Kennedy. Almost alone, the GUARDIAN has from the outset presented the news in the best tradition of a newspaper. One day, when history views this dark chapter in our nation's story, the media of America will have to face up to their abdication of their responsibilities. On that day the NATIONAL GUARDIAN can raise its head unashamed."

THE GAME OF DEATH

The war in Vietnam ground on. As American involvement increased, the folder of clippings and notes I took home every weekend became bulkier—articles from the American press, and from the world press sent in by Cedric and our correspondents in Paris, New Delhi, Peking, Melbourne. Out of these I made my own notes for what became in effect a weekly editorial-review of the war and Washington policy. How did one break through with a dissenting view, confronted by a paper curtain behind which the American press tailed American policy, with an occasional yelp for an end to official ambiguity? Trust us a little more, the newspapers seemed to be saying to Washington: we're on your side. But with their own ambiguity, it emerged in print with a slightly different emphasis. Isn't it time, asked the Washington *Post* in January 1964, "for the Administration to show more faith in the intelligence and good faith of the American people?" In the issue of February 13, 1964, I wrote:

What would such a plea for truth entail? It would mean telling the American people (and here the press itself stands indicted with the Administration it rebukes) this: The writing is on the wall for the U.S. misadventure in South Vietnam. The struggle may be long drawn, but this is a war the U.S. cannot win. The Americans will spill more blood, their own and others, destroy more villages, wipe out more rice fields and buffalo, but that is about all. The people of Vietnam are against them, disciplined, organized, courageous and experienced. No matter what combination of puppets the U.S. may stick together and jerk into action, the end result cannot be changed.

This is the high road to oblivion. It starts from the blind premise that the people of South Vietnam (read: Cuba, Panama, South Korea, the Dominican Republic and a host more) prefer our invitation to death to the opportunity to build their own lives in their own land under governments of their own choosing.

Until the people of this country are made aware of the utter falsity of Washington's line, there will be no change. Until the peace groups, the churches, the progressive press—until every organization and institution which hopes for peace in the world comes to a realization that the U.S. must get out and stay out of Vietnam, and starts immediately to see that this is done, our nation faces a grave threat. Stated simply, it is that the mindless men who sit in positions of power may yet succeed in blowing us all to Kingdom Come for an evil crusade in a country 7,000 miles from our shores.

When that was written there were 15,500 U.S. troops in Vietnam.

On August 5, 1964, the Senate of the United States abdicated its constitutional mandate to declare war and by a vote of 88 to 2 passed what became known as the Tonkin Gulf Resolution. The pretext was an alleged attack by North Vietnamese gunboats upon the warships of the U.S. fleet illegally patrolling the Gulf of Tonkin off North Vietnam. The attack was subsequently unmasked as a monstrous fraud, concocted to provide the United States with an excuse for extending the war to the north and landing thousands more troops in the south. The House had already voted unanimously for the resolution, which authorized President Johnson "to take all necessary measures to repel any armed attack against the forces of the U.S. and to prevent further aggression."

The two Senate votes against the resolution were those of Wayne Morse of Oregon and Ernest Gruening of Alaska. Only Morse spoke in the "debate," and only the GUARDIAN, in the issue immediately following the vote, published a full page of excerpts of the speech.

On August 10, Gruening delivered the first address on the floor of the Senate advocating withdrawal of American troops from Vietnam. It was a reasoned, factual presentation of the circumstances of American involvement and in the daybook of any newspaper surely was an event to be noted. Yet the next morning, when Gruening sought out newspaper accounts of his speech, he found none in the New York *Times* or the Washington *Post*. Had he been able to repeat the exercise with most if not all other newspapers in the country that day, the search would have been equally futile. The *Times,* which saw no reason to place either Morse's or Gruening's speech in its record of the news, on the contrary perceived "an ominous perspective . . . the beginning of a mad adventure by the North Vietnamese Communists."

But the mad adventurers were on the other side, as became clear

THE GAME OF DEATH

in America's escalation of the war immediately after the congressional abdication. The pretext of American "advisers" was ignored as U.S. marines swarmed ashore through floodgates smashed open by the resolution. In the weeks that followed, Johnson would take visitors for a stroll through the White House Rose Garden, pull a copy of the resolution out of his breast pocket and shout at the captive audience: "It says, *all, all measures!*" It was his justification for mass murder.

The GUARDIAN's coverage kept pace with the escalation. In January 1965 a cablegram arrived from Burchett: JUST BACK FROM SEVERAL WEEKS WITH LIBERATION FORCES SOUTH VIETNAM. THINNER BUT WISER. SENDING NEW SERIES MORE SENSATIONAL THAN LAST. TEN ARTICLES. Because of their urgency we doubled them up for publication in five weeks; we knew they comprised one of the most important journalistic documents we had ever published. They were in effect a primer explaining why defeat was certain for the U.S. forces and their South Vietnamese mercenaries: a detailed survey of a revolution-in-progress based in the people of South Vietnam, led by battle-trained revolutionaries who had never lost faith in their people.

Burchett gave a general setting of the circumstances under which he traveled and worked in South Vietnam (with photographs), and an unimpeachable account of the battle of Bien Hoa, which destroyed many U.S. planes and resulted in enormous casualties. There was an interview with National Liberation Front President Nguyen Huu Tho, a description of the growth of the guerrilla forces from tiny groups to regiment size, their morale, training, and battle planning, a Saigon officer's story of why he had deserted to the NLF, an analysis of U.S. air power, and the NLF's terms for negotiation. The stories profoundly contradicted Washington's reports of the progress of the war.

Once again, to ensure the widest possible circulation, we sent out to the press and wire services prepublication galleys of the first two articles, accompanied by a release dated February 1 describing the entire series. Nothing was published in the United States outside of the GUARDIAN. The Washington *Post* published a Reuters dispatch under a Tokyo dateline quoting Burchett's account of Bien Hoa (as contained in the GUARDIAN's first article). Reuters had picked it up from *Mainichi Shimbun,* which had Japanese rights to the Burchett series; the *Post* could have had the full story a week earlier if it had been willing to use the GUARDIAN galleys.

The *Times,* noting the *Post* story, reacted after receiving a second release from the GUARDIAN dated February 10. The foreign news desk called to ask for a look at the whole series. As we hastened to prepare the material, a second call came from the *Times:* no need to rush; they would wait until we published the full series. By coincidence, the United States had ordered massive bombings of North Vietnam and publication in the *Times* of the Burchett information would have pulled the rug out from under Washington's justification for the bombings. The Burchett series in the *Guardian* came to an end in late February—and so did the *Times*'s interest.

The antiwar campaign then began in earnest. In late February there were protest rallies in thirty cities and plans were afoot for a great demonstration in Washington in April. The "international communist conspiracy" theme, slumbering in the early 1960s, was shaken awake. In the vanguard were Senator Eastland (worried about an alliance of the growing black freedom movement with the antiwar forces) and the columnists. Evans and Novak were particularly fretful about the GUARDIAN; they scolded the Rev. C. T. Vivian, an assistant to Rev. Martin Luther King Jr., for having appeared as an honored guest at an annual GUARDIAN dinner. The *Congressional Record* was brimful with the hardy perennial descriptions of the GUARDIAN as a "virtual propaganda arm" of the Soviet Union and "flamboyantly" pro-Chinese. Aware that these were permanent fixtures, we wrote in the issue of March 27, 1965:

"We accept these characterizations as evidence that we know a conspiracy when we see one—a conspiracy to discredit the Negro freedom movement with a red label—and we should like to assure the members of the gang, legislative as well as journalistic, that we will remain a propaganda arm of any movement that seeks to gain equal rights for all Americans, and we will be flamboyantly active in pursuit of this goal."

Sensing a campaign to divide the protest movement generally into "respectables" and "radicals," we cautioned: "The policy of exclusion is a destructive force in any forward-looking movement—for peace, civil liberties, or civil rights—and we oppose it wherever it is found. There is room for all shades of opinion, on the side of decency, in the fight for progress in America."

Our April 17 issue, coinciding with the Washington rally, devoted nine of its twelve pages to the war in Southeast Asia, including a prophetic warning by Owen Lattimore and an article by Jean-Paul Sartre explaining his rejection of a speaking tour of the United States. More than 25,000 people came to Washington for the largest protest demonstration since the end of World War II and the largest picket line in history around the White House. It was the culmination of months of letters to Congress, the press, and the President, of ads in newspapers, formation of new groups on campuses, and a petition by 2,500 clergymen saying to the President: "In the name of God, *STOP IT!*"

Most significantly, the Washington demonstration had been initiated and organized by a new campus group, Students for a Democratic Society (SDS), forming the youth section of the League for Industrial Democracy, a group known for its hostility to communism. And it was the first public manifestation of the disenchantment of young people with capitalism. Paul Potter, SDS president, asked in his Washington speech what kind of a system it was that permitted such evil as the United States had created in Vietnam. He said: "We must name that system. We must name it, describe it, analyze it, understand it, and change it. For it is only when that system is changed and brought under control that there can be any hope for stopping the forces that create a war in Vietnam today."

The government/press efforts to isolate and discredit the radical protesters, plus a growth in sentiment such as Potter's, moved important leaders in the peace movement, mainly those with social democratic orientation, to yield to the pressure. Warnings were raised against cooperating with "groups and individuals . . . committed to any form of totalitarianism [or] drawing inspiration or direction from the foreign policy of any government." The reference was clear: a kind word for the Soviet Union or the People's Republic of China was an automatic exclusion clause. The GUARDIAN responded:

"The attempt to split the movement into 'respectable' and 'unrespectable' sections is in effect an effort to split it into 'manageable' and 'unmanageable' sections, as far as the war hawks are concerned. Any peace advocate who participates in this process can only weaken the fight against aggression in Vietnam. The urgent need is for unity in the peace movement against the mounting domestic attacks and the growing danger of spreading war."

Only weeks later the GUARDIAN had a direct confrontation on this issue with the leadership of the National Committee for a Sane Nuclear Policy (SANE) which had projected a rally at Madison Square Garden on June 8, 1965. Although we recognized the limited scope of the rally's objectives (there was to be no demand for withdrawal of U.S. forces from Vietnam) we supported and publicized it.

A Women Strike for Peace (WSP) group had reserved space for a large ad in the May 29 GUARDIAN in support of the meeting. Submitting their copy to SANE for approval, they were told that if they placed the ad "there would be trouble." A SANE representative ordered the GUARDIAN to "kill the ad." We responded that only WSP could tell us that—and WSP did shortly thereafter. Asked why SANE had pressured WSP to withdraw the ad, Donald Keys, executive director of SANE, said: "We must be effective, and to be effective we operate within this framework of decision-making: what can SANE best do to have a useful impact politically in Washington? We are most effective when we operate as close to a 'Mr. and Mrs. America' position as possible."

We published a full-page report of the meeting attended by 18,000 people, a majority of whom (judging from reactions to the speeches) seemed to support the GUARDIAN's more militant position. We also reported about the controversy over the ad. In a letter to the GUARDIAN some weeks after the rally, Keys charged us with creating "some sort of cause célèbre." He said the groups participating in the meeting—the academic community, Democratic clubs, national church groups, among others—raised protests "of far more value and political impact than those of the radical left. Responsible criticism and constructive advocacy are bound to be more effective than plain 'aginism.' "

Keys wrote approvingly of I. F. Stone's division of the peace movement into three general groups (*I. F. Stone's Weekly,* June 28). That drew the issue "very clearly," he said. No basic entente was possible among these groups, he concluded, and urged that this "not be allowed to become a source of acrimony and misunderstanding among the three groups."

We too felt that the issue had been clearly drawn, but not as Keys and Stone had interpreted it. I prepared an editorial titled "How many paths to peace?" for publication in the same issue (July 31, 1965) with Keys's letter. I believe it stands the test of time as a statement of principle on non-exclusion going far beyond the issue of the SANE rally. A major section of the editorial follows:

The GUARDIAN remains unalterably opposed to any effort to make the fight for peace divisible, and the presence in Madison Square Garden June 8 of thousands of persons who are militant pacifists or radical peace workers indicates that the peace workers have a far greater understanding of the urgency of the times. They supported the rally despite the attitude of the leadership of SANE. They understand, if the leadership of SANE does not, that in the galloping crisis situation which confronts the nation today over the escalation of the war in Vietnam and the danger of World War III, it is suicidal to indulge in a sorting-out process in the peace movement.

There are of course differences among the liberals, pacifists, and radicals in the peace movement, and particularly on the question whether world peace can be secured without a basic change in the power structure in the U.S. But faced with the immediate danger of a headlong drive to oblivion, which will carry with it persons of all political persuasions, it seems folly to set out a mathematical division, with an implied loyalty means test, when the impelling need is for all the peace forces immediately to seek to brake the drive to oblivion.

More disturbing than Keys's prescription for a peace movement is I. F. Stone's simplistic analysis and judgment of the effectiveness of his three-part peace movement: (1) the "democratic forces"; (2) the "religious witnesses"; and (3) "those who want to express their solidarity with the Viet Cong . . . by doing all they can to obstruct the war effort in this country." In Stone's view, only the first group can be effective in changing public opinion for the better.

Stone's description of the radicals is a loaded one. We cannot speak for all the groups that would find a place in this area, but we will place the GUARDIAN there and speak for ourselves—with a more accurate description of the aspirations of the radicals in the peace movement. We would define the radicals thus:

Those who insist that the U.S. withdraw its forces from South Vietnam . . . are doing their utmost to persuade the people of this country to do all they can to end the war and further the right of self-determination of all peoples, including the Vietnamese.

Until such time as the government of the United States can be persuaded or forced to end its intervention in the affairs of sovereign states, it is the right and duty of peace workers to demonstrate as vigorously and as forthrightly as possible that they will not be accomplices to unwanted wars. These are actions of conscience against killing people who have never hurt us.

If this means expressing sympathy for and understanding the aspirations of people seeking the right of self-determination, we would hope only that these valiant people would in turn sympathize with and understand a similar struggle by our people if the situation were reversed.

Stone asserts that the peace workers in his category 3 can "only fill the role of agents provocateurs, giving the government an excuse for repression [and] strengthening the widespread mania about a Communist conspiracy." This is an astonishing statement from a journalist with such an exemplary record in the fight against McCarthyism. Radical activity does not foment anti-Communist hysteria. Rather, the hysteria is fomented by the propaganda of the repressive forces who fear exposure of their aims by the activity of the radicals.

In a recent article Washington columnist Doris Fleeson said that "a sickness like McCarthyism is stirring again in the country." It is clearest, she said, "in the ugly accusations of appeasement being hurled by the self-styled hardliners against those who urge alternative policies. Also coming back into vogue [is] the conspiratorial theory of history. . . . Pavlovian reflexes to the word 'Communist' are being played on with increasing frequency by government sources and columnists who know better."

THE GAME OF DEATH

Far from being instruments of "hate and hysteria," as Stone implies, the radicals in the peace movement have presented the most consistent and valid political analysis and protest on the war in Vietnam and U.S. motives.

But if persuasion must be augmented by methods of civil disobedience, then perhaps this is a necessary if jarring step in the process of reawakening a sense of feeling—of outrage—in a numbed public which has not yet been able to comprehend the meaning of murder and destruction that the forces of hate and hysteria in Washington have visited upon Vietnam. A premature American anti-imperialist named Thoreau understood this.

Persuasion is of course the most desirable means of debate. But let Stone tell us, if he will, how one reasons together with Johnson, McNamara, Rusk, and Bundy. And would he suggest that Jean-Paul Sartre and his colleagues in the intellectual life of France were agents provocateurs during the Algerian War, when they urged the youth of France to refuse to serve in any army engaged in that dirty war?

Would he describe as purveyors of hate and hysteria the militant young leaders of the freedom movement who stepped out ahead of their own conservative leaders to say to the black people of America: The time is now? They were acting in the noblest radical tradition, and certainly they identify themselves with the oppressed peoples of the world—not, as Stone quaintly puts it, "in a curious melange of Maoism and Stalinism with Negro nationalism," but in the spirit of brotherhood of people fighting to be free.

Having witnessed, as Stone says, "the wonderful students at the various teach-ins [who] have achieved more than anyone had dreamed possible a few months ago," Stone must know that these students would be the first to reject his categorical judgment of the peace movement of the U.S. The students have neither the time nor the patience for his tendentious reasoning. They have a sense of urgency about their lives and their future which will sweep aside the calculated delineations between "persuasion and provocation." They know that their campaigns on the campuses have won for them the label of rebel in the high seats of conformity and they couldn't care less. Now they are seeking to instill their new-found strength and energies in the communities of the country.

More power to them and their non-categorized life and work. Let those who sit in categorical judgment join them in the streets.

I spoke from firsthand experience because just weeks before I had returned from a fifteen-day tour during which I had spoken at twenty-four meetings (nine on college campuses) culminating in the great teach-in at the University of California at Berkeley on May 21. Not since the earliest GUARDIAN days had I sensed such an atmosphere of concern and involvement, particularly on the issue of war and peace—the dawn of a national reawakening to the need for new forms of direct moral and political action. The deepest impression was the excitement on the campuses shared by students and faculties: at Stanford, a conservative university where 1,700 filled the teach-in hall and an equal number listened on the lawn in the soft evening; at Orange State in the heart of John Birch country; at the University of California Medical School in San Francisco where lab technicians of Japanese, Filipino and Korean origin joined the students. In a fluid situation whose dominant characteristic was protest, the political vacuum was becoming apparent in the acknowledgement that protest by itself cannot be sufficient.

At Berkeley there were 12,000 in the audience when I spoke from the same platform as I. F. Stone, Norman Thomas (a leading exponent of the Keys position), and many others. In the blazing sun there was a sea of paper hats formed of GUARDIANS distributed to the audience; I provided one for the gleaming bald pate of Isaac Deutscher, biographer of Stalin and Trotsky, who had come from London for the event. He had no quarrel with the GUARDIAN's position on the antiwar movement, either on his head or in his hand.

On my return I tried to convey to the staff my sense of excitement, and there was a spirited discussion of the GUARDIAN's role in forming an independent political opposition. Evident at that session for the first time was the political division that was to cause so much internal havoc in the next two years. But for the moment, and for the staff, I wrote this Report to Readers in the issue just before the SANE rally:

We feel that the changing mood in America is in a sense a vindication of the GUARDIAN's position (advocating independent and direct political action) and that the GUARDIAN now more than ever has a vital role to play. In no small measure it is to act as a bridge between a newer generation which must lead, and an older generation—with much to offer in both experience and moral commitment—which has persevered through a dark and trying time.

If the dialogue would be difficult "in the family," it would be even more difficult with Donald Keys's "Mr. and Mrs. America," as an incident in July 1965 showed. The Democrats had organized a gigantic Tri-State (Ohio, Indiana, Kentucky) Ox Roast at the Carthage, Ohio, Fair Grounds to raise funds among the 150,000 persons present. The Cincinnati Committee to End the War in Vietnam had received permission to provide a speaker and a literature table on which were 350 copies of the GUARDIAN. The Democratic leadership forced cancellation of the speaker (author-lecturer Sidney Lens) and hecklers forced the officials in charge to order the dismantling of the literature table. When the table attendants resisted, city police threatened arrest and seized 40 pounds of literature, including the GUARDIAN. The table tenders were dragged to the ground and the GUARDIANS disappeared from a car into which the police had thrown them. One Democratic official said: "I don't care how they get the bastards out just so long as they get them out."

Postscript [**C.B.**] The shock of President Kennedy's assassination, and the circumstances under which the shock came, make November 22, 1963, a memorable day for everyone. Mexican radios were erupting with the news as Mary and I entered a furniture store to begin our exile home—a peaceful one, we hoped. The U.S. sources were stressing Oswald's membership in a pro-Cuba committee and, driving off with a cargo of chairs, we asked ourselves if this wasn't America's Reichstag Fire. If so, tomorrow the Dachaus and Buchenwalds for our U.S. comrades. . . .

It was another false alarm, but in the days that followed we heard Mexicans referring to the United States as "the country where they kill Presidents." The custom of "magnicide" (top-level assassination) was not unknown in either country's history; in Mexico it had fallen into disuse, but in the United States it continued with the murders of Malcolm X, Martin Luther King Jr., and Robert Kennedy—none of them, of course, committed by a leftist. At the same time American "nobodies" were being murdered under equally horrible and criminal circumstances—by the thousands in Southeast Asia, by dozens on the home fronts where the battle against racism was reaching its climax.

I can add nothing important except to express the pride I felt in Jim's conduct of the GUARDIAN through those bloody years, perhaps the most difficult of all periods for a radical editor to keep head on shoulders and eye on ball. We corresponded regularly on questions of policy but my only solid contribution was an attempt to deepen American awareness of their government's atrocities south of the border. Under the "Alliance for Progress" mask, the series of U.S-blessed military coups, which by now have turned most of Latin America into a neo-Nazi chamber of horrors, began in Brazil in 1964.

I was mindful of Jim's agonies as he wrestled with the space problem, so integral a part of the problem of survival. Yet he managed, week by week, to cover almost all that demanded covering and say all that demanded to be said about it. I have no hesitation in calling these years the GUARDIAN's finest hour. My only persistent beefs up to 1965, in letters to Jim, were about the increasingly careless proofreading. "We're getting as bad as the New York *Times*," I wrote. Jim had more than enough on his plate—he did most of the fund-raising on top of everything else—and I wondered what the staff did on press day.

Then letters started coming to me from members of the staff, beefing about Jim and seeking my sympathy. . . .

Entrances and Exits

The time ahead must . . . be a time of experimentation in the techniques of political action and independent organization. Although a new political party must inevitably be the goal and the consequence of these efforts, it is just as inevitable that there must be a long and thorough prologue of varied independent political action, day by day, issue by issue, and area by area. The pattern will be—and ought to be—flexible, allowing for trial and error in form, content, timing, and method.

—*National Guardian,* November 7, 1964

[**J.A.**] That editorial comment was published immediately after the "consensus" election of Lyndon Johnson to a full term—more accurately, the consensus defeat of Barry Goldwater. It was titled: "The job ahead for the U.S. Left."

Ten months later, on September 18, 1965, we began publication of a series on "the New American Left," an expository examination and analysis of the form, content, thinking, and methods of a still-developing phenomenon in the nation's political life. We were not heralding a new "Gideon's Army," as seemed to be the case when the GUARDIAN came into existence in 1948, but candidly assessing the radical turn of America's youth who were coming to the conclusion that the existing political machinery offered no hope for the vast majority of people.

This new generation groped toward political maturity while an older one, tested in the tough years since the end of World War II, still sought a political base for action. The debate developing between the two was marked by increasing antagonism and diminishing dialogue. Despite defections in the ranks of the "Old Left" (a term which the GUARDIAN employed sparingly), where disillusion sometimes kept pace with mounting affluence, there were many veterans of the political wars eager to develop with young people a viable political alternative. We were among them, with a staff now almost evenly divided between younger and older, and with a unique vantage point at a critical juncture in history. We had made our share of miscalculations in the political and journalistic trials of the past two decades. But we believed as firmly as ever in independent radical political action as the ultimate instrument for change.

During the 1964 presidential election campaign, we had been caught up in a debate within the staff and among the readership which was perhaps the most abrasive in our history. Internally and externally, there was a division whether to 1) endorse Johnson; 2) denounce Johnson and urge abstention or a vote for a minor party, 3) lay out the situation and make no recommendation.

I chose the third position on the ground that most of our readers, alarmed by Goldwater's bristling campaign, would vote anyway for Johnson and his pledge to seek peace, so that a positive stand against Johnson could cause a perilous breach between the GUARDIAN and its readership. We had for weeks presented the background of the Johnson administration, seeking to puncture any illusions that he would effect major changes in policy. Yet I felt that there were times when a newspaper had to listen rather than harangue. The third position prevailed.

In retrospect I believe I was wrong. The outlines for Johnson's blunderbuss pursuit of the Vietnam War were already in place, and that alone was reason for denunciation in the polling place as well as in the week-to-week comment on policy. While such a position would have had no effect on the outcome, it would have maintained without compromise a sixteen-year principle of opposition to the lesser-evil theory. For once I was not mindful of Eugene Victor Debs's classic admonition: "Better to vote for what you want and not get it than to vote for what you don't want and get it."

It was in any case a lesson well absorbed. In the editorial quoted at the head of this chapter, I noted that the GUARDIAN had been conceived in the enthusiasm of the birth of a new party when the standard of Roosevelt's New Deal (for better or for worse) was held high. We had set as our editorial point of view a continuation and development of the progressive tradition set by FDR, but "in the intervening seventeen years we have seen a consistent distortion and betrayal of progressive traditions by the very persons who have campaigned in their name." If the ideals of the New Deal were valid for America at the time of the GUARDIAN's founding, "the actions of the succeeding administrations, the changing character of the forces for peace and civil rights at home, and the alignment of a majority of the world's people for socialism have rendered them inadequate for the world of 1965." Therefore:

"We hold with the movers of the New Left in America that the need of the hour is the development of a movement, radical in content and form, which must set about to shake the foundations of the power structure. We are aware that such a development is in the beginning stages and that it faces mighty obstacles. But we have enough faith in the basic common sense of the people of this country to believe that it can succeed. Toward this end, the GUARDIAN reaffirms its dedication to the struggle for a radical alternative for this nation."

Our series on the New Left was written by Michael Munk, appropriately one of the youngest staff members and himself typifying the makeup of the new movement. He was the son of a university professor (a profession he was later to follow himself), raised in a middle-class intellectual environment, who had acquired his radical views on the campus. The series accurately presented the new movement, spearheaded by Students for a Democratic Society, as the most exciting and potentially most powerful political phenomenon in U.S. radical history since the rapid growth of the

Communist Party in the 1930s. But there was no certainty that it "would move toward developing the popular political strength to constitute an effective challenge to the existing order."

SDS's organizational strength of about 12,000 indicated that there were perhaps 200,000 students committed in varying degree to radicalism. While the movement shared the broad perspectives of the Left rooted in the 1930s, it spurned the organizations of the Old Left and regarded most of its adherents as unwilling or unable to adapt to the changed environment of the 1960s "in a forthright and radical manner, both because of [their] loss of moral authority and because of their almost negligible impact on the 'silent generation' of the 1950s." In short, the New Left regarded the Old Left as "irrelevant to the radical needs of today." The first article in our series compared the Old Left and the New:

There is a common element in the histories of these two social movements influencing two different radical generations. Both highlight the cooptive nature of the corporate system: that is, its ability to absorb protest movements by rewarding them with concessions rather than permitting a political challenge to develop. A specific charge often made by the New Left against the Old is that the Communist Party's great contribution to the labor movement of the 1930s did not concentrate on radicalization of the workers but championed their short-range goals in return for organizational power. Thus the Old Left never developed a wide ideological following among the workers, and was routed when counterattacks began in earnest after 1945. The lesson that some on the New Left draw from this is that centralized organization is 'manipulative,' and that their main emphasis must be on radicalization of individuals, who will then make their own decision on organization.

Having set forth the main differences between Old and New, the new movement said its "theory of action" was directed toward "community organization formed around the immediate issues that affect people's lives"—a concept that sounded remarkably similar to the Old Left's "short-range goals" so roundly criticized. The principles of community organization, as formulated by SDS, were described in our articles in a manner that makes my blue pencil twitch as I read them after an interval of more than ten years. The strange terminology could only create a gap between the new organizers (who did not believe in organization) and the people they sought to organize:

Such counter-community groups . . . are built on the principles of "participatory democracy" to counter the threat of co-optation of their most militant members by the local power structure. Basically, this means "let the people decide" on what issues should be attacked, on what level, and how deeply. Organizers attempt to avoid leadership positions in the community groups that could lead to what some call 'manipulation' of the poor—i.e., the imposition of programs and tactics from above and from outside the social group. A tenet of participatory democracy is that persons who are drawn into activities where they are responsible for the major decisions will (1) become radicalized by confrontation at various points with the power structure as they realize that they have no fundamental power over basic decisions that affect their lives . . . and (2) that their awareness of the facts will lead to a commitment to radicalism that will not be destroyed by token concessions and co-optative offers from the power structure.

Munk pointed out that these ideological and tactical approaches to radical social change consciously rejected the existing political parties of the Left and were developing a style, vocabulary, and even mystique which distinguished them from the socialist youth groups that identified with the New Left. Unfortunately it also distinguished them from the community people they sought to radicalize. Few of the new crusaders had ever been poor or involuntarily unemployed; even fewer were black or of Hispanic origin, the dominant color and condition of the people to whom they were directing their attention. In a sense, this style and mystique carried with them the seeds of the eventual dissolution of the New Left. This is said without in any way discounting the high-mindedness of the new radicals, or their impressive social impact on the decade of the 1960s and thereafter, particularly in the struggle against the war in Vietnam.

They had without question helped force the nation to face up to the moral questions of the war, the gross inequality of life in the inner cities, and the dehumanization of mass production. And they acted directly upon their commitment. But unorganized confrontation was not enough, and the endless debates in the inner circles (one was not permitted to say "leadership") in the name of participatory democracy produced fatigue, anger, and indecision—and little continuing activity. The community projects for the most part rarely survived the planning stages, and the young black militants and the Hispanic–Americans were going their separate ways with their own leadership. The slogan "Black and White Unite and Fight" was in discard. The new themes were "Black Power" and "Free Puerto Rico." The black and the poor were seeking their own organizational forms: even without political lessons they understood the futility of protest activity without a base organization to transform confrontation into effective political action. The New Left spoke of a "radical center" which miraculously would evolve out of the protest movements. But of course none would without effort toward organization, and organization was an Old Left anathema.

The dilemma was never resolved. Indecisiveness resulted in needless waste of lives, efforts, and ideals, in intramural frustration, in bitterness and hate, whose end products were division and impotence.

This finally came about at an SDS convention (in June 1968 in Chicago), a panorama of self-cleaving in a bedlam atmosphere which could only have brought joy to the hearts of the counterinsurgency headquarters in Washington and their branches throughout the country. (Their agents in the youth movement had already done their job efficiently, playing with Machiavellian skill on the neuroses and political immaturity of the students.) The ancient and foul-smelling Coliseum was filled with screams and shouts, the chanting of slogans and raising of ikons to exorcise heretical devils. Speakers degraded women as sexual vessels. Half a convention hall was expelled by the other half in flagrant violation of a democratic constitution. There was neither inclination nor opportunity to discuss, much less formulate, a program to enlist the support of fellow Americans toward the urgent tasks of altering the system —the stated goal of SDS. And finally there was an election to "leadership" of a man of undoubted courage and much less proven acumen and ability, who acknowledged that he was a "press-created" leader whom the media had made a "symbol of the New Left." * Accepting his media-created role, he said: "The movement needs leadership, the movement needs symbols. My name exists as a symbol. I think that's a good thing."

Actually it was a poor thing. One could welcome and applaud the radical formulations of the New Left as a replacement for the reformist formulations of the Old Left, while at the same time deploring the romantic rhetoric of revolution that permeated much of the new movement. It misled young radicals (and persons finding their way to radicalism) into regarding spontaneous confrontation with the "power structure" as the final battle with American imperialism. The power structure may have been worried, but it was enormously strong. The potentially revolutionary forces were almost entirely unorganized or in disarray; and those sectors that were organized had no program—socialist or otherwise.

I recall the words of young Paul Potter at the great Berkeley teach-in in May 1965. Suppose, he said, the Administration abruptly abdicated and said: We've made a mess of things. It's all yours. Do what you can. "We wouldn't know what to do," Potter declared. "We would have no program. We would have no plan."

Internally, the indecisions of the new movement were at first reflected at the GUARDIAN as natural growing pains. We were cognizant of great changes taking place with the rise of the young black freedom movement, and our reporters followed the action in the South with such intimacy that occasionally one became a "case" and landed in jail or was run out of town by a constabulary determined to maintain the separation of press and public. The mushrooming peace movement rendered obsolete the SANE mentality of respectability and exclusion. The revolt against established politics was intermingled with the revolt against customs

---

* Mark Rudd, a leader of the 1968 uprising at Columbia University who later became a Weatherman and disappeared from public view. He surfaced in 1977 to face the various charges against him in a calmer political climate.

and manners: hair grew longer, beards sprouted, sex came out of the closet, chemical and herbal drugs blossomed into widespread use, and psychedelic art and rock music produced a "counter-culture," seemingly revolutionary in content, but actually adding to the confusion of programs and plans because it diverted young people away from meaningful politics. It was a time of extraordinary ferment, and the GUARDIAN sought to record it without endorsing euphoria as a short-cut to revolution.

The standing of the paper was high as we entered the mid-1960s. Because of our independence and resistance to the more obvious conformities of the older radical movement, and particularly the Communist Party, the young radicals seemed to trust us. They knew that the GUARDIAN was the one constant to which they could turn for factual news of what was going on and as a bulletin board for what might be taking place. Wherever there was action—a march in Selma or a demonstration in Washington—there were bundles of the paper for distribution in addition to reporters covering events. This fact was duly noted by the hatchet columnists and in cliché-sodden entries in the *Congressional Record*.

Throughout this period we emphasized that unorganized and unstructured activity was far less effective than organized but unauthoritarian programing, but we acknowledged the prevailing mood among the young radicals and accepted that it was up to them to alter their course—if they would. Increasingly, internal problems were exacerbated by external currents, especially as they affected the housekeeping chores of a radical newspaper. In concert with Cedric, with thom I shared all problems in correspondence and in an annual visit to Mexico, I felt that the GUARDIAN had an awe-inspiring political job to do in the world situation existing at the time. We had vaguely anticipated this at the turn of the decade, but hardly conceived what a load history would dump on our shoulders by 1965. Nonetheless we were aware that the GUARDIAN would play an effective role only to the extent that it could heal disunity in the ranks of the radicals and break through to a new generation of Americans who had rarely been exposed to decent,

320   ENTRANCES AND EXITS

sober, and positive ideas. Finding the correct ways and means remained a problem to which none of us had the exact answer. No formula would provide it, but the need to work together in a mature way was more urgent than ever.

In the past, the staff had been acutely conscious of the need to hang together through the stresses and storms that threatened the life of the paper. The marvel was not that differences had arisen, but that they were resolved before the ship could stray dangerously off course. This was quite an achievement when one considers that there had been no organizational star to steer by and that we rejected the imposition of any set of prefabricated views. It was also an achievement to have continued providing, through the period of setbacks and failures on the Left, a modest living wage every week for more than a score of people for what was almost extinct in the journalistic field—an honest job.

These achievements were made possible because there were always enough people among staff and management (though it was not always unanimous) who understood what working together on such an enterprise meant. Obviously it meant readiness to listen respectfully to other points of view, to compromise as well as criticize, and in general to be flexible. In this atmosphere we had set a low record for the Left on major blunders and gained steadily in prestige. The point was and remained that if we wanted to be an influence for unity on the Left outside the newspaper, we had to start by practicing it inside. Those who understood this tried to appraise carefully what their own job was, to give their best to it, and to respect the jobs of others within the responsibility and competency of each. The best periods of the paper were when the greatest number of staff people were functioning along these lines.

At all times we had sought to maintain a democratic structure, with authority but not authoritarianism. We knew that neither an army nor a revolution nor a heretical publication could be run without good captains and sergeants. If there were too many front-seat and back-seat generals, disaster followed. The most serious flaw in the concept of participatory democracy, we felt, was that the whole army would be comprised of generals without insignia, each insisting on the correctness of his or her strategy and tactics.

As the 1960s wore on, job applications poured into the GUARD-IAN. Some of the older people were leaving mainly for economic reasons, and several younger ones were hired. My own aim had always been to attract young people who might be trained for a future with the paper or elsewhere in radical journalism. We neither had nor wanted a monopoly. The new members caused a sharp decline in the average age of the staff and a concomitant rise in conflicts between older hands with political experience of another era and younger hands without political experience of any era, but with strongly held views of present and past politics. Interestingly, the debate soon crossed generational lines, and the divisions at the weekly editorial conferences often did not conform to age categories. Often, too, seemingly high-minded ideological positions served as a cover for lower-minded personal grievances and power ploys clad in the canonicals of politics.

Complicating the internal exacerbations was a very old issue which had never before been a problem: the question of thirty shares of stock of Weekly Guardian Associates Inc., issued to Cedric, Jack McManus, and myself at the incorporation of the paper in 1948. When Cedric was forced to leave the United States in 1955, on lawyer's advice he turned over to Jack and me his ten shares of stock, which had never earned a dividend and were always good for a bit of heavy corporate levity at our annual "board of directors" meetings. This left Jack and me with fifteen shares each.

When Jack died of a heart attack in November 1961, he left no will. Automatically his ten shares went to his widow, Jane (who later became a valuable member of the staff). Feeling she had no right to the stock, Jane, through our attorney Gibby Needleman, turned it over to me. Thus, by deportation and death, I became sole owner of the NATIONAL GUARDIAN, a status I did not relish and had already resolved to alter by sharing ownership with the staff.

But the immediate problem following Jack's death—a devastating blow to the paper and to me personally—was his replacement. After weeks of discussion and search, I offered the post to Russ

Nixon, then legislative representative in Washington for the United Electrical and Machine Workers Union. A sharp observer of the Washington scene, well known in the corridors of Congress, he held a doctorate in economics from Harvard. He had been writing on national politics for the GUARDIAN.

I told Nixon I wanted him to share equally with me in directing the GUARDIAN, as Jack had done; the stock shares were not mentioned. He agreed to take the job early in 1962. He was a strong personality and his arrival stirred a flurry of excitement—meetings and memos abounded. The staff was impressed, yet many were at the same time uncomfortable over Nixon's approach, a combination of standard corporate enterprise and ultra-left politics. Preoccupied with editorial concerns, I tended to attribute the discomfiture to the contrast with Jack's easy and open manner, which had endeared him to us all.

Gradually, however, the unease became contagious and various incidents caused me to consider more closely Nixon's penchant for decision-making without consultation, his executive-suite style and, above all, an awareness that he was at the root of divisions in the staff which occurred seemingly without cause. This was a gratuitous development superimposed on the understandable differences caused by the shifting political winds on the left.

In September 1964 Nixon asked for a private session with me. Since he had been engaged as Jack's replacement, he said, he felt he was entitled to Jack's fifteen shares of stock. This abrupt request, almost two and a half years after his arrival, produced in me a reflective pause. Consultation with the staff produced a temporary closing of ranks and an expression of unanimous opposition to the idea. It matched my own, and I so informed Nixon. He submitted to me a letter of resignation as general manager. Believing (again with staff concurrence) that a possible public dispute over such an odd issue would hardly benefit the paper, I proposed various alternatives within the framework of my determination to share the stock with the staff. None suited Nixon, and it was becoming indisputably clear that what he was after was personal power. In that case, he was not the man for the job.

Late in June 1965 I accepted Nixon's resignation. He sought immediately to withdraw it, but it was too late and the staff, by resolution, accepted the fact of Nixon's departure. It expressed full confidence in the future of the paper under my editorship and the prospect of equal joint ownership of the GUARDIAN. The resolution asked that Nixon be given a grace period of three months (retention of title with pay but without function) to seek new employment.

Nixon used the time to the fullest extent. He circularized the financial contributors to the paper in his behalf, wrote to notable public figures among the readership and to correspondents in the United States and abroad and, with some degree of success, pressured staff members to change their minds. His efforts caused considerable concern and confusion (I refused to be drawn into public debate), but they ultimately failed. His departure became final in September 1965 but the internal damage lingered severely for me and, more importantly, for staff unity.*

Mindful of portents of trouble ahead, I proceeded with the plan to share the ownership with the staff despite the misgivings of attorney Needleman and sage friends and advisers, who felt that equal ownership (50 percent of the stock in my hands and 50 percent in the staff's) might result in an unresolved deadlock situation, to the detriment of the paper.

I recognized the soundness of this, but minimized the likelihood of it happening. Should it happen, my long-held position was that if a majority of the staff disagreed with my general point of view, and there was no way to resolve the differences, I would withdraw from the paper. Therefore, just before Christmas 1965, following discussion with the staff-management committee,† I asked Needle-

---

*The head of the committee at the time was Edward T. Zusi, the GUARDIAN's news editor. An old friend whom I had first encountered while working at the New York *Herald Tribune,* Zusi resigned from the San Francisco *Chronicle* in 1962 to come to work with us. A first-rate editor, he was equally sound and sage in his counsel on the internal affairs of the GUARDIAN. While we sometimes had to be on opposing sides in staff/management affairs (his principled trade unionism was staunch), my respect and love for him never diminished.

†Soon after he left, Nixon became associate director of New York University's Study of the Unemployed. He went from there to Columbia University as an associate professor of social work, and a consultant on manpower problems. In December 1973 he suffered a fatal heart attack. He was 60.

man to draw up an agreement transferring to the staff fifteen shares of the stock. If I were to withdraw, my fifteen shares would revert to the staff; if the staff should withdraw en masse, their fifteen shares would revert to me.

There was a ceremony at my home with the entire staff present. Toasts were drunk to a bright new future and pledges of cooperation flowed with New York State (in keeping with our nonbudget) champagne. The most ardent pledges came from those who had been pressing me to share the stock in the spirit of the new participatory democracy. Their fervor touched a core of my being which, at the same time, sounded an instinctive warning: the enthusiasm might be channeled in a direction that would exclude my participation in the new democracy.

For the rest of the winter harmony prevailed, but with the first breath of spring restlessness set in—an Era of Memoranda, a paper barrage interspersed with lengthy meetings, which was to last for more than a year. The apparent cause of contention was that the GUARDIAN had not kept pace in circulation and influence with the growth of "the movement." To give the flavor of the memoranda, I quote one from a staff member dated March 21, 1966:

America, at the height of its power, is in crisis. The "American dream" is shattering. An illusion, however, dies slowly. Liberalism, where the ideals of this illusion are most pronounced and therefore most vulnerable, is being dashed against the rocks in our universities, our slums, and our back-country hovels. It is, for all its seeming grandeur, in obvious decay. A new radicalism is developing in its wake. . . . But the GUARDIAN, the newspaper best suited to the interests of this new and revitalized radicalism, has been virtually rejected. . . . The GUARDIAN has not developed in step with the new radical movement. It must become a "new" newspaper.

There followed a five-page single-spaced critique of the GUARDIAN with various suggestions to improve content, circulation, and advertising, many of which had been tried out at one time or another during our eighteen years. There was one new suggestion: that I become the publisher (I was being "crushed by the day-to-day affairs of the paper" and my "responsibilities had become diffused") and that a new editor be named. In subsequent staff meetings the memo-writer proposed himself as my replacement.

Other proposals were to dispense with contributors deemed to be "irrelevant to the needs of the new radicalism." Among these were Anna Louise Strong, then sending to the paper the only dispatches from China by an American correspondent; Alvarez del Vayo, the last foreign minister of Republican Spain, one of the world's most respected commentators on foreign affairs; Carleton Beals, untiring advocate of understanding Latin America, a lost continent to the American press—and Cedric Belfrage, editor-in-exile, then receiving a princely $50 a week for his coverage of Latin America and the world, for which he paid his own travel expenses. (His last journey as editor-in-exile was to Berlin in 1966, to receive with Burchett the annual International Organization of Journalists awards for professional service to peace.)

I recall vividly the meeting at which these last proposals were made. Until then I had maintained calm and patience because I genuinely believed, however much I might disagree with some suggestions, that it was proper that they be aired and investigated. This time, however, I exploded with a lecture on arrogance, the continuity of history, and respect. Would they propose, I asked, if he were alive that we also dispense with W. E. B. DuBois as irrelevant? Did they not know that none of us would be sitting in that room that day if Cedric, with the tenacity of a bulldog eighteen years before, had not clung to the idea of a new radical paper, inspiring me to leave the New York *Times* to join forces with him, and then been torn from his newspaper and his adopted land for his persistence and courage? Was this the root spirit of the new radicalism? I quoted Chou En-lai: "The past not forgotten is a guide to the future." A major reason for the "rejection" of the GUARDIAN (an inappropriate word in any case), I suggested, was that the new movement was for the most part rejecting the history of radicalism in its own country, and any movement that did so was quickening the pace of its own destruction. None of the recommended departures would take place with my approval, I said, and if they were forced, then I would depart too.

My lecture was met with remarkable passivity by the proponents of the changes, who then represented a minority of the staff. But the session was instructive, and I knew there were hard times ahead.

In June I distilled all the suggestions for a "new" paper made in the preceding six months, added several of my own, and presented an eighteen-point program for changes in content, format and staff. In a preamble, I wrote:

The position of the GUARDIAN fundamentally is one of independent radical politics, with a flexible point of view countenancing the regional differences in the country and even the possibility of supporting candidates of the existing parties, including of course the minority parties. The fact that we have never in our history supported the candidate of a major party demonstrates our general position. In international politics, the position is and should continue to be one of sympathy and friendship for the socialist world, yet maintaining the right to principled criticism when warranted, and outright disagreement.

I said I felt many of the general suggestions by staff members had been positive, and accepted the idea of a more specialized focus for the paper geared to nurturing the new movement. The program was all-encompassing and could have been the basis for a final discussion. Instead, some weeks later, the staff members of the staff–management committee produced a document titled "Draft Recommendations on Changes" that simply ignored the fact that I had offered a program.

Once again their approach was that a "new" GUARDIAN was needed, that the task was to shatter the image of a paper that was irrelevant, stodgy, and unimaginative, and to create a new, lively controversial organ serving the new radicals, a paper that would gain circulation by relating directly to the "New Left."

The basic error, in my opinion, lay in the assumption that the paper was a complete failure, hence needing drastic renovation to achieve a mysterious "relevance" to American radicalism. In fact the GUARDIAN was more relevant to the new movement, and carried more news of its activities, than any paper of general circulation. We had persevered and served a useful purpose through eighteen years of political turbulence. We had shunned left-wing polemics. Our role had been to carry information of left and radical activities in world and national affairs, with meaningful interpretations conveyed in the choice of news, how it was prepared and in commentaries about the news.

The staff-committee document cited the slow growth of GUARDIAN circulation and compared it unfavorably with the growth of the radical movement, "which we assume is our constituency." This constituency (the "radical movement") was described as encompassing the black people in general, poor whites, ghetto inhabitants, and the "student generation." The choice, the document said, was between serving this constituency and serving "the middle-class," again the assumption being that most present GUARDIAN readers were middle-aged, with well-paying jobs, homes and gardens, who read the paper to demonstrate that they were still "in there."

This was as grossly simplistic as it was to regard all blacks, poor and oppressed, as radical. Of course we reached some in all of these groups and much of their leadership. But increasingly—and this was a major reason for the slow circulation growth—these groups were seeking leadership among their own and, like the new radicals, were beginning to publish on their own. A phenomenon of the period was the surfacing of the misnamed "underground press," a new and spontaneous journalism attuned to the student rebellions, the protest against the war in Indo-China, and the militant black freedom movement (although few blacks were involved in underground press activities). This development was facilitated by low-cost offset printing presses (the GUARDIAN was publishing in a union shop out of principle and with concomitant higher costs) and by street vendors who sometimes were allowed to keep up to 80 percent of the sale price. The new papers provided a market for advertising recordings by rock stars and groups, and for stores and mail-order houses offering the accoutrements of underground life. Their readers regarded them as the troubadours of a new life in a new world.*

*For a full treatment of the underground press, see James Aronson's *Deadline for the Media* (New York: Bobbs-Merrill, 1972).

I felt, as did those on the staff who held with me, that to make the GUARDIAN a paper specifically serving the New Left was misguided on several points. The whole question of news coverage had to be placed in the perspective of a world in which the United States had become the center of a still enormously powerful capitalism facing revolutionary movements on three continents. Life in America reflected the strength and desperation of capitalism—decadent, violent, neurotic, anticultural. The student movement, while courageous and a source of hope, was at that time in the United States far weaker than student movements elsewhere. It was marked to a large extent by romantic protest and lack of ideology. The black movement was far more significant, but neither it nor the student or peace movement offered the likelihood of a genuine revolutionary turn. Nevertheless these groups were vital as the main opposition to the U.S. drift to totalitarianism.

The point seemed to be this: The GUARDIAN was called upon to help guide these movements to deeper political awareness, to report and interpret their activities without cease, to provide their leaders with important information on world and national political currents, and to cultivate awareness that what happened in the Soviet Union, China, Vietnam, Cuba, and Africa had a significant influence upon what happened in the United States.

But clearly the internal debate, while still couched mainly in political terms, was becoming more personal than ideological: there had developed in the staff a concentrated group who wanted simply to take control—in the name of the staff, of course. Some, I believe, genuinely felt there was a possibility of converting the paper into a mass-circulation organ of the New Left, and they were successfully converting waverers to this belief. Others were governed purely by power drives, and this became the dominant divider, however much it was disguised.

A *cause célèbre* was created when one of the newer and more influential staff members resigned—with a mimeographed letter circulated to the staff before the original was given to me. An articulate opponent of the system's "co-optive" tactics to defuse opposition, he said in the letter that he could no longer work for a publication whose "editorial direction is not sufficient to guide a respected, vital publication in today's political conditions." The paper's lack of editorial courage and radical perspective, he said, gave him no alternative but to leave. What neither the staff nor I knew then was that the departing member had already accepted a university job at a vastly higher salary, in a federally funded program whose purpose could only be to persuade the disadvantaged of the virtue of the system.

Even this demonstrable hypocrisy failed to bring about any change in the internal alignment. The battle of memoranda went on, the meetings became lengthier and more acerbic, and the lines hardened. In late summer 1966, I described the atmosphere in a letter to Cedric:

"The word 'cooperation' is a subject of derisive laughter, and the aim of several on the staff seems to be to score off one another. Kindness is a myth and tolerance a crime. They speak of revolution and know not what they speak of. Revolution on these terms would collapse in a sea of hatred. I should tell you that I am seriously thinking of giving the whole thing one last try and, if it fails, to leave. I have reached the point where there is no pleasure in work, no sense of a joint effort, and as far as I am concerned, very little hope of a future with the present group."

In November 1966 a thousand people came to the dinner marking the GUARDIAN's eighteenth year. The theme reflected the contents of the paper in the preceding year: a celebration of the nation's "militant minority." The honored guests represented a cross-section of the radical movement: Jane Adams, an assistant national secretary of SDS; Dr. Charles V. Hamilton, then of Lincoln University, a leading theoretician of the black freedom movement; Carl Braden, who had spent a year in prison for defying the Un-American Activities Committee, executive director of the Southern Conference Educational Fund; Grace Mora Newman, a leading activist of the draft resisters' movement; Lincoln Lynch, associate director of the Congress of Racial Equality; Arthur Kinoy, civil rights and civil liberties attorney. Felix Greene, author and film maker increasingly devoting his attention to China, sent a message. In a keynote I summarized the GUARDIAN's role:

"To encourage the emergent radicalism toward a unified, non-sectarian goal of socialism; to expose the chief obstacle to this goal—U.S. monopoly capitalism and imperialism; to stress for an essentially white readership the validity of the concept of black power and the positive aspects of all people's revolutions; and the affinity and importance of the world revolutionary movements to our own efforts to effect a basic change in the structure of our own society. Finally, to say to all of our friends on the Left: Enough of fratricide; An end to political popery!"

Consciously or unconsciously I was speaking to that faction of the staff hell-bent on fratricide. They had boycotted the dinner and sneered at it as an "elitist" event geared to a "tired, middle-class audience." Their attitude and comments so angered our indispensable director of events/fund raiser Vita Barsky that she resigned. I characterized the attitude as inverse snobbism that could only halt the flow of sorely needed funds. If their rejection was based on the middle-class composition of the audience, to what class did they think they belonged? The dinner participants in fact included people who had waged some of the great union battles in the 1930s, fought in the civil war in Spain, resisted the witch-hunters of the 1950s, and gone South with the first waves of civil rights workers as doctors, nurses, and lawyers.

It was becoming a Kafka-like situation. The prestige of the paper had rarely been higher among young and old alike. The editor of the *Boston University News,* one of the most militant college newspapers in the country, wrote that he sought to model his paper after the GUARDIAN. European and Asian correspondents called repeatedly for permission to reprint our articles on the New Left and came in person to use our research facilities. I was more than ever mindful of Max Werner's stricture to us back in 1949 to "make the *Guardian* the kind of newspaper that no informed person could do without."

On March 23, 1967, I received a letter signed by eleven members of the staff ("with a dedication and concern to the paper") charging me with "evasion and delay" in effecting changes. It amounted to a virtual ultimatum to agree to their demands (as vague and generalized as ever) or face a situation in which they were determined "through our own initiative and through others concerned with the paper's well-being and growth," to effect the changes. The paper, they said, was "in crisis."

The same day a letter came from Cedric who wrote: "From your account there seems from here no doubt that these people are deliberately scheming to drive you insane or into a heart attack." He urged me to fly to Mexico for a face-to-face session with him—the mails took too long, and the phone was impossible.

Thus, on my 52d birthday, in the last week of March, we sat among the bougainvilleas in Cuernavaca seeking a "final solution" for the NATIONAL GUARDIAN—twenty-two years after we had dreamed of its birth in a rain-soaked Army billet on Franklin D. Roosevelt Allee in Bremen. When we had examined every option for my continuing with the paper, Cedric said: "I see no alternative to your leaving; otherwise it may mean your life."

"I have come to that conclusion myself," I said, "painful as it is. But what about you? After all, it has been your life as well as mine, and I refuse to let my decision influence yours."

He looked at me as though I were peculiar and said: "I wouldn't remain a day after you left. We'll resign together."

As simple as that. We drafted separate letters of resignation, and I flew back to New York. On the weekend before returning to work, I went over my letter carefully and had a final draft ready that Sunday night. The next morning, as I was leaving the house, Grambs walked to the door with me and said: "If you change your mind, you'll have to reckon with me." It was the first time in our relationship that she had ever expressed herself so inexorably about my work. The letter of resignation, dated April 5, 1967, was addressed to the full staff:

"After carefully considering the letter dated March 23 from eleven of your colleagues, I am informing you today of my decision to relinquish my duties as editor of the NATIONAL GUARDIAN and president of Weekly Guardian Associates Inc. In view of the internal situation as reflected in the letter, I believe that my action is in the best interests of the paper and of my own future useful-ness in the radical movement.

"I cannot agree that the GUARDIAN is in crisis in the sense expressed by the signers of the letter—that is, that the Left is growing but the GUARDIAN is not. On the contrary, I believe that the GUARDIAN's prestige remains remarkably high at a time when the Left still shows little sign of maturing in any meaningful fash-ion.

"I do agree that the paper is not as good as it should be, but that is not due fundamentally to differences between the staff and edi-tor on the question of changes and improvements. There has been agreement on many proposals put forward. In a collective en-terprise such as ours, the responsibility for implementing them must be collective. It has not been.

"In one major sense, I do agree that the GUARDIAN is in crisis. But I believe the crisis in internal. I refer to the persistent bitter-ness and inability to find common ground, which have undoubt-edly been reflected in the work of the staff and the quality of the paper. Further, it has caused the voluntary departure of valuable staff members.

"If this rancor and division continue, the prospects for the paper would be dim indeed. I have obviously been unable to end them. My departure is in accordance with the principle I have expressed in the past—that if a majority of the staff expressed a lack of con-fidence in me and I saw no hope of restoring a spirit of harmony and unity, I would withdraw.

"My decision after nineteen years with the GUARDIAN is not taken lightly. It was reached with considerable sadness. But I have no regret at all; rather, I leave with a sense of gratification for the years of work toward a most desirable goal. And whatever work I undertake in the future will be toward this same goal."

I decided to make no statement in the paper about my reasons for resigning. Aside from an unwillingness to make public issues that would titillate a hostile press and government, I knew that the new directorate at the paper would counter whatever I had to say and thus open the floodgates for a public controversy without possible resolve. In the issue of the GUARDIAN dated April 29, 1967, the last under my editorship, there appeared a brief two-column boxed story on page 2 announcing my resignation and Cedric's. I wrote it myself.

It was a break in the Long March, but not the end of the road.

Postscript [**C.B.**] As I watched from afar the "New Left" coming to the boil against the "Old Left," I had gray presentiments about its effect on our citadel of Zusammenarbeit. As always, renovation based on study of past errors was necessary, but what else was new? The "Stalinist" label, rendered more than meaningless by Left fissions without end, was one that the "New Left" then stuck on the "Old Left." Writing nine years after the explosion at the GUARDIAN, I note without comment that the people who took over our paper—after a Pilgrim's Progress all over the political map— ended as securely in Mao's corner as the CP once was in Stalin's, to the extent of restoring Stalin to the pantheon after the Chinese model. I also note that in 1976 the GUARDIAN began fraternally (and to my mind justifiably) criticizing aspects of China's policy— a move back toward our position which gave me pleasure.

Some of the paper barrage of 1966 reached me in Mexico, and I added to it in what I hoped was worth two cents. "What seems beyond a doubt," I wrote to the staff (all personally unknown to me), "is that our *non-sectarian* radicalism—an approach we were the first to take in 1948—is the main basis of the support we receive. . . . The U.S.A. is our primary concern but, as internationalists, we reject the patriotism that stops at frontiers. As realists and not mystics, we reject the infallibility of any country or sect. As socialists we are, however, partisan toward those who err in the fight for socialism, believing that our mission is not to magnify their errors but to accent whatever is positive."

I suggested that with the greater diversity of positive elements now in the struggle, perhaps we hadn't gone far enough in this. "One example: extremely important elements now exist within the Catholic church which the Left has traditionally anathematized in toto. Another: we did well in not maintaining the total anathema against Trotskyists, a word at which millions of progressives learned to shudder like Pavlovian dogs. But the time has come for clearly expressed repudiation of all such sectarian mystiques. The USSR and China may find justification for maintaining the angels-and-devils theory of men and history, but we don't need it and will broaden our influence the more candidly we discard it. Wherever there is a broadening trend on the Left, we should be in the vanguard of it—always within the boundaries of those 'Left proprieties' which we set for ourselves.''

As for style, balance of content, and other points in controversy, I agreed with some of the staff beefs and differed with others. My letter announcing that I would resign if Jim did, after his visit to Cuernavaca, began:

''Any comments by me on this conflict must be measured by the fact that Jim is my oldest and closest friend. Some will feel that this makes my views too subjective to have any value. Others may wish to consider that my opinions about him are based on twenty-two years of working and personal association. The extent of his exhaustion and depression when he arrived here distressed me very much. . . . The general theme [of the staff paper-barrage] is that Jim is a bad editor and an impossible person. . . . If [the barrage] reflects the majority mood of the staff, in my view Jim has no other course than to resign and there is little for me to say. I have made no secret of my admiration for Jim's professional competence, personal integrity, and maturity of political judgment. I do not find that he has changed, and I have seen no evidence that any member of the staff compares with him in any of these qualities.''

I was especially baffled by the fusillade against Jim with regard to overlong articles and lack of humor. ''Is it suggested,'' I wrote, ''that the GUARDIAN writers are turning in short pieces which Jim then proceeds to lengthen, or humorous pieces from which he removes the humor?'' Who but those who wrote the pieces were complaining? Yet such criticism from anyone else would have had validity. In these and other areas the paper's quality had been dropping. The reason was that many of the staff were on a semi-sitdown and leaving too much in Jim's harassed, overloaded hands.

All this is water long over the dam, and all of us have survived doing our Thing. The mills of the gods of social change still grind slowly while the atom-armed gods of reaction gallop toward destruction—not, unfortunately, of themselves alone.

The sad thing about the GUARDIAN explosion of 1967—a very small element in the total process—was that it rang down the curtain on nineteen years of functioning Zusammenarbeit on the left. Wonderful years for all of us who participated, and a record over the course in recent newspaper history. I have been privileged to see for myself how magnificently Jim, as guide-philosopher-friend to journalism students at Hunter College, is fulfilling his pledge to "work toward this same goal in whatever I undertake in the future." At 72, my contribution as an author is waning, but "if there remain but two. . ."

Autopsy

There is nothing finer than gallant rearguard actions, and besides, we may not know how strong we are.

—Thomas Mann (1934)*

[**J.A., C.B.**]† On the masthead of its May 6, 1967, issue the GUARDIAN carried a new label—"The Progressive Newsweekly" had become "An Independent Radical Newsweekly." We had already agreed to the change in designation but had regarded it as more nearly cosmetic, for the content was always radical, "progressive" being the commonly used word for our point of view when we started out. An announcement said the staff "reaffirms its journalistic and political commitment to a growing American Left and sets a radical perspective for fulfilling that commitment. . . . As it sharpens its coverage, so the GUARDIAN believes, it will sharpen its relevance to the time." A longer statement gave a familiarly rhetorical background to the dispute and promised great things to come.

Spokesmen for the new GUARDIAN asked that we allow our

---

*In a letter commending, as one voluntary exile to another, Rene Schickele's journalistic struggle against Nazism.

†The "I" in this chapter is J. A., who wrote it; I have merely edited it. The "we" is both of us, who agree on its contents, hence no postcript. —C.B.

names to stay on the masthead as founders, but we declined. While the request may have indicated tentative ambivalence about a severance with the past, the acrimonious course of the dispute suggested rather an opportunistic move to retain support of contributors whom our departure might alienate.

We had both sent copies of our resignation letters to all of the *Guardian*'s correspondents and representatives in the United States and abroad, and to persons who had been particularly close to the paper over the years. Their reaction was overwhelmingly one of dismay. Many worried about our personal futures, and offers of help were as generous as they were moving; but the prime concern of the letter-writers and callers—most of whom also received documents from the new managers outlining ambitious plans for increased circulation and advertising—was the future of the paper. None placed any hope in the vision of a commercially viable radical newspaper—a clear contradiction in political terms, they felt. The reaction that most warmed my heart came from the composing-room foreman of the plant that printed the GUARDIAN. A quiet man of Italian origin and a superb craftsman, he offered his services free of charge for any publication venture I might undertake.

My departure stirred more journalistic curiosity than my nineteen-year tenure. Even before the resignations were made public, the *Times* was on the phone. The four-column headline over its report was quaint: NATIONAL GUARDIAN EDITOR QUITS IN FORMAT DISPUTE. The story was factual but sketchy, owing partly to my unwillingness to respond in detail to the reporter's questions. I had resolved not to discuss the experience publicly until I could write about it without bitterness and with the perspective of time and distance. (The first article was in response to a request from Carey McWilliams, editor of *The Nation;* it was published on February 5, 1968, with the title: "Editing on the Left: Memories and Convictions.")

Although we made no attempt to influence them, almost all the correspondents and contributors felt they could not continue without us. Among them were Carleton Beals, our roving corrrespondent Ursula Wassermann, and Anne Bauer in Paris. The new managers sent urgent appeals to Anna Louise Strong and Alvarez del Vayo (whom a year earlier they had sought to dump on the ash heap of history) to carry on, and they acquiesced for reasons we accepted without question: the need for an outlet, in the hostile sea of American journalism, for fairly presented news about China and the liberation struggles generally. Wilfred Burchett, with close ties to both of us, was especially disturbed about our leaving and proposed to diminish his contributions and then depart himself. But after a visit to Hanoi, where he saw freshly made craters of American benevolence, he concluded that he had an obligation to both the Vietnamese and American peoples to tell the truth through any vehicle available to him. There was no other, and we approved.

Predictably the GUARDIAN shifted its viewpoint according to the fortunes of dominant groups within the New Left—first rejecting a "Marxist–Leninist" approach as incorrigibly Old Left, then becoming a virtual adjunct of Students for a Democratic Society, then veering away from a strictly New Left approach when SDS disintegrated into warring factions. "We are movement people acting as journalists," the new managers said. "The duty of a radical newspaper is to build a radical movement." But in the absence of an organized framework, this task was impossible.

In February 1968, with fanfare to demonstrate the break with the past, "NATIONAL" was removed from the name of the paper, and it became "the GUARDIAN." We never grasped the significance of this action, even symbolically, because of a curious continuing ambivalence in the new directorate. On the one hand they constantly emphasized changes in style, content, and direction; at other times—for example, the issue marking "twenty continuous years of publication"—there was a proud reminder of the NATIONAL GUARDIAN's record, with reproduction of headlines, stories, and pictures of notable campaigns and editorials. They were beholden to the past whether they approved or not.

For the most part the tone was one of exhortation to the thinning activist ranks of the New Left to stand fast at the barricades while their brothers and sisters in Third World liberation movements hastened the demise of American imperialism. In the absence of an American program toward this end, that was a recurrent theme. The stress was on events abroad; the decline in analysis of the American experience was apparent. And those events within the United States which were covered produced a flow of letters critical of inaccuracies in the coverage. Articles scorned in the "old" GUARDIAN as too long became longer. Humor, which had declined precipitously during the great internal debate, vanished altogether. Editorial discipline was sorely lacking.

Within a year of our resignation the staff had been almost entirely replaced, and reports of internal conflict were prevalent. In the GUARDIAN of December 14, 1968, after a turbulent "twentieth anniversary" meeting, an editorial declared: "The movement itself is split in numerous camps. There is no ideological cohesion. A relevant strategy for the next years has not been formulated." The GUARDIAN itself shared the plight of the movement. Group resignations continued, causing a second almost complete turnover, and in 1970 a large part of the staff went on strike and then left to form a *Liberated Guardian.** In October 1971 the GUARDIAN's paid circulation was listed in the mandatory annual notice as 14,000, half the figure at the time of our departure, and advertising content had diminished considerably. Many left groups felt it useless to place their meeting notices and service advertising in the GUARDIAN, because of its intense partisanship.

---

*The record is incomplete without mentioning "The Split at the *Liberated Guardian,"* as described in February 1972 by *Liberated Guardian* loyalists after a walk-out by nine rebels who proceeded to "put out their 'liberated' *Liberated Guardian."* The loyalists accused the rebels of a "profoundly anti-working class bias," the "treacherous thing" about which was that it was "not explicit." Support or nonsupport of the "Weather Underground's" bomb-and-sabotage tactics apparently figured in the split. Citing neither Marx nor any other departed prophet, the loyalists' 8-page manifesto ended: "We feel that everyone who is serious about the struggle against capitalism must become a part of and work to build the world wide proletarian revolution."

The *Liberated Liberated* vanished without trace, but the *Liberated* was appearing in 1977 renamed the New York City *Star.* The latter little resembles the paper we published, but the general desire to perpetuate our name, shown by leftists with a yen to publish, was a sort of compliment.

At about this time the paper abruptly adopted a firm "Marxist–Leninist" line. It began to examine and find wanting the programs and policies of just about every avowed Marxist group in the country, particularly the CPUSA, with its allegiance to the Soviet Union. Commentary and even news articles became intensely polemical. Film reviews were laced with Marxist terminology: V. I. Lenin faced down John Wayne at High Noon. GUARDIAN theoreticians announced as the basic task of the American Left the formation of a "new communist party." While exhortation toward this end was profuse, a program for implementing it was missing—as it had to be, since the conditions for such a party were also missing.

Ideological correctness became the first order of business. Where once the paper had sought to rise above the bickering of dogmatists who had isolated themselves from the mass of Americans, the new GUARDIAN seemed to relish the battle in the quicksands of orthodox insularity. It had indeed finally broken with our founding principle, that a radical newspaper should provide facts for all radicals to fight with and positive commentary aimed to close rather than widen breaches among them.

The actual time span of this book, with a prologue for background into the 1940s and an afterword into the 1970s, is 1948 to 1967. As this final chapter was set down in 1977, there was a temptation to assess the record of radical journalism in the intervening decade, and thereby perhaps vindicate positions strongly held in these pages. But our book was not undertaken in a spirit of self-justification. We thought it would be more useful to review our own record as objectively as possible, measuring "success" and "failure" not in terms of size or circulation, but in the context of the times and the role we sought to play in them: a radical newspaper in a struggling movement beset by monumental opposition at home and by a historic cleavage in the world of socialism. Only within this framework can criticism and self-criticism have valid meaning.

It is important therefore to look back at the 1950s and the first half of the 1960s through the eyes of younger radicals, particularly journalists, trying to understand why certain positions were taken by an independent radical publication and why certain lines of inquiry were not. The questions come primarily from serious-minded intellectual workers (as we prefer to call them) who were in the universities (and for the most part remained to graduate) in the 1960s. Many of them today are engaged in serious research into the nature of American imperialism and its institutions, the kind of study which has already been of great help to activists and historians seeking alternatives to the present system.

Why, some of them ask, did the NATIONAL GUARDIAN not criticize the Communist Party more sharply when our disagreement with major CP positions was so clear? Why was there so much "uncritical acceptance of the Soviet Union's positions," so much "overzealously favorable portrayal of the socialist nations under Stalinism?" as one put it.

Many of the questioners come from families whose parents were Communist Party members, and there is implied in their questions a sense of betrayal. We were weaned, they seem to be saying, on the belief that Stalin could do no wrong, and the CPUSA encouraged this feeling. Then came the disclosures of the crimes of the Stalin era, not only in the Soviet Union, but throughout Eastern Europe. Why were these things not reported earlier?

Such questions are too valid not to demand confrontation. Some can be answered fully, if they ever will be, only by persons who were in the CP leadership at the time, or were informed members. None of the NATIONAL GUARDIAN's managers fell into those categories.

Some of the questions bear the mark of the scapegoat theory of history: the need to ascribe blame to one group, or several groups, for events which were beyond those groups' control. They also tend to deny the continuity of history. The questioners in this vein stand apart from the history of events except where they themselves are immediately and currently involved. They view past events from a perspective not in accordance with the reality of the time in which the events occurred, but almost entirely from hindsight influenced by subsequent events and current conditions. This approach is scientifically unsound. Conditions in the 1950s for the American left were quite different from those of the 1970s. The Soviet Union is a prime example. The aim of American foreign policy in the 1950s was to destroy the Soviet Union and prevent the self-determination of peoples anywhere in the world if it interfered with the profitable functioning of American finance capital. The obligation of a radical newspaper was to impress upon its readers the right of the Soviet Union to exist—of *any* socialist nation to exist—without fear of destruction; and the right of any country to adopt a socialist system.

The most effective way to do this, we believed, was to focus the attention of as many Americans as possible on the policies and goals of their own government. The goal of Soviet foreign policy, as we interpreted it, was peaceful coexistence with other nations, including the capitalist nations. The Russians did not then seek to emulate Dulles in reverse by attempting to contain capitalism. They were in any case preoccupied with repairing the devastation of World War II. They sought to fashion a protective belt around the perimeters of the Soviet Union to forestall another invasion. Only a distorted mind could find this unreasonable.

Those who attacked Soviet policy in those years did so not as friends of socialism. They sought to give aid and comfort to American policy. Of such critics "on the Left" (it is actually a perversion to place them on the Left) I wrote in *The Press and the Cold War* (Bobbs-Merrill, 1970): "The so-called democratic socialists . . . believed neither in democracy for dissenters nor in socialism for the country. So firmly were they in thrall to anti-communism that their press at times was a virtual propaganda arm of Washington foreign policy."

We did not regard Soviet policy as flawless, but generally we held with Anna Louise Strong that the Soviet Union "carried the hope of mankind," with stress on the word *hope*. The Soviets' internal problems were and are more complex, and they pose a challenge to every radical, communist and non-communist, to explore them with utmost seriousness both in order to understand the past and to confront the future. To say that the facts about the ugly aspects of the Stalin era were not available may sound like a subterfuge, but it is to a large extent a fair statement. There were no sources of non-adulatory information from inside the Soviet Union which, by our socialist standards, could be called reliable. On various occasions we tried to impress upon Soviet journalists in the United States that news from their country was too hyperbolic to be usable. Some of them agreed and promised to discuss it when they returned home, but nothing changed. From this one could and did draw increasingly dim inferences, but no facts.

Meanwhile reports of repression within the Soviet Union were common currency—from sources that were almost always virulently anti-Soviet and anti-Communist. Much of the information was patently contrived and easily disproved. The chief channels were persons who, formerly in the CP themselves, had become professional anti-Communists, profitably employed by the Hearst and Scripps-Howard press or serving as "Kremlinologists" to less obviously biased newspapers. They were in the business of peddling hate, and it was not only the Soviet Union, but any dissenting movement in the United States, that they sought to destroy.

The question of what was right or wrong for a radical newspaper is also subjectively related to the military time factor. During more than three decades when the first nursery of socialism remained vulnerable to its far more potent enemies, genuine socialists spontaneously and naturally defended it. This became a habit which, with the end of the U.S. A-bomb monopoly, socialists shed too slowly. Thus, by the 1950s, we can now see it as wrong to have dismissed without careful investigation (however difficult such inquiry would have been) reports of grievous injustice and terror inside the Soviet Union. If the reports could have been verified and protests registered by sympathizers of socialism, some of the horror might have been prevented or ameliorated, as was the case with our persistence in the mistreatment of Anna Louise Strong. Injustice, wherever it occurs, has to be exposed. If radical Americans sought help throughout the world, including the Soviet Union, in the case of Ethel and Julius Rosenberg, then victims of

Soviet injustice should be able to turn with expectation of support to American radicals.

The relationship of an independent radical publication to the CPUSA was more tangible and hence more manageable. It was clear to us in the prepublication stages that leaders of the CP looked with suspicion on our plans. We were independent, untested, unpredictable. There was no overt hostility, but the non-availability of financial aid in certain areas was eloquent. Individual Communists, however, welcomed the new paper and were among our earliest subscribers and boosters. They found refreshing our abstinence from sectarianism, clichés, and cant.

A founding principle of the NATIONAL GUARDIAN was that we would not be the organ of any existing party, nor would we favor any segment of the radical movement, domestic or foreign, to the exclusion of others. We insisted that we had no enemies on the left, however great the disagreement about certain tactics or policies. The Communist Party was part of the left, at that time unquestionably (as shown by its priority status for J. Edgar Hoover) the leading part.

Our major disagreement with the Communists, as we have noted earlier, was on electoral politics. We wanted to help lay foundations for an independent radical political movement, and kept insisting on it. We felt that the responsible way to demonstrate such disagreement with the CP was not in denunciatory debate, but in presenting our own point of view as constructively and effectively as possible.

In 1973 the CP finally seemed to be abandoning its "mainstream" thesis of politics in favor of an independent socialist alternative. Unfortunately its shift in strategy was announced without a candid analysis of its electoral role in the previous two decades, a study which could have been of singular service both to the CP and to all radicals. Further, the CP remained bound by its belief in the need to support unswervingly any position adopted by the Soviet Union. This in itself severely limited its appeal not only to the American public generally but to American radicals particularly.

One young radical suggested to me that the NATIONAL GUARD-

IAN refused to attack the CP because 99 percent of the press was already doing so. While the percentage estimate was accurate, the reason was not. We refused to attack the CP as a matter of principle. It was an easy path to "respectability," a goal that we were not pursuing. We wanted rather to demonstrate to the American public that it was respectable, without quotation marks, in the finest American tradition, to be radical—and that included the right to be a communist with a lower-case or upper-case "C."

We applied this principle generally. We published advertising submitted by the Socialist Workers Party (Trotskyist) as well as by the Communists and other left groups. While it may seem absurd today to report this fact, intolerance on the left in the 1950s had reached a point where publication of such news and advertising often was met with severe criticism and even threat of boycott. Intolerance? We recall an episode early in our paper's life when some staff members protested acceptance of advertisements from an organic orange grower because he grew his oranges in Florida, a state notorious for discriminating against blacks. The grower, incidentally, was a devoted reader who placed NATIONAL GUARDIAN subscription blanks in every crate he shipped out.

Intolerance and absolutism, to our minds, are twin enemies of the left, pernicious, draining, demoralizing. They render impossible the harmony and collaboration without which radical movements cannot long exist, let alone grow. We read much of the radical press today with a sense of dismay. The sects continue to proclaim themselves the true and singular heirs of Marx and Lenin, or of Marx, Lenin, Stalin, and Mao, or of Marx, Lenin, and Trotsky, or whatever other pantheon they have selected. Having canonized or diabolized these thoroughly human beings, the sects then become preoccupied with jockeying for the vanguard role of the most faithful. Meanwhile the most faithful enemy, finance capitalism, goes about its work almost unchallenged except by those radicals who apply their "ism" without theology. The theists are of no concern or danger to the imperialists because they so rarely leave the cathedral.

An American radical newspaper can transmit the experiences of the Chinese revolution without making Mao's theories sound like Talmudic liturgy. It is, in fact, a disservice to the American radical movement *not* to translate the Chinese experience in terms applicable to American conditions. One can criticize the Soviet Union's medieval attitudes toward its cultural figures without dismissing the Bolshevik revolution as a failure because its heirs have abandoned its principles. Not to be critical is to betray the principles of revolutionary freedom.

For American radicals who are in a sense a colonized group within their own imperial country, there is much to be learned from the revolutionary experience of the peoples of North Korea, Vietnam, and Cuba. There revolutionaries have resisted and defeated American colonialism and imperialism *with* the help of the large socialist countries but *without* the loss of sovereignty or socialist independence.

A radical newspaper dedicated to the cause of revolutionary change in the United States can be an articulate instrument for such change if it acts in the interest of cohesion and unity. If it pursues a divisive course, it can become counterrevolutionary. A radical newspaper must, as a primary obligation, fix its attention not on the merits or demerits of revolutionary systems or movements abroad, but on the enemy of revolution at home. Otherwise it ends up, in effect, doing the work of the political police.

In a nation which has so recently marked the bicentennial of its bourgeois revolution, a radical newspaper must see as its socialist-revolutionary priority the creation of a political force comprising diverse but cooperating elements—white, black, Hispanic, Indian, poor people from city and country, organized workers and unemployed, individual and organized professionals—any and all groups in our society which, working separately or together, will accept a common unity of purpose pervasive enough to bring about fundamental change in the system. An entrenched American capitalism will do its utmost to prevent such a force from being realized. It will be assisted in its effort if any one group seeks to impose its policy as the dominant and only "correct" one.

We do not believe that there can be an overall "correct" policy

for a national radical movement today except in the acknowledgement that the overriding issues are imperialism, racism, and
sexism; and even here there will be differences on methods of
struggle against them. The first objective, it seems to us, must be a
working relationship among all groups and organizations which are
potential participants in such a movement—with tolerance, understanding, a seeking after knowledge of one another's problems and
aspirations and, above all, a knowledge of history.

I recall a clear-headed commentary by the late teacher and
theoretician Paul Baran in a symposium on "Cooperation on the
Left" in the *Monthly Review* (July 1950). Discussing the "manipulative ability" of the American ruling class to sustain the decline
of radicalism in the United States, Baran wrote:

"There is hardly any room for political cooperation on the Left
in the present movement because there are no politics on the Left.
The time will perhaps come, possibly sooner than we think. But
just now the issues are ideological, and ideological problems cannot be solved by organizational makeshifts. . . . What is
needed—let us say it again and again—is clarity, courage, patience, faith in the spontaneity of rational and socialist tendencies
in society. At the present historical moment in our country—'better smaller but better.' "

In the 1960s there was a great deal of politics on the left, much
of it spontaneous but euphoric, and the slogan seemed to be "bigger and quicker." But there are no short cuts to revolution, and a
movement without popular support, as the activists discovered, is
not at all revolutionary. This applies precisely to the problems of a
radical newspaper, and it was well understood in the radical movement more than sixty years ago.

The *Appeal to Reason,* whose history the founders of NATIONAL
GUARDIAN studied, reached its height about 1912, when the Socialist Party had a membership of 150,000 and Gene Debs won
nearly a million votes for the Presidency out of 15 million cast.
During strikes, free speech battles, elections, and jailings,
hundreds of Socialist locals ordered bundles of the *Appeal* and distributed them free door-to-door on Sunday mornings. In the period

of the great trials—Moyer-Haywood-Pettibone in Idaho, and the McNamara brothers in Los Angeles—the paper had press runs of a million, almost all paid for by Socialist Party locals and trade unions and distributed free. Every Socialist local had a "literature agent" selling the paper at union halls, street corner meetings, picket lines, and demonstrations. Debs went on tours for the *Appeal*, attracting thousands in each city with his dynamic manner. With the admission charge came a subscription to the *Appeal*, ranging from four to forty weeks. It was the result of hard work by a solid, organized movement with a common basic ideal. In the intervening years there have been hundreds of radical publications, yet with the exception of the *Appeal*, all were forced to go to their readers for survival money because of lack of organizational support.

In the spirit of Baran's "better smaller but better," and without elitist connotation, we believe that a new force is emerging in the late 1970s. It is comprised of both older and younger generations, battle-hardened by the domestic and foreign wars of the last four decades, and of still younger people now absorbing the facts of history. They accept the positive changes wrought by the upheavals of the 1960s without endorsing drugs, bizarre dress, electronic sound, or pornography as heralds of national liberation. They do not regard themselves as culpable for the state of the nation or the world today—the comforting universal-guilt promulgations of the liberals—but feel a responsibility to bring about change.

Among the newest adherents to this force, many of them political novices but eager to learn, as I have come to see through my work in the universities in the last ten years, there is an earnest striving to understand the institutions of our society through honest intellectual endeavor and life experience of the community. These young people do not reject America; they reject the system and symbols of the American establishment. They believe with us, as they look about them at nations with far less freedom, far more savage and cynical injustice, that here there remains something to guard as well as to rebel against. They have no desire to isolate themselves in superior sects, yet they know they may for a long time to come be forced to suffer the slings and arrows directed at a vulnerable minority. They understand the problems of the generation gap but do not refuse dialogue between the generations. They have a greater understanding of the psychological problems of their own generation—yearning after idols, ego drives, frustration of careers, still prevalent color barriers—but try to deal with them in a spirit of fraternity.

They seek not the destruction of the university but to open its incomparable facilities to all; and they welcome, for all that it may or may not be worth to them, the guidance of faculty members who share their hopes and aspirations. They have no firm faith in the electoral system but understand the relevance to the community's immediate needs of electing black mayors and honest liberals. They accept the division between black and white as a necessary concomitant of a system which created the division in the first instance, but they are confident of a time when it will be appropriate—nay, essential—to join in a common struggle.

A national liberation movement—that is in essence what it must be—will not develop easily or without great cost in America. Fifty years after the death of John Brown, pioneer American radical, W. E. B. DuBois wrote in his biography of the Old Man: "John Brown taught us that the cheapest price to pay for liberty is its cost today." Sixty years after DuBois wrote that, the cost continues to rise each day. But an indispensable part of it, whenever it comes to be reckoned, will be the price of establishing a genuinely radical press to stir the nation's conscience and achieve its liberation.

Index

Jefferson, Thomas, 17
Jencks, Clifford and Virginia, 66, 73-74
Jenner, Sen. William, 217-19
Jerome, V. J., 62-63
Johnson, Lyndon, 292, 296, 313
Johnson, Mordecai (Howard University), 147
Jordan, Dr. Virgil, 195
Joseph, Joe, 89
Joyce, Robert, 23, 54
Jugger, Ocie, 142
Juliao, Francisco, 275

Karnow, Stanley, 54, 69
Karp, Samuel, 163-64
Kaufman, Judge Irving R., 164, 172-74, 189
Kearney, Rep. Bernard W., 179
Keller, Helen, 147
Kennedy, John F., 104-5, 266, 272, 277-78, 288, 295, 311
Kennedy, Robert, 182, 312
Kent, Rockwell, 239
Keys, Donald, 306-7, 310-11
Khrushchev, Nikita, 91, 103, 221-22, 237-38, 242-43, 255-56, 272, 277, 280-85
Kilgallen, Dorothy, 281
Kim Il Sung, 106-7, 126, 128
King, Martin Luther Jr., 148, 312
King Yo-ling (Peking), 248-50
Kinoy, Arthur, 330
Knowles, Clayton, 217
Koch, Ilse, 88, 161
Koje Island (Korea), 113
Korean Peace Ctee. and Journalists Union, 125-26
Koreans in U.S., 120
Korean war, 59, 98, 106 *passim,* 159, 173, 177, 184-85
Kramer, Ione, 54
Kremlin (Moscow), 243-44
Krock, Arthur, 173
Kwak, Choon Cha and Chungsoon, 119-29, 197, 245
Kyle, Rev. A. B., 135

Labor Party (UK), 15, 93, 102-3
Labour Monthly (London), 97
Lambert, Tom, 293
Lamont, Corliss, 67, 99, 194, 227
Lane, Mark, 296-300
Lanham, Rep. Henderson L., 143
Laos, 288-89, 292
Lardner, John, 23
Lardner, Ring Jr., 23, 66
Latin America, stirrings & repressions, 232, 261-75
Lattimore, Owen, 66n, 195, 305
Lawrence, William, 281
League for Industrial Democracy, 305
League of Nations, 33, 89, 92
Lee, Roger (Harvard), 40
Lehrer, Tom, 271
Lenin, 43-44
Lens, Sidney, 311
Lerner, Max, 174
Levitt, Victor, 15, 22, 29, 31, 34-35, 51, 154, 166, 189, 228-29
Liang Sze-chen (Peking), 248-50
Liberated Guardian, 340
Libération (Paris), 298
Liberty, Statue of, 104, 197
Liberty Book Club, 202
Lidice (Czechoslovakia), 24
Lieu, N. N., 248
Life (magazine), 104
Light, Robert E., 14, 53, 278
Lincoln, Abraham, 17, 28
Little, Brown & Co., 178
Lloyd, Jessie, 67, 267n
Lodge, Henry Cabot, 282
Loeser, Franz, 238
Los Angeles Times, 293
Lotto, Jack, 298
Lovejoy, Elijah P., 219
Loyalty boards and oaths, 8, 15
Luce, Henry (Time Inc.), 39
Lynch, Lincoln, 330
Lynchings, 140-43, 195
Lyons, Leonard, 174
Lysenko, T. D., 77

MacArthur, Gen. Douglas, 97, 110, 114
MacDougall, Curtis, 39-40
MacLaine, Shirley, 282
Macy's (N.Y.), 176
Mailbag (N.G.), 71-83, 115, 153, 165, 222
Mailer, Norman, 24, 54, 70
Mainichi Shimbun (Tokyo), 292, 304
Malcolm X, 312
Malenkov, Georgi, 100-1
Mallard, Amy, 141
Maltin, Aaron, 200-1
Manchester Guardian, 240
Mann, Thomas, 89-90, 199
Mao Tse-tung, 26, 96, 195, 244, 252, 256-58
Marcantonio, Rep. Vito, 13, 16, 19, 50, 59-60, 93, 107-8, 111, 138, 143, 175, 199, 287
Marine Cooks & Stewards Union, 109
Marshall, Daniel (lawyer), 188
Marshall, George (Civil Rights Congress), 118
Marshall Plan, 27
Martinsville (Va.) Seven, 141
Marx, Karl and Marxism, 43, 76-77, 229, 252, 257, 270, 341
Marzani, Carl, 66
Matchan, Don C., 15
Matusow, Harvey, 199
McCarran, Sen. Pat and McCarran Internal Security Act, 15, 85, 108, 114-15, 214, 220
McCarthy, Sen. Joseph R., 47, 108, 111, 114-16, 156, 161, 177-85, 191-92, 194-95, 198, 202, 210, 213
"McCarthyism," 114, 192, 203-4, 308
McClure, Brig. Gen. Robert A., 162, 167
McCormick, Cyrus, 32
McCormick, Robert R., 36, 39, 42-44
McGee, Willie and Rosemary, 142
McGrath, Atty. Gen. J. Howard, 114
McManus, John T., 16-20, 23, 135, 144, 170, 180, 183-84, 189, 191, 208, 212-13, 220-21, 229, 231,

261-62, 275-77, 287, 322; candidate for governor, 11, 60, 155, 227; dealings with Anita Blaine, 35-42; dealings with Newspaper Guild, 18, 47-50; dealings with PP and CP, 17, 30-32, 60, 100; devices and projects, 154-58; probed by Eastland, 216-17
Meeropol, Michael and Robert, 171-72, 192-95
Meet the People (revue), 187
Melvin, Murry, 189
Mexican and Hispanic Americans, 66, 119, 122, 318
Mexico, C.B. settles in, 273-75
Middleton, Peggy A., 238, 240
Miller, Arthur, 66*n*
Minneapolis *Daily Star,* 287
Missile crisis (Cuba), 105
Mitchell, Bessie, 130-33
Moisseyev dancers, 237-38
Monde, Le (Paris), 173
Monthly Review and MR Press, 19, 67, 206, 218, 348
Mooney-Billings case, 143
Moore, Mr and Ms Harry, 142
Moos, Elizabeth, 137
Morford, Rev. Richard, 118
Morris, Rev. Stuart, 196
Morse, Sen. Wayne, 302
Movement for Colonial Freedom (London), 236
Mundt, Sen. Karl, 15
Munk, Michael, 315
Murphy, Justice Frank, 197
Murphy, Joseph P., 216
Murphy, Thomas J., 48
Muste, A. J., 226

Nagy, Imre, 223, 230-31
Nation, The, 205-6, 338
National Association for Advancement of Colored People (NAACP), 131, 138, 142, 148
National Committee for a Sane Nuclear Policy, 306-10, 319
National Education Association, 33

Schomburg Collection (N.Y. Public Library, Harlem), 146-47
Schuman, Frederick L., 13, 15, 69, 95
Schuman, Julian, 218
Scott, Helen, 14-15
"Scottsboro Boys," 131, 143, 149
Scripps-Howard newspapers, 47, 49, 112, 175, 344
Scully, Frank, 200-2
Seeger, Pete, 46, 67
Seeman, Ernest, 72, 135
Seldes, George, 111, 153-54
"Self-Determination of the Black Belt," 133
Shah of Iran, 244
Shaughnessy, Edward J., 205-6, 210
Shaw, G. B., 14, 108
Sherwood, Robert E., 116
Sholokhov, Mikhail, 282
Shostakovich, Dmitri, 90
Sibley, Mulford Q., 226
Sichl, Rabbi Gustav (Prague), 95
Sihanouk, Prince, 244
Silverman, Sydney (MP), 102, 175
Simon, Abbott, 137
Sing Sing prison, 172, 174, 192
Smedley, Agnes, 69, 96-98, 106, 250
Smith Act and trials, 15, 27-29, 59, 65*n*, 86, 118, 160, 194, 207
Sobell, Morton, 164-65, 170, 193-94, 239
Sobell, Rose, 239, 249
Socialist Party (U.S.), 8, 226-27, 349
Socialist Workers Party, 296, 346
Social Security payments (N.G.), 154-55
Souphanouvong, Prince, 288-89
Sourwine, Jay C., 214-19
South China Morning Post, 254
Southern Conference Educational Fund, 330
Southern Negro Youth Conference, 149
Soviet Union: antisemitism, 221, 230; C.B. in, 126, 230, 241-45, 251; China relations, 87, 245-46, 254-59; Cuba crisis, 105, 272; delegates at N.Y. conference, 89-90; effects of cold war, 7-10, 103, 105, 117, 342-45; internal tensions and fake trials, 56, 91; "peace offensive," 173, 199, 201; A. L. Strong case, 86-87, 98-102; 20th CP Congress and after, 222-24, 229-31
Spain, 162, 196
Spanish Republican refugee committee, 118
Spectator, The (London), 298
Spellman, Cardinal Francis, 117
Stageberg, Susie, 286-88
Stalin, 14, 43-44, 90-92, 106, 133, 173, 199, 204, 334; N.G. views of, 23, 95-96, 342-44; posthumous indictments, 221-22, 242-43; "Titoist plots," 28, 92-93
Stander, Lionel, 202
Starobin, Joseph, 99-100
Steinbeck, John, 201
Steven, Stewart, 91*n*
Stevenson, Adlai, 103, 224-26, 261
Stockholm Peace Appeal, 75
Stokes, Rose Pastor, 62
Stone, I. F. and *Weekly,* 69, 93, 108, 119, 182, 202, 206, 300, 307-10
Stone, John B., 15
Stone, Shepard, 9
Stover, Fred W., 13, 69, 286
Strong, Anna Louise: N.G. correspondent in Far East, 15, 107, 256, 258, 289-91, 326, 339; correspondence in USSR, 24, 240, 343-44; Kremlin denunciation and return to U.S., 69, 77, 86-88, 98-100, 128, 229; cleared of charge, 101-2, 199; views on 1956 convulsions, 233-34
Students for a Democratic Society, 305, 315-16, 339
Subversive Activities Control Board, 115
Sulzberger, Arthur Hays, 215
Summit, Leon, 14, 175
Sweezy, Paul, 67
Swing, Gen. Joseph, 206, 210

Symington, Sen. Stuart, 180-85, 192
Syracuse (N.Y.) *Post-Standard,* 220

Taft-Hartley law, 85
Taiwan, 255
Ta Kung Pao (Peking), 231
Teachers Union (N.Y.), 178, 234
Tempo (Milan), 298
Tenney, Sherman, Bentley & Guthrie (Chicago lawyers), 35
Thackrey, Ted O., 39, 48
Thomas, Norman, 310
Thompson, Dorothy, 165
Thoreau, Henry David, 224-28
Time (magazine), 18, 23-24, 27, 158, 236n, 292
Times, The (London), 112, 244, 298
Tito, 28, 85, 92-93, 242-44
Town Hall (N.Y.), 298-300
Townsend, Peter, 15, 96
Trade Union Service, 15, 22, 54, 99
Treason trials, E. Europe, 90-96, 101, 103, 128
Trenton Six, 98, 130-33, 141-42, 156
Tribune des Nations (Paris), 111, 201
Trotsky and Trotskyists, 87, 226, 296, 334-35
Trujillo, Gen. Leonidas, 268
Truman, Harry S., 8, 26-27, 47, 108, 110, 173-74, 211
Trumbo, Dalton, 66
Tsai Shen-ling (interpreter, China), 246-47
Tugwell, Rexford G., 13
Turner, Jack, 13, 87
Twain, Mark, 108, 207

Unitarians, 88
Unitarian Service Committee, 92
United Fruit Co., 196
United Nations and UN Charter, 9, 10, 56, 89, 101-2, 106-7, 111, 115, 143, 204, 232, 277-78
United Press International, 297
United States, political barriers at airports, 262, 268, 274-77

U.S. Farm Assn., 286
U.S. Information Agency, 177, 180
University of California: witch-hunts, 117; teach-ins, 310
University of Chicago, 33
University of Marburg, 6-7
University of Massachusetts, 140
University of Moscow, 243
Uphaus, Willard, 66
Urey, Harold C., 172-73

Valley City (N.D.) *Times-Record,* 15
Variety, 200
Van Kleeck, Mary, 69, 137
Vayo, Alvarez del, 326, 339
Velde, Rep. Harold H., 176-79, 198, 210
Vietnam, 97, 104, 110-11, 193, 195, 288-94, 301-8, 314, 317
Vinson, Justice Fred M., 189, 211
Vishinsky, Andrei, 101
Vivian, Rev. C. T., 304
Von Braun, Wernher, 262

Waldorf-Astoria conference (N.Y.), 89-90
Wallace, Henry A.: A. Blaine and N.G. financing, 30, 34, 40; heads PP, 9-14, 104, 138; 1948 vote, 26-27; on press and campaign, 22, 24; supports Korea war, 77, 108-9
Wall Street Journal, 111, 239
Walter, Rep. Francis and Walter-McCarran Immigration Act, 115, 200, 205, 209, 214, 238
Warfield, William S. III, 35, 42
Warren, Justice Earl and Warren Commission, 296-97, 300
War Resisters League, 226
Washington, Paul, 142
Washington *Post,* 47, 211, 216, 278, 280, 284, 291, 300-4
Wassermann, Ursula, 57, 95, 222-23, 338-39
Watergate hearings, 182
Weathermen, 319n, 340n

Wechsler, James, 177-78, 202, 210-11

Weekly Guardian Associates Inc., 22, 155, 220, 229, 322

Weinfeld, Judge Edward, 187, 191, 198

Werner, Max, 15, 110-11, 116, 331

West, Don, 144

West St. Federal House of Detention (N.Y.), 204-9, 212

Wheeler, Eleanor and George, 15, 94, 124-25, 127-28

White, William L., 174

Whitfield, Rev. Owen H., 15, 134

Whitman, Walt, 72, 81, 207

Wiggins, J. R., 211

Wilder, Col. Billy, 167

Wilkins, Roy, 148

Williams, Rev. Claude C., 10, 117, 135, 144, 149, 195, 200, 202

Winchell Walter, 116, 169, 174, 298

Winiewicz, Ambassador Joseph, 101

Winnington, Alan, 113n

Women's International Democratic Federation, 126, 198

Women Strike for Peace, 306

Worker, The and *Daily* (N.Y.), 28, 50, 65, 87, 99, 149, 162, 178, 226-27, 238

World Government Foundation, 33

World Marxist Review, 103

World Peace Council, 251

World Youth Congress (Moscow), 243-45

Worthy, William, 245

WQXR radio (N.Y.), 175

Wright, Fred, 27, 154

York (Pa.) *Gazette and Daily,* 13-16, 211

Young Communist League, 177-78

Young Progressives of America, 162

Zenger, John Peter, 219

Zilliacus, Konni MP, 15, 85, 88, 91-95, 102-5, 128, 230-31, 234, 237

Zionist "plots," 92, 94

Zorach, William, 146

Zusi, Edward T., 324n

362